152

X

AUTHOR BRAMBELL, F. W. R.	CLASS No. 571.9619
TITLE The Transmission of Passive immunity from Mother to Young	BOOK No. 470017346

THE TRANSMISSION OF PASSIVE IMMUNITY FROM MOTHER TO YOUNG

NORTH-HOLLAND RESEARCH MONOGRAPHS

FRONTIERS OF BIOLOGY

VOLUME 18

Under the General Editorship of

A. NEUBERGER

London

and

E. L. TATUM

New York

Consultant for Immunology

E. J. HOLBOROW

Taplow

NORTH-HOLLAND PUBLISHING COMPANY

AMSTERDAM · LONDON

THE TRANSMISSION
OF PASSIVE IMMUNITY
FROM MOTHER TO YOUNG

F. W. ROGERS BRAMBELL

Emeritus Professor of Zoology, University College of North Wales,

Bangor, Caerns., United Kingdom

1970

NORTH-HOLLAND PUBLISHING COMPANY
AMSTERDAM · LONDON

Library of Congress Catalog Card Number: 72-108282

ISBN 7204 7118 4

PUBLISHERS:
NORTH-HOLLAND PUBLISHING COMPANY – AMSTERDAM
NORTH-HOLLAND PUBLISHING COMPANY, LTD. – LONDON

SOLE DISTRIBUTORS FOR THE U.S.A. AND CANADA:
AMERICAN ELSEVIER PUBLISHING COMPANY, INC.
52 VANDERBILT AVENUE, NEW YORK, N.Y. 10017

PRINTED IN THE NETHERLANDS

Previous volumes in the series **FRONTIERS OF BIOLOGY**

Editors' preface

The aim of the publication of this series of monographs, known under the collective title of '*Frontiers of Biology*', is to present coherent and up-to-date views of the fundamental concepts which dominate modern biology.

Biology in its widest sense has made very great advances during the past decade, and the rate of progress has been steadily accelerating. Undoubtedly important factors in this acceleration have been the effective use by biologists of new techniques, including electron microscopy, isotopic labels, and a great variety of physical and chemical techniques, especially those with varying degrees of automation. In addition, scientists with partly physical or chemical backgrounds have become interested in the great variety of problems presented by living organisms. Most significant, however, increasing interest in and understanding of the biology of the cell, especially in regard to the molecular events involved in genetic phenomena and in metabolism and its control, have led to the recognition of patterns common to all forms of life from bacteria to man. These factors and unifying concepts have led to a situation in which the sharp boundaries between the various classical biological disciplines are rapidly disappearing.

Thus, while scientists are becoming increasingly specialized in their techniques, to an increasing extent they need an intellectual and conceptual approach on a wide and non-specialized basis. It is with these considerations and needs in mind that this series of monographs, '*Frontiers of Biology*' has been conceived.

The advances in various areas of biology, including microbiology, biochemistry, genetics, cytology, and cell structure and function in general will be presented by authors who have themselves contributed significantly to these developments. They will have, in this series, the opportunity of bringing together, from diverse sources, theories and experimental data, and of integrating theses into a more general conceptual framework. It is unavoidable, and probably even desirable, that the special bias of the individual authors will become evident in their contributions. Scope will also be given for presentation of new and challenging ideas and hypotheses for which complete evidence is at present lacking. However, the main emphasis will be on fairly complete and objective presentation of the more important and more rapidly advancing aspects of biology. The level will be advanced, directed primarily to the needs of the graduate student and research worker.

Most monographs in this series will be in the range of 200–300 pages, but on occasion a collective work of major importance may be included somewhat exceeding this figure. The intent of the publishers is to bring out these books promptly and in fairly quick succession.

It is on the basis of all these various considerations that we welcome the opportunity of supporting the publication of the series '*Frontiers of Biology*' by North-Holland Publishing Company.

E. L. TATUM

A. NEUBERGER, *General Editors*

Preface

The need for a comprehensive review of the transmission of passive immunity from mother to young has been apparent for some years. It has become more insistent with the very rapid growth of the subject and of the widely scattered literature bearing upon it. The author has wished to try to provide this review for the last ten years with a growing sense of urgency but, despite several starts, he has been frustrated by the demands of certain government committees which have absorbed nearly half his time; direction of research and teaching absorbed the rest. Release from these duties during the past year provided the welcome opportunity to write this book. He hopes it will be of use to those engaged in this fascinating field and that it may stimulate others to enter it.

This is a field that is attractive scientifically because it is concerned ultimately with the relation of protein molecular structure to the ways in which cells transport or degrade these large preformed molecules. It throws light on the relationship of molecular structure to cell function. There are illuminating resemblances between the reactions of cells to γ-globulins during transmission, anaphylaxis and γ-globulin catabolism. This is also a field that has importance for human and veterinary medicine. Passive immunity derived from the mother provides the neonatal animal with its resistance to disease; it can inhibit or hinder the prophylactic immunization of the young animal so long as the maternal antibody persists; it can cause disease of the newborn when the mother transmits antibodies to those antigens of her offspring which they have inherited from their father and which she lacks.

The plan has been to review for each species, or group of similar species, the route of transmission including the development and arrangement of the foetal membranes which are involved in transmission before birth and the mammary secretion of antibodies and structure of the neonatal intestine which absorbs them when transmission is after birth; the kinds of molecules that are preferentially transmitted; how they can interfere with each others transmission; the duration and termination of transmission; the waning of passive immunity and the beginning of active immunity. A separate chapter has been devoted to the comparative treatment of haemolytic disease in man and animals. The final chapter deals with the resemblances between the phenomena of transmission, anaphylactic sensitization and γ-globulin catabolism and offers a working hypothesis to account for transmission and, possibly, γ-globulin catabolism.

The author's interest in this field began with the chance observation, while working in collaboration with Dr. (now Professor) I. H. Mills on prenatal mortality in wild rabbits, that fibrinogen was present in the yolk-sac fluid of the rabbit blastocyst before implantation and the realisation that it must have been of maternal origin. Researches on the route and nature of transmission of immunity in rabbits followed and soon led to extension of the work to rats and mice. Much of the work has been in collaboration with senior friends expert in the various disciplines involved, especially Dr. Irene Batty, Professor R. A. Kekwick, F.R.S., Professor C. L. Oakley, F.R.S., Professor R. R. Porter, F.R.S., and Mr. W. T. Rowlands, to all of whom the author is greatly indebted. A large part has been done by his colleagues and pupils, especially Dr. D. R. Bamford, Dr. R. Halliday, Dr. W. A. Hemmings, Dr. Megan Henderson, Dr. B. Morris, Dr. I. G. Morris and Dr. A. Wild and to them belongs the credit for many of the advances. It is a particular pleasure to acknowledge the unfailing and continuous support of the work by the Agricultural Research Council, who provided the Unit of Embryology which made such team work possible. The author's thanks are due also to the Trustees of the Wellcome Foundation for the provision of additional accommodation and to the Rockefeller Foundation for additional equipment.

Dr. W. A. Hemmings, Dr. B. Morris, Dr. I. G. Morris, Professor C. L. Oakley, F.R.S., Professor R. R. Porter, F.R.S. and Dr. R. R. Race, F.R.S. read and constructively criticised parts of the manuscript of this book, for which the author is most grateful, though they are in no way responsible for errors or omissions or for the views expressed. Thanks are due also to all those authors referred to in the legends of figures or headings of tables who have given permission for the use of these and especially to those who provided the photographs for the plates. The author is indebted also for permission to reproduce material to the following publishers: Academic

Press, Inc. *(Advances in Immunology, Arch. Biochem. Biophys., Devl Biol., J. Ultrastruct. Res., Proc. Soc. exp. Biol. Med.);* The American Academy of Pediatrics *(Pediatrics);* The American Dairy Science Association *(J. Dairy Sci.);* The American Physiological Society *(Am. J. Physiol., Handbook of Physiology);* The American Society of Animal Science *(J. Anim. Sci.);* The American Society of Biological Chemists, Inc. *(J. biol. Chem.);* The American Society for Clinical Investigation Inc. *(J. clin. Invest.);* Athlone Press *(Antibodies and Embryos);* Blackwell Scientific Publications, Ltd. *(Immunology, Res. vet. Sci.);* The British Society of Animal Production *(Anim. Prod.);* The British Veterinary Association *(Vet. Rec.);* Butterworth & Co. (Publishers) Ltd. *(Colston Papers);* Cambridge University Press *(Biol. Rev., J. Embryol. exp. Morph., J. gen. Microbiol., J. Hygiene, J. Physiol., Quart. J. Microsc. Sci.);* Carnegie Institution *(Contrib. Embryol.);* Elsevier Publishing Co. *(Biochim. Biophys. Acta);* IPC Magazines Ltd. *(New Scientist);* Lancet *(Lancet);* E & S Livingstone Ltd. *(Quart. J. exp. Physiol.);* MacMillans (Journals) Ltd. *(Nature);* New York State Veterinary College *(Cornell Vet.);* The Pathological Society of Great Britain and Ireland *(J. Path. Bact.);* The Rockefeller University Press *(J. Cell Biol., J. exp. Med.);* Royal Veterinary College, Copenhagen (Den kgl. Veterinær- og Landbohøskole) *(Kgl. Vet.- og Landbohøskole, Arsskr.);* Springer-Verlag *(Handbuch der speziellen pathologischen Anatomie und Histologie, Z. Zellforsch.);* University of Adelaide *(Aust. J. exp. Biol. med. Sci.);* The Williams and Wilkins Co. *(J. Immunol.);* The Wistar Institute of Anatomy and Biology *(Am. J. Anat., Anat. Rec.).*

Full reference to this material is given in the bibliography.

The completion of this book would have been delayed and it might never have been finished, were it not for a grant from the Royal Society to provide secretarial assistance for this purpose, for which grant the author wishes to express his thanks. Finally, and by no means least, the author's thanks are due to Mrs. G. Marshall for her skilful assistance in the preparation of the manuscript, bibliography and index.

Department of Zoology   F.W.R.B.
University College of North Wales, Bangor

Contents

Chapter 6. *Transmission of immunity in the guineapig, cat, dog and hedgehog*   *142*

Chapter 7. *Transmission of immunity in the pig and the horse*   *166*

Chapter 11. *Conclusions and hypotheses*   *299*

CHAPTER 1

Introduction

1.1. The nature of immunity

Adult mammals normally are equipped with powers of resistance to those diseases to which they are liable. This immunity, as it is called, resides in part in the cellular elements of the tissues and in part in antibodies which are present in solution in the blood stream. It is this latter serological kind with which we are concerned. The infective agents of protozoan, bacterial or virus diseases when they enter the body act as antigens which stimulate the animal to produce and to liberate into the blood antibodies which will react specifically with them. Large molecules such as proteins, polysaccharides and nucleic acids can act as antigens also. Proteins which differ from those which the individual itself produces, such as those from another species or another individual of the same species, or even the individual's own proteins which have been altered by attachment to the molecules of a foreign chemical group, when introduced into the body may act as antigens and induce the production of antibodies to them. The antibodies are very specific and react only with the particular kind of antigen which stimulated their production or with a closely related one which has a similar antigenic structure.

An animal during its normal life is exposed continually to germs of many kinds which enter the body through the mucous surfaces of the respiratory, digestive or urinogenital tracts and through the skin. Although these organisms may not be in a state, or in sufficient quantity, to produce any other apparent effect they can start the process of antibody production. Sometimes the organisms will establish themselves and cause disease but more often they will produce no apparent effect, being either insufficient in quantity or in an uninfective state. Yet whether the animal develops the disease and

1

recovers or shows no ill effects the process of antibody formation is likely
to have been started. Man and his domestic animals are subject to injections
for clinical reasons of sera, vaccines, etc., and to transfusions of blood from
other individuals which contain antigenic substances that likewise may
induce the formation of antibodies. If the production of antibodies is started,
even on a small scale, in any of these ways by a first or primary exposure to
a particular antigen then any subsequent exposure to the same antigen after
an interval is followed normally by a copious production of antibody, which
soon appears in the blood. This secondary response is marked both by a
more copious and a more lasting production of antibody. Such an animal is
said to be actively immune to that particular antigen. If the antigen is
pathogenic the animal then can resist even a heavy subsequent infection.
An actively immune animal will continue to produce the antibody for a
long time or even throughout life, though in gradually declining quantity
unless it is exposed again to the antigen. Thus an animal during its life
builds up powers of resistance to each of the antigens to which it has been
exposed and its total equipment of antibodies reflects the sum of its past
antigenic experience.

1.2. *Varieties of antibodies*

Antibodies can be classified conveniently according to the ways in which
they react with their antigens as agglutinins, lysins, opsonins, precipitins and
antitoxins. The first three are antibodies to cellular antigens, such as bacteria
or foreign red blood corpuscles. Agglutinins cause these to stick together
in clumps or agglutinate, and may be called bacterioagglutinins or haemagglutinins according to the nature of the antigen. Antibodies have at least
two similar reactive sites on each molecule and if it becomes attached by
these to two antigenic cells it will link them together and clumps of antigen
and antibody will be formed. These are called complete agglutinins and
they can bring about agglutination of the antigen in saline solution. Sometimes, however, agglutinins are formed which are able to attach to the surfaces of the antigenic cells in a similar manner but fail to cause agglutination
in clumps in saline solution, though they can do so in undiluted serum or in
a colloidal medium. These are called incomplete agglutinins and special
techniques are necessary to demonstrate them. Lysins, in the presence of
another serum component called complement, dissolve or lyse the cell
membranes of the antigen. Both bacteriolysins and haemolysins occur.

Opsonins also attach to the cell surface of the antigen and facilitate phago-cytosis. Precipitins are antibodies to soluble antigens, such as foreign proteins or polysaccharides, causing them to precipitate. Antitoxins are produced in response to toxic substances such as bacterial toxins, snake venom, etc., and render these non-toxic to the body. Other antibodies, as well as lysins, when they react with antigen may bind complement. Complement is a very complex component of serum, the quantities of which vary greatly from species to species. It can be destroyed by heat treatment at a lower temperature than affects the antibodies and it can be supplied by adding guineapig serum, in which it is particularly plentiful.

1.3. The serum proteins

The proteins of blood serum are of several kinds, which can be characterised and separated by various physical and chemical means, such as by electro-phoresis, ultracentrifugation, diffusion, fractional precipitation and chro-matography. Protein molecules in solution in an electric field migrate towards the anode or cathode according to whether they carry a negative or positive charge. The rate of migration depends on the current, the charge on the molecules and a frictional component. Suitably buffered they will migrate at characteristic rates in free solution, or in a gel of starch, agar or other suitable material, or in saturated filter paper. Four principal compo-nents of serum can be distinguished in free solution in this way (fig. 1.1). The fastest major component is albumin, then α-, β- and γ-globulins in that order. Under favourable circumstances these components can be further subdivided into α_1 and α_2, β_1 and β_2, etc. Most of the antibody in an immune serum generally is in the slowest component, though some of the immune globulin moves in free solution in the β-globulin region.

The ultracentrifuge provides a means of determining the sedimentation constants (S_{20}) of the serum proteins. Most antibodies are in the fraction sedimenting at 7S with molecular weights of c. 150,000 but some antibodies are macroglobulins sedimenting at 19S and with molecular weights of near 1,000,000. Electrophoretically macroglobulin antibody migrates faster, in the β-globulin region, than 7S antibody.

Diffusion, especially in gels, combined with immunological methods provides another means of distinguishing antibody activity in different serum protein fractions. The Ouchterlony double diffusion method consists in putting an immune serum in a well in an agar gel and its antigen in solution

in a neighbouring well. The antibody and the antigen diffuse slowly outwards
from their respective wells and a line of precipitate is formed in the gel at
the point where they meet. The number of separate concentric arcs so formed
indicates the number of types of antibody and of antigen molecules with
different rates of diffusion. The technique of immunoelectrophoresis com-
bines the advantages of electrophoresis and diffusion. Longitudinal wells

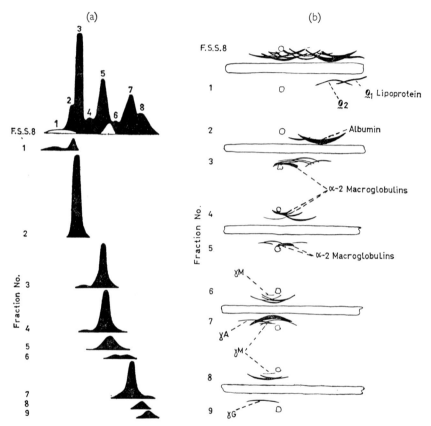

Fig. 1.1. The electrophoretic profile of squirrel serum in fluid agar at pH 8.6 is shown at
(a) together with the fractions into which the proteins were cut by Porath zone electrophoresis on starch. The white areas represent lipoprotein. Peaks 1 and 2 represent preal-
bumins, peak 3 albumin, peaks 4 and 5 α_1- and α_2-globulins respectively, peaks 6 and 7
β_1- and β_2-globulins and peak 8 γ-globulin. Immunoelectrophoretic diagrams of the whole
serum and of the fractions are shown at (b) and indicate that more than one component
is present in every fraction, with the exception of 9 which contains only γG-globulin.
(After Wild 1965b.)

are cut in an oblong agar gel, leaving strips of gel an inch or so wide between them. The serum to be analysed is run electrophoretically in these strips and when the run is complete and the current switched off a solution of the appropriate reactant is put in the wells and diffuses in, forming arcs of precipitate where the reaction takes place. If an immune serum is run in the strip and the soluble antigen is put in the well the electrophoretic fractions with antibody activity can be distinguished. If the intention was to distinguish as many protein fractions as possible in a serum, without reference to its antibody content, then an antiserum to the whole serum prepared in another species is put in the wells (fig. 1.1).

Fractional precipitation with sodium or ammonium sulphate, or by an aqueous ethyl ether system (Kekwick and Mackay 1954) or fractionation on a chromatographic column can be used to separate the serum protein fractions from whole serum.

1.4. Active and passive immunity

An animal that has produced antibody in response to an experience of an antigen is said to be actively immune to that antigen. This state is long lasting. There is, however, always an interval after primary exposure to an antigen before antibody appears in the circulation. The minimum interval appears to be about 3–4 days in mammals. If the antigen is an infective organism it can multiply during this period when the host is unprotected. Antibodies formed in an immune individual can be transferred to the circulation of another individual of the same or another species and will confer upon it a passive immunity which is immediate (fig. 1.2). Advantage

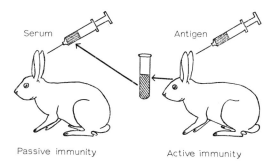

Fig. 1.2. Diagrammatic representation of active and of passive immunity with homologous serum in rabbits.

has been taken of this method of passive immunization in human and veterinary medicine to combat virulent infections, which could be lethal before the patient had time to develop an effective level of active immunity. Passively acquired antibody can provide resistance itself or can reinforce the animal's own active immunity when this has been developed. Passive immunity, although immediate, is short lived, persisting only so long as the transferred antibody remains in the patient's circulation. If the transferred antibodies were prepared in another species, which is commonly necessary in human medicine, then the antibodies, being themselves foreign proteins, will act as antigens in the patient and after an interval antibodies against them will be formed and will accelerate their elimination from the circulation. This will occur when any foreign γ-globulin is injected into an animal, irrespective of whether it displays antibody activity or not.

1.5. The molecular structure of immune globulins

The immune glublins comprise three principal classes of γ-globulin, γG-, γM- and γA-globulins, of which only the γG-globulin corresponds to the classical γ-globulin of free-boundary electrophoresis. The γM-globulin or macroglobulin moves on free-boundary electrophoresis with the β_2-globulins

TABLE 1.1

Nomenclature of immunoglobulins.

Terms used	Old equivalent
γG	7Sγ, γ_2
γA	β_2A, γ_1A
γM	β_2M, 19Sγ, γ_1M
γD	—
γE	—
γ-chain	7Sγ heavy chain
α-chain	γ_1A heavy chain
μ-chain	γ_1M heavy chain
κ-chain	Type 1 or B light chain
λ-chain	Type 2 or A light chain
Fab-fragment (resulting from papainisation)	Fragment I or II (rabbit), S-fragment (human)
Fc-fragment (resulting from papainisation)	Fragment III (rabbit), F-fragment (human)
F(ab′)₂ (resulting from pepsinisation)	Pepsin refined antibody

and for a long time was known as $\beta_2 M$, and the γA-globulin moves close behind it and ahead of the γG-globulin. The terminology became very confused until in 1964 international agreement under the auspices of the World Health Organisation was reached and this nomenclature will be used in this book wherever possible (table 1.1). The last decade has seen great advances in our knowledge of the chemistry of the immune globulins and it is now evident that all three principal classes of immune globulins are essentially similar in structure and share certain characteristics.

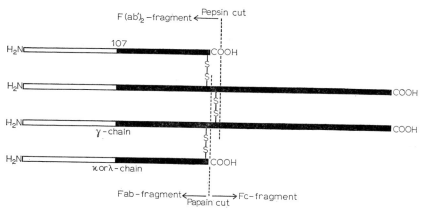

Fig. 1.3. Diagram of a γG-globulin molecule showing how the two heavy and two light chains are held together by disulphide bonds. The light chains contain *c.* 220 amino acid units and the heavy chains *c.* 430. The N-terminal parts of all four chains consisting of about 107 units each, represented in white, have a very variable sequence of units, and the C-terminal parts represented in black, a remarkably constant sequence. The points where the molecule is cleaved by the enzyme papain into two Fab- and one Fc-fragment and by pepsin into one F(ab')$_2$-fragment and small degradation products of the C-terminal halves of the heavy chains are shown. (Based on Porter 1967.)

The unit of γG-globulin has a molecular weight of *c.* 150,000 and consists of 1300 ± 40 amino acid residues arranged in four polypeptide chains, two heavy chains and two light chains, joined by disulphide bonds (fig. 1.3). The light chains, which are almost exactly half the length of the heavy chains, are each joined to a heavy chain by a single disulphide bond near its C-terminal end to the middle of a heavy chain and the heavy chains are joined together by one or more disulphide bonds a little further towards the C-terminal end as shown in the diagram fig. 1.3. The light chains are of two principal kinds, κ and λ, both of which occur in any individual and which are both common to all three classes of immune globulins. Both the light chains in any one molecule are of the same kind. The heavy chains, on the other hand, are distinctive of each class, hence there are three classes of heavy chains, γ, α and μ, corresponding to γG-, γA- and γM-globulins. A further complexity is that there are four kinds of γ-chains in human γG-globulin that differ in minor respects, and similar sub-types of γ-chain are known to occur in other animals. Inherited allelic variants of both heavy and light chains occur also; in the human there are the Gm characters on the C-terminal half of the heavy chains and the Inv characters on the C-terminal half of the light chains. Those individuals which are homozygous for one of these characters will have it on all their γ-chains, or on all their light chains, as the case may be, but those who are heterozygous for one of them will produce both the allelic types. Finally an individual may produce a chain that varies in some respect from the pattern of the species and is unique to himself; such variation is known as idiotypic.

Much of the advance in the chemistry of γ-globulins derives from digestion of the molecules with enzymes. It has been the practice for many years to refine antitoxins prepared in horses for human therapeutic use by controlled digestion with pepsin. This treatment reduces the size of the molecule by about one third without impairing its antibody activity and has the advantage that it greatly reduces its antigenic properties when injected into another species of animal. It is known now that it cleaves the heavy chains close to, but on the C-terminal side, of the disulphide bonds that hold them together and results in the degradation of their C-terminal halves. The N-terminal halves of the heavy chains remain attached to each other and to the light chains, forming the F(ab')$_2$-fragment. Since this retains the antibody activity it is clear that the active sites must be situated on the duplicate halves of this fragment, and since much of the antigenic activity is lost it must have resided in the C-terminal halves of the heavy chains which have been removed. A further advance that provided the starting point of much of the recent work came when Porter (1958, 1959) found that by digestion of rabbit γ-globulin with crystalline papain the heavy chains could be cleaved on the N-terminal side of the bonds between them, cutting the molecule into three parts of nearly equal size, two duplicate pieces, the Fab-fragments, each consisting of the N-terminal half of a heavy chain with a light chain attached to it, and one piece, the Fc-fragment, consisting of the two C-terminal halves of the heavy chains still bonded together. Separation of the Fab- from the Fc-fragments was achieved. It was found that the Fab-fragments of antibody globulin retained their capacity to unite with antigen though they had lost the power to precipitate it. The Fc-fragment could be crystallized and it reacted with antibody prepared in another species to whole rabbit γ-globulin. Similar studies have since been carried out on human and some other γ-globulins.

The disease of myelomatosis occurs in man and in mice and is a lymphoid neoplasm which results in a massive overproduction of γ-globulin. A great step forward in the elucidation of the structure of γ-globulin was made when it was realised that the molecules overproduced in this disease were uniform both as regards their heavy and their light chains. The myeloma protein was not a mixture of all those varieties of molecule that have been referred to and which constitute normal γ-globulin. This uniformity arises from their being the product of a single neoplastic clone of cells. The disease provides the further convenience for the chemist that the free light chains are secreted in the urine of the patient. These are known as Bence-Jones proteins and they provide a rich source of uniform light chains. There is reason to think that the myeloma proteins are abnormal in no other respect than their overproduction and uniformity in each individual. These proteins and the crystallizable, and hence uniform, Fc-fragments obtained by papain digestion have provided the starting point for amino-acid sequence studies of both light and heavy chains, after breaking these down further into smaller polypeptides.

It has been shown by these means that the C-terminal halves of the light chains and the C-terminal three-quarters of the heavy chains of any one kind have a remarkably constant sequence. The differences between the classes of heavy chains, or between κ and λ light chains in a given species are substantial, those between the sub-classes of heavy chains somewhat less. Moreover, the differences between the corresponding chains of different species are comparable to the species differences found in other proteins, such as haemoglobin; for example the C-terminal octadecapeptide of the heavy chains of rabbit, human and horse γG-globulin differ in only two or three of the 18 amino-acid residues, a difference no greater than exists between the different classes of heavy chains in man. This similarity between the C-terminal ends of the heavy chains of widely different species has particular significance when we come to consider the phenomenon of selective transmission of globulins in later chapters. The N-terminal parts of both heavy and light chains, consisting of one hundred or so amino-acid

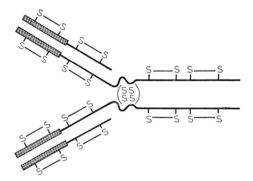

Fig. 1.4. Diagrammatic representation of the twelve loops in chains, two in each light chain and four in each heavy chain, formed in a molecule of human γG-globulin by intra-chain disulphide bonds. (After Frangione, Milstein and Pink 1969.)

residues, display a still more surprising variability within each class or sub-class of chain in each individual. Although the Bence-Jones proteins from one individual are uniform, those from no two individuals are identical. The inference is irresistible that the variability of these parts of the chains provides for the immense variety of antibodies that the individual can produce according to the antigenic stimuli experienced. The exciting problem of how the genetic mechanism provides for the control of the synthesis of polypeptide chains, part of each of which is constant and part immensely variable, is attracting much attention and awaits solution, but is beyond the scope of this book.

A molecule made up of long polypeptide chains like those of γG-globulin, the light chains containing 220–240 residues and the heavy chains 420–440 (Porter 1967), must be folded in a complex manner. The precise configuration of the molecule is not known, but some features are emerging. It appears that in human γG-globulin (fig. 1.4) there are at least 12 loops on the chains, made by intrachain disulphide bridges and each including about 60 residues (Frangione, Milstein and Pink 1969). Four of these are in each heavy chain,

Plate 1.1. Electron micrograph of the complex of γG-antibody with the antigen bis-dinitrophenyl octamethylene diamine. The antigen molecules are too small to be seen but they link together the antibody molecules, each of which has become Y-shaped, the arms being linked to the antigen molecules and the stem sticking out from the complex as a small knob is believed to be the Fc piece. Three antibody molecules linked together by antigen produce the triangular shapes, four the diamond shapes and more polygons. × 350,000. (From Green 1969.)

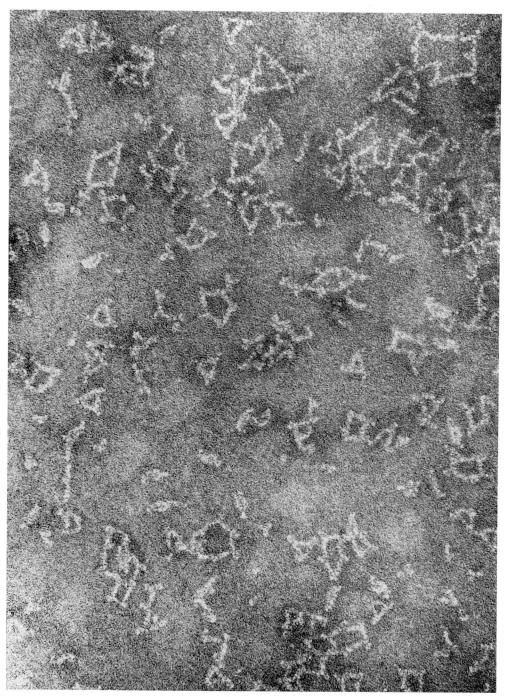

PLATE 1.1

two in the Fc part (C-terminal half) and two in the Fd part (N-terminal half), one of which is in the variable region. Two loops are in each light chain, one in the variable and one in the invariable region. The disulphide bonds joining the heavy chains are variable according to the particular type of molecule; thus of the four kinds of human γG, there are two disulphide bonds close together in γ_1G and γ_4G, four in γ_2G and five in γ_3G. Electronmicrographs of rabbit antibody/antigen complexes have shown (plate 1.1) that the antibody on union with antigen tends to take up a Y shape, the Fc region being the stem and Fab regions, uniting with the antigen molecules, being the arms; the region in the neighbourhood of the inter-heavy chain bonds forming the hinge about which these open (Valentine and Green 1967). This flexibility appears to be facilitated by the high concentration of proline residues in this region of the heavy chains (Smyth and Utsumi 1967).

Much of the information outlined above relates to γG-globulin, which normally occurs in the form of separate molecules with a molecular weight of the order of 150,000 and sedimenting in the ultracentrifuge at 7S. The molecules of γM-globulin have a molecular weight nearer 1×10^6 and sediment at 19S. It is now known that these molecules are polymers of five units, each built on a similar plan to the γG molecule and linked together by disulphide bonds between their μ chains situated very near the

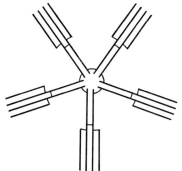

Fig. 1.5. Diagrammatic representation of the way in which the five units, each consisting of two heavy (μ) chains and two light (κ- or λ-) chains are linked by disulphide bonds to form a polymer of γM-globulin.

C-terminal ends of these chains (fig. 1.5). These bonds are broken and the polymers reduced to 7S units by treatment with mercaptoethanol, the antibody activity being lost or changed in the process so that a macroglobulin agglutinin for example, fails to agglutinate antigen after such treatment.

Sensitivity to mercaptoethanol is therefore regarded as evidence of an antibody being a macroglobulin. In serum γA-globulin appears to occur largely as dimers or higher aggregates but these are not held together by covalent bonds, as are the polymers of γM. Normal human serum contains c. 10 mg/ml of γG-globulin, 1.6 mg/ml of γA-globulin and 1.1 mg/ml of γM-globulin (Tomasi 1965). In addition to the three principal classes of immune globulins, two others have been identified in human sera, γD- and γE-globulin, about which comparatively little is known as yet. It is known that γE-globulin carries the reagin activity and sensitizes homologous cells and some account has been given of its chemical structure (Johansson, Bennich and Wide 1968). Antibody activity after active immunization may be spread between all these fractions of γ-globulin but its distribution appears to depend on many factors, including whether the stimulus is primary or secondary, the nature of the antigen, the age and the species of animal concerned. After a primary exposure to antigen the first antibody to appear in the circulation is largely or exclusively γM-globulin and this is followed by the production of γG-antibody. After secondary exposure there is little or no increase in the amount of γM-antibody but the γG-antibody may show a large increase. In man the ABO blood group isoagglutinins and Rhesus (Rh) blood group complete agglutinins are largely γM-globulins, whereas Rh incomplete agglutinins and bacterioagglutinins are mainly γG-globulins (Kekwick and Mollison 1961). In rabbits the haemagglutinins to sheep red cells are largely γM-globulins (Paić 1938; Stelos 1956; Hemmings and Jones 1962), whereas bacterioagglutinins, precipitins and antitoxins are predominantly γG-globulins. In the mouse antibodies formed to haemocyanin and to pneumococcal polysaccharide are mainly γG-globulin, but antisheep-red-cell haemolysins are γM-globulins (Fahey and Humphrey 1962). The horse, unlike the rabbit and the mouse, produces antibody to pneumococcal polysaccharide which is largely γM-globulin, though antitoxins are mainly γG-globulins (Kekwick and Record 1940). *Brucella* as a primary antigen induces the formation of γM-antibody followed by some γG-antibody, but even hyperimmunization with it in some species fails to produce large amounts of γG-antibody, whereas in the same species hyperimmunization with *Salmonella* antigen produces a massive rise in titre of γG-antibodies. These differences in distribution of antibody activity between the various kinds of γ-globulin in different sera may be of great importance in determining their transmission from mother to offspring and could go a long way to account for selective transmission.

One other matter concerning the molecular structure of immune globulins is of importance in relation to the transmission of passive immunity; γA-globulin is preferentially secreted by various glands including the mammary glands, salivary glands, etc. The γA-globulin in secretions is in the form of dimers attached to a special molecule called secretory piece, which can also be found free in these secretions. Secretory piece is not present in the dimers of γA-globulin in serum, which differ from those in colostrum, milk and saliva in this respect. The secretory piece of human colostrum has a molecular weight of *c.* 76,000 and the γA-dimers with secretory piece a molecular weight of *c.* 393,000 and a sedimentation constant of 11.73 (Newcomb, Normansell and Stanworth 1968).

1.6. Transmission of passive immunity to the young

The newborn animal has little capacity to make antibodies in response to antigenic stimuli and has emerged from an environment where, even if it had this capacity, it was sheltered from most antigenic stimuli which could call forth such a response. Therefore the newborn animal lacks active immunity and would have little resistance to disease during this critical period of its life if it were not equipped with passive immunity derived from the mother. Antibodies actively produced by the mother are transmitted from her circulation to that of her offspring and provide it with a ready made immunity to those antigenic stimuli which she has experienced. These passively transferred antibodies persist longer in the circulation of the young animal than they would do in that of an adult and tide it over the period until it can respond itself adequately to those antigens which it encounters. Thus the transmission of passive immunity from mother to young plays an important part in neonatal survival.

The transmission of passive immunity from mother to young may occur before birth, or after birth or at both these times (table 1.2). Human infants and the young of monkeys, rabbits and guineapigs are born well equipped with passive immunity. Often at birth the maternal antibodies in the circulations of the young of these species are at an equal, or even a greater, concentration than they are in the mother's own circulation. The young animal grows quickly, with increase in blood volume and consequent dilution of the maternal antibody concentration, yet there is little, if any, augmentation of the passive immunity after birth. The maternal antibodies have been transmitted to the young in these species while they are still in the

TABLE 1.2

Time of transmission of passive immunity.

Species	Transmission of passive immunity	
	Prenatal	Postnatal
Horse	0	+++ (24 hr)
Pig	0	+++ (24–36 hr)
Ox, goat, sheep	0	+++ (24 hr)
Wallaby (*Setonix*)	0	+++ (180 d)
Dog, cat	+	++ (1–2 d)
Fowl	++	++ (< 5 d)
Hedgehog	+	++ (40 d)
Mouse	+	++ (16 d)
Rat	+	++ (20 d)
Guineapig	+++	0
Rabbit	+++	0
Man, monkey	+++	0

uterus across the membranes which enclose the foetus and constitute the maternal/foetal barrier (table 1.3).

The young of cattle, sheep, goats, horses, donkeys and pigs are born with no passive immunity or, at best, only trace amounts and they derive their

TABLE 1.3

Routes of transmission of passive immunity.

Species	Route	
	Prenatal	Postnatal
Fowl	Yolk-sac	Yolk-sac
Rat (and mouse?)	Yolk-sac	Gut
Guineapig	Yolk-sac	None
Rabbit	Yolk-sac	None
Hedgehog	Unknown	Gut
Dog	Unknown	Gut
Cat	Unknown	Gut
Man and monkey	Placenta	None
Horse	None	Gut
Pig	None	Gut
Ruminants (ox, goat and sheep)	None	Gut
Wallaby	None	Gut

compliment of maternal antibodies from the colostrum or milk during their first few hours of independent life. Maternal antibodies secreted in the colostrum are transmitted rapidly to the circulation of the newborn animal across the walls of the digestive tract. The young animal's capacity to absorb the antibodies intact from the gut contents is transitory, lasting only a few hours. If colostrum is not fed to them until 48 hr after birth, it is then, as a rule, too late because the antibodies will be digested, instead of being transmitted, and only their degradation products will reach the circulation. The newborn calf, for example, depends for its passive immunity on being fed with the antibody-rich colostrum within a few hours of birth and to deprive it of this is to rob it of much of its powers to resist infection. At this time the antibodies are at such a high concentration in the colostrum and are transmitted so rapidly from the gut to the circulation of the calf that they attain within a few hours a concentration in its blood equalling or exceeding that in the blood of the mother.

Rats, mice, hedgehogs, cats and dogs form an intermediate group between these two in which passive immunity is transmitted from mother to young both before and after birth. Although a significant amount is transmitted across the foetal membranes to the foetal circulation before birth in these animals, the greater part is transmitted after birth by way of the colostrum and the milk. The postnatal transmission is not limited to a few hours after birth in rats, mice and hedgehogs but continues for a long period or even throughout lactation. It terminates abruptly by the gut of the young animal becoming impermeable to antibodies, although these are still present in quantity in the milk.

Passive immunity is transmitted from mother to young in birds, as well as in mammals and in them the antibodies are secreted in the ovary and incorporated in the yolk of the egg before it is ovulated. The antibodies are stored in the yolk until the later stages of incubation when they are absorbed by the embryonic membranes and transmitted to the circulation of the chick.

Generally the young animal is not making appreciable quantities of antibody itself while it is still receiving passive immunity from its mother. This may be due largely to the immaturity of its lymphoid system and to being wholly or partly sheltered from antigenic stimuli, but it is becoming increasingly evident that it can respond to appropriate antigens at much earlier ages, even during foetal life in some species, than was generally thought. However this may be, there is normally a period after the transmission of passive immunity has ceased during which the decline in passively acquired γ-globulin exceeds the synthesis of autologous γ-globulin and which results in the γ-globulin concentration of the young animal falling to a minimum at a considerable interval after birth.

1.7. Methods of labelling serum proteins

It is evident that the first essential for studying the transmission of immunity in living animals is to have some method of labelling or marking the molecules so that they can be recognised and their movements followed. The label must be such that it cannot normally be reproduced in the organism, so that confusion with counterfeit labels cannot arise. There are several different methods of labelling protein molecules so that they can be distinguished from all the other protein constituents of the animal's body, but no known method is ideal. Three methods have proved most useful and our knowledge of transmission is due largely to their use, singly or in combination.

First, the natural biological activities of some proteins, such as antibodies, enzymes or hormones, can be used as a means of recognising them by their reactions with antigen, substrate or target organ respectively. Antibodies are the most convenient of these in practice because of the highly specific nature of the antibody/antigen reactions and the sensitivity of the methods of measuring them. Provided the antibody is prepared in one individual and used in another, which is not immune or likely to become immune to the particular antigen employed, it provides a nearly ideal label of those globulin molecules which display the activity. No label could be better for studying the movements of antibodies than the antibody activity which they themselves display. Maternally produced antibodies in the young animal in effect are labelled proteins, since it does not produce them itself. Since antibody activity is a property of the surface configuration of a part of the molecule it provides a label which enables the molecule to be recognised so long as it retains this configuration intact, but if it is denatured or degraded it may lose its activity and be no longer recognisable. It is a label of the substantially intact molecule rather than of a small component part.

Secondly, the antibody/antigen reaction can be used in the reverse manner for the recognition of the specific antigen. The chosen protein antigen is first employed to immunize an animal which will produce an antiserum that can be used as a reagent for identifying small quantities of the same antigen in samples of the body fluids of other animals. This method has the advantage that any antigenic protein, and not only immune globulins, can be recognised. It has the disadvantage that it cannot be used for the recognition of proteins belonging to the same species as the experimental animal to which they are administered, because the antiserum would react indiscriminately with the animal's own proteins as well as with those which it was desired to recognise.

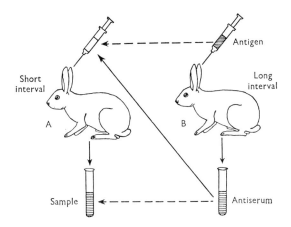

Fig. 1.6. Diagrammatic representation of the ways in which the immunological activity of molecules may be used as labels to recognise them. Rabbit B will become actively immune and develop antibodies after injection of antigen. These antibodies can be withdrawn in the serum from rabbit B. This serum can be injected, as shown by the solid arrows into rabbit A which is not immune and subsequently recognised in samples of its body fluids or those of its foetuses by its ability to react *in vitro* with the antigen. Alternatively the antigen can be injected into rabbit A and recognised by its reaction *in vitro* with the immune serum of rabbit B, as indicated by the broken arrows. (From Brambell 1958.)

Both these methods, which are represented diagrammatically in fig. 1.6, are very specific, sensitive, reliable and easy to use in practice, but whereas both can be used for labelling heterologous γ-globulins, only the first can be used for labelling homologous γ-globulins and only the second for serum protein fractions other than those containing antibody. A whole range of immunological and serological techniques, such as titration, skin and ana-phylactic tests, immunodiffusion, immunoelectrophoresis and the use of fluorescent antibodies, etc., can be adapted to the recognition and measurement of antibody/antigen reactions with either of these methods, but the description of these techniques is beyond the scope of the present work.

Thirdly, protein molecules can be labelled by attaching radioactive isotopes to them. This method is still more senstitive than the immunological methods but it is less specific, because denaturation or degradation of the labelled protein molecule does not destroy the isotope, which remains as a marker of the altered molecule or of the fragment of the molecule to which it was attached. This may be an advantage for some purposes, such as studying the metabolism of a protein, but it is a disadvantage where the purpose is to follow the movements of the intact protein. One of the most useful isotopes for labelling proteins is ^{131}I because it can be coupled readily to the protein *in vitro*. Labelling *in vitro* has great advantages in convenience but inevitably produces a change, however small, in the natural structure of the molecule. A level of iodination of 0.5 atoms ^{131}I/molecule protein, provided the technique is adequate, does not appear to produce an appreciable change in the behaviour of the molecule *in vivo* or in its biological activity. The iodine unites with the tyrosine of the protein to form iodotyrosine. If the iodinated protein is degraded in the animal, the labelled tyrosine is not resynthesized into protein and is eliminated from the body fairly rapidly, provided the animal has been maintained on a diet with excess iodide. This often is an advantage because the isotope will not be incorporated in other proteins, so labelling them and causing confusion. Other isotopes, especially ^{14}C and ^{35}S can be administered to an animal in such forms that they are incorporated *in vivo* in the proteins as they are synthesized. These proteins labelled *in vivo* are entirely natural, except that they are radioactive. The isotope can be provided in a form, such as a selected amino acid, in which it will act as a marker of a specific part of the molecule, or in the case of ^{14}C, in a form in which it will be randomly distributed amongst all the carbon atoms and is not a marker of any one particular part of the molecule. Moreover, the degradation products of the protein containing ^{14}C may be reutilized by the organism and synthesized into other carbon containing compounds. This renders the method of limited use for the purpose of following the transmission of immune globulins, with which we are concerned, though it is an advantage in following the utilization of proteins.

All these three methods are very sensitive and can be used on a micro scale, so that traces of a protein can be detected and measured in very small samples of body fluids. It is possible in certain circumstances to use all three labels simultaneously on one sample of protein, as is represented diagrammatically in fig. 1.7, so that each can be used to check the others.

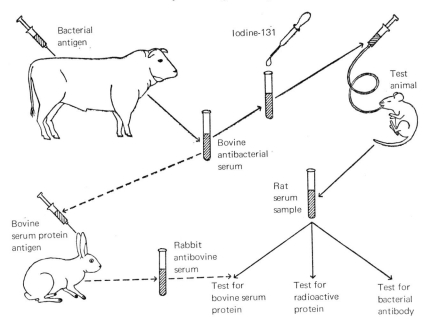

Fig. 1.7. Diagram illustrating three methods, used together, of tracking an immune serum globulin through the gut-wall of a young rat. The immune serum globulin is prepared in an ox against a bacterial antigen and subsequently is labelled with the isotope iodine-131 *in vitro* before feeding to the young rat. Meanwhile an antibovine globulin serum has been prepared in a rabbit. A sample of serum from the young rat is tested for (a) antibody to the bacterial antigen used to immunize the ox, (b) isotopically labelled protein, and (c) bovine globulin by means of the rabbit antiserum. It will be noted that the ox is actively immunized, whereas the rabbit is passively immunized with the antibody made by the ox. However, after a time, the rabbit will become actively immune to the bovine protein, not to the bacterial antigen, and it is these antibovine antibodies that are used in the test. (From Brambell 1960.)

Collectively they provide a very effective tool for studying the problems presented by the transmission of immunity, though they involve the use of a considerable range of technical skills and equipment.

CHAPTER 2

Transmission of immunity in birds

2.1. Introduction

Representatives of all the classes of vertebrates have the capacity to react immunologically, but it is only in relation to birds and mammals that our knowledge of the extent of this capacity is substantial. Immunity is highly developed in birds, both cellular immunity, displayed for example in tissue graft rejection reactions, and serological immunity; the fowl being a particularly good producer of antibodies.

It has been known since the work of Klemperer (1893) that passive immunity to tetanus toxin is transmitted from mother to offspring in the fowl; this was only a year after Ehrlich (1892) had demonstrated for the first time the transmission of passive immunity in mammals. The newly hatched chick is, in fact, well equipped with maternal immunity. Moreover it is known that immunity is transmitted from mother to young in many other species of birds. Clearly in oviparous animals transmission of passive immunity can occur only by way of the egg and there is ample evidence that it does so by way of the yolk, and not the white, of the egg. Two stages in the process must be involved, first the passage from the maternal circulation into the yolk of the egg before laying and secondly the passage from the yolk into the circulation of the developing chick. These two stages will be considered separately in that order.

2.2. The growth of the oocyte

The single ovary of the adult hen contains very large numbers of small oocytes, each in its own follicle. At sexual maturity the largest of these are only about 1 mm in diameter. Thereafter, in the laying hen a small number of these at any one time have entered upon a period of rapid growth and development which normally culminates in ovulation. It is during this period that the vast stores of yolk are accumulated in the oocyte. At first, growth and yolk-formation proceed relatively gradually until the oocyte has attained a diameter of about 6 mm. The remainder of the growth from 6 mm in diameter to 35 mm in diameter, which is the approximate final size, is accomplished in a period of 6 days preceding ovulation. Once ovulated the ovum takes about 24 hr to pass down the oviduct, the albumen, shell membranes and shell being formed around it as it does so, and then to be laid. Normally a laying hen produces one egg per day and the next largest oocyte is released from the ovary and engulfed by the infundibulum of the oviduct within a few minutes of the laying of the previous egg.

The final growth of the oocyte is astonishingly rapid since it increases its volume by about 200 times in six days. All the material for this growth must cross the follicle to reach the oocyte. Bellairs (1965) gives the thickness of the follicular epithelium as 7 μ around an oocyte of 6 mm diameter and 3 μ around a mature oocyte of 35 mm diameter. Hence the follicular epithelium must transmit its own volume of material to the oocyte at an average rate of once every $1\frac{1}{4}$ minutes. It is inconceivable that it could synthesize material at this rate and it is evident that a large part of the material transmitted by the follicle to the maturing oocyte has been synthesized before it reaches the follicle. A part of this prefabricated material that is transferred by the follicle from the maternal circulation to the oocyte consists of serum proteins. Although the follicle cells are not responsible for synthesizing these materials they appear to play an essential role in selecting the kinds and determining the amount of each that is transmitted.

2.3. *The structure of the ovarian follicle*

The structure of the avian follicle has been described by van Durme (1914), Marza and Marza (1935) and more recently, with the aid of the electron microscope, by Bellairs (1965). The wall of the follicle is composed of several layers of tissue. The follicular epithelium is the layer nearest the oocyte and consists of a simple cubical epithelium in both small and large follicles but reaches a maximum thickness in follicles of medium size, when it appears to be stratified or pseudostratified. It rests upon a thin basement membrane, the membrana propria which is surrounded by a rich vascular network in the theca of connective tissue. Inner and outer layers can be distinguished in the theca of the larger follicles, the latter containing smooth muscle fibres. At first the cell membranes of the oocyte and of the follicle cells lie close together but in the later stages more complex structures are formed which separate them. The first formed and innermost of these under the light microscope appears radially striated and has been called the zona radiata or zona striata, but under the electron microscope it is seen to consist of microvilli on the surface of the oocyte forming a close pallisade around it, like the pile of velvet. This layer therefore appears to arise from, and to be a part of, the oocyte itself. Later another outer membrane is secreted around the oocyte, the vitelline membrane. At least two layers can be distinguished in this (Bellairs 1963), the innermost of which is secreted by the follicle before the oocyte is ovulated and the outermost appears to be added by the oviduct after ovulation. Together they constitute the firm, translucent membrane which contains the yolk intact during the early stages of embryogenesis and prevents it mixing with the white of the egg.

Bellairs (1965) has shown that in small follicles the cell membranes of the follicle cells and the oocyte lie close together and many desmosomes can be seen attaching the surfaces of the follicle cells to that of the oocyte as well as to those of each other. The follicle cells are complex in structure, with well developed rough endoplasmic reticulum and Golgi apparatus and they are rich in ribonucleoproteins. They appear to be actively synthesizing, and possibly secreting, material into the oocyte. Vesicles, probably pinocytotic, are numerous in the periphery of the oocyte. As growth proceeds, long processes of the follicle cells deeply indent the surface of the oocyte and extend some distance into its cortex, although there is no evidence that the continuity of the cell membranes of either oocyte or follicle cell is interrupted. These processes of the follicle cells contain curious osmiophil, and hence electron-dense bodies resembling, but more extensive than, half-desmosomes, attached to the inner surfaces of their cell-membranes. It is possible that the tips of these processes become detached as vesicles donated to the oocyte. It is interesting that, before electron microscopy was available, bodies that were osmiophil and argentophil, were described as passing from the follicle cells into the cortex of the oocyte at these stages (Brambell 1925). These were thought to be derived from the Golgi bodies of the follicle cells, but in the light of Bellairs' work, it seems probable that they were the follicle cell processes containing her 'lining-bodies', as she suggests. These processes of the follicle cells are not interrupted by the vitelline membrane, which is deposited around them.

2.4. The serum proteins of the yolk

The cytoplasm of the maturing oocyte becomes so heavily laden with yolk that cytoplasmic movement must be reduced to a minimum. The yolk is laid down in concentric layers and these appear to represent successive increments between which little mixing occurs. This is an important consideration when sampling the yolk to test for the presence of ingredients that may have been in the circulation for only a short time, because these could be present in relatively high concentration in the layer of yolk secreted at that time and absent from other regions. Hence, if a sample is to be representative of the whole oocyte, the yolk should be well mixed before it is taken so as to ensure even distribution.

Extraction of the yolk of an egg with saline results in the separation of a water-soluble livitin fraction from a water-insoluble vitellin fraction. The soluble proteins of livitin can be separated by free-boundary electrophoresis into α-, β- and γ-livitin, which closely resemble and probably are identical with the serum proteins. Shepard and Hottle (1949) found the proportions to be: α-livitin 17.3%, β-livitin 32.7%, and γ-livitin 50.0%, whilst Gorini and Lanzavecchia (1955) found α-livitin 18.7%, β-livitin 44.1% and a minor fraction 4.8%, and γ-livitin 32.4%. Shepard and Hottle found the corresponding peaks in hen serum to be respectively 53.3%, 18.3%, and 28.3%. Thus there appears to be relatively much more β- and γ-livitin as compared to α-livitin in yolk than of the corresponding components in serum. Jukes and Kay (1932) compared the livitin proteins with the serum globulins by their anaphylactic and precipitin reactions and concluded that they were very closely related, if not identical, although the complement fixation test did indicate some difference. Nace (1953) found that livitin absorbs the antibodies from rabbit antisera to fowl serum albumin and fowl γ-globulin and hence contains proteins immunologically similar to these. Williams (1962) identified the livitin proteins with serum proteins by immunoelectrophoresis, starch-gel electrophoresis and comparison of peptide patterns. He identified by these means α-livitin with serum albumin, β-livitin with serum α_2-glycoprotein and γ-livitin with serum γ-globulin. Transferrin was found to be present in livitin but ovalbumin was absent. All antibodies were removed from anti-livitin serum by absorption with serum proteins, and from anti-serum-protein serum by absorption with livitin, however not all antibodies were removed from an anti-serum-globulin serum by absorption with livitin. It was concluded that although the proteins present in livitin were present in serum, some serum proteins may be absent or present at only very low concentrations in livitin. The relative proportions of the proteins in livitin were not the same as those in serum. Patterson, Youngner, Weigle and Dixon (1962a) found that the concentration of γ-globulin in the yolk was many times that of serum albumin and concluded that γ-globulin is preferentially transferred from the circulation to the yolk of the egg by the follicular epithelium. They found that this transfer occurred largely during the final four to five days preceding ovulation.

Patterson et al. (1962a) demonstrated the passage of fowl γ-globulin, trace labelled with ^{131}I and injected into the circulation, to the yolk of the egg. Autoradiographs of sections of the yolks of the eggs showed that the labelled material was concentrated in a peripheral or more central zone according to the interval when it was taken after injection. Dispersal of the labelled material appeared to occur very slowly in yolk and consequently, to measure the total activity in the yolk, it is necessary to mix the whole yolk very thoroughly before sampling. These authors (1962b) also showed that no activity is present in the yolks of eggs laid one day after intravenous injection into the mother, as might be expected since injection would have coincided with ovulation and the egg would have spent the whole of the interval in the oviduct. Protein-bound activity is detectable in eggs laid two days after injection, reaches a peak in eggs laid five days after injection, and declines in eggs laid after longer intervals. Therefore, transmission of γ-globulin to the yolk takes place mainly during the final rapid phase of growth of the ovarian oocyte. The amount of labelled γ-globulin in the yolks of ovarian eggs of various sizes 24 hr after intravenous injection into the mother was determined also and it was found that the amount increases with yolk-volume to a maximum at about 10 ml and declines or levels off thereafter (fig. 2.1). Taking into account the dilution effect of the volume of yolk present at the time of injection, it is evident that transmission to the yolk becomes increasingly rapid during the final growth of the oocyte.

2.5. *The transmission of antibodies to the yolk of the egg*

Ramon (1928) immunized laying hens by subcutaneous injection of tetanus toxin and found that antitoxin was detectable in the serum on the 14th or 15th day after injection and in the yolk on the 25th day. The amount of antitoxin in the yolk reached a maximum on the 30th day. Antitoxin passively administered to the hen increased the amount in the yolk of eggs laid subsequently. Jukes, Fraser and Orr (1934) also observed the passage of anti-toxin to the yolks of eggs laid by hens immunized with diphtheria toxoid. They observed some correlation of the concentrations in the yolk and the serum respectively.

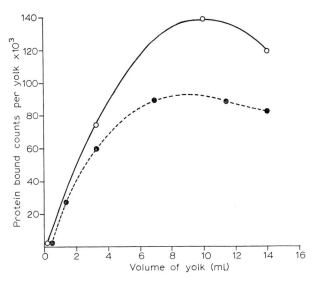

Fig. 2.1. The yolk content of ^{131}I-labelled homologous γ-globulin in the developing ovarian oocytes of two hens 24 hr after intravenous injection. (After Patterson, Youngner, Weigle and Dixon 1962b.)

Antiviral antibodies also are transmitted from the circulation to the yolk of the egg. Brandly, Moses and Jungherr (1946) found antibodies to New-castle disease virus in the yolks of the eggs of hens which had been vaccinated for this disease as well as of hens which had recovered from the disease. Schmittle and Millen (1948) invariably found the yolks of the eggs of hens which gave positive haemagglutination-inhibition serum reactions to be positive also, whereas none of the eggs from a Newcastle disease-free flock were positive. Kissling, Eidson and Stamm (1954) found antibodies to eastern equine encephalomyelitis both in some of the sera and in some of the eggs of a colony of white ibises that they examined. Patterson et al. (1962b) found that antibody induced by a single injection of influenza virus sus-pension was transmitted to the yolk of the egg and attained peak levels in it 5 days after the peak level had been attained in the serum.

Bacterioagglutinins are transmitted also from the circulation to the yolk of the egg. Buxton (1952) found that hens from a flock chronically infected with *Salmonella pullorum* produced eggs with agglutinin titres in the yolk about equal to those of the maternal sera. However, the agglutinin titre of the yolk bore no close relation to that of the serum and was usually very much lower with hens immunized by killed suspensions of *S. pullorum* or *S. typhi*. Hens experimentally infected with *S. gallinarum* produced eggs even after an interval of nearly a year which had yolk-titres of both agglutinating and non-agglutinating antibodies equalling or exceeding those of the maternal sera. Non-agglutinating antibodies appeared in the yolks of the eggs of birds immunized with killed suspensions of *S. pullorum* at titres about equal to those of the maternal sera. Brierley and Hemmings (1956) also found that the agglutinin titres of the yolks of the eggs of hens immunized to killed suspensions of *S. pullorum* were considerably lower than those of the maternal sera, but they did not test for non-agglutinating antibodies.

TABLE 2.1

Relation of serum and egg-yolk titres of immune laying hens. The figures indicate the number of eggs tested. (From Brierley and Hemmings 1956.)

Titre of antibody in fowl serum	Titre of antibody in egg-yolk					
	$\frac{1}{10}$	$\frac{1}{20}$	$\frac{1}{40}$	$\frac{1}{80}$	$\frac{1}{160}$	$\frac{1}{320}$
$\frac{1}{2560}$					1	2
$\frac{1}{1280}$			1		1	
$\frac{1}{640}$		2	4	5		
$\frac{1}{320}$			1			
$\frac{1}{160}$		11	1			
$\frac{1}{80}$		2				

The titres of the agglutinins in the yolks (table 2.1) were nearly linearly related to those of the maternal sera, and approximated to $\frac{1}{8}$. Malkinson (1965) examined the transmission to the yolk of both naturally occurring and induced antibodies to *Escherichia coli*. Fowl erythrocytes were sensitized with an alkaline extract of *E. coli* bacteria; agglutination of these by the fowl sera was evidence of the presence of complete antibody, and agglutination by dilute rabbit antiserum to fowl serum was evidence of incomplete antibody. Hens immunized by a single injection of a suspension of killed

E. coli bacteria produced complete antibody which was 2-mercaptoethanol sensitive and hence taken to be a macroglobulin antibody. No 2-mercaptoethanol sensitive antibody was found in the yolks of the eggs of such birds. Incomplete antibody, which was not 2-mercaptoethanol sensitive, was found in the yolks of the eggs of both the control and the immunized birds at levels which were correlated with those of the sera. Consequently it was suggested that the incomplete antibody which was transmitted was in the 7S γ_2-globulin fraction and that transmission was selective as between $\gamma_1 M$ and 7S γ_2 globulins.

Orlans (1967) studied the antibodies naturally occurring in fowl serum to sheep erythrocytes and those produced after primary and secondary immunization. Agglutinins, non-agglutinating antibodies and haemolysins were examined. Non-agglutinating antibodies were found in the yolks of the eggs at titres between $\frac{1}{2}$ and equality with those of the maternal sera, whereas agglutinins were on average at titres of about $\frac{1}{16}$ of those of the corresponding sera. Haemolysins could not be detected in the yolk at all, even when they were present in the maternal serum at high titres. The yolk antibodies reached peak levels at 5 days after the serum antibodies.

Patterson et al. (1962b) studied the transmission to the yolk of immune precipitins to bovine serum albumin. The antibody appeared in the yolks of eggs laid 4 days after it appeared in the serum and reached peak levels 5–6 days after the peak serum levels. The recovery of antibody from the yolk was estimated at 70–80% by adding known amounts to normal yolks. The yolk consists of about 50% solids. Correcting for these factors the peak antibody levels of the aqueous phase of yolks were estimated to equal or exceed the peak serum level.

2.6. *Persistence of antibody in the yolk of egg during storage and incubation*

Antibody in yolk appears to be remarkably stable and persistent, although proteolytic enzymes are known to be present. Thus Brandly, Moses and Jungherr (1946) found the titre of antibody to Newcastle disease virus to be well maintained in eggs that had been stored for 6 months at 6–8 °C. Brierley and Hemmings (1956) found that the yolk titre of bacterioagglutinins does not appear to fall even during incubation. Thus the residue of yolk in the yolk-sacs of 1–4 day old chicks, hatched from the eggs of actively immunized hens, had titres of $\frac{1}{80}$ to $\frac{1}{320}$, which were as high as those observed in new-laid

eggs of these birds. Similarly, antibodies injected into the yolk-sac on the
6th day of incubation were present in the yolk-sac of the newly-hatched
chick. To discover if there was any significant decrease in titre due to proteolysis of antibodies in yolk when incubated *in vitro*, these authors mixed
immune sera with yolk withdrawn from freshly laid eggs and from developing
eggs on the 6th day of incubation and incubated the mixture under sterile
conditions at 39 °C for 13 days. No fall in titre of antibody was observed.
Thus it appears that although the quantity of antibody in the yolk-sac
presumably declines with the quantity of yolk, the concentration in the
residue does not decline appreciably.

2.7. *The transmission of heterologous proteins from the circulation to the egg*

Ramon (1928) injected tetanus toxin subcutaneously into laying hens.
He was unable to detect the toxin in eggs laid the following day, either in
the albumen or in the yolk, but it was present in the yolks of eggs laid two
days after injection and increased in amount in those laid on successive days
to a peak in those laid on the 5th day, declining in those laid thereafter.
Knight and Schechtman (1954) injected intravenously in laying hens rat
serum, crystalline bovine albumin, bovine γ-globulin and lobster serum.
All were recognised in the yolks of the eggs laid by the hens by positive
precipitin reactions with rabbit antisera to these antigens. The rat serum and
bovine albumin antigenic activity were not precipitated by antilivitin sera.
The bovine albumin and γ-globulin were found in eggs laid 2–3 days after
injection, appeared to reach maximal concentrations in eggs laid 5–7 days
after injection and were present in eggs laid up to 15 days after injection,
but not thereafter. The electrophoretic properties of bovine albumin and
γ-globulin were retained after transmission to the yolk and so also was the
ultracentrifugal behaviour of bovine albumin. So far as could be determined
these proteins appeared to be unchanged by transmission to the yolk of the
egg. Patterson et al. (1962b) also demonstrated the passage of bovine serum
from the circulation to the yolk of the egg. Bovine serum albumin trace-
labelled with ^{131}I appeared in the yolks of eggs laid 3–4 days after intravenous injection. It was also demonstrated immunologically with rabbit
antiserum by double gel diffusion and ring precipitin tests.

2.8. *The structure of the embryonic membranes of the chick*

A knowledge of the structure of the embryonic membranes, and especially of the yolk-sac, of the chick is essential for an understanding of the transmission of immunity from the yolk to the circulation. The following account has made much use of the description of Romanoff (1952). Meroblastic cleavage of the fertilized ovum occurs as the egg traverses the oviduct and results in the formation of a small disc of cells, the blastoderm, lying on the surface of the yolk at the animal pole of the ovum. The embryo arises from the central region of the blastoderm only and the peripheral tissues are extraembryonic and give rise to the membranes which envelop the embryo and enclose the yolk and ultimately the albumen. The cells of the margin of the blastoderm differentiate into outer and inner layers, the ectoderm and endoderm respectively. Mesoderm differentiates and extends peripherally between ectoderm and endoderm. The extraembryonic coelomic cavity, or exocoel, in the mesoderm extends with it almost to its margin, separating it into an outer somatic layer, lining the ectoderm, and an inner splanchnic layer covering the endoderm. The margin of the blastoderm grows rapidly and during the third day of incubation has extended well beyond the equator of the ovum, by the 10th day all the membranes are established and the whole of the contents of the egg enclosed by them.

A fold of extraembryonic ectoderm and somatic mesoderm begins to form around the embryo in the middle of the second day of incubation. It grows up over the embryo and by the end of the third day its margin has contracted and closed over the dorsal surface of the embryo two-thirds of the way back. The inner wall of this fold is the amnion, which immediately envelops the embryo and encloses the amniotic fluid. Thus the amnion is lined on the side next to the embryo by ectoderm and covered with somatic mesoderm. The outer wall of this fold is the chorion, the outermost membrane of all, composed of ectoderm on the outside and lined by somatic mesoderm. The amnion is separated from the chorion by the exocoel except at the point of final closure of the fold, where the amniotic and chorionic ectoderm remain in continuity, forming the sero-amniotic connection.

The endoderm next to the yolk and its covering of splanchnic mesoderm gives rise to the yolk-sac. This is in continuity with the embryonic gut of which it is really an extraembryonic extension. The connection between gut and yolk-sac becomes reduced to a narrow tube as the embryo becomes delimited, entering it through the umbilicus; this is the yolk-sac or vitelline stalk. As the blastoderm extends around the yolk, the yolk-sac wall and the chorion are continuous at its margin, until the envelopment of the yolk is complete and the extension of the exocoel separates them. Cells in the splanchnic mesoderm of the central area of the yolk-sac wall give rise both to blood vessels and blood cells on the second day of incubation. These 'blood islands', as they are called, coalesce and give rise to the network of blood vessels, containing clumps of blood-forming cells, that constitute the area vasculosa of the yolk-sac wall. Vitelline arteries and veins develop and connect it through the yolk-sac stalk with the developing heart. The limit of the area vasculosa is marked by a marginal vessel, the sinus terminalis. Blood begins to circulate in the area vasculosa when the embryo has attained the 16-somite stage in the middle of the 2nd day. The area vasculosa extends gradually, occupying half the surface of the yolk-sac on the sixth day and covering it all by the end of the 14th day. The blood vessels with their covering of endoderm protrude into the cavity of the yolk-sac as folds or ridges, which thus increase the internal absorptive surface. The external surface area of the yolk-sac increases rapidly at first, but then, owing to the absorption of yolk and the folding of its walls it decreases in size. It attains its maximum weight at the middle of the third week of incubation and by the day before hatching has lost about half its weight. It is then retracted into the body of the embryo, through the umbilicus, together with about $\frac{1}{3}$ of the yolk, which is still unabsorbed. In the newly hatched chick the flaccid and crumpled yolk-sac lies immediately within the body wall on the ventral surface of the intestine. It is gradually absorbed during the succeeding 5 days, the nutriment it provides enabling the chick to go without food for a considerable interval after hatching. It is very easy to make injections into the yolk-sac of the newly hatched chick as it is clearly visible through the thin body wall when the down is damped.

The allantois starts to develop on the second day of incubation as a small evagination of the yolk-sac wall into the exocoel just behind and beneath the embryo. This grows out as a stalked sac into the exocoel, where it expands. Its wall consists of a lining of endoderm and a covering of splanchnic mesoderm and it is connected by the tubular allantoic stalk through the umbilicus to the hind gut of the embryo. It is vascularised by the allantoic vessels which grow out in the splanchnic mesoderm covering it. It expands rapidly till it nearly fills the exocoel and on the fifth day of incubation its outer wall comes in contact with the inner surface of the chorion, with which it fuses to form the allantochorion. Nearly the whole of the chorion is converted in this way into allantochorion, which becomes richly vascularised by the allantoic vessels. This membrane therefore consists of ectoderm on the outside, fused layers of somatic and splanchnic mesoderm in the middle and endoderm on the inside. The inner wall of the allantois fuses with the amnion in the region of the sero-amniotic connection but is otherwise freely exposed in the exocoel. Folds of allantochorion grow out around the albumen and close to form the albumen sac by the 12th day of incubation. The floor of this sac is formed by the only remaining part of the chorion which has not been converted into allantochorion and which adjoins the

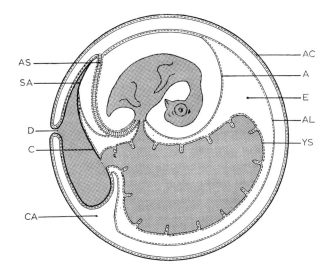

Fig. 2.2. Diagram of the arrangement of the fully established embryonic membranes of the chick. Much of the yolk has been absorbed and the yolk-sac splanchnopleur (YS) folded. The albumen has been surrounded by folds of the allantochorion (AC) in an albumen sac (D) which still communicates with the yolk-sac. The allantoic stalk (AS) encircles the outside of the amnion (A) and the allantois (AL) has fused with the chorion (C) over almost its whole extent to form the allantochorion. The allantoic cavity (CA) is extensive and its expansion has reduced the extent of the exocoel (E). The amnion and chorion are continuous over a small area of sero-amniotic connection (SA). (After Lillie 1927.)

sero-amniotic connection (fig. 2.2). The sero-amniotic connection opens on the 11th day and allows albumen from the albumen sac to flow into the amnion and mix with the amniotic fluid.

2.9. *The functions of the embryonic membranes of the chick*

The embryonic membranes, characteristic of the Amniota, are an adaptation to enable the embryo to develop on land within the closed system of the cleidoic egg. They have to provide for the conservation and utilisation of the water and nutritive stores within the egg, for respiratory exchange with the surrounding air, for isolation and storage until hatching of the excretory products, and for the provision of a fluid environment in which the early embryo can develop. The function of the yolk-sac is primarily that of a yolk-containing and yolk-absorbing organ. Absorption of the yolk appears to take place entirely within it and there is no passage of yolk from it to the intestine through the yolk-sac stalk. The retraction of the yolk-sac into the body of the embryo before hatching ensures the conservation of all the yolk and provides reserves for the first few days of life after hatching. The yolk-sac wall is also the principal blood-forming organ in early stages of development and its consequent very vascular nature provides for the transport of the materials absorbed from the yolk. The function of the amnion is to surround the embryo with a fluid environment, which supports it hydrostatically, lubricates its surface and prevents adhesion of the membrane, prevents dessication and provides a cushion against shock. Since the very soft tissues of the early stages have a specific gravity close to that of the amniotic fluid the embryo is able to develop in an almost weightless state in this environment. Smooth muscle in the amniotic wall enables it to pulsate, contractions beginning on the fourth day and reaching a maximum on the twelfth day, after which they decrease and finally stop. Probably this pulsation assists in preventing adhesions. Swallowing movements of the embryo, when they start on the 9th day, result in the amniotic fluid, with which albumen has mixed, being ingested. Although there are villous processes on the wall of the albumen sac probably most of the absorption of albumen is from the embryonic intestinal tract. The allantois functions as a

---

Plate 2.1. Electron micrographs of the yolk-sac endoderm of a chick at 3 days of incubation. A whole cell is seen at A with its small, basally situated nucleus (N), mitochondria (M) and vacuoles that contained yolk droplets (arrows). The cell rests upon a basement membrane adjoining the splanchnic mesoderm. The free surface of the cell is indented with caveoli (C) and pinocytotic vesicles (V) are present in the apical cytoplasm, as shown at higher magnifications in B and C. A desmosome (D) connecting two adjoining cells is seen in B. An artefact (F) is caused by a fold in the underlying carbon film. A × 5200, B × 16,000, C × 59,000. (From Bellairs 1963.)

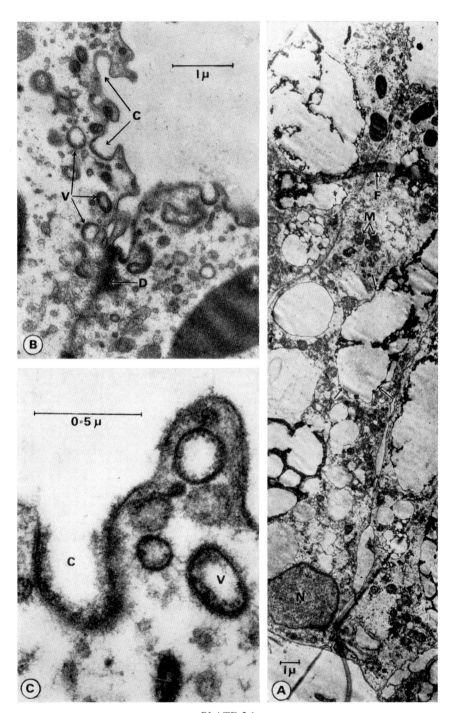

PLATE 2.1

reservoir for the mesonephric excreta which drain into it. Most of the nitrogenous waste is in the form of uric acid, which precipitates out as urates that are retained in the allantoic cavity and are left with the membranes in the shell at hatching. The allantois also functions as a route by which the allantochorion is vascularised, thus providing for respiratory exchange between the outermost membrane, through the porous shell to which it adheres, and the surrounding air.

Water movements between the compartments of the embryonic membranes are extensive. At first the albumen is the main reservoir of water. The yolk-sac absorbs water from the albumen and by the 10th day of incubation it has accumulated several ml. Thereafter it loses water and little remains in the yolk at the time of hatching. Fluid appears in the amnion shortly after its formation and by the 5th day of incubation it is tense. It reaches a volume of 3–6 ml, or even more, after the entry of the albumen, by the 13th day, then decreases gradually until the 16th day and thereafter very rapidly. Fluid begins to collect in the allantois on the 4th day and mesonephric excretion is added from the 5th day, so that it may contain about 1 ml on the 7th day and 6.5 ml by the 13th day. Thereafter it decreases and little is left at the time of hatching. Throughout incubation there is, of course, some loss of water by transpiration through the shell.

2.10. *The cytology of the yolk-sac endoderm*

The changes in the yolk-sac of the chick during early stages of development have been examined with the electron microscope by Bellairs (1963). At first the endoderm cells in the peripheral zone of the blastoderm tend to be separate and scattered in the periphery of the yolk, but by 3 days of incubation they have undergone extensive changes and become arranged as epithelium. The tall columnar cells of this epithelial endoderm may be 50μ or more in height, with relatively small nuclei situated basally (plate 2.1). They rest on a basement membrane, which separates them from the overlying splanchnic mesoderm. They are attached to their neighbours by desmosomes and have interlocking processes. Their free surfaces, next to the yolk, have many indentations and small vesicles beneath the surface, suggesting pinocytosis. The membrane of these indentations and vesicles has a thick fuzzy lining of electron dense material, such as is often met with in pinocytosis. Mitochondria are numerous and the endoplasmic reticulum is well developed. At this stage the intracellular yolk droplets are beginning to show unmistakable signs of digestion. Unfortunately no description is available of the electron microscopy of the endoderm cells in later stages of development.

2.11. *The passage of serum proteins from the yolk to the chick embryo*

Serum proteins can be detected early in development in the embryo and embryonic membranes of the chick. The very early appearance of these strongly suggests that they are of maternal origin, but except in so far as maternal antibodies or labelled serum proteins have been used this cannot be said to be demonstrated, since the possibility of foetal synthesis is not formally excluded. Nace (1953) using rabbit antisera to fowl serum proteins, which had been carefully absorbed and tested for specificity, was able to detect immunologically antigens resembling serum albumin on or before the 5th day of incubation, those resembling $\alpha\beta$-globulins about the 6th day and those resembling γ-globulin between the 9th and 12th days. Brandly, Moses and Jungherr (1946) found that the embryonic tissues and membranes early in development displayed virus neutralizing and inactivating properties when they were from eggs of Newcastle disease immune birds, which would appear to indicate the passage of antibodies from the yolk at these stages. It is probable, therefore, that maternal serum proteins, including antibodies, may be transmitted intact to the tissues of the developing chick at early stages of development before circulating antibodies can be detected in the embryonic serum.

2.12. *The transmission of homologous antibodies from the yolk to the serum of the chick*

Ramon (1928) showed that tetanus antitoxin is transferred from the yolk to the serum of the chick and indeed he came to the conclusion that all the antitoxin present in the yolk reaches the serum. Antiviral antibodies have been shown to be transferred to the chicks of a variety of birds, as well as fowl, including pigeons and doves, sparrows, crows, swallows, herons, ibises, magpies, etc. (Kissling, Eidson and Stamm 1954; Reeves, Sturgeon, French and Brookman 1954; Sooter, Schaeffer, Gorrie and Cockburn 1954). Maternal opsonins, both natural and immune, are transmitted to the circulation of the chick (Karthigasu, Jenkin and Turner 1964). Both natural and immune antibodies in fowl serum to sheep red cells are transmitted from the yolk to the circulation of the chick, but non-agglutinating antibodies were transmitted more readily to the yolk than agglutinins and haemolysins were not transmitted at all, and in consequence it was mainly non-agglutinating antibody which reached the circulation of the chick (Orlans 1967). Anti-bacterial antibodies are transmitted to the circulation of the chick also. Thus both naturally occurring and immune antibodies to *Escherichia coli* are transmitted, but those reaching the circulation of the chick were not 2-mercaptoethanol sensitive, and presumably were exclusively 7S antibodies (Malkinson 1965). Both agglutinating and non-agglutinating antibodies to *Salmonella* are transmitted to the circulation of the chick (Buxton 1952; Brierley and Hemmings 1956), but the non-agglutinating antibody appears

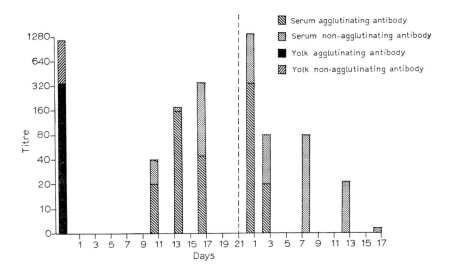

Fig. 2.3. Diagram of the transmission of agglutinating and incomplete antibodies to *Salmonella* from the yolk to the circulation of developing embryonic and young chicks of actively immunized hens. The yolk-titre is shown on the left. It will be noted that the maximum serum titre is attained on the first day after hatching and that the incomplete antibody titre is then 4 times that of the agglutinating titre, and that both titres are as high as those of the yolk. (After Buxton 1952.)

to be transmitted the more readily (Buxton 1952) (fig. 2.3). Immune agglutinins to *Brucella abortus* are also transmitted (Brierley and Hemmings 1956).

2.13. The transmission of heterologous antibodies from the yolk to the serum of the chick

Brierley and Hemmings (1956) showed that transmission of antibodies occurred from immune fowl serum injected into the yolk-sac either of the embryo at the 6th or 8th day of incubation, when this operation on the egg is most readily performed, or into the retracted yolk-sac of the newly hatched chicken. Using this technique these authors tested the transmission of a variety of antibodies from immune sera prepared in various species. Antibodies to *Brucella abortus* prepared in fowl when injected into the yolk-sacs on the 6th or 8th day of incubation in doses of 0.5 to 1.0 ml of antiserum were transmitted to the circulations of the chickens which hatched from these eggs. The concentration of antibody in the serum of the newly hatched chicken relative to that in the serum injected (C.Q.) was $\frac{1}{32}$ to $\frac{1}{256}$. Transmission was better when the injection was performed on the 8th day of incubation than on the 6th, possibly because the yolk-sac was then less turgid and consequently the serum was less liable to leak from the puncture. Injection into the retracted yolk-sac of the newly hatched chick was much easier and transmission of antibodies to both *Salmonella pullorum* and to *Brucella abortus* was observed at C.Q.'s of $\frac{1}{32}$ to $\frac{1}{256}$. When bovine antiserum was injected into the yolk-sac on the 6th day of incubation no antibody could be detected in the sera of the newly hatched chickens at C.Q.'s of $\frac{1}{128}$ or better, although antibody was still present in the yolk-sac in quantities of the order of those injected. A more sensitive test was then employed by injecting bovine or equine anti-diphtheric serum into the yolk-sac on the 6th day of incubation and testing the sera of the newly hatched chickens for diphtheria antitoxins. No bovine antitoxin could be detected at C.Q.'s of 0.0002, but in one chick serum equine antitoxin was present at a C.Q. of 0.00004. Antisera to *Brucella abortus* prepared in rabbit, bovine and pigeon were injected into the retracted yolk-sacs of newly hatched chickens. Neither of the mammalian antibodies could be detected in the sera of the chicks subsequently, although in each case 10 were tested at a C.Q. of $\frac{1}{128}$, and 5 at a C.Q. of $\frac{1}{256}$. The pigeon antibodies were transmitted, but much less readily than fowl antibodies.

It appears, therefore, that there is a selection by the yolk-sac of antibodies transmitted from the yolk to the circulation of the chick, both as between antibodies produced in the fowl, where the selection probably depends on the γ-globulin fractions in which the activity resides, and as between antibodies prepared in different species, where mammalian antibodies are not transmitted at all, or only at such very low levels as to be scarcely detectable even as antitoxins, and where pigeon antibodies are transmitted but significantly less readily than fowl antibodies.

2.14. The time and place of transmission of antibodies to the circulation of the chick

Traces of γ-globulin were detected in the embryonic serum by Kaminski and Durieux (1956) on the 14th day of incubation and it was definitely present on the 17th day. Buxton (1952) found that non-agglutinating antibodies to *Salmonella* from the yolk are present in the embryonic serum from the 11th day of incubation but that agglutinating antibodies are seldom transmitted before the 17th day (fig. 2.3). Brandly et al. (1946) were unable to detect antibodies to Newcastle disease virus in the embryonic serum until the 18th day of incubation. It is clear from the work of Brierley and Hemmings (1956) that transmission continues from the retracted yolk-sac after hatching and that it is then at least as rapid as it is at the end of incubation.

The yolk-sac is connected to the gut of the chick by the yolk-sac stalk, which appears to have a patent lumen although, according to Lillie (1927) yolk does not pass through it. However, Karthigasu et al. (1964) finding opsonins which were labile to mercaptoethanol, and hence assumed to be macroglobulins, in the sera of chicks after hatching but not in embryonic sera, suggested that these were transmitted only by the intestine, whereas the 7S antibodies were transmitted by the yolk-sac. However they provide no direct experimental evidence of this route of transmission and it is not even possible to be sure that the antibody in question was of maternal origin; it is possible that it was actively produced by the chicks themselves. Buxton (1952) in order to test the possibility of transmission by the intestine, administered immune anti-*Salmonella pullorum* fowl serum orally to newly hatched chicks and found only very low titres in the circulation. He concluded that most of the transmission is by way of the yolk-sac. Brierley and Hemmings (1956) administered immune fowl anti-*Brucella* serum by stomach tube to 41 newly hatched chicks and could detect no antibody at a C.Q. of $\frac{1}{128}$ in any of their sera, all of which were negative. It must be concluded that transmission occurs mainly, probably entirely, by way of the yolk-sac and that transmission by the intestine, if it can occur at all, can do so only at a very low level. Moreover there is no evidence that maternal antibody ever reaches the intestine directly from the yolk.

2.15. *The transmission of passive immunity and the development of immune competence*

It is often stated that the transmission of passive immunity from the mother is to provide the offspring with resistance to disease until such time as they can develop their own active immunity. No doubt this statement is true but it is often misinterpreted to mean that the offspring are incapable of active immunological response during the period when they are dependent on maternal passive immunity. This has given rise to the idea that the young animal is incapable of active immunization at least throughout the period it is receiving passive immunity. Much evidence has been accumulating that tends to show that the capacity to respond immunologically to a variety of stimuli is developed much earlier than was supposed and that it overlaps and is unrelated to the transmission of passive immunity, except in so far as the presence of maternal antibody to a given antigen hinders active immunization with that antigen. Obviously the full range and intensity of immunological responses characteristic of the adult are developed gradually in the young animal and may not be fully achieved until long after maternal passive immunity has waned but even the embryo displays some powers of immune response to challenge.

It would be more accurate to state that the embryo in the egg, or the uterus, as the case may be, is normally so sheltered from antigenic challenge that it has little opportunity of becoming actively immune before hatching or birth and that as an interval is required after challenge before an active immunity can be developed it is normally dependent on maternal passive immunity at first to tide it over this interval at least. In this way the young animal is provided with the product of the mother's accumulated antigenic experience but its own developing capacity to be actively immunized by those antigens with antibodies for which it has been provided by the mother is temporarily inhibited or impaired. Thus the whole problem of the development of immunological competence in the young animal is bound up with the transmission of passive immunity from the mother, but for reasons that are largely other than its incapacity to react.

2.16. *The development of cellular immunity*

The chick embryo is capable of both cellular and serological immune responses. Karthigasu and Jenkin (1963) found that bacteria, provided they are opsonized by antibody passively acquired either from the mother or by injection, are phagocytosed by the embryonic tissues from at least 10 days of incubation until hatching. At the beginning of this period the membranes account for most of the phagocytosis but their activity declines with age as that of the liver increases and from about 15 days incubation the liver is responsible for most of the phagocytosis. Van Alten and Schechtman (1963) found that the introduction of rabbit serum or human γ-globulin into 12 day old embryos sensitized them at some time before 3 days after hatching when a further injection of the same antigen produced anaphylactic shock. This they attributed to a cellular, rather than a humoral, immunity. Following up this finding van Alten (1966) injected chick embryos with either human or bovine γ-globulin on the 12th day of incubation and harvested blood from them 3 days after hatching. By injecting 2-day old chicks that had not been previously sensitized with this blood he was able to sensitize them and produce an anaphylactic response by injection of the antigen at 3 days of age. Transfer of serum alone did not sensitize these chicks but transfer of buffy coat or of between 700,000 and 1,500,000 mononuclear leucocytes did sensitize. He concluded that the embryonic sensitivity is cell-bound and associated with the lymphocytes.

Another approach to the problem of the time of appearance of cellular immunity in the chick embryo is provided by the homograft reaction. Enlargement of the spleen occurs when lymphoid cells of another strain are injected into a chick embryo and the amount of splenomegaly is a measure of the intensity of the graft-against-host reaction. Solomon (1964) has shown that for a given dose of donor cells maximum splenomegaly is obtained when they are injected at 13 days of incubation and suggests that this is because at later ages a host-against-graft reaction reduces the effect of the graft-against-host reaction and that at earlier ages vascularization of the spleen is incomplete. This conclusion is supported by the fact that maximum tolerance to subsequent skin homografts is produced by prior injection of whole blood from the skin donor at 13 days of incubation. The onset of the homograft response in the chick begins at about 15 days of incubation and continues to increase until 2 days after hatching, when it is well developed. That cells capable of becoming sensitized are present soon after 15 days of incubation was shown by injecting a small number of lymphoid cells initially, followed after an interval by a second exposure to cells from the same donor. An initial exposure at 15 days of incubation resulted in (a) a reduction in splenomegaly and (b) an accelerated rejection of skin grafts on second exposure, showing that sensitization had occurred.

Immunologically competent lymphocytes are present at 2 days after hatching, as shown by skin grafts of 2-day old and older chicks of one parental strain being rejected by adult F_1 hybrids, whereas skin from 1-day old parental strain chicks was not rejected. Clearly, as the F_1 host, though adult, could not react against the parental strain skin this reaction must have been due to competent cells in the graft reacting against the other parental strain antigens in the F_1 host.

Thus it appears that some cells capable of being sensitized are present from 15 days of incubation, as shown by the very sensitive splenomegaly test, and that competent cells are sufficiently numerous in a skin graft by 2 days after hatching to result in rejection.

2.17. *The development of serological immunity*

It appears to be possible also to induce serological immunity in the chick embryo from about 15 days of incubation. Solomon (1966a) claims that the rate of clearance of goat erythrocytes from the circulation of the chick is a very sensitive measure of the amount of opsonizing antibody present. Injection of goat erythrocytes into the embryo could result in the production of antibody as early as the time of hatching and that production was vigorous by 3 days after hatching. This antibody production could be induced by injection of the erythrocytes as early as 12 days of incubation and was most readily induced by injection at 15 days of incubation. Antibody production was poor in response to injection of goat erythrocytes between the 15th day of incubation and 15 days after hatching, due to inhibition resulting from the presence of maternal opsonizing antibody passively acquired. The less sensitive test for immune agglutinins (Solomon 1966b) showed that after injection of chicks soon after hatching with goat erythrocytes agglutinins first appeared at 11 days of age and that by 17 days of age several kinds, including macroglobulin and 7S antibodies, and possibly γA antibodies, were present. The amount of antibody produced increased from 5 to 24 weeks of age. This agrees fairly well with what is known of the synthesis of γ-globulins in the chick. Seto and Henderson (1969) found that some newly hatched chicks and practically all week-old chicks were capable of producing agglutinins to rabbit, rat, mouse, hamster and sheep red cells, whereas 14–18 day embryos were unresponsive. Natural agglutinin levels were low in embryos and in chicks up to two weeks of age. Patterson et al. (1962a) state that the amount of γ-globulin synthesis is low during the first 2 weeks after hatching, but that the rate of synthesis has increased by the end of the 1st month, as shown by the rise in the serum γ-globulin level. Asofsky, Trnka and Thorbecke (1962) used the incorporation of radio-actively labelled amino acids in serum proteins, identified by immunoelectrophoresis coupled with autoradiography. These authors were unable to find any evidence of the synthesis in chicks from 17 days of incubation to 12 days after hatching of either macroglobulin or the major 7S γ-globulin components, but three other minor components of intermediate mobility were labelled. Since exposure to antigenic stimuli plays so large a part in determining the amount of γ-globulin synthesis, it would be better to look for synthesis in animals which had been subjected to a known antigenic challenge. Stone and Boney (1968) found that 2-day old chicks passively immune to Newcastle disease virus were more difficult to protect by vaccination than controls lacking passive immunity, but that this refractoriness could be surmounted by vaccination with an antigen–antibody complex.

Patterson et al. (1962a) found that the half-life of γ-globulin in the circulation of the newly hatched chick was 72 hr, as compared to 35 hr in the adult. Thus, there is a sparing of γ-globulin in the young chick which would tend to increase the duration of passive immunity as well as conserving γ-globulin that is being synthesized.

CHAPTER 3

Transmission of immunity in the rabbit

3.1. The functional significance of the anatomy of the foetal membranes

The method of transmission of immunity from mother to foetus has been investigated more thoroughly in the rabbit than in any other mammal, not excluding man, in which transmission occurs before birth. This is because of the suitability and availability of this animal for surgical experiments upon the pregnant uterus. Appreciation of the significance of the evidence obtained requires a knowledge of the development and final arrangement of the foetal membranes. Indeed, an experimental approach to problems of maternal/foetal interchange in any species must necessarily rest on such knowledge and the experimenter must be equipped with a sufficiently extensive acquaintance with the comparative anatomy of the foetal membranes to be able to exploit the characteristics of each available species. This is an obvious truism; yet it is surprising how often physiologists expect foetal membranes that are widely different in origin and structure to have similar functions. For example, there is little or no justification for assuming similarity of function for the placentae of rabbit and man, even though they are both classed as haemochorial, because their structures and the arrangements of the other foetal membranes associated with them are so widely different. Yet because immunity was known to be transmitted before birth in both it was for long assumed to be transmitted by the same route: across the placenta. It will be shown that it is now known to be transmitted in the rabbit by way of a membrane that is unrepresented in man, except by a rudiment, and that is separate and distinct from the placenta. No further apology is necessary for introducing the subject of transmission of immunity in the rabbit by way of a fairly full account of the development and structure of the foetal membranes. It will be convenient to break off this description at the time when the embryo has become implanted and to deal then with the experimental evidence of the transmission of proteins from the mother to the yolk-sac cavity of the early embryo, before dealing with the further development and final arrangement of the membranes as a preliminary to consideration of transmission to the foetal circulation and other foetal fluids.

3.2. Early uterine development and implantation of the embryo

The developing eggs in a rabbit reach the uterus as small blastocysts three days after copulation. Each blastocyst is surrounded by the zona pellucida, a tough hyaline mucoprotein membrane, secreted by the ovary, that is about 3 μ thick at this stage, and by a much thicker gelatinous layer of mucoprotein on the outside, the so-called albumen, secreted by the lining of the Fallopian tube during transit. During the succeeding four days the blastocysts remain free in the uterine cavity and receive a further coating of mucus. They become spaced out fairly evenly along the length of the uterus. They expand with increasing rapidity and have attained an average diameter of about 3.5 mm by the beginning of the 7th day. Each is then a little thin-walled vesicle still surrounded by its membranes and filled with liquid, the yolk-sac fluid. The expansion of the blastocyst stretches the covering membranes to such an extent that they are exceedingly thin at this time. The wall of the blastocyst itself consists of a cellular layer of ectoderm, the trophoblast, lined by a very thin membrane of endoderm cells. At one side is the thicker embryonic plate from which the mesoderm will spread later, between the trophoblast and the endoderm, until it reaches the equator. It does not extend further and the abembryonal hemisphere of the yolk-sac omphalopleur remains bilaminar.

Early on the seventh day the blastocyst begins to implant (fig. 3.1). The literature dealing with this process has been reviewed recently by Böving (1963) and an excellent electron microscopic study of the process has been published by Larsen (1963a), who has also described the structure of the uterine epithelium both during oestrus and pregnancy (1962a). Ciliated cells are numerous in the uterine epithelium at oestrus but these have disappeared by the 6th day of pregnancy. The rapidly expanding blastocyst is orientated with the embryonic plate towards the mesometrium. Owing to its expansion it fills and then distends the uterine cavity on the antimesometrial side,

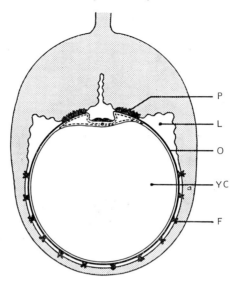

Fig. 3.1. Diagram of the implanting blastocyst of the rabbit at 8 days after conception. The bilaminar omphalopleur (O) which forms the wall of the yolk-sac (YC) is attached to the uterine mucosa antimesometrially at a number of points (F) where the trophoblast is invading the maternal tissues. Mesometrially the amniotic folds are not yet closed but the trophoblast of the chorion is invading the mucosa in the region that will become the placenta (P). The uterine cavity is shown (L).

where the uterine wall is thinnest, forming a spherical chamber around itself. The trophoblast of the bilaminar wall of the yolk-sac adheres to the antimesometrial uterine epithelium at a number of isolated points over the abembryonal hemisphere of the blastocyst, the thin enveloping membrane disappearing first. Trophoblast cells appear to form little clusters or knobs at these points. Meanwhile the cells of the uterine epithelium over the region of attachment have fused to form a symplasma (plate 3.1). The trophoblastic knob, adhering to this, becomes syncytial and then fuses with the symplasma, bulges into the mouths of the uterine glands and, in places, penetrates the uterine epithelium and envelops the adjoining maternal capillaries. Careful examination with the light microscope suggests that the endothelial walls of these capillaries are eroded in places and that the maternal blood circulates in channels in the trophoblast, as it does in the placenta itself at later stages (Parry 1950). Recently electron microscopic examination has thrown doubt on this, suggesting that the endothelium remains intact

(Larsen 1963a). Uninucleate or binucleate giant cells are budded off from the invading tongues of trophoblast to form the obplacental giant cells which persist in the lateral and antimesometrial sub-mucosa until late in pregnancy (Larsen 1963a). The regions of the bilaminar wall of the blasto-cyst, intervening between these fusion areas, remain separate from, though close to, the uterine epithelium.

The blastocyst continues to expand while it is implanting and attains a size of nearly 1 cm in diameter by the end of the 8th day. Meanwhile the uterine glands have continued to secrete, the lining of their deeper parts remaining cellular and not transforming into symplasma. The secretion distends the glands and protrudes from them to form large lacunae in the trophoblast (Larsen 1963a). On the 9th day the symplasma becomes detached from the uterine wall and disintegrates. It is probable that this superficial layer of the mucosa which is sloughed off and lost, and beneath which a new uterine epithelium is regenerated, is comparable to the decidua capsularis of rodents (Morris 1950). Then the whole of the bilaminar wall of the yolk-sac begins to break down. The trophoblast breaks down first and the endoderm persists for a time, but it too has disappeared by the 13th day, cell debris and rem-nants of the uterine symplasma, and of the bilaminar omphalopleur in the uterine lumen being all that remains. Reichert's membrane, a non-cellular hyaline membrane developed between the endoderm and the trophoblast of the bilaminar omphalopleur in many mammals, is not found in rabbits. Consequently the disintegration of the trophoblast and endoderm of the bilaminar omphalopleur opens up the yolk-sac cavity to the uterine lumen and exposes the endodermal lining of its splanchnic hemisphere, which has been everted. Meanwhile a new cellular uterine epithelium has been re-generated by the spread of the epithelium lining the deeper parts of the glands over the areas denuded by the break-down of the symplasma. The obplacental giant cells, of trophoblastic origin, are enclosed in the mucosa beneath this regenerated epithelium, where they enlarge and form a conspicuous feature of the pregnant uterus until near full term.

It will be appreciated from this account that the yolk-sac of the rabbit is a closed vesicle from the time when it arrives in the uterus until the ninth day. Thereafter it is difficult to determine the exact time at which the delicate endoderm of the bilaminar omphalopleur becomes disrupted. During the first three days after arrival in the uterus the blastocyst is free in the cavity and is enclosed in the zona pellucida. This membrane is shed early on the seventh day when the blastocyst becomes attached. Thus the blastocyst is naked and attached to the mucosa during the remaining three days. This is an important distinction because, before the seventh day, the blastocyst can only absorb substances that are contained in the uterine fluid and to which the zona pellucida is permeable, whereas after attachment and shedding of the membrane this barrier is removed and substances may also be absorbed direct from the uterine tissues. Moreover before attachment, even on the 6th day, the blastocysts are so small that only minute samples of yolk-sac fluid can be harvested for analysis, whereas by the 8th day as much as 0.5 ml can be obtained from each, making analysis easier.

3.3. The protein content of the yolk-sac fluid

Our interest in the transmission of immunity was aroused by finding clots in the yolk-sac cavities of the blastocysts of wild rabbits that had been killed at stages shortly after implantation. These clots resembled fibrin microscopically. It was appreciated that if fibrinogen was present in the yolk-sac fluid it must be of maternal origin, since the embryo could scarcely be supposed to synthesize it at so early a stage of development when the vascular system had not yet begun to differentiate. Such clots were not observed in blastocysts before they had started to implant. The presence of fibrin was verified by aspirating into sodium citrate solution the fluid from recently implanted blastocysts of tame rabbits approximately 9 days after copulation. This fluid did not clot on standing, but the addition of a solution of human thrombin caused it to do so (Brambell and Mills 1947). The fibrinogen content

---

Plate 3.1. A. Photomicrograph of a region of first contact between the trophoblast (EC) of the rabbit blastocyst and the uterine symplasma (US) on the 7th day. The endoderm (EN) forms a thin lining to the yolk-sac (YS). A uterine gland is shown (UG). × 205. B. Photomicrograph of the attachment of the bilaminar wall of the yolk-sac to the uterine tissues on the eleventh day. 'Arcades' are formed by the uterine symplasma and the syncytial trophoblast (EC) and enclose the mouth of a uterine gland. The uterine epithelium is being regenerated from that of the glands and has almost displaced the degenerating symplasma. The endoderm (EN) of the bilaminar omphalopleur is still intact and lines the yolk-sac (YS). × 93.   C. Electron micrograph of an area similar to those regions of contact shown in A. The line of fusion between the trophoblastic cytoplasm and the uterine symplasma is indicated by arrows. Vacuoles (V) are present in the trophoblastic cytoplasm and the trophoblastic nuclei (NE) are larger and more irregular than those of the symplasma (NU). The basement membrane (BM) of the trophoblast is discontinuous and many basal processes of the trophoblast protrude through it. × 3,250. (From Larsen 1963a.)

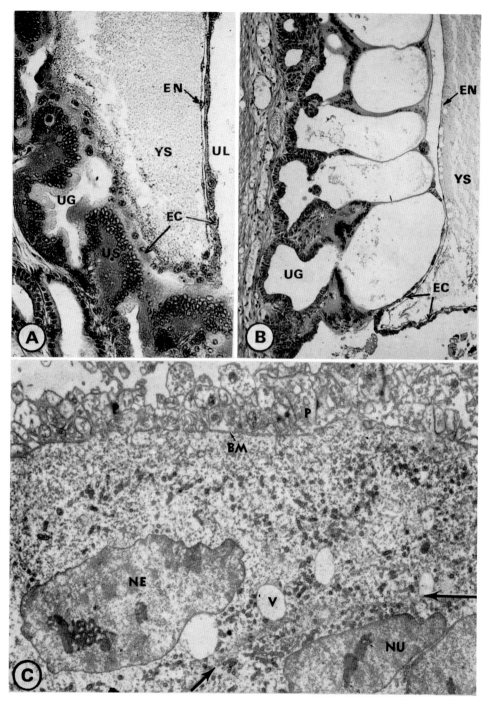

PLATE 3.1

was estimated by nitrogen determinations of the dried clot and was found to represent a concentration in the yolk-sac fluid of 30–40% of that of the maternal plasma. The nitrogen content of the residue of the yolk-sac fluid after clotting was equivalent to nearly 60% of that of maternal serum and suggested the presence of other proteins. To determine the nature of these, free-boundary electrophoretic and ultracentrifugal studies were undertaken (Brambell and Hemmings 1949; McCarthy and Kekwick 1949). Since there is a small risk of slight contamination of fluid harvested by aspiration, an improved method of collection was adopted. The whole uterus of a freshly killed rabbit was frozen rapidly at -47 °C by immersion in isopentane cooled in solid CO_2. The blastocysts could then be easily shelled out as spheres of ice from which the tissue could be removed completely by polishing. The frozen fluid was then thawed in sodium oxalate solution. Electrophoretic examination showed that this fluid contained albumin, α-, β- and γ-globulins and fibrinogen in proportions similar to those in the maternal plasma but at a concentration of about 50% of that in plasma. Two components were observed in the ultracentrifuge sedimenting in a similar manner to those in plasma. So far as the proteins were concerned the fluid resembled dilute plasma and that these were derived from the maternal circulation was an obvious assumption.

More recent work has confirmed and extended these results. Sugawara and Hafez (1967) examined the proteins in the fluid from blastocysts of 6 to 8 days of age by electrophoresis in cellulose polyacetate at pH 8.8. The proteins appeared in the fluid in succession according to the stage of development, albumin being detectable at 6 days, β-globulin at 7 days, α- and γ-globulins at $7\frac{1}{4}$ days and fibrinogen at $7\frac{1}{2}$ days. The electrophoretic distribution of the proteins at $7\frac{1}{2}$ days was qualitatively, but not quantitatively similar to maternal serum. This was considered evidence of the selective absorption of the proteins by the blastocyst. Beier (1968) found that the blastocyst fluid at 6 days contains 8–14 μg protein. Six proteins were identified in the fluid, prealbumin, albumin, uteroglobulin, β_1-globulin, β_2-globulin and γG-globulin. The fluid resembled uterine fluid fairly closely, but only the albumin and γG-globulin were identical with serum.

3.4. *Transmission to the yolk-sac fluid*

The dye Evan's blue (T-1824) when injected into the circulation becomes firmly and selectively attached to the albumin fraction of the serum proteins.

Accordingly 30 mg of the dye was injected into each of a number of pregnant rabbits from 7 days 20 hr to 9 days after copulation and the yolk-sac fluid of the embryos was harvested from 1–2 hr thereafter. The dye was found to pass rapidly into the yolk-sac fluid from the maternal circulation at 7 days 20 hr and in declining but detectable concentrations until 8 days 20 hr. Thereafter it could not be detected in the yolk-sac fluid. The dye was still attached to the albumin fraction in the yolk-sac fluid, as was shown by electrophoresis (Brambell and Hemmings 1949; McCarthy and Kekwick 1949). Since the yolk-sac fluid is increasing in volume very rapidly over this period, the ratio of surface to volume of the blastocyst increasing by about three times, the decline in concentration of the dye in the fluid could be accounted for largely by increasing dilution, and might not represent a significant change in transmission per unit area of yolk-sac wall. These observations strongly support the assumption that albumin with the dye attached is transmitted from the maternal circulation to the yolk-sac fluid at these stages, though the possibility is not formally excluded that the dye could be detached from the maternal albumin before passage through the membrane and reattached to foetal albumin thereafter.

Conclusive evidence of the transmission of serum protein from the maternal circulation to the yolk-sac fluid was obtained by actively immunizing female rabbits to *Brucella abortus* killed carbolised antigen and mating them when their serum contained a high titre of agglutinins (Brambell, Hemmings and Rowlands 1948). They were killed at 8 days 16 hr after copulation and the yolk-sac fluid of the blastocysts was harvested and titrated. Agglutinin titres varying from equality to $\frac{1}{16}$ of those of the maternal serum at the time of killing were found. Pregnant rabbits that were not actively immune to *B. abortus* were passively immunized by intravenous injection of high titre rabbit or bovine anti-*B. abortus* serum on the 7th day after copulation. They were killed 10 to 17 hr later and the yolk-sac fluid of the blastocysts was titrated. All those exposed to bovine agglutinins and most of those exposed to rabbit agglutinins had significant titres of agglutinins in the fluid (table 3.1). Agglutinins were not found in the yolk-sac fluid of blastocysts of rabbits passively immunized with bovine anti-*B. abortus* serum at 9 days after copulation and harvested 12 hr later, a finding in line with that obtained with Evan's blue on the transmission of albumin at this age. The passage of heterologous serum proteins from the maternal circulation into the yolk-sac fluid on the 7th to 9th days has been observed by Smith and Schechtman (1962). Pregnant rabbits were injected intra-

TABLE 3.1

Agglutinin titres of the yolk-sac fluid of rabbit embryos on the 9th day after copulation relative to those of the maternal serum following active or passive immunization. (Brambell F. W. R., W. A. Hemmings and W. T. Rowlands, 1948, Proc. Roy. Soc. B. *135*, 392–398.)

Reciprocal of titre of yolk-sac fluid/ reciprocal of titre of maternal serum	Number of embryos		
	Bovine antibody	Rabbit antibody	
	Passive	Passive	Active
$\frac{1}{16}$	—		2
$\frac{1}{8}$	5	$(3 > \frac{1}{4})$	—
$\frac{1}{4}$	6	3	9
$\frac{1}{2}$	6	1	7
1	9	—	6

venously with human or guineapig serum. Using continuous paper electrophoresis and precipitin reactions to identify the fractions, they found that all the components of both these sera passed from the maternal circulation into the yolk-sac fluid on the 7th to the 9th days. Their finding of passage on the 9th day was due no doubt to the greater sensitivity of the precipitin reaction as compared to agglutination. It is interesting that they found some evidence of selective passage as between human and guineapig proteins and between the different fractions of guineapig serum proteins even at this stage. Comparison of the results we obtained with rabbit and with bovine agglutinins provided no indication that the membrane transmits these differentially and the close correspondence in the relative proportions of the various fractions of the rabbit plasma proteins in the yolk-sac fluid with those in the maternal plasma suggests that there is no significant selection between these. However this may be, it is evident that both homologous and heterologous plasma proteins do pass relatively freely from the maternal circulation of the pregnant rabbit through the bilaminar omphalopleur of the embryo into the yolk-sac fluid on the 7th and 8th days after copulation, and probably in reduced quantities on the 9th day.

3.5. *Expansion of the blastocyst and composition of the yolk-sac fluid*

It would be interesting to understand the mechanism of the rapid expansion of the blastocyst at this stage. This is due mainly to an accumulation of yolk-sac fluid. Although its wall is so thin it retains its essentially globular form throughout this period, becoming somewhat flattened on the mesome-trial side, where the greater thickness of the uterine tissues might be expected to present a greater resistance, and blowing out the thinner antimesometrial side like a bubble. It is not easy to see how it can achieve this expansion at a time when its wall is permeable to such large molecules as proteins. It was found by Hafez and Sugawara (1968) that the mean volume of fluid in the blastocyst increased from 1.5 μl at 5 days to 375 μl at 9 days, the greatest increase being between the 7th and 8th days. There was great individual variation in the size of blastocysts, expecially on the 8th and 9th days and this was influenced by the physiological state of the mother, whether she was nulliparous, multiparous, etc. The average weight of the tissues of the blastocyst increased from 0.87 mg at 6 days to 20.1 mg at 9 days. The average weight of the intact blastocyst increased from 0.68 mg at 5 days to 446 mg at 9 days. Much valuable information on the non-protein composition of the yolk-sac fluid and on the permeability of its wall to small molecules and ions has been provided by the work of Lutwak-Mann and her colleagues (Lutwak-Mann and Laser 1954; Lutwak-Mann 1954; Lutwak-Mann, Boursnell and Bennett 1960). The blastocyst fluid at 6 days has a high bi-carbonate content, which declines steadily during the two succeeding days. The fluid withdrawn from 6 and 7 day blastocysts becomes distinctly alkaline on standing for a few minutes, whereas that from 8 day blastocysts does not do so but remains at an approximately constant pH 7.8, presumably because of buffering. Normal yolk-sac fluid has a glucose concentration of 18.25 mg/100 ml at 7 days which rises to 90–99 mg/100 ml at 10 days, fructose and inositol being absent. Glucose, fructose, sucrose and sulphapyridine failed to pass from the maternal circulation to the yolk-sac fluid before implantation but did so freely after implantation, although thiocyanate did not. Glucose entered more readily at first than either fructose or sucrose. Isotopically labelled ions, $^{32}PO_4^{3-}$, $^{35}SO_4^{2-}$, $^{24}Na^{1+}$, $^{42}K^{1+}$ and $^{131}I^{1-}$ were freely secreted from the circulation into the uterine fluid in roughly equal proportions. They entered the yolk-sac fluid much less readily and at different relative rates. Some, such as PO_4^{3-}, Na^{1+} and SO_4^{2-} reached peak values in the yolk-sac at a time when the permeability of the wall to proteins is maximal. It was concluded that the composition of the yolk-sac fluid is determined and maintained by the cells of the embryo itself to a considerable extent. Hafez and Sugawara (1968) found that the concentration of glucose in the blastocyst fluid reached a maximum, comparable with the maternal blood level, at 8 days of age, when the mean absolute amount per blastocyst was 380 μg. Lactic acid levels were similar to those of glucose, with a maximum mean absolute amount of 282 μg. The amount of protein in the fluid increased dramatically until 7 days, and at 9 days the mean amount was 8968 μg per blastocyst. The ratio of non-protein N to total N reached a peak at 6 days and then declined. The information available at present is inadequate to determine the functional significance to the embryo of the composition of the yolk-sac fluid. The most obvious feature is the achievement of a relatively large size, while the total mass of embryonic tissue is very small, by the expansion of the thin-walled vesicular blastocyst; clearly the composition of the fluid contents must reflect the means by which the volume of this fluid is increased so rapidly. If, as seems probable, the yolk-sac fluid provides for the nutrition of the embryo, its isolation is curiously transient since the break-down of the bilaminar omphalopleur results in what remains being merged with the uterine fluid by the 13th day. Smith and Schechtman (1962) state that human serum protein already in the yolk-sac before the 9th day passes into the foetal circulation from the 9th to 13th day and, as will be shown later, protein is absorbed thereafter by the yolk-sac splanchnopleur from the uterine fluid. However, the further development and final structure of the foetal membrane and placenta must be considered before dealing with transmission to the foetal circulation.

3.6. *Development of the foetal membranes*

Soon after the blastocyst becomes attached by its abembryonal hemisphere to the antimesometrial wall of the uterus, the mesoderm begins to extend outwards from the embryonic plate between the endoderm and the tropho-blast. The exocoel extends with the mesoderm, separating an outer somatic layer of mesoderm next to the ectoderm from an inner splanchnic layer of mesoderm next to the endoderm of the yolk-sac. The mesoderm and exocoel extend almost to the equator of the blastocyst. Blood islands develop in the splanchnic mesoderm of the yolk-sac and a circular vessel forms around the margin of this area vasculosa during the 8th day. The sinus terminalis is situated at the furthest limit of the coelom, where the yolk-sac splanchnopleur and the chorion join the bilaminar omphalopleur; when the latter breaks down a narrow fringe is left, encircling the equator and immediately ad-joining the sinus terminalis. Amniotic folds are formed around the embryonic plate on the 8th day from the outer wall of the blastocyst (fig. 3.1). They consist of ectoderm lined with somatic mesoderm. These folds have closed over the embryonic region by the beginning of the 10th day, their inner walls forming the amnion, which envelops the embryo and is separated by the exocoel from the chorion, formed from their outer walls. The trophoblastic ectoderm of the chorion adjoining the two folds of uterine mucosa, which project into the cavity on the mesometrial side, thickens, and its outer part becomes syncytial. It fuses with the uterine symplasma covering these folds to form the rudiment of the placenta, even before the amniotic folds have closed. The syncytial trophoblast invades and fuses with the uterine symplasma (Larsen 1961) and penetrates deeply into the uterine glands, destroying their epithelium, and penetrating into the sub-epithelial tissues to form the disc-shaped chorionic placenta on the mesometrial wall of the uterus.

The area vasculosa of the yolk-sac splanchnopleur is connected to the embryo, as it becomes delimited, by the yolk-sac stalk, in which the vitelline arteries and veins run. The heart begins to beat and the vitelline circulation to the yolk-sac is established early on the 9th day. Meanwhile the allantois grows out from the embryo into the exocoel. It is a pear-shaped bag of endoderm covered with splanchnic mesoderm. It extends around the outer surface of the amnion until its distal wall comes into contact and fuses with the inner surface of the chorion over the circular area of the placental rudiment. Thus the vascular splanchnic mesoderm covering the allantois joins the non-vascular somatic mesoderm lining the placental chorion and the allantochorionic placenta so formed is vascularised by the allantoic blood vessels. These grow out from the embryo along the allantoic stalk. The yolk-sac stalk and the allantoic stalk join close to where they enter the embryo at the umbilicus, both running around the amnion from opposite sides to do so (fig. 3.2).

3.7. The structure of the placenta

The syncytiotrophoblast grows into the glands and it penetrates the symplasma in these and on the surface. It invades the connective tissue of the mucosa and envelops the maternal blood vessels of the placental region. Maternal perivascular cells in the deeper part of the placenta enlarge and give rise to multinucleate giant cells which become laden with glucose. The syncytiotrophoblast destroys the endothelium of the maternal capillaries with which it comes in contact so that the maternal blood flows in channels in it. The cytotrophoblast and foetal mesenchyme then grow inwards be-

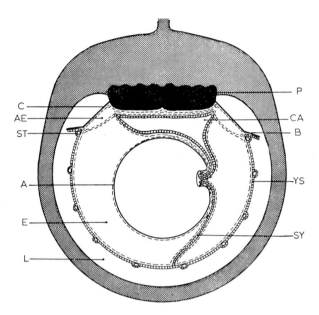

Fig. 3.2. Diagram of the final arrangement of the embryonic membranes of the rabbit. The bilaminar omphalopleur (B) forming the outer wall of the yolk-sac has disappeared except for a small tag adjoining the sinus terminalis (ST) thus exposing the endoderm (cross hatched) of the vascular splanchnic wall of the yolk-sac (YS) to the uterine lumen (L). The vesicular allantois (CA) has joined the chorion in the placental region (P) to form an allantochorion and a sheet of vascular allantoic mesoderm has grown down from it to the region of the sinus terminalis cutting off an accessory exocoelomic cavity (AE) from the main cavity of the exocoel (E). The expansion of the amnion (A) will later reduce the extent of the exocoel. The stalk of the yolk-sac (SY) runs from the umbilicus across the exocoel to join the yolk-sac splanchnopleur antimesometrially. A band of chorion (C) intervenes between the yolk-sac and the placenta.

tween the tongues of syncytiotrophoblast, which become split up into large numbers of tubules, perpendicular to the placental surface, in each of which maternal blood flows. The maternal arteries, entering the placenta from the mesometrium, penetrate through it to the foetal side and there break up over the surface into numerous arterioles. These join the tropho-blastic tubules, through which the blood flows back towards the maternal side, where groups of tubules join to form larger channels opening into the maternal placental veins. The allantoic arteries branch in the walls of the tent-like allantois, before reaching the placenta, on the surface of which they branch further into small arterioles. These run through to the maternal side of the placenta in the foetal mesenchyme between the tubules and there break up into capillaries which envelop the walls of the tubules and carry the blood back to the foetal side, where they join to form the allantoic veins. Consequently the direction of flow of the foetal blood in the capillaries is opposite to that of the maternal blood in the tubules, an arrangement that has been shown to be the most favourable for exchange by diffusion (Mossman 1926) since it allows the foetal blood to come into equilibrium with the maternal arterial blood. Since the foetal capillaries closely invest the trophoblastic tubules, only the foetal endothelium and a thin layer of syncytiotrophoblast intervene between the two circulations. Indeed, it has been claimed that in places in the fully established placenta the foetal capillaries project through the syncytiotrophoblast into the maternal blood, so that at these points only the foetal endothelium intervenes. However electron-micrographs suggest (Wislocki 1955; Larsen 1962b) that even at these points a thin investment of trophoblast, invisible with the light microscope, persists (plate 3.1.A). Depending on this distinction the placenta of the rabbit may be said to be haemochorial, if the maternal blood is confined to direct contact with the chorionic trophoblast, or haemoendothelial if it is in contact with the foetal endothelium. It is of the labyrinthine type in which the maternal blood flows in narrow trophoblastic channels, as distinct from the lacunar type of haemochorial placenta, characteristic of the apes and man, in which the maternal blood is contained in large caverns in the trophoblast. Although both are spoken of as haemochorial, they are distinct in structure and must have been evolved independently.

The maternal decidual giant cells form the basal part of the placenta below and extend as tongues between the trophoblastic tubules. Beneath the decidua, between it and the uterine muscle, is a zone of connective tissue containing many sinuses. The base of the placenta becomes slightly constricted, in line with this zone, by the ingrowth for a short distance beneath its margin of the regenerated uterine epithelium. This forms a natural zone of weakness from which the placenta readily peels away at parturition. Contraction of the uterus then reduces the naked area, so that scarcely any bleeding occurs and healing is rapid. More detailed descriptions of the development and structure of the placenta of the rabbit, and references to the literature, are available in the works by Duval (1889, 1890), Chipman

(1903), Mossman (1926), Amoroso (1952), Larsen (1962b, 1963b) and Larsen and Davies (1962).

3.8. The structure of the yolk-sac

The growth of the foetus and the expansion of its enveloping amnion and of the exocoel presses upon and inverts the upper or splanchnic hemisphere of the yolk-sac within the lower hemisphere of bilaminar omphalopleur. The disappearance of the latter exposes the endoderm of the splanchnic wall to the uterine cavity, which it nearly fills. Although the endoderm is pressed close to the regenerated uterine epithelium it neither fuses with it, nor is even in contact with it, at any stage. The narrow intervening space is filled with uterine fluid containing the secretion of the glands and the debris of the uterine symplasma and bilaminar omphalopleur. The endoderm of the yolk-sac splanchnopleur consists of a simple low columnar epithelium

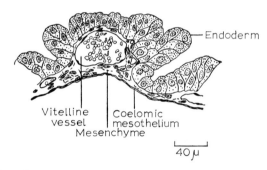

Fig. 3.3. Drawing of a part of the yolk-sac splanchnopleur of a 24-day rabbit foetus, showing a large vitelline vessel in the mesenchyme, the endodermal epithelium of large cells on the outside next the uterine lumen and the thin squamous mesothelium on the inside next to the exocoel. (From Morris 1950.)

(Morris 1950). The cells are large with nuclei in their basal regions (fig. 3.3). Each is provided with a brush border of microvilli (Luse 1958; Larsen 1963a). They rest upon a distinct basement membrane. Each cell is linked to adjoining ones near their apical surfaces by desmosomes (Luse 1958; Larsen 1963a) but intercellular spaces occur between the cells more basally, internally to these (plate 3.2B). The cells are rich in ergastoplasm, situated mainly in their basal regions. The Golgi elements are apical to the nuclei and mitochondria are scattered throughout the cytoplasm. Many vacuoles and canaliculi of varying size, probably indicating pinocytosis, are present in the apical halves of the cells. Invaginations between the bases of the microvilli and the apical vesicles and canaliculi have a thickened filamentous lining that, it has been suggested, may represent a special surface for protein attachment (Deren, Padykula and Wilson 1966). Beneath the basement membrane of the epithelium is a loose mesenchymal connective tissue containing blood islands and foetal blood vessels. The vessels lie very close to the membrane and the larger ones cause the endoderm covering them to project as ridges on the surface. The inner surface of the yolk-sac splanchno-pleur, adjoining the exocoel, is covered by a very thin squamous mesothelium. The margin of the yolk-sac splanchnopleur is bounded by the sinus terminalis and persisting fringe of bilaminar omphalopleur. The blood vessels radiate from the yolk-sac stalk which joins the splanchnopleur near its centre. There is no continuous yolk-sac duct in the stalk.

3.9. The structure of the chorion, amnion and allantois

A broad zone of chorion joins the margin of the discoid placenta to the margin of the yolk-sac and the sinus terminalis (Morris 1950; Larsen and Davies 1962). This zone of chorion remains unattached to the uterine tissues and its free surface is covered by cellular trophoblast. During the second half of gestation this chorionic trophoblast proliferates multinucleate spherules which are set free into the uterine cavity and there degenerate. Beneath the trophoblast is a thin, non-vascular layer of somatic mesoderm. About the 13th day allantoic mesoderm grows down from the margin of the placenta over the inner surface of this chorionic mesoderm, as far as the sinus terminalis. Between these two layers of mesoderm, somatic and

---

Plate 3.2. A. Electron micrograph of the placenta of a rabbit at full term showing a foetal vessel separated from the maternal blood (MB) by the foetal mesenchyme (FM), the cytotrophoblast (CT) resting on its basement membrane (BT), and a sheet of syncytial trophoblast (ST). The two sheets of trophoblast are connected by desmosomes (D). A nucleus (NE) and cytoplasm (CE) of the foetal endothelium and the basement membrane (BE) on which it rests are shown. × 10,900. (From Larsen 1962b.) B. Electron micrograph of the apical region of an endoderm cell of the yolk-sac splanchnopleur of a rabbit foetus of 28 days gestation. The free surface of the cell is covered with microvilli (MV) and caveoli can be seen between the bases of some of them. The apical cytoplasm contains many canaliculi (C) and absorptive vacuoles (AV). The intercellular space (IC) is enlarged and adjoining cells are held together by desmosomes (D). × 21,000. (From Deren, Padykula and Wilson 1966.)

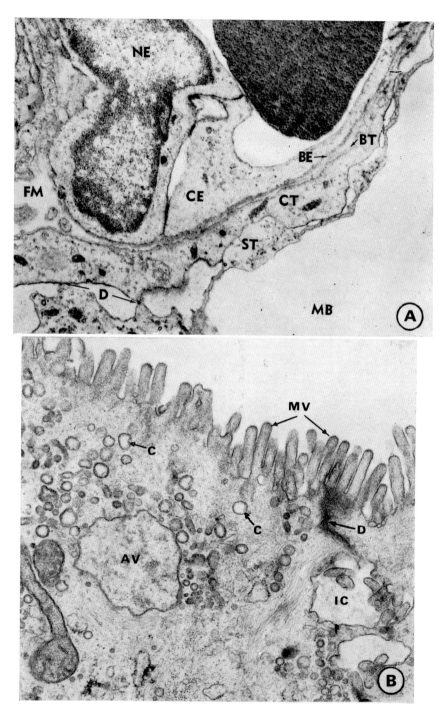

PLATE 3.2

splanchnic respectively, a cleft appears by the 16th day, separating the outer non-vascular layer next the trophoblast from an inner vascular sheet. This cleft forms an annular accessory exocoelemic cavity that is separated from the rest of the exocoel by the vascular sheet of allantoic mesoderm. Small blood vessels in this allantoic mesoderm anastomose with the sinus terminalis, so establishing connections peripherally between the allantoic and vitelline circulations. Although Duval (1889, 1890) noted these anastomoses, they have tended to be overlooked since then.

The mesothelial lining of the exocoelomic spaces does not appear to rest on a basement membrane and the cells are not joined by desmosomes, so that there are sometimes spaces between them, according to Larsen and Davies (1962). These authors describe the endodermal epithelium lining the allantois as a single layer of flat cells resting on a basement membrane, which separates it from the thin layer of mesenchyme and the coelomic mesothelium which form the remainder of its wall. The endodermal cells have a few short microvilli on their free surfaces. The ectodermal epithelium lining the amnion consists of a single layer of large cells resting on a basement membrane. Microvilli are present on the free surfaces of these cells. The cells are joined by many desmosomes. The mesodermal part of the amnion consists of a thin layer of mesenchyme and the coelomic mesothelium, and does not differ essentially from the corresponding part of the allantoic membrane. The allantoic fluid at the 20th day of gestation is opalescent and hypotonic to the maternal serum, with a higher concentration of urea and potassium and a lower concentration of sodium and chloride than the maternal serum; facts which suggest that it may be largely metanephric excretion (Dickerson and McCance 1957).

3.10. *Orientation and accommodation of the foetuses*

The foetuses are orientated within their membranes with their cephalo-caudal axes at right angles to the longitudinal axis of the uterus until about the 22nd day, when they rotate through 90° and lie lengthwise along the uterus (Reynolds 1946, 1947). Prior to this rotation the individual conceptuses are contained in distinct sub-spherical uterine chambers, with constrictions between them, but thereafter these merge so that the uterus becomes cylindrical and evenly distended (fig. 3.4). This change in shape is accompanied, and probably caused, by a slackening of uterine tension. This is of practical importance in foetal experimental surgery, since it is very difficult to prevent

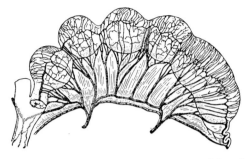

Fig. 3.4. Drawing of the uterus of a rabbit on the twenty-second day of pregnancy showing the transformation of the form of the uterus from a chain of separate spherical conceptuses to a continuous cylinder. (From a drawing by Mr. James F. Didusch in Reynolds 1947.)

extrusion of a conceptus through a uterine incision while the wall is tense before the 22nd day, and relatively easy while it is slack thereafter, until near full term when foetal growth results in maximal distension.

3.11. The route of transmission to the foetal circulation

It has been shown (Rodolfo 1934) that maternal circulating bacterioagglutinins and haemagglutinins are transmitted to the foetal rabbit and that the titres of these antibodies in the foetal serum rise continuously from the 22nd day of gestation to full term, the rate of increase in titre reaching a maximum on the 27th day. Transmission, therefore, must be supposed to continue after the disruption of the bilaminar wall of the yolk-sac about the 16th day. That this occurs was shown by active immunization of pregnant rabbits to *Brucella abortus* after the 15th day and the presence of resulting antibody in the blood of the new-born young (Brambell, Hemmings and Rowlands 1948). All the young had titres approaching, equalling or even exceeding that of the maternal serum. The route by which this transmission of immunity occurs during the second half of gestation needed investigation. Either it could occur across the placenta, directly from the maternal to the foetal circulation, as had been generally supposed, or it could occur by secretion from the maternal circulation into the uterine cavity, from where antibody could be absorbed by the inverted yolk-sac splanchnopleur and be transported by the vitelline circulation or it could traverse the chorion and enter the exocoelomic fluid. Since only the margin of the placenta is exposed to the uterine lumen, passage from there via the placenta appeared improbable. Consequently high titre anti-*Brucella* serum prepared in rabbits was injected into the lumen of one uterine horn of non-immune rabbits on the 24th day of gestation, the other horn of the uterus serving as a control. After trials the amount of serum injected was standardised at 1 ml per conceptus in the experimental horn. The animals were autopsied 24 hr after injection and agglutinins were found in the sera of all the foetuses from the experimental horns and from none of those from the control horns (Brambell, Hemmings, Henderson, Parry and Rowlands 1949).

It was found possible to interrupt the vitelline circulation surgically. Pregnant rabbits on the 24th day of gestation were used; fully mature animals having a first pregnancy were chosen as it was found that the uterine wall was more transparent in these than in parous animals. The uteri were exposed under ether anaesthesia using aseptic precautions. It was then possible to see through the antimesometrial uterine wall the point where the yolk-sac stalk joined the yolk-sac splanchnopleur and from which the vitel-

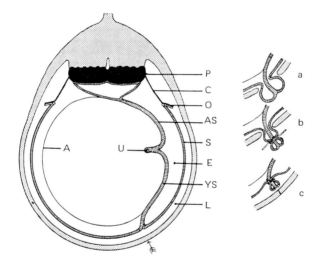

Fig. 3.5. Diagram of the foetal membranes of a rabbit in late pregnancy to show the method of ligaturing the vitelline vessels of the yolk-sac. The uterine wall is incised at the point marked by the arrow and the yolk-sac splanchnopleur, at the point where the vitelline vessels in the yolk-sac stalk join it, allowed to protrude as at a. These are then ligatured without perforating the membrane as at b and returned to the uterine lumen and the uterine incision closed as at c. P, placenta; C, chorion; O, tag of omphalopleur; AS, allantoic stalk; S, yolk-sac splanchnopleur; E, exocoel; YS, yolk-sac stalk; L, uterine lumen; U, umbilicus; A, amnion. (From Brambell 1958.)

line vessels radiated. A small radial incision in the uterus immediately over this point allowed the yolk-sac wall to bulge through and the yolk-sac stalk to be ligatured securely, as shown in fig. 3.5, without perforating the membranes. These were then returned to the uterus and the incision in it sutured and ligatured. In the majority of cases this procedure resulted in haemostasis throughout the area vasculosa of the yolk-sac splanchnopleur, but in a minority the circulation was maintained over part, usually a small part, of the area, probably by means of the small vessels that may occur in the splanchnic mesoderm beneath the chorion, linking the sinus terminalis with the placental circulation. The completeness of haemostasis could be determined by the blackening of the vessels. Several embryos were treated in this way in one uterine horn, care being taken to leave at least alternate embryos intact as controls. High titre immune rabbit serum to the amount of 1 ml/foetus was then injected into the lumen of the experimental uterine horn as in the previous experiment, the uteri were returned to the body cavity and the body-wall was sutured. Some mortality of foetuses was experienced, deaths apparently occurring at the time of operation either through temporary interruption of the uterine circulation arising from pressure on the vessels while the uterus was exteriorised or through the affects of anaesthesia, but this affected the control, as much as the experimental, foetuses. The majority of the foetuses survived and the experimental ones appeared as large and as active as the controls at the end. At autopsy after 24 hr or 48 hr maternal and foetal sera were harvested and titrated. The results are given in table 3.2 and show that ligation of the vitelline circulation completely stops the transmission of immunity in the majority of experimental foetuses,

TABLE 3.2

Intra-uterine injection of immune serum at 24 days. (From Brambell, Hemmings, Henderson, Parry and Rowlands 1949.)

Uterine horns	Foetuses	Total number of foetuses	Dead foetuses	Surviving foetuses (titre $\frac{1}{32}$ of serum injected)	
				Negative	Positive
Experimental	Intact	32	8	0	24
	Ligatured	22	5	12	5
Control	Intact	34	8	26	0

although transmission at a reduced level occurred in a few, probably because of incomplete vitelline haemostasis referred to above. No transmission occurred to the foetuses in the control uterine horn, showing that absorption of antibody from the uterine lumen into the maternal circulation was insignificant.

A further series of experiments, involving similar ligation of the vitelline circulations of some of the foetuses, was performed in which the immune serum was administered intravenously to the mother, instead of being injected into the uterine lumen. It is clear from the results, shown in table

TABLE 3.3

Intravenous injection of immune serum at 24 days. (From Brambell et al. 1949.)

Foetuses	Total number of foetuses	Dead foetuses	Surviving foetuses (titre $\frac{1}{16}$ of maternal serum at autopsy)	
			Negative	Positive
Intact	28	1	0	27
Ligatured	19	1	10	8

3.3 that in many cases transmission to the experimental foetuses was stopped completely, though to others transmission at a reduced level occurred, no doubt through incomplete vascular stasis of the area vasculosa. These results demonstrate that passive immunity is not transmitted in the rabbit by way of the allantochorionic placenta at levels that could be detected by the methods employed, that maternal circulating antibodies are secreted into the uterine cavity during late stages of gestation, as well as at the time of implantation, and that transmission occurs by absorption of antibodies by the yolk-sac of the foetus. Uterine fluid was collected from an intact non-gravid uterine horn of an experimental animal and was found to contain antibodies at a titre of $\frac{1}{8}$ that in the maternal circulation, thus precluding the possibility that antibodies reached the cavities of the experimental uterine horns only by transudation resulting from the surgical trauma. This observation shows also that the presence of a placenta in the uterus is not necessary for the occurrence of antibodies in the uterine fluid.

The route of transmission of proteins from the maternal to the foetal circulations in the rabbit has been confirmed subsequently by Schechtman and Kulangara (Schechtman and Abraham 1958; Kulangara and Schechtman 1962). They injected intravenously into the mother human and bovine serum albumin and human γ-globulin and identified these as antigens in the uterine fluid and in the serum of intact foetuses. These proteins were not detectable in the sera of foetuses in which the vitelline vessels had been ligatured. It is interesting that the allantochorionic placenta of the rabbit does not appear to be permeable to γ-globulins in either direction. Hemmings and Oakley (1957) after intravenous injections into foetuses of antitoxins and of isotopically labelled globulin were only able to detect traces, that could account for at most 1 % of the dose, in the maternal circulation after 24 hr, an amount that could have been derived very easily from slight leakage at the point of injection.

3.12. *The relative concentration of antibody attained in the foetal serum*

The titres of the foetal sera 24 hr after exposure to immune serum injected into the uterine lumen at 24 days *post coitum* are related to the titres of the sera to which they have been exposed (Brambell, Hemmings, Henderson and Rowlands 1950). This correlation for rabbit hyperimmune anti-*Brucella* or anti-sheep red cell sera is shown in table 3.4. The relation can be expressed as the reciprocal of the titre of the foetal serum divided by the reciprocal

TABLE 3.4

Correlation of titre of foetal serum 24 hr after injection into the uterine cavity at 24 days *post coitum* of immune rabbit serum. (From Brambell, Hemmings, Henderson and Rowlands 1950.)

Titre of serum injected	Titre of foetal serum						
	$\frac{1}{10}$	$\frac{1}{20}$	$\frac{1}{40}$	$\frac{1}{80}$	$\frac{1}{160}$	$\frac{1}{320}$	$\frac{1}{640}$
$\frac{1}{20480}$						4	
$\frac{1}{10240}$							
$\frac{1}{5120}$					2	1	2
$\frac{1}{2560}$			1	4	12	9	
$\frac{1}{1280}$		1	8	8	5		
$\frac{1}{640}$	1	2	4		5		
$\frac{1}{320}$		5	11	1			

of the titre of the serum to which it was exposed, a quantity which we have called the concentration quotient (C.Q.). It represents the relative concentration of antibody and provides a convenient means of correcting for the titre of the immune serum employed in a given experiment. Expressed in

TABLE 3.5

Titre of foetal sera relative to that of the immune serum to which they were exposed at 24 days *post coitum*. (From Brambell et al. 1950.)

Relative titre C.Q.	Intra-uterine injection	Intravenous injection
$\frac{1}{64}$	7	
$\frac{1}{32}$	16	
$\frac{1}{16}$	30	1
$\frac{1}{8}$	27	8
$\frac{1}{4}$	6	13
$\frac{1}{2}$		5

this way, it can be seen from table 3.5 that the foetal sera have a C.Q. of $\frac{1}{16} \pm 2$ dilutions after intrauterine injection of the immune rabbit serum at 24 days *post coitum* but that they have a higher C.Q. in relation to that of the maternal serum at the time of killing after intravenous injection. This difference is not surprising. Intrauterine injection of immune serum does not ensure continuous exposure of the foetuses for the whole period of the experiment, for the dose may be exhausted before the end or possibly drain away through the cervix, whereas intravenous injection will result in continuing exposure to a maternal serum titre that will be greater immediately after injection than at the end of the experiment, when it was measured.

3.13. Time of transmission

Immunity is transmitted in the normal rabbit during the second half of pregnancy, as has been shown by actively immunizing rabbits after the 15th day of gestation (Brambell, Hemmings and Rowlands 1948). In these circumstances the serum titres of the newborn young approximate to those of the mothers. It has been shown (Kulangara and Schechtman 1962) that human γ-globulin administered intravenously to the mother is transmitted to the foetuses at 19 days *post coitum* but it transmitted much more rapidly at 24 days *post coitum*. This agrees with the finding that the rate of transmission of rabbit antitoxin injected into the uterine cavity increases nearly linearly from a low level at 20 days *post coitum* to a maximum at 26 days *post coitum*, and declines thereafter. It appears, however, that some transmission to the foetal circulation can occur at still earlier stages, for Smith and Schechtman (1962) showed by injection of human serum proteins intravenously into pregnant rabbits that these could be identified in the foetal serum from the 9th day. They concluded that proteins already in the yolk-sac fluid before the 9th day were transmitted to the foetal circulation from the 9th to the 13th day, when the bilaminar wall of the yolk-sac disappears, and that thereafter transmission directly from the maternal circulation occurs.

Transmission appears to occur very rapidly at later stages. Cohen (1950) found that rabbit antibodies injected intravenously into the mother could be detected in the foetal serum in 1 hr and that the foetal titre equalised with that of the mother in 4 hr. He found that human and bovine γ-globulins were transmitted more slowly. Similarly Kulangara and Schechtman (1962) were able to detect human γ-globulin injected intravenously into the mother in the foetal circulation after 1 hr, though the concentration in the foetal serum increases up till 48 hr after injection, both at 19 days and 24 days *post coitum*.

3.14. *Changes in concentration of foetal serum proteins*

Foetal rabbit serum has a lower protein concentration than maternal serum. Thus at 25 days *post coitum* the mean foetal concentration was found to be 25.5 mg/ml compared to a mean maternal concentration of 45.4 mg/ml (Brambell, Hemmings, Henderson and Kekwick 1953). It has been estimated that the foetal concentration doubles between the 23rd and 28th days *post coitum* (Daffner and Schreier 1961). More recently the concentration (fig. 3.6) has been shown to rise continuously from *c.* 12 mg/ml at 20 days *post coitum* to about 34 mg/ml at 28 days *post coitum* (Wild 1965a). These changes in total concentration are accompanied by changes in the relative concentrations of the various components (fig. 3.7). Foetal serum contains relatively, as well as absolutely, less albumin and γ-globulin than maternal serum, due to a notably large amount of globulin which was found by free-boundary electrophoresis to move as a complex peak in the β region but which was

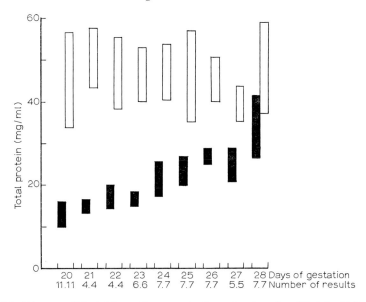

Fig. 3.6. Diagram of the total protein concentrations of maternal and foetal rabbit sera at successive stages of gestation. The maternal concentrations are shown in white and the foetal in black. (From Wild 1965a.)

unresolvable (Brambell et al. 1953). Using a variety of modern techniques Wild has shown that most of this is α_2-globulin; an identification in agreement with those of Osorio and Myant (1958), Myant and Osorio (1959) and Daffner and Schreier (1961). At 20 days *post coitum* the concentration of α_2-globulin actually exceeds that of albumin; however, whereas the α_2- and β-globulins increase in concentration only slightly from the 20th to the 28th day, the albumin, α_1- and γ-globulins increase substantially, especially from the 24th day. Unfortunately information is lacking on the developmental changes in the serum proteins of suckling rabbits.

It is possible to estimate from the known growth rate of rabbit foetuses (Huggett and Widdas 1951) and the concentration of γ-globulin determined electrophoretically the normal daily increment in total foetal γ-globulin (Brambell et al. 1953). Assuming that the transmission of antibody is representative of the transmission of γ-globulin, then the amount transmitted is ample to provide both for the growth increment and for a reasonable level of catabolism. It has been shown by intravenous injection into the foetus of isotopically labelled globulin and of antitoxin that its rate of disappearance from the circulation is no greater than in the adult (Hemmings and Oakley 1957). Although the rabbit foetus may synthesize small quantities of γ-globulin, it need not be assumed that it does so, as most of its γ-globulin is transmitted from the mother. However, Daffner and Schreier (1961) found a high rate of labelling of the γ-globulins in foetuses between 22 and 28 days *post coitum* after they had been injected with ^{14}C-labelled glycine.

A component known as homoreactant is present in normal adult rabbit serum which reacts with the Fab- or Fab^{1}-fragments of rabbit γ-globulin produced by treatment with papain or pepsin, but not with the intact γ-

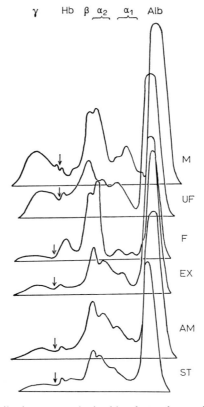

Fig. 3.7. Protein distribution curves obtained by electrophoresis in fluid agar of maternal serum (M), uterine fluid (UF), foetal serum (F), exocoelomic fluid (EX), amniotic fluid (AM) and stomach contents (ST) of a rabbit at 24 days of gestation. The exocoelomic and amniotic fluids and stomach contents were concentrated. Arrows indicate the points of application of the samples. (From Wild 1965a.)

globulin molecule. It behaves like an antibody directed to antigenic sites that are normally buried in the γ-globulin molecule but are exposed by enzymic digestion. It is, therefore, naturally occurring but appears to be similar to the actively produced antibody resulting from immunization with Fab fragments. It is believed to be a γ-globulin and can be titrated by the agglutination which it effects with erythrocytes sensitized with the Fab- or Fab[1]-fragments of a rabbit anti-erythrocyte serum. Recent work (Mandy, Woolsey and Lewis 1968) has shown that homoreactant is passively transmitted from mother to young before birth in rabbits. Newborn rabbits have serum titres of homoreactant comparable to those of the mother. These decline steadily to a very low level during the first four weeks of life and during this period are mercaptoethanol resistant and presumably 7S γG-globulins. Thereafter the titres rise gradually to adult levels due to synthesis, but during the period 4 to 10 weeks most of the homoreactant synthesized is mercaptoethanol sensitive and presumably γM-globulin; later only mercaptoethanol resistant antibody is produced. It would appear from these results that autogenous antibody is at a very low level at 4 weeks of age and that synthesis is only beginning to reach a significant level then; moreover, in this instance of homoreactant the synthesis would appear to be of macroglobulin initially.

3.15. *Variety of proteins transmitted*

The evidence available suggests that all kinds of maternal antibodies are transmitted to the foetal circulation in rabbits. Reference has been made already to the transmission of bacterio- and haemagglutinins, and antitoxins. Antibodies protecting against cholera, resulting from vaccination with live vibrio, are transmitted (Panse and Dutta 1964); so also are antibodies resulting from skin homografts, as has been demonstrated by the quicker rejection of homografts by the offspring of mothers sensitized to the same donor (Halasz and Orloff 1963) and by the identification of maternal cytotoxic antibodies in the sera of newborn animals (Lanman and Herod 1965). Rabbit hyperimmune anti-sheep red cell haemolysins are also transmitted (Brambell et al. 1950) although, after primary immunization, these have been shown to be predominantly in the γ-macroglobulin fraction (Paić 1938). The passage of maternal macroglobulin antibodies to human red cells of Group A has been confirmed subsequently, using more refined methods (Hemmings and Jones 1962). The sera of almost all adult normal rabbits contain natural anti-sheep red cell or Forssman haemolysin. Both this natural haemolysin and that resulting from injection of sheep-red cells are in the γM-globulin. They are transmitted from mother to foetus and are present in the newborn young at titres approximately the same as the maternal titres (Aitken 1964). Their half-life in the young rabbit is 8 to 9 days.

Rabbit albumin, α-, β- and γ-globulins, separated by zone electrophoresis and isotopically labelled with ^{131}I, are transmitted, the albumin being transmitted in substantial amounts, though at a lower level than the γ-globulin, whereas the α- and β-globulins are transmitted at very low levels (Hemmings 1961). It is interesting that rabbit γ-globulin, iodinated even at very low levels, appears to be transmitted at a lower rate than rabbit antibody (Hemmings 1956), a finding that might be due to the effect of the treatment involved in iodination. The transmission of ^{131}I-labelled rabbit serum albumin near term in rabbits has been studied at intervals of 1 to 24 hr after intravenous injection (Winkler, Fitzpatrick and Finnerty 1958). Negligible amounts were found in the foetal serum after intervals of one, and of six, hours but considerable quantities were found after 16 and 24 hr. Labelled rabbit γ-globulin was found to be transmitted on the 28th day twice as readily as labelled rabbit albumin, whereas labelled transferrin transmission was only about $\frac{1}{20}$ of that of the labelled albumin (Morgan 1964).

Transmission is not confined to homologous serum proteins for Holford (1930) was able to detect in the sera of new born rabbits egg-albumin, and equine and bovine serum proteins after these had been injected into the mothers near term. He tested for these as antigens by means of precipitin reactions and noted the variation between young even in the same litter. However, he was unable to demonstrate any transmission of equine haemoglobin.

The passage of all the protein components of human serum to the foetal circulation after intravenous injection into the mother was found to occur from the 9th day *post coitum* by Smith and Schechtman (1962), as mentioned already, but they failed to demonstrate passage of guineapig serum proteins at those early stages. Cohen (1950) records the transmission of both human and bovine γ-globulin and Kulangara and Schechtman (1962) record the transmission of both human and bovine albumin at 19 and 24 days. The transmission of human macroglobulin, and of its monomeres as well as of 7S γ-globulin, after injection into the uterine lumen has been demonstrated by Kaplan, Catsoulis and Franklin (1965). Indirect evidence of the passage of human γ-globulin is also provided by the production of tolerance in young rabbits to this protein by subcutaneous inoculation of the mothers late in pregnancy (Trench, Gardner and Green 1964). The passage of ^{131}I-labelled bovine albumin and α-, β- and γ-globulins has been demonstrated also (Hemmings 1961).

3.16. Selective transmission

It appears probable that all antibodies produced in rabbits are transmitted equally readily to the foetal circulation. No significant differences have been detected in the transmission of complete agglutinins to *Brucella abortus*, *Salmonella pullorum* or sheep red cells, of haemolysins to sheep red cells or of antitoxins to diphtheria or tetanus toxoid, provided these have been prepared in rabbits (Brambell et al. 1950, 1952; Batty, Brambell, Hemmings and Oakley 1954). This is the more remarkable because the antibodies to sheep red cells, at least after primary immunization, are predominantly macro-globulin and those to bacteria predominantly 7S γ-globulin (Brambell et al. 1950). There can be no doubt of the transmission of the macroglobulin antibodies since they have been identified as such in the foetal circulation (Hemmings and Jones 1962). Moreover human macroglobulin and its monomeres, produced by treatment with mercaptoethanol followed by iodoacetamide, have been shown to be transmitted in the rabbit (Kaplan et al. 1965). It appears, therefore, that the size of the molecule is not important in transmission.

Transmission of the various protein fractions of homologous serum, however, is by no means uniform. When these are trace-labelled with ^{131}I it has been shown that, although rabbit albumin is transmitted in consider-able quantities, it is transmitted only about half as readily as the γ-globulin, whereas the α- and β-globulins are scarcely transmitted at all (Hemmings 1961).

Heterologous serum protein fractions appear to be transmitted less readily than the corresponding fractions of rabbit serum and the rates appear to be characteristic for each donor species. It was shown first that bovine anti-bodies were transmitted very much less readily than rabbit antibodies at 24 days *post coitum*, though the difference appeared to be less significant at 20 days *post coitum* (Brambell et al. 1950). At the same time it was shown that human and bovine γ-globulins, testing for these as antigens, were transmitted much more slowly than rabbit antibodies (Cohen 1950). More precise comparisons of the rates of transmission of antibodies prepared in a variety of species were obtained by using antitoxins (Batty et al. 1954). Antitoxins to diphtheria and to tetanus toxoid, and to the α-toxin of *Clostridium welchii* were employed and by injecting suitable mixtures of these into the uterine cavity it was possible to compare the transmission of those prepared in two or more donor species at the same time across the membranes of the same foetuses. It was found that the antitoxins were transmitted according to the donor species in the order: rabbit > human > guineapig > dog > equine > bovine, where the transmission of the rabbit antitoxin was about 100 times that of the bovine antitoxin (fig. 3.8). No differences

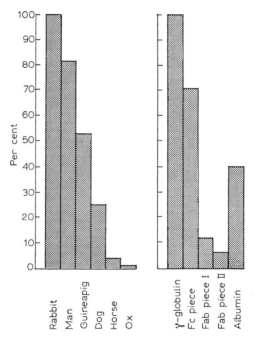

Fig. 3.8. Diagrams showing the selective transmission of immune globulin and its fragments by the yolk-sac of the foetal rabbit. The histogram on the left represents the rates of transmission of antitoxins prepared in various species expressed as percentages of the transmission of rabbit antitoxin. (Data from Batty et al. 1954.) The histogram on the right represents the rates of transmission of ^{131}I-labelled papainised fragments of rabbit γ-globulin and of rabbit serum albumin expressed as percentages of the rate of transmission of whole rabbit γ-globulin similarly labelled. (Data from Brambell et al. 1960; Hemmings 1961.)

were found in the transmission of antitoxins prepared against different toxins in any one species, although at the time it was thought that such a difference was detected between human diphtheria and tetanus antitoxins this difference was subsequently found to be due to a technical error in testing arising from the very low concentration of one of them. The differences in the amounts transmitted to the foetal circulation could not be accounted for by differences in the amounts absorbed by the foetal yolk-sacs from the uterine lumen. If this were the case there would be a change in the relative concentrations of the antitoxins in the residue of serum in the uterus and that this was not so is shown by the equality in the uptake of the antitoxins, irrespective of donor species, into both the maternal circulation and into the foetal exocoelomic and amniotic fluid, passage to all of which occurs directly without the intervention of the foetal circulation. However, it is clear also, that the selection occurs before the antitoxins are released by the yolk-sac into the foetal circulation, for when rabbit and bovine antitoxins and trace-labelled γ-globulins were injected intravenously directly into the foetal circulation they were still at the same relative concentrations in the foetal serum after 24 hr (Hemmings and Oakley 1957). Therefore the differential selection must occur within the cells of the foetal yolk-sac.

The relative transmission to the foetal circulation of rabbit and bovine γ-globulins trace-labelled with ^{131}I is closely comparable to that of antitoxins from these donor species (Hemmings 1956).

Trace-labelled bovine serum albumin is transmitted from the uterine lumen to the foetal circulation of the rabbit at 24 days *post coitum* at about $\frac{1}{3}$ the rate of similarly labelled rabbit serum albumin (Hemmings 1961). Thus there appears to be a clear selection as between serum albumins according to the donor species, but this selection is not so marked as that between γ-globulins, for bovine γ-globulin is transmitted at only about $\frac{1}{100}$ the rate of rabbit γ-globulin. Whereas rabbit γ-globulin is transmitted twice or three times more readily than rabbit albumin, bovine albumin is transmitted much more readily than bovine γ-globulin. It has been found also (Kulangara and Schechtman 1962) that human serum albumin is transmitted about twice as readily as human γ-globulin from the uterine lumen to the foetal circulation at 19 days *post coitum*, but that both are transmitted at very nearly the same rate at 24 days *post coitum*. These authors found that bovine serum albumin was not transmitted quite as readily as human serum albumin at either age. These authors' determinations were based on precipitin tests for the heterologous proteins as antigens in the serum. Thus it appears that both γ-globulin and albumin whether homologous or heterologous, are transmitted in the rabbit, but at characteristically distinctive rates, and that selection according to donor species occurs in both but is much more marked with the γ-globulins than with the albumins.

3.17. Selection of fragments of γ-globulin

It had been observed in the pregnant guineapig (p. 148) that whereas natural homologous diphtheria antitoxin is transmitted readily from the maternal to the foetal circulation, the antitoxin when pepsin-digested and refined is transmitted at such low levels as to be barely detectable. To determine if pepsin-refined antitoxin behaved similarly in rabbits, diphtheria antitoxin prepared in rabbits was digested with pepsin and prepared by the standard methods. This refined antitoxin was mixed with natural unrefined rabbit tetanus antitoxin and the mixture injected into the uterine cavities of rabbits 24 days pregnant. It was found that whereas the natural antitoxin was transmitted at the levels expected from previous work (Batty et al. 1954), the pepsin-refined antitoxin was not transmitted in detectable amounts and certainly many times less readily than the natural antitoxin (Brambell, Hemmings and Oakley 1959). Pepsin-refining cleaves the heavy chains about the middle and degrades the C-terminal halves, while the N-terminal halves, with the light chains attached to them, remain intact and bonded together. Thus the molecular weight of the molecule is reduced to about $\frac{2}{3}$ without loss of antibody activity, although much of the antigenic activity of the original molecule has disappeared. This suggested to us that the part of the molecule lost in the process of pepsin-refining, and which is the more antigenic when injected into another species, might be the part of the molecule which determines the rate of transmission of the whole. It was about this time that Porter (1958, 1959) succeeded in splitting rabbit immune γ-globulin molecules into three fragments with papain and in separating and recovering these. Two of these fragments, known as the Fab pieces, are similar, with a molecular weight of c. 50,000 and have the antibody activity. It has been demonstrated since that these, when bonded together by a disulphide linkage, correspond approximately to the pepsin-refined moiety (Nisonoff, Wissler, Lipman and Woernley 1960). The third fragment, known as the Fc piece, corresponds to the part of the molecule lost by pepsin-refining. It has a molecular weight of c. 80,000, lacks antibody activity and retains much of the antigenicity of the original molecule. This Fc-fragment, therefore, was the part which we thought might be responsible for transmission and Porter's discovery provided an opportunity for testing this hypothesis. The Fc- and Fab-fragments of papain-digested rabbit γ-globulin were trace-labelled with ^{131}I and their rates of transmission from the uterine cavity to the foetal circulation compared with that of whole rabbit γ-globulin similarly labelled (Brambell, Hemmings, Oakley and Porter 1960). It was found in accordance with expectation that the Fc piece was transmitted nearly as readily (c. 70%) as the whole molecule whereas the Fab piece was transmitted at a rate about an order less (fig. 3.8). The transmission of the pepsin-refined antitoxin would not have been detectable at the level observed for the isotopically labelled Fab piece, so that these results are compatible. Thus it appears that the Fc piece of rabbit γ-globulin, comprising the C-terminal halves of the two heavy chains linked together by a disulphide bond, which lacks antibody activity but retains much of the antigenicity of the intact molecule, is the part mainly responsible for transmission and that constitutes the 'recognition unit' or 'handle' that determines its acceptability for transmission by the cells of the foetal yolk-sac.

Confirmatory results have been obtained with the fragments of human γ-globulin (Kaplan et al. 1965) in rabbits. These were injected into the uterine cavities of rabbits 24 days pregnant and the foetal sera harvested after 24 hr. It was found that the pieces of human γ-globulin after papain digestion (F(B)), corresponding to the Fc pieces of rabbit γ-globulin, or whole heavy chains (obtained from a patient with H-chain disease) were readily transmitted to the foetal circulation at rates that appeared to even exceed those of the whole molecules. Conversely the pieces (AC), corres-ponding to the Fab pieces of rabbit γ-globulin, or the light chains alone (Bence-Jones protein) of human γ-globulin were transmitted at best in barely detectable amounts.

3.18. *Quantitative estimation of γ-globulin transmission*

The mean concentration of rabbit antitoxin in the foetal serum is 7.2% of that in the solution injected at 24 days *post coitum* into the uterine cavity 24 hr previously in quantities of 1 ml/foetus (Batty et al. 1954). This repre-sents transmission of approximately 20% of the dose of γ-globulin adminis-tered, assuming the total foetal γ-globulin space to be about 2.5 ml. It has been shown with isotopically labelled rabbit γ-globulin (Hemmings 1956) that about 25% of the dose is present in the foetuses as breakdown products and, since these are likely to be quickly eliminated, the total amount degraded probably is substantially more. Slightly more degradation products are found in the foetuses when isotopically labelled bovine γ-globulin is used although only about 1% as much intact protein reaches the foetal circulation. Labelled rabbit γ-globulin, injected into the uterine cavity after ligation of the cervix, to prevent escape by that route, is not absorbed during oestrus but in the non-gravid horn during pregnancy 11 to 33% of the dose is absorbed (Hemmings 1957) over a 24-hr period. In a gravid horn, however, 83 to 96% of the dose is absorbed over a similar period, irrespective of whether the labelled globulin is rabbit or bovine. Clearly most of the dose is absorbed by the conceptuses. Since only a small part is transmitted to the foetal circulation as protein, the greater part must be degraded. No significant proteolysis could be demonstrated in the uterine cavity and the conclusion was inescapable that degradation occurred after absorption by the foetal cells and before liberation into the circulation. The evidence indicates that rabbit and bovine globulin are absorbed equally readily by the cells of the foetal membrane, that a small part is transmitted as protein to the circulation, the amount depending on whether it is rabbit or bovine globulin, and that the greater part, comprising all the residue not so transmitted, is degraded by the cells. Examination of the proteolytic enzymes of the cells of the yolk-sac splanchnopleur has shown that at least three cathepsins and three exopeptidases are present (Jones 1966). These cells are much richer in cathepsins than the cells of the other embryonic membranes. The enzymes were shown to be capable of hydrolysing bovine albumin and γ-globulin and rabbit γ-globulin.

3.19. *The proteins of other foetal fluids*

The foetal membranes of the rabbit enclose fluids in the separate compartments of exocoel, amnion and allantois. During the later stages of pregnancy, when the foetal swallowing reflex has been established, the stomach is full, as a rule, with a viscous fluid derived largely from ingested amniotic fluid. The first investigation of the protein content of some of these fluids electrophoretically showed that they contained the principal components of serum (Brambell et al. 1953). The exocoelomic and amniotic fluids and the stomach contents at 25 days *post coitum* contained similar components in closely similar proportions, though the total concentrations were different, being lower in the amniotic fluid than in the exocoelomic fluid and higher in the stomach contents than in either. Although the components resembled those of the sera in electrophoretic mobility, their relative concentrations differed widely from those both in maternal and in foetal sera. Wild (1965a), using more sophisticated techniques that permitted better resolution of the globulins, confirmed these general findings. It was shown that the protein concentration was greater in the exocoelomic fluid, and less in the allantoic fluid, than in the amniotic fluid and that there was a progressive increase in concentration from the 23rd day onwards. All these fluids and the stomach contents contained proteins of similar mobility in similar proportions. These proportions were different both from those of the maternal and of foetal serum, but resembled those found in the uterine fluid during the 24–26 day period; the only time when samples could be obtained. These fluids all contained a higher proportion of albumin and a lower proportion of γ-globulin as compared to maternal serum, and α_1- and α_2-macroglobulins and lipoproteins appeared to be absent from them. The α_2-globulin present appeared to be of low molecular weight, like that in foetal serum. Antiserum to rabbit amniotic fluid, prepared in the rat, and absorbed with maternal serum, showed this component in the foetal fluids, including foetal serum, although it was apparently absent from maternal serum, suggesting that it is of foetal origin. Previously, Lambotte (1963) had identified an α-globulin-component in amniotic fluid and foetal serum, which persisted in the circulation of the young rabbit until 20 days of age, but was absent from the serum of older animals. This would appear to be the same component as the α_2 of Wild, although Lambotte classed it as α_1.

Antibodies often can be detected in the amniotic fluid and in the stomach contents, as well as in the exocoelomic fluid, after intrauterine or intravenous injection of the mother with immune serum. The titres observed in the amniotic fluid approximate to those in the exocoelomic fluid, but those of the stomach contents are frequently much higher, sometimes upwards of 100 times. No doubt these are attained by concentration through absorption of water from amniotic fluid which has been swallowed. Nevertheless a correlation was demonstrable between the titres of stomach contents and amniotic fluid, but not between those of stomach contents and of foetal serum (Brambell, Hemmings, Henderson, Oakley and Rowlands 1951), indicating that there was no transfer either way between serum and stomach contents. The much higher concentration of protein in the stomach contents as compared to the amniotic fluid was observed by Wild (1965a) also. The entry of antibodies prepared in different species from the uterine cavity into the exocoel, amnion and stomach is not selective, in striking contrast to their entry to the foetal circulation (Brambell, Hemmings, Henderson and Oakley 1952). The non-selective entry of various antitoxins to the amniotic fluid and stomach contents after intrauterine injection of a mixture of two or more prepared in different species is clearly brought out by the graphs in figs. 3.9 and 3.10 (Batty et al. 1954). Clearly these proteins must enter

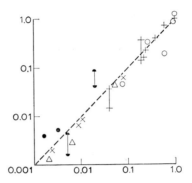

Fig. 3.9. Diagram of the rates of transmission of antitoxins prepared in various species from the uterine lumen to the amniotic fluid and stomach contents of foetal rabbits relative to those prepared in rabbits. The rates are expressed as concentration quotients (C.Q.'s) to correct them for the concentrations in the mixtures of immune sera injected into the uterine lumen and are on a logarithmic scale. The values for the rabbit antitoxins are plotted on the abscissa and for the heterologous antitoxins on the ordinate. The broken line represents the expectation if the values for the heterologous antitoxins were equal to those of the rabbit antitoxin. Key to symbols: Rabbit/human ● = amniotic fluid; ○ = stomach contents. Rabbit/dog △ = amniotic fluid; + = stomach contents. Rabbit/horse × = amniotic fluid. (From Batty et al. 1954.)

from the uterine lumen direct, without the intermediary of the foetal circulation and the most probable route is through the avascular chorion into the exocoel, and from there through the amnion into the amniotic fluid and so, through swallowing reflexes, to the stomach. A similar conclusion as to the route of entry into these compartments was arrived at by Kulangara and Schechtman (1962). This probability has been greatly strengthened by the use of the chorion, amnion and yolk-sac membranes *in vitro* for dialysis experiments (Wild 1965a). It was shown by this means that proteins passed across them in both directions but that, under these circumstances, the amnion and chorion were much more permeable than the yolk-sac splanchnopleur. When serum was dialysed the proportions of the dialysates were similar, irrespective of which membrane was used or in which direction the transfer occurred. Molecular size appeared to influence the rate of dialysis, as the proportion of albumin was higher, and of α- and γ-globulins lower, in the dialysate than in the serum dialysed.

The possibility that maternal serum proteins might reach the foetal circulation directly from these compartments, without traversing the yolk-sac splanchnopleur, was explored. Immune serum was injected into the exocoelomic cavities of alternate foetuses at 24 days *post coitum* (Brambell, Hemmings, Hemmings, Henderson and Rowlands 1951). The injections were made through the uterine wall and a small air-bubble was injected with the serum. The uterine wall was sufficiently transparent to enable the larger vitelline vessels to be avoided and to be reasonably confident that the injection, as indicated by the air-bubble, had indeed gone into the exocoel. It was not possible to be certain at the time of injection that the amnion had not been perforated, but at autopsy it was found to be distended as a rule, whereas the exocoel was often empty, indicating that the amnion had not been punctured. The condition of the exocoel indicated that the perforation in the yolk-sac splanchnopleur did not seal itself and that the exocoelomic fluid containing the immune serum injected leaked out into the uterine

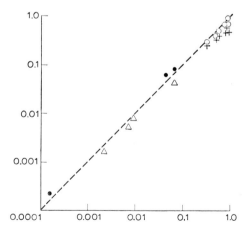

Fig. 3.10. Diagram similar to fig. 3.9 but showing the relative rates of transmission of pairs of heterologous antitoxins from the uterine lumen to the amniotic fluid and stomach contents of foetal rabbits. The values for horse antitoxin are plotted on the abscissa and for guineapig or bovine antitoxin on the ordinate. Key to symbols: Horse/guineapig ● = amniotic fluid; ○ = stomach contents. Horse/bovine △ = amniotic fluid; + = stomach contents. (From Batty et al. 1954.)

cavity. At the conclusion of the experiment 24 hr after injection it was found that the antibody titres of the sera of experimental and control foetuses did not differ significantly (table 3.6), presumably because the absorptive surfaces of the yolk-sacs of both had been bathed by the fluid in the uterine

TABLE 3.6

Comparison of serum titres of control and experimental embryos. (From Brambell, Hemmings, Hemmings, Henderson and Rowlands 1951.)

Experimental embryo serum titre	Highest control embryo serum titre from same uterus												
	$\frac{1}{10}$				$\frac{1}{20}$			$\frac{1}{40}$			$\frac{1}{80}$		
	−	+	++	+++	+	++	+++	+	++	+++	+	++	+++
$\frac{1}{80}$ +++	.	.	.	.	.	.	.	.	.	.	.	.	2
$\frac{1}{80}$ ++	.	.	.	.	.	.	.	.	.	1	.	.	.
$\frac{1}{80}$ +	.	.	.	.	.	.	.	.	.	3	2	.	.
$\frac{1}{40}$ +++	.	.	.	.	.	.	1*	3	1	3	.	.	.
$\frac{1}{40}$ ++	.	.	.	.	.	.	.	.	.	1	.	.	.
$\frac{1}{40}$ +	.	.	.	.	.	.	.	.	.	.	.	.	.
$\frac{1}{20}$ +++	.	.	.	1*	.	4	4	.	.	.	.	.	.
$\frac{1}{20}$ ++	.	.	.	.	.	.	.	.	.	.	.	.	.
$\frac{1}{20}$ +	.	.	.	.	.	.	1	.	.	.	.	.	.
$\frac{1}{10}$ +++	.	.	1	.	.	.	.	1	.	.	.	.	.
$\frac{1}{10}$ ++	.	.	.	.	.	.	.	1	.	.	.	.	.
$\frac{1}{10}$ +	.	.	.	.	.	.	.	.	.	.	.	.	.
$\frac{1}{10}$ −	2	.	.	.	.	.	1	.	.	.	.	.	.

* Titre of injected embryo 1 dilution higher than that of control.

cavity which had leaked from the exocoels of the experimental foetuses. Since the inner or exocoelomic surfaces of the yolk-sac of the experimental foetuses were exposed to the antibodies, whereas those of the control foetuses were not, it was clear that no significant entry of antibody to the circulation from the exocoel occurred.

Apparently antibodies cannot be transmitted from the gut to the circulation of the foetal rabbit, since even when very high concentrations were attained in the stomach contents of experimental foetuses, no correlated increase in the concentration in the serum was observed. Since antibodies are transmitted from the gut to the circulation of both foetal and neonatal rats, it might be expected that similar transmission might occur in the foetal rabbit, but this is not the case. It has been shown that the foetal rabbit intestinal epithelial cells develop microvilli by the 25th day and appear to display pinocytotic vesicles in the apical cytoplasm, and that these are very well developed by full term (Deren, Strauss and Wilson 1965). Moreover these authors have shown that the cells can absorb various sugars and amino-acids at these stages. The pinocytotic uptake of ferritin by these cells in the new-born rabbit has been demonstrated also (Kraehenbuhl, Gloor and Blanc 1967). However, the new-born rabbit does not augment materially the passive immunity, transmitted before birth, by absorption of antibodies from the colostrum or milk (Vaillard 1896; Remlinger 1899; Romer 1901). Recently, nevertheless, the transmission of isotopically labelled homologous and heterologous γ-globulins has been demonstrated, though at a very low level, after oral administration in both the new-born and the adult rabbit. The transfer after oral administration to adult rabbits of hyperimmune horse anti-diphtheria antitoxin has been shown also, using the Schick test (Mouton, Margadant, Collet, Rowinski and Bein 1957). Since serum γ-globulins are secreted in the colostrum and milk of rabbits (Feinstein 1963; Askonas, Campbell, Humphrey and Work 1954), it would appear that the possibility of some transmission to the circulation occurring after birth requires to be reinvestigated with modern methods. Whether or not any transmission to the circulation occurs after birth, maternal antibodies in the colostrum and milk could well be of importance to the neonatal animal in providing it with protection in the lumen of its alimentary canal against enteric pathogens. The recent work of Genco and Taubman (1969) is of interest in this context. They immunized female rabbits before and during pregnancy to 2.4-dinitrophenylated bovine γ-globulin, using complete Freund's adjuvant, either by injection into the foot pads or into the mammary tissue. The colostrum of both groups contained anti-DNP antibody in the γM- and γG-globulins, but γA antibody was present in the colostrum only of those that had been injected in the mammary tissue. This suggests that local immunization regularly induces secretory γA antibodies.

CHAPTER 4

Transmission of immunity in the rat and the mouse before birth

4.1. Introduction

The transmission of immunity from mother to young was demonstrated originally by Ehrlich (1892), using mice. The rat and the mouse resemble each other sufficiently closely in the manner in which this transmission occurs for it to be possible for us to consider them together, simply indicating where the information available relates to one species only. Both species transmit some immunity before birth and in both most of the transmission occurs after birth and continues throughout the greater part of lactation. Both species are particularly convenient experimental material for studying the transmission of immunity after birth because of the ease with which the sucklings can be given immune serum or protein solutions orally by means of stomach tube. Each of these two species has certain distinctive features which render it more convenient for certain kinds of experiments than the other species. The rat, for example, because it is larger is more convenient for surgical experiments and for those in which the size of the serum sample that can be harvested is important; consequently information concerning the route of transmission before birth is confined to this species at present. The mouse has the advantage that many highly inbred and genetically uniform lines are available, the use of which reduces individual variation in the results. Mice are also particularly valuable because of the occurrence of myelomas in them which result in the overproduction of some one particular category of immune globulin by the neoplastic clone of lymphoid cells which has given rise to the disease. This characteristic, shared with man, has resulted in a more extensive knowledge of the varieties of immune globulins in these two species than in any others.

Transmission of immunity to the foetus and to the suckling are very different processes that must be considered separately. Much less is known concerning transmission before birth in these animals than in the case of the rabbit, mainly because their small size renders them less convenient experimental material, but also because their early development and the details of the arrangement of the foetal membranes are less favourable in some respects. It follows that a description of early development and of the arrangement of the foetal membranes is an essential preliminary to consideration of transmission before birth (see Duval 1891; Jenkinson 1902; Sobotta 1903, 1911; Mossman 1937; Amoroso 1952).

4.2. Early development of the rat and mouse

Fertilized mouse eggs have attained the morula stage by the time they reach the uterus three days after ovulation. Shortly afterwards the zona pellucida is shed and after remaining free in the uterine cavity for about one day under normal circumstances, during which period they have become sub-equally spaced out along its length, implantation begins. The embryos are small blastocysts at this stage, their diameter not greatly exceeding that of the unfertilized egg, and each becomes lodged in the cleft-like antimesometrial extremity of the uterine lumen. Implantation is therefore eccentric and antimesometrial, unlike the central implantation of the comparatively large blastocyst of the rabbit. Almost as soon as the trophoblast begins to adhere to the uterine epithelium, the latter breaks down and disintegrates in the immediate vicinity of the blastocyst and the trophoblast invades and penetrates into the sub-epithelial tissues of the mucosa. At the same time the connective tissue cells of the mucosa, in a spherical region surrounding the implanting blastocyst, undergo enlargement and transformation into decidual cells and give rise to a dense uniform tissue and a microscopically recognisable swelling on the antimesometrial side of the uterus marking each implantation site. Meanwhile the blastocyst in its implantation chamber in the centre of this mass becomes orientated with its inner cell mass situated mesometrially. It has been shown by Kirby, Potts and Wilson (1967) that this orientation is brought about, after a randomly orientated initial attachment of the blastocyst, by migration of the cells of the inner cell mass within the shell of trophoblast, rather than by a rotation of the whole blastocyst, the trophoblast of which appears to be firmly attached to the uterine tissues. Soon after it has become orientated, the cells of the trophoblast overlying the inner cell mass increase and become heaped up to form the ectoplacental cone, projecting mesometrially into the cleft-like uterine lumen, laterally compressed by the development of the decidual mass. The further development of the decidual tissue so compresses the uterine lumen, mesometrially to the ectoplacental cone or träger, that the uterine epithelium disintegrates and the lumen disappears, so that the embryo is completely enclosed in the decidual mass. Between adjacent implantation sites the uterine lumen remains patent and persists.

The inner cell mass lengthens in the mesometrial–antimesometrial direction at the same time as the ectoplacental cone is forming and in consequence of these two changes the whole blastocyst assumes a cylindrical shape, known as the egg-cylinder. The endoderm, differentiating first as a covering layer around the inner cell mass, spreads around the inner surface of the trophoblast and lines the yolk-sac cavity into which the inner cell mass projects. Between the endoderm and the trophoblast a continuous hyaline membrane is secreted and is known as Reichert's membrane. It may play an important part in determining, when it is present, what substances of maternal origin can reach the yolk-sac cavity. Between this membrane and the maternal decidua a layer of giant cells is formed, the origin of which has been much disputed, some authors attributing to them a trophoblastic origin and others a maternal decidual origin. On balance it appears probable that at least the majority are of trophoblastic origin though some may be maternal. These cells appear to be phagocytic and migratory, causing destruction of the maternal tissues in their vicinity and rupture of the capillaries, the maternal blood being liberated into the spaces between their long interdigitating processes, so that the whole forms a layer of loose vascular tissue around the developing and expanding embryo. The giant cells have been shown (Wislocki, Deane and Dempsey 1946) to be rich in alkaline phosphatase.

4.3. The development of the foetal membranes

The way in which the amnion arises is very different to that in the rabbit, where the embryonic ectoderm is exposed on the surface of the large blastocysts and the amnion and chorion are formed by the upgrowth and closure over it of amniotic folds. Perhaps because of the early implantation and small size of the murine blastocyst the amnion arises from a closed cavity within the inner cell mass and the embryonic ectoderm is never exposed. As the egg-cylinder lengthens, a longitudinal cleft appears in the ectoderm in the centre of the inner cell mass. The mesoderm differentiates between the ectoderm and endoderm of the embryonic region of the inner cell mass and the coelom appears in it. Mesoderm and coelom extend mesometrially around the ectoderm of the inner cell mass to the base of the träger and then laterally around the mesometrial hemisphere of the yolk-sac. Midway along the length of the inner cell mass the exocoel expands and constricts the cavity in it into two, an antimesometrially situated cavity above what will become the embryonic ectoderm, which is the rudiment of the amnion, and a mesometrially situated cavity beneath the base of the ectoplacental cone, which is known as the ectoplacental cavity and which is transitory. Between these two ectodermal cavities is the exocoel in the mesoderm. Meanwhile the ectoplacental cone has expanded and invaded the maternal decidual tissue on the mesometrial side of the uterus, where the uterine lumen has been obliterated, forming the rudiment of the placenta. A solid process of mesoderm grows out from the posterior extremity of the primitive streak into the exocoel. This is the homologue of the allantoic mesoderm of, for example, the rabbit although it contains no endodermal diverticulum. The ectoplacental cavity collapses and disappears and the allantoic mesoderm, growing across the exocoel, reaches and fuses with the splanchnic mesoderm beneath the ectoplacental cone, which is thus converted into allantochorion and becomes vascularised by the allantoic blood vessels.

The uterine lumen persists between conceptuses. As development proceeds, the parts of the lumen on each side of a conceptus extend antimesometrially around it between the decidual tissue and the muscularis and, joining with the basal remnants of the uterine glands in this region, ultimately meet and re-establish the continuity of the cavity. Thus, the cavity of the yolk-sac becomes separated from the restored uterine cavity by a layer of tissue which becomes stretched and thinner as development proceeds and which finally disappears. At first, this layer consists, from within outwards, of the very thin endoderm of the bilaminar hemisphere of the yolk-sac, Reichert's membrane, the trophoblast, and the remains of the maternal decidua, now stretched to form the thin decidua capsularis. First the cellular layers disintegrate and disappear and finally, about the 15th day of gestation, Reichert's membrane also ruptures and recoils to the sides of the placenta, exposing the splanchnic wall of the yolk-sac. This splanchnic wall has become inverted by the growth of the foetus and amnion. It completely encloses the exocoel, amnion and foetus, except where the allantoic stalk joins the placenta and is closely invested by it. Folds appearing in sections like branching villi are developed on the yolk-sac splanchnopleur. They

project into the uterine lumen, particularly facing the placenta on the mesometrial hemisphere of the yolk-sac from the equator to the point where
it invests the allantoic stalk. Each has a mesenchymal core containing blood
vessels and is covered by the columnar endodermal epithelium. They may
increase the absorptive capacity of the yolk-sac by greatly increasing the
area of endoderm exposed to the contents of the uterine cavity. The bilaminar
omphalopleur of the yolk-sac joins the margin of the splanchnic wall around
the allantoic stalk and invests the whole surface of the placenta, extending
around its margin. This part of the bilaminar omphalopleur persists until
term. At its margin the ruptured and recoiled Reichert's membrane, all that
is left of the rest of the bilaminar omphalopleur, forms a frill around the
placenta. At the points where the chief branches of the allantoic arteries
from the allantoic stalk penetrate into the placenta blind tubular extensions

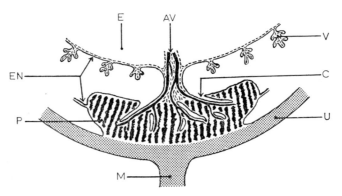

Fig. 4.1. Diagram showing how the endodermal crypts of Duval (C) follow the major
allantoic blood vessels from the allantoic stalk (AV) into the depth of the placenta (P)
of the rat. EN = endoderm of yolk-sac; E = exocoel; M = mesometrium; U = uterine
wall; V = villi of the yolk-sac splanchnopleur.

of the bilaminar omphalopleur accompany them for some distance (fig. 4.1).
These are known as the crypts of Duval after their discoverer. Each crypt
nearly surrounds the foetal artery, from which it is separated only by a thin
layer of foetal mesenchyme. The endoderm on the side of the crypt away
from the artery rests on an extension of Reichert's membrane, which separates it everywhere from the trophoblast of the placenta.

The final arrangement of the embryonic membranes (fig. 4.2) is comparable to that in the rabbit, although attained in a remarkably different manner,

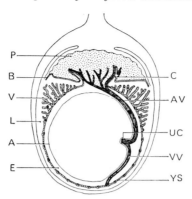

Fig. 4.2. Diagram of the foetal membranes of the rat. A = amnion; B = tag of bilaminar omphalopleur; L = uterine lumen; UC = umbilical cord; VV = vitelline vessels in yolk-sac stalk; YS = yolk-sac splanchnopleur; other letters as in Fig. 4.1. (From Brambell and Halliday 1956.)

probably due largely to the eccentric implantation of the blastocyst while it is still very small. It differs from the rabbit in the absence of a zone of chorion intervening between the margin of the placenta and the margin of the yolk-sac, in the greater development of splanchnic villi, in the investment of the surface of the placenta by the bilaminar omphalopleur and the presence of crypts of Duval, and in possessing a well developed Reichert's membrane. Consequently it is surgically impracticable to isolate the bilaminar omphalopleur of the yolk-sac of the rat or mouse from the placenta, and hence to determine whether substances absorbed from the uterine lumen by this part of the endoderm are transmitted to the foetus, since they would be transported by the allantoic vessels of the placenta. The splanchnic wall of the yolk-sac can be removed surgically and as the vitelline circulation to this region is through the yolk-sac stalk, which only joins the allantoic stalk at the umbilicus, it is possible to distinguish its functions from those of the placenta, as in the rabbit.

Excellent accounts of the development and structure of the yolk-sac of the mouse and rat have been provided recently by Friedrich (1964) and by Padykula, Deren and Wilson (1966) respectively, and reference should be made to these for more detailed descriptions. The structure and histochemistry of Reichert's membrane, and of the basement membranes of the endoderm and serosal epithelium of the splanchnic wall of the yolk-sac of the rat have been described by Wislocki and Padykula (1953). The fine structure of that part of the parietal wall of the yolk-sac which invests the surface of the placenta and persists after the rest has disappeared has been described by Jollie (1968). The endoderm cells of this region do not form a continuous layer so that Reichert's membrane, on which they rest, is exposed in places to the yolk-sac cavity. The trophoblast beneath Reichert's membrane also is fenestrated by the 22nd day, so that the maternal blood in the placenta comes into direct contact with Reichert's membrane, which forms the only barrier between the maternal blood and the cavity of conjoined yolk-sac and uterine lumen. Ferritin injected intravenously readily traversed the membrane and was phagocytosed by the parietal endoderm cells but thorotrast did not traverse the membrane.

4.4. *The placenta*

The placenta is discoid in shape and is labyrinthine in structure, since the maternal blood circulates in a system of narrow channels in the trophoblast. The maternal arteries traverse the thickness of the placenta and discharge near its foetal side into large lacunae in the trophoblast, the blood percolating back through the small channels in columns of trophoblast perpendicular to the surface. Similarly the foetal allantoic arteries traverse the thickness of the placenta to the maternal side, where they branch and the foetal blood returns in capillaries forming a network around the trophoblastic columns containing the maternal blood. Mossman (1937), using the light microscope, claimed that these capillaries actually projected through the trophoblast in places into the maternal blood so that only the foetal capillary endothelium separated the two circulations. Consequently on the principles of Grosser's (1927) classification of placentae, he suggested that these should be called haemoendothelial. More recent work with the electron microscope on several species has failed to confirm this interpretation and indicates that there is always a layer of trophoblast between the foetal capillaries and the maternal blood, though this layer may be very attenuated (see Wislocki and Dempsey 1955). On this basis the placenta of the rat or mouse is probably more correctly described as haemochorial. The blood from the foetal capillaries is gathered into the allantoic veins on the foetal side of the placenta. Thus the foetal and maternal bloods are flowing in opposite directions where they are in closest proximity in the trophoblastic columns. This counter-current flow favours exchange by diffusion between the two circulations.

4.5. *The fine structure of the yolk-sac splanchnopleur*

The fine structure of the yolk-sac splanchnopleur of the rat has been studied by electron microscopy and with the use of cytochemical methods. Reference should be made to the excellent descriptions provided by Wislocki and Padykula (1953), Wislocki and Dempsey (1955), Calarco and Moyer (1966), Padykula, Deren and Wilson (1966) and Lambson (1966). This description is based largely on the two last mentioned accounts, which agree remarkably closely.

The endodermal epithelium of the splanchnic wall of the yolk-sac is composed of columnar cells which are very complex in structure. These cells are closely linked together near their free surfaces by desmosomes and present a continuous cellular membrane to the cavity. Their outer surfaces are clothed with a pile of microvilli from the 10th day of gestation to term (plate 4.1). These villi at first are slender but late in gestation they are often branched and swollen. They are clothed with a fuzzy coat which gives a strong periodic acid-Schiff reaction and may be glycoprotein. Between the bases of the microvilli are numerous indentations or caveoli; both these caveoli and many small vesicles in the apical cytoplasm have a lining similar to the fuzzy-coat of the microvilli and 200–300 Å thick, the fibres of which appear to be arranged perpendicularly to the surface. As development proceeds these invaginations and vesicles become more numerous and give the impression of an interconnected system of channels with dilations and lined throughout by the fuzzy material. They are connecting with the surface of the cell, continuously or intermittently by the caveoli between the bases of the microvilli. Thus the apical regions of these cells present the appearances recognised as characteristic of active pinocytosis. Beneath this region of thick walled canals and vesicles, larger thin-wall vesicles are present, into which it is probable that the thick-walled vesicles and canals may discharge.

The nuclei of these cells are situated in the basal halves of the cells and the cytoplasm is rich in rough endoplasmic reticulum, ribosomes, mitochondria and Golgi elements. The latter are paranuclear and often adjoin the lateral plasma membrane. Golgi vesicles can be seen containing a material resembling that in the intracellular spaces in later stages. The lateral borders of the cells have numerous irregular and interlocking processes. Lipid is accumulated and stored in the basal cytoplasm from the 13th to 15th day of gestation but subsequently until term it is glycogen that is stored in this region. Sorokin and Padykula (1964) noted the presence of alkaline phosphatase in the apical border, and succinic dehydrogenase, adenosine triphosphatase and non-specific esterase in the cells, but found that all these enzymes declined in quantity towards the end of gestation. These authors also found the cells to be rich in acid phosphatase, which did not decline in quantity towards term, and considered that this indicated that some of the granules or vesicles in the cytoplasm are lysosomal in character. Johnson and Spinuzzi (1966) investigated the enzymes in homogenates of the yolk-sac splanchnopleur of rats from 10 to 20 days pregnant. They also found acid phosphatase, non-specific esterase and malate and lactate dehydrogenases, but the relative concentrations changed with time. The intensity of the dehydrogenases was greatest at ages of 11 to 13 days, whereas that of the acid phosphatase and esterase was greatest late in gestation. More recently (Johnson and Spinuzzi 1968) it has been shown by gel electrophoresis that three molecular varieties of alkaline phosphatase occur in the yolk-sac of the rat. The variety of highest mobility remained constant from the 10th day throughout gestation, that of intermediate mobility appeared on the 13th day and increased in activity at the end of gestation on the 18th to 20th day, and that of lowest mobility was present from the 10th to 13th day, then declined in activity and was undetected after the 16th day. Similarly four molecular varieties of glucose-6-phosphate dehydrogenase could be distinguished. The slowest was the principal variety throughout gestation, attaining a maximum on days 12 to 14 but declining on days 16 to 20. The three faster varieties all attained their greatest intensity during the third week of gestation. The cathepsins of the endoderm cells of the yolk-sac splanchnopleur of the rat do not appear to have been investigated, but it may be recalled that Jones (1966) found that these enzymes were plentiful in the endoderm cells of the yolk-sac splanchnopleur of the rabbit.

The endodermal epithelium rests on a well-developed basal membrane, the visceral basement membrane, and similarly the thin mesothelium lining the exocoelomic surface of the yolk-sac splanchnopleur, rests on another basement membrane, the serosal basement membrane (Wislocki and Pady-

---

Plate 4.1. Electron micrographs of the apical regions of endoderm cells of the yolk-sac splanchnopleur of foetal rats near term. In A the microvilli on the surface and the complex interconnecting system of apical canaliculi (C) are apparent. A large vacuole (V) is present and desmosomes can be seen joining adjacent cells. × 9,400.   B is after ferritin injection and shows ferritin granules indicated by arrows in the glycocalyx of caveoli and canaliculi.
× 58,500. (From Lambson 1966.)

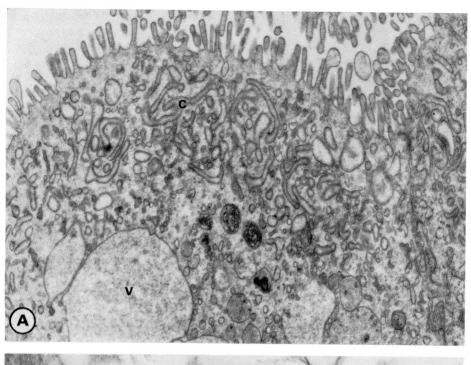

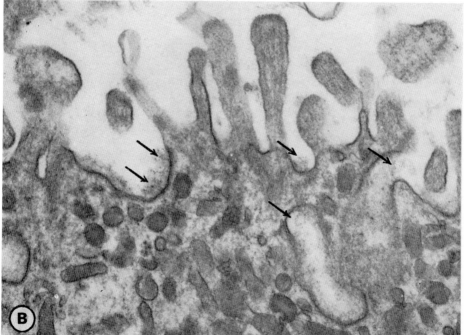

PLATE 4.1

kula 1953). Between these two basement membranes is the vascular mesen-chyme containing the sinusoidal blood vessels. These vessels are endothelial tubes of large diameter the walls of which are composed of overlapping and closely apposed endothelial cells, which may be as thin as 0.1 μ in places. At 13 to 14 days of gestation erythroblasts occur in these vessels but ery-throcytes prevail near term.

Materials passing from the uterine lumen to the blood in the vitelline vessels of the yolk-sac splanchnopleur must traverse the endodermal endo-thelium, the visceral basement membrane, the intervening loose mesenchyme and the vascular endothelium; to reach the exocoel direct they would have to traverse the serosal basement membrane and the exocoelomic mesothelium as well.

4.6. *Experimental evidence of pinocytosis by the yolk-sac endoderm*

It is apparent from the cytological structure of the endodermal cells of the yolk-sac splanchnopleur, as revealed by the light and electron microscopes, that all the characteristics of pinocytosis are recognisable. There is also much experimental evidence of the pinocytotic absorption of colloidal materials by these cells. Everett (1935) carried out vascular perfusion experiments on the uterus of the pregnant rat and claimed that the maternal blood bathes the surface of Reichert's membrane. He found that both trypan blue and toluidine blue, when added to the perfusion medium, readily penetrated Reichert's membrane and entered the apical regions of the endoderm cells. Toluidine blue was reduced to the leuco-base in these cells and was trans-mitted to the foetal circulation by this route before it appeared in the allan-toic vessels. Bridgman (1948a, b) found also that trypan blue appeared to be ingested by the yolk-sac endoderm cells. Wislocki, Deane and Dempsey (1946) found that iron secreted by the uterine glands and resulting from the break down of maternal erythrocytes was absorbed by the cells of the endoderm. They were of opinion that these cells absorbed protein which was apparent as granules in the cytoplasm. Calcium, on the other hand, appeared to be absorbed by the placenta and not by the yolk-sac.

Sorokin and Padykula (1964) successfully cultured *in vitro* yolk-sacs removed from rats at various stages of development from the 12th day of gestation to term, but principally at the 13th day. The explants, whether whole or subdivided, survived and appeared healthy for two weeks, considerably longer than they would have survived *in vivo* had they remained to term. The endoderm cells in the explants retained the lipoid that they contained at the time of transplantation and accumulated glycogen during the culture period. These cells were actively phagocytic and absorbed colloidal materials, such as cholesterol and trypan blue, from the medium. Padykula, Deren and Wilson (1966) studied the uptake by the endoderm cells of vitamin B_{12}, isotopically labelled with ^{58}Co, in such cultures. This uptake was increased up to sevenfold in the presence of rat gastric intrinsic factor in the medium and was 10 to 100 times greater per gram of tissue than is the uptake in the adult intestine. Neither hog intrinsic factor nor rat blood plasma had any effect on the uptake of the vitamin. Both the endodermal and mesothelial surfaces of the yolk-sac splanchnopleur absorbed the vitamin. The amount of uptake varied by as much as 50% between embryos from different litters but the variation was less between embryos from the same litter and was remarkably constant between the two halves of a single yolk-sac when these were cultured separately. The uptake per gram of tissue was greatest in yolk-sacs at 13 days of gestation age and declined in older yolk-sacs until full term, but the simultaneous increase in the mass of the yolk-sac tissue during this period more than compensated for the declining rate of uptake so that the absolute amount absorbed by the whole yolk-sac increased slightly towards term. The yolk-sac splanchnopleur *in vitro* did not transport against a concentration gradient either isotopically labelled L-valine or α-methylglucoside. Intravenous injection of the labelled vitamin into the pregnant mother resulted in a high initial concentration of it in the placenta, which declined rapidly over 24 hr, whereas the concentration in the yolk-sac splanchnopleur increased during this period. The authors were not able to exclude the placenta as a normal route of the transmission of the vitamin from the mother to the foetus but nevertheless they were inclined to regard the yolk-sac as specialised for the transmission of large molecules.

Several workers have exposed the yolk-sac *in vivo* to materials which could be visualised in the cells. Lambson (1966) injected ferritin intravenously into rats pregnant 10 to 21 days. He found that the ferritin reached quickly the uterine lumen and was absorbed by the endoderm cells. It was found within the apical invaginations, canals and vacuoles at all stages of development examined, mainly being present in the fuzzy-lining of these but also being free in their cavities. Only on the 20th and 21st day of gestation was it observed in the more basal regions of the cells, being present in small dense vacuoles, often near the basal or lateral plasma membranes. At this time it was present also within the basement membranes, the endothelial cells of the capillaries and even in some exocoelomic mesothelial cells. Carpenter and Ferm (1966) injected thorotrast into the uterine cavities of golden hamsters on the 13th, 14th and 15th day of gestation and examined with the electron microscope the yolk-sac tissues harvested 15 min to 48 hr after injection. They found that the endoderm cells rapidly and progressively took up the thorotrast by way of the fuzzy-lined apical invaginations. The apical regions of the cells became filled with heavily labelled vacuoles by 1 hr after injection and many of these vacuoles subsequently coalesced. No thorotrast was found at any stage in the other tissues or in the vitelline blood vessels. Beck, Lloyd and Griffiths (1967) injected horseradish peroxidase intravenously into rats at stages of from $8\frac{1}{2}$ to $20\frac{1}{2}$ days of pregnancy. It was taken up by the endoderm cells pinocytotically and digested in them by the fusion of lysosomes with the phagosomes. Little intracellular digestion occurred in the invasive trophoblast or its derivatives and it did not cross the foetal membranes in any case. It was shown subsequently that the horseradish peroxidase undoubtedly is degraded within the cells (Parry, Beck and Lloyd 1968). The peroxidase was injected intraperitoneally into 17 day pregnant rats and after 6 hr pieces of foetal yolk-sac were harvested and cultured *in vitro* in a system adapted to biochemical analysis. Samples of the cultures were assayed for the peroxidase at 10 min and at 19–24 hr. The net loss of peroxidase in the interval was 70–80%. Since none was present in the medium, in which it was shown to be stable, degradation must have been in the cells, in which the presence of the enzyme was demonstrated histochemically.

4.7. *Transmission of immunity before birth*

The pioneer work on transmission of passive immunity from mother to young was that of Ehrlich (1892). He immunized mice with plant toxins and found that the young of these animals had a measure of resistance to the toxins. He considered that there was some transmission of immunity *in utero* but that the greater part occurred after birth by way of the milk, a conclusion which has been amply confirmed subsequently, although a few workers have failed to detect transmission before birth. Boucek (1928) immunized female rats to guineapig red blood corpuscles before mating them and gave them further injections during pregnancy. Despite maternal titres of 300 to 400 he was unable to demonstrate haemolysins in the foetal sera, but provided no information of the stage of development at which the foetal sera were tested. He also failed to find natural haemolysins, present in maternal sera at a titre of 10, in the foetal sera. A possible explanation of his negative results is that the antibodies were predominantly in the macro-globulin fraction, but there is no clear evidence that such antibody would not be transmitted before birth, though it is known not to be transmitted after birth in the rat. Positive evidence of transmission before birth in the rat is provided by the work of Culbertson (1938). He found that the young of mothers which had recovered from infections of *Trypanosoma lewisi* were resistant at birth to infection with this parasite. He showed that the foetuses were not infected by the parasite *in utero* and so could not be actively immune. Moreover the resistance was specific to *T. lewisi*, as the animals were susceptible to *T. cruzi*. Kolodny (1939) using mothers actively immunized by recovery from infection with *T. cruzi* was unable to detect any resistance in the young of such animals transferred at birth to normal foster mothers. Thompson and Meyers (1950) studied the transmission of antibody from mother mice actively immunized with Lansing poliomyeli-tis virus to their offspring and found that although most was transmitted after birth the possibility of some transmission before birth was not elimina-ted. Jo (1953) demonstrated the transmission of complement fixing anti-bodies from rats actively immunized with *Reckettsia*, alive or as a dead vaccine, or passively with rabbit antisera to this antigen, to the young *in utero*. Bruce-Chwatt and Gibson (1956) immunized rats by infecting them with *Plasmodium berghei* and found that immunity was transmitted to their young before birth, though most was transmitted after birth. Kosunen and Halonen (1963) studied the transmission of maternal immunity to tetanus to the offspring by challenging them with toxin. The young were obtained by Caesarean section, yet they tolerated *c.* 100-fold the lethal dose of toxin for normal newborn mice. Similarly Malkinson (1967) studied the protection against vaccinia virus passively transferred from actively immunized mice to their offspring, using the technique of cross-fostering the offspring on the day of birth when a challenge dose of virus was given. This dose was lethal to all the young born and suckled by unvaccinated mothers, but almost all the young born and suckled by vaccinated mothers survived. Few of the young born to unvaccinated mothers but fostered on vaccinated mothers survived but more than three times as many of the young of vaccinated mothers fostered on unvaccinated mothers survived. These results show that in the conditions of the experiment the prenatal transmission of protection was more effective than the postnatal, but it must be remembered that the former preceded challenge and the latter accompanied incubation of the infection; nevertheless it is clear that effective protection was transmitted before birth. Kaliss, Dagg and Stimpfling (1963) immunized C57 BL mice, which lack the H-2 (histocompatibility) antigen, with A strain mouse tumours which have this antigen. They found that both haemagglutinating and tumour enhancing isoantibodies were transmitted *in utero* to the foetal sera and haemagglutinating antibodies to the amniotic fluid (see also, Kaliss 1968; Kaliss and Rubinstein 1968). They commented on the lack of correlation of the values obtained for haemagglutinins and for enhancement, but suggest that this might be occasioned by the test for enhancement probably being much more sensitive than that for haemagglutination *in vitro*. Carretti and Ovary (1969) injected intravenously $\gamma_1 G$ and $\gamma_2 G$ mouse antibodies to dinitrophenyl into pregnant mice near term and found that both these fractions are transmitted to the foetuses and can be detected in their circulations after 6 hr.

This work, reviewed above, shows plainly that a variety of antibodies are transmitted before birth from mother to young in rats and mice but it is essentially qualitative in character and provided little quantitative information. The first satisfactory quantitative information concerning transmission before birth in rats was provided by Halliday (1955b). He hyperimmunized female rats to killed *Salmonella pullorum* antigen and mated them 2 to 10 days before the final injection of antigen. Some of these were killed on the 17th, 18th and 20th day of gestation and others were allowed to litter but not suckle, and still others were allowed to suckle for varying periods before the sera were collected for testing. In all cases the maternal serum was collected at the same time as that of the offspring, the titres of which were expressed as a fraction of that of the maternal serum (concentration quotient). Seventeen days of gestation was found to be the earliest stage of development at which sufficient samples of foetal sera could be obtained. The combined amniotic and exocoelomic fluids and the stomach contents of the foetuses were sampled at the same time. The results are given in tables 4.1 and 4.2. Foetuses of 17 days gestation had a small, but significant, amount of antibody in their sera, averaging $\frac{1}{128}$ of the concentration in the maternal sera. This relative concentration had increased by a factor of $\times 8$ at birth and by a further factor of $\times 8$ by a few days after birth, thereafter remaining relatively constant throughout lactation. Many sucklings had titres in their

TABLE 4.1

Occurrence of antibodies in the sera of foetal, newborn and suckling young of immune mother rats. (From Halliday 1955b.)

Concentration quotient	Gestation in days				Birth	Lactation in days																				
	17	18	19	20		0	1	2	3	4	5	6	7	8	9	10	11	12	13	14	15	16	17	18	19	20
2	.	.	.	.	.	.	.	1	.	.	2	.	.	.	.	1	.	.	.	.	2	.	.	.	.	3
1	.	.	.	.	.	.	.	2	1	1	6	.	.	.	.	4	.	.	.	.	2	.	.	2	.	5
$\frac{1}{2}$	.	.	.	.	.	1	1	.	2	1	2	.	.	.	.	5	.	.	.	.	6	.	.	.	.	8
$\frac{1}{4}$	.	.	.	.	.	6	6	2	5	.	2	.	.	.	.	.	.	.	.	.	.	.	.	.	.	1
$\frac{1}{8}$	.	.	.	.	3	6	.	.	.	.	1	.	.	.	.	.	.	.	.	.	.	.	.	.	.	.
$\frac{1}{16}$	.	.	.	2	7	2	.	2	.	.	.	.	.	.	.	.	.	.	.	.	.	.	.	.	.	.
$\frac{1}{32}$	.	.	3	5	2	.	.	.	.	.	.	.	.	.	.	.	.	.	.	.	.	.	.	.	.	.
$\frac{1}{64}$	1	.	8	3	.	.	.	.	.	.	.	.	.	.	.	.	.	.	.	.	.	.	.	.	.	.
$\frac{1}{128}$	3	.	4	.	.	.	.	.	.	.	.	.	.	.	.	.	.	.	.	.	.	.	.	.	.	.
$\frac{1}{256}$	1	.	.	.	.	.	.	.	.	.	.	.	.	.	.	.	.	.	.	.	.	.	.	.	.	.

TABLE 4.2

Occurrence of antibodies in the body of the foetuses of immune mother rats. (From Halliday 1955b.)

Concentration quotient	No. of observations		
	Serum	Amniotic and exocoelomic fluid	Stomach contents
$\frac{1}{16}$	2		
$\frac{1}{32}$	8		
$\frac{1}{64}$	12	2	
$\frac{1}{128}$	7	6	
$\frac{1}{256}$	1	4	
$\frac{1}{512}$		8	
$\frac{1}{1024}$		3	5
$\frac{1}{2048}$		1	2
$< \frac{1}{2048}$			8

sera equalling those of their mothers and a few had titres double those of their mothers. Antibody was present also in the combined amniotic and exocoelomic fluid samples, but at concentrations several dilutions lower than in the sera. The presence of very low concentrations of antibody in the stomach compared to the amniotic fluid contrasts with findings in foetal rabbits, in which the antibody concentration of the stomach contents often greatly exceeded that in the amniotic fluid. This difference probably was due to rapid absorption of antibody by the foetal rat gut, similar to that which occurs after birth, whereas such absorption has been shown not to occur in the foetal rabbit, with a consequent build up of concentration in the stomach in this species.

The transmission from mother to foetuses of homologous transferrin, albumin and γ-globulin, labelled with ^{131}I, was studied by Morgan (1964). He injected the isotopically labelled proteins intravenously into rats on the 20th day of pregnancy and sampled the foetal sera 6 and 20 hr after injection. He found relatively high concentrations of all three proteins in the foetal sera, the albumin and transferrin being transmitted approximately equally readily and the γ-globulin about 3 times as readily as either.

Recently Koch, Boesman and Gitlin (1967) have injected intravenously into pregnant rats and mice γG-globulins from rats, mice, guineapigs, bovines and man in pairs, one being trace-labelled with ^{131}I and the other with ^{125}I, and have determined their relative rates of transmission to the foetal circulation. Human serum albumin was used also. They found that in both species guineapig γ-globulin was transmitted most readily, and human γ-globulin less readily, whereas rat, mouse and bovine γ-globulins were transmitted much less readily, and human serum albumin least of all. In the mouse, rat γ-globulin was transmitted more readily than the homologous mouse γ-globulin, and in the rat, mouse γ-globulin was transmitted more readily than the homologous rat γ-globulin. There was thus a selective transmission of γ-globulins according to species of origin. This is the only clear evidence available that transmission before birth in rats and mice is selective.

Gitlin and Koch (1968) injected intravenously ^{131}I-labelled human albumin or human γ-globulin into mice on the 18–20 day of gestation and harvested the foetuses and maternal serum 24 hr later (fig. 4.3). The trichloracetic acid precipitable activity of the maternal serum and total foetal homogenate were determined. A wide range of doses was used and maternal serum concentrations at harvesting varied from 0.03 to 935 mg/100 ml for albumin, and from 0.01 to 2,000 mg/100 ml for γ-globulin. Over this wide range of concentrations it was found that with albumin the foetal TCA-precipitable

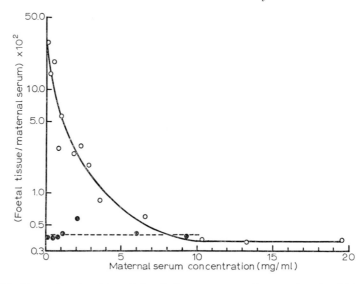

Fig. 4.3. The ratio of activity of foetal tissue to maternal serum in mice 24 hr after intravenous injection of ^{131}I-labelled human albumin or human γG-globulin at varying maternal serum concentrations of these proteins. The ratios on the ordinate are × 100. (From Gitlin and Koch 1968.)

activity was directly and linearly proportional to that of the maternal serum and could be expressed as

$$F = 4.25\ M \times 10^{-3}\ \text{ml/g}$$

where F = foetal tissue concentration in mg/g, and M = maternal serum concentration in mg/ml. The foetal γ-globulin concentration showed a much more complex relation, increasing rapidly as the maternal serum concentration increased at first and then decreasing to a minimum when the maternal serum concentration was about 7 mg/ml and becoming directly and linearly proportional to the maternal serum concentration when this exceeded 11 mg/ml, the relation being expressed as

$$F = 3.80\ M \times 10^{-3}\ \text{ml/g}$$

where F = foetal tissue concentration in mg/g, and M = maternal serum concentration in mg/ml. It was suggested that the transfer of human albumin, and that of human γ-globulin at high maternal concentrations was a first order relation, but that that of human γ-globulin at lower maternal concentrations was consistent with a carrier or enzymic process. This is the only quantitative information available concerning transmission before birth in the mouse and the difference between the transmission of albumin and γ-globulin is particularly interesting. It should be remembered in considering these results that transmission from the one circulation to the other is a two-stage process, involving transmission first across maternal tissues and then foetal tissues, secondly that the high maternal concentrations greatly exceeded physiological levels, and thirdly that the foetal determinations were on tissue homogenates, not serum, and there is no evidence that the precipitable protein was unaltered.

Gitlin and Morphis (1969), in another series of similar experiments on mice 15–17 days pregnant, injected intravenously in pairs, mouse, bovine, rabbit, guineapig and human γG-globulins and human albumin, the one labelled with ^{131}I and the other with ^{125}I. The activities in the maternal serum and foetal homogenate were determined after 24 hr and expressed as a F/M (foetal/maternal) ratio. Hypogammaglobulinaemic, normal and hypergammaglobulinaemic mice with γG-globulin concentrations ranging from 2.5 mg/ml to 10 mg/ml were used. It was found that the F/M ratio was very much higher for guineapig, human and rabbit than for mouse and bovine γG-globulins and was lowest for human albumin. The endogenous γG-globulin concentration had no effect on the human albumin F/M ratio, but for mouse and bovine γG-globulins the ratio was significantly higher in hypogammaglobulinaemic mice than in normal or hypergammaglobulinaemic ones and for human and rabbit γG-globulins the ratio was similar in hypogammaglobulinaemic and normal mice but was significantly lower in hypergammaglobulinaemic ones, as it was also with guineapig γG-globulin. Loading the circulation of normal mice with heterologous γG-globulin to bring the total γG-globulin concentration to about 10 mg/ml when bovine γG-globulin was used had only a small effect on the F/M ratio of all the labelled γG-globulins, comparable to that in mice with similar concentrations of mouse γG-globulin, but when human, rabbit or guineapig γG-globulins were used the F/M ratios of all three of these labelled γG-globulins were reduced drastically to a level similar to mouse and bovine γG-globulins (fig. 4.4). Loading with human or bovine albumin had little effect. When the maternal serum concentration of any one of these five γG-globulins is about 5 mg/ml the F/M ratio of that γG-globulin is $\frac{1}{100}$ whether it is of human, rabbit, guineapig, bovine or mouse origin. The F/M ratio for mouse γG-globulin in normal mice (5 mg/ml) is low when bovine γG-globulin is also present but is high when human, rabbit or guineapig γG-globulin is present. The authors conclude that there may be two different systems for the transfer

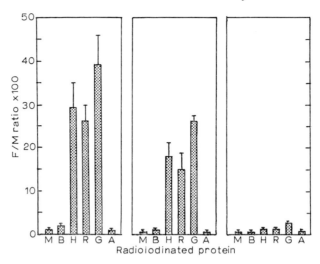

Fig. 4.4. Histograms of the average foetal/maternal ratios for mouse (M), bovine (B), human (H), rabbit (R) and guineapig (G) γG-globulins and for human albumin (A) in normal mice on the left, in mice loaded with 100 mg of bovine γG-globulin in the centre and in mice loaded with 100 mg of human γG-globulin on the right. (From Gitlin and Morphis 1969.)

of γG-globulins from mother to foetus in the mouse, one of which operates for mouse and bovine globulins and the other for human, rabbit and guineapig globulins.

Determination of the route of transmission in the rat clearly required experimental investigation. Noer and Mossman (1947) showed that it was surgically feasible to interrupt the circulation to the yolk-sac of the foetal rat by ligaturing the vitelline vessels without apparent effect on the foetus, which survived the operation for up to 4 days, when death appeared to be due to the effect of compression by the dead membranes. Ligation of the allantoic vessels to the placenta, on the other hand, resulted invariably in death of the foetuses within 4 hr, presumably from anoxia. This work showed that a surgical approach to determining the route of transmission in the rat was practicable. Accordingly, such an investigation was carried out (Brambell and Halliday 1956). First, rat anti-*Salmonella pullorum* serum of high titre was injected at laparotomy into the cavity of one of the two uterine horns of rats 19 days pregnant. The foetal sera were sampled 24 hr later and those of all the foetuses in the injected uterine horns had antibodies at concentration quotients of $\frac{1}{256}$ to $\frac{1}{1024}$, whereas those of all the foetuses in the control uterine horns were negative. The amniotic fluids of all the foetuses in the experimental uterine horn of one animal also contained antibodies at approximately the same titres as in the sera, those of the foetuses in another animal gave only trace reactions which may have been non-specific. The amniotic fluids of all the foetuses in the control uterine horns were negative. Clearly antibodies can enter the foetal circulation and the amnion from the uterine lumen, and since there is no chorion, as in the rabbit, and the endoderm of the yolk-sac is the only foetal tissue exposed to the uterine lumen, entry must be effected by traversing it. Two possible routes to the circulation are then possible; either the antibody could enter the vitelline vessels of the yolk-sac splanchnopleur directly or, after reaching the amniotic fluid by way of the exocoel and amniotic membrane and being swallowed by the foetus it could be absorbed from the gut, as happens after birth. Immune serum was administered by stomach tube to 19 day foetuses and the possibility of regurgitation obviated by ligaturing their mouths. The foetuses were maintained in the body cavities with their pla-centae and allantoic circulations intact for periods of 2 to 5 hr and their sera were then sampled. All the experimental foetuses had antibodies in their sera at concentration quotients of $\frac{1}{8}$ to $\frac{1}{512}$, whereas the controls were negative or showed only trace reactions which were believed to be non-specific. Evidently antibody is absorbed and transmitted to the circulation quickly and efficiently by the gut of the 19-day foetal rat. Another experi-ment was performed to determine if transmission to the circulation occurs also in the yolk-sac. Rats 19 or 20 days pregnant in both uterine horns were opened and kept under deep anaesthesia. One uterine horn of each animal was opened throughout its length, the foetal membranes were opened and the mouths of all the foetuses ligatured to prevent swallowing. The vitelline vessels of alternate foetuses were ligatured and the whole of the yolk-sac splanchno-pleur dissected away and removed. The peritoneal cavity of the mother was then filled with immune serum and the preparation maintained for periods of 2 to $6\frac{1}{2}$ hr, the limit to which the mothers could be kept alive under deep anaesthesia. The maternal and foetal sera were then sampled. The sera of the foetuses in the opened uterine horns with yolk-sacs and vitelline circulations had antibody titres averaging two dilutions higher than either the alternate foetuses without yolk-sacs in the opened horns or the foetuses in the intact control horns, both of which groups had similar titres. This result provided clear evidence that the yolk-sac and vitelline circulation is an important route of transmission of immunity in the rat. However, since both the foetuses without yolk-sacs and vitelline circulations and the control foetuses had significant titres it was clear that some other route must exist. Theoretically antibody could reach the sera of the foetuses without yolk-sacs only through the allantoic circulations of the placentae or through their skins, since their mouths were occluded. The immune serum in the peritoneal cavity had free access to the endoderm of the bilaminar omphalopleur covering the surface of the placenta and lining the crypts of Duval. If the antibody was absorbed by these endoderm cells it might be transmitted to the allantoic vessels in the crypts of Duval without having to traverse Reichert's membrane. Alternatively, if the maternal serum was of high titre, owing to rapid absorption from the peritoneal cavity, antibodies might have been transmitted across the allantochorionic placenta into the allantoic circulation. It was not feasible to distinguish experimentally between these possibilities and transplacental passage is not formally excluded as a route of transmission in the rat.

Somewhat similar experiments were performed on rats 19 to 21 days pregnant by Quinlivan (1964), who opened the uteri and removed the membranes from some of the foetuses, leaving the others intact. He injected homologous γ-globulin trace labelled with ^{131}I intravenously into the mother and harvested the samples from 1 to 6 hr later. All the foetuses, both experimental and controls, had labelled γ-globulin in their sera, the amount in the experimental foetal sera being on average 85 to 88% of that in the control foetal sera. Whole body counts of the experimental foetuses average 78 to 83% of those of the control foetuses. These differences are small and were interpreted as showing that transmission took place mainly by way of the placenta. Certainly this appears to be valid evidence of placental transmission, but it is very doubtful if it can be taken as evidence of the placental route of transmission being more important than the yolk-sac route in the intact animal. The experiments were of such short duration after intravenous injection into the mother of the labelled material that it is very doubtful if much of it would have been secreted by the uterus or into the peritoneal cavity in the time, and so reach the yolk-sac; any such delay in secretion would favour the placental route. Moreover, if transmission were purely transplacental, the experimental foetuses might have been expected to have not only as high a concentration in their sera, but a higher concentration than the controls, because their blood volume had been substantially reduced by removal of the vitelline blood. Thus the experimental design was such as might be expected to minimise yolk-sac transmission.

It has been shown by Anderson (1959) that ^{131}I-labelled homologous γ-globulin intravenously injected into rats 11, 15 and 17 days pregnant quickly reached the yolk-sac splanchnopleur at all these stages, both before and after the rupture of the bilaminar wall of the yolk-sac. Autoradiographs showed that the γ-globulin probably encountered a barrier at the placental trophoblast but that it entered the endoderm cells of the yolk-sac splanchnopleur in small amounts. Mayersbach (1958) injected fluorescent-labelled whole rat and human serum into rats in late pregnancy and identified all the proteins serologically and electrophoretically in the foetal serum and amniotic fluid. He found that the proteins crossed the uterine epithelium and yolk-sac splanchnopleur and reached the vitelline circulation. Transmission across the placenta was not found but absorption by the crypts of Duval and by the foetal skin was considered possible.

Recent work suggests that maternal cells, probably lymphocytes, may be able to invade the mouse foetus *in utero*. Tuffrey, Bishun and Barnes (1969) transplanted blastocysts of the inbred CFW strain of white mice into early pregnant CBA/T$_6$T$_6$ agouti mice. The young resulting from the transplanted ova could be distinguished at birth. The host strain has a characteristic chromosome marker which enables cells to be distinguished at mitotic metaphase. Examination of cell squashes from liver, spleen, thymus, lymph nodes and bone marrow of the transplanted young showed that seven out of eight were chimaeras containing a significant proportion of cells of the host strain with the chromosome marker. These must have been derived either from the foster mother or, much less probably, from those siblings which were her own offspring. It was not possible to definitely identify the type of cell involved.

CHAPTER 5

Transmission of immunity in the rat and the mouse after birth

5.1. Transmission of antibodies from immune mothers

Following the demonstration of the transmission of passive immunity in rats to *Trypanosoma lewisi* by Minning (1936), the researches of Culbertson (1938, 1939a, b, 1940) provided a firm outline of the process after birth in rats and mice, which subsequent work has confirmed. Using mother rats which had been actively immunized by recovery from an infection with *Trypanosoma lewisi*, Culbertson (1938) showed that young of normal mothers fostered upon the immune mothers rapidly become resistant to infections with this parasite. At one day of age and within 24 hr of suckling upon an immune foster mother these young had become wholly resistant to an injection of 1×10^6 parasites. Young, born and nursed by normal mothers which had become infected with the parasite and developed antibodies to it during the nursing period, themselves become immune. Hence he concluded that maternal antibodies are secreted in the milk as well as the colostrum and are absorbed into the circulation of the suckling from the intestine for a period of at least 15 days after birth. The transmitted immunity is specific, as the young of mothers immune to *T. lewisi*, although resistant to this parasite, are as susceptible as normal young to infection with *T. cruzi*. Subsequently, Culbertson (1939b) showed that young rats, suckling upon a mother, passively immunized by intraperitoneal injections of immune serum on days 1 to 5 after delivery, acquired resistance, showing that circulating antibody, whether actively or passively acquired, is transmitted through the milk to the young. He showed also (1939a) that antibody from immune serum administered orally to suckling rats confers immunity upon them. Groups of young rats aged 10, 15, 20, 25, 40 and 60 days were given doses of 0.25 ml per 10 g body weight of immune serum *per os*. The day following they were challenged by an intraperitoneal injection of 1×10^6 *T. lewisi* per 100 g body weight. Each group included one control which was not immunized and one which was immunized by intraperitoneal injection of the immune serum. Daily examinations of the blood were made. It was shown that the young rats could be immunized by oral administration of immune serum throughout the usual nursing period of 21 days, although late in this period immunization was progressively less effective. It was indicated that the loss of the capacity to be immunized by oral administration of immune serum could be due either to the intestine becoming impermeable to the antibody or to the denaturation of the antibody in the gut.

Subsequently Culbertson (1940) carried out precisely similar experiments with mice, the mothers being actively or passively immunized to *T. duttoni* and the technique of fostering the young being employed. The results showed that the transmission of passive immunity in the mouse after birth is closely similar to that in the rat except that the period during which it occurs is shorter, being limited to 15 days after birth.

The year following Culbertson's first paper (1938), Kolodny (1939) confirmed his results on transmission of immunity after birth in the rat, using *T. cruzi* as antigen. He showed also that the passive immunity acquired by the young reared by actively immunized mothers persists for at least 10 days after weaning and then declines rapidly, and that the smaller the number of young in the litter reared the greater the immunity which they acquire. Transmission after birth of passive immunity to *Plasmodium berghei* in rats has been demonstrated by fostering experiments by Bruce-Chwatt and Gibson (1956) and by Terry (1956). The latter author found that transmission could not be secured after 22 days of age and that the passive immunity derived from the mother had disappeared by 7 weeks after weaning. Transmission after birth of passive immunity to *Reckettsiae* (Worth 1951; Jo 1953), to *Toxoplasma* (Lewis and Markell 1958), to *Salmonella* (Widal and Sicard 1897; Halliday 1955b), to *Brucella abortus* (Halliday and Kekwick 1960), to the cestode *Cysticercus fasciolaris* (Miller 1932), to the nematode *Trichinella spiralis* (Mauss 1940), and to homologous tumours (Sekla 1958) has been demonstrated also.

Transmission of passive immunity after birth in the mouse has been demonstrated also to tetanus (Kosunen and Halonen 1963); the young of normal or immune mothers suckled by immune foster mothers were able to withstand a challenge with toxin 10,000 times that lethal to normal young when 1 to 2 weeks old. Transmission of passive immunity after birth in mice to a wide variety of viruses has been demonstrated, including blue-tongue virus (Svehag and Gorham 1963), herpes simplex virus (Berry and Slavin 1943), Coxsackie virus (Melnick, Clarke and Kraft 1950), foot-and-mouth disease virus (Skinner, Henderson and Brooksby 1952; Campbell 1960), influenza virus (Nossal 1957), Friend virus (Mathot and Scher 1968) and various strains of encephalomyelitis and poliomyelitis virus (Smith 1943; Smith and Geren 1948; Fenner 1948; Curley and Gordon 1948; Anderson and Bolin 1949; Gordon and Curley 1949; Von Magnus 1951; Thompson and Meyers 1950). Transmission of immunity to the mouse cestode, *Hymeno-lepis nana*, has been shown also (Larsh 1942). Transmission of haemaggluti-nating and enhancing isoantibodies to the H2 histocompatibility antigens has been demonstrated in mice (Kaliss, Dagg and Stimpfling 1963; Kaliss 1968).

It has been mentioned previously (p. 93) that Halliday (1955b) investi-gated the titres of antibody in the blood of young rats at ages from the 17th day of gestation to 20 days after birth that were born and reared by mothers actively immunized to *Salmonella pullorum*. The results are given in table 4.1 (p. 94) as concentration quotients, which serve to correct for variations in the maternal serum titres. It can be seen that the relative concentration of antibody in the serum of the new-born continues to rise from birth to about 3 days of age and that it remains thereafter remarkably constant throughout the period up to 20 days of age. Similar results were obtained by Jordan and Morgan (1967) by injection of isotopically labelled γ-globulin into lactating rats. Individual relative concentrations vary from double that in the maternal serum to $\frac{1}{8}$ in one case, but the majority are equal to or $\frac{1}{2}$ that of the maternal serum. During this period the young rat is growing rapid-ly from a mean live body weight of *c*. 5.4 g at birth to *c*. 32.7 g at 20 days, increasing its weight by a factor of *c*. ×6. The serum volume will increase nearly proportionately (Trávníčková and Heller 1963) and consequently the absolute amount of antibody in it must increase proportionately also if the relative concentration is to remain constant. It is evident, therefore, that transmission of maternal antibody must continue throughout this period.

It has been shown (Halliday 1956) that the failure of immune mother rats to transmit antibodies to their sucklings after 20 days of age is not due to a failure to secrete antibodies in the milk. Normal young rats of 6 to 9 days of age were fostered for 3 days on immune mothers which had been lactating for 21 to 25 days and whose own young therefore would have ceased to acquire passive immunity. These fostered young, however, acquired antibody and had titres in their sera from $\frac{1}{2}$ to 2 times those of the maternal sera. Clearly antibodies are still present in quantity and available to the young in the milk after transmission normally stops. Five young rats 22 or 23 days of age were then fostered for 7 days on immune mothers, which had been lactating for 9 or 10 days and had high antibody titres in their sera, but acquired no detectable antibody in their blood. Two young rats 20 days of age fostered for 7 days on an immune mother which had been lactating for 14 days acquired antibody at concentrations of $\frac{1}{32}$ and $\frac{1}{64}$ of that of the maternal serum. Evidently some residual capacity to absorb antibody from the mother's milk is present in young rats at 20 days of age which has disappeared by 22 days of age.

5.2. *Transmission of antibodies after oral administration*

Culbertson (1939a) was the first to show that young rats absorb antibodies from immune serum administered orally as readily as from their mother's milk, and young mice have since been shown to do so with equal facility. The discovery opened the way for experimental investigation of intestinal transmission of immunity because immune serum or isotopically labelled γ-globulin preparations could be administered orally with minimal disturbance to the animal and so conveniently. It is remarkable that comparatively little use was made of this opportunity until Halliday started to exploit it in 1955, sixteen years later. He found that doses could be administered readily and in precise amounts direct to the stomach of the suckling by means of a stomach tube of fine-drawn polythene attached to a 2-ml syringe operated by a weighted plunger so as to deliver the dose under constant pressure. The required degree of flexibility can be obtained, for use with suckling rats or mice of any chosen age from birth, or even foetuses, by drawing polythene tubing of 2 mm bore and 0.55 mm thick wall over a flame. This technique has enabled the transmission of antibodies or γ-globulin from the gut *in vivo* to be quantified and has increased greatly our knowledge of the process. It is a good example of how some discovery of little intrinsic importance, by opening the way to technical refinement, can be the starting point of an important advance in knowledge.

Young rats varying in age from 1 to 30 days were each fed a single dose of 0.25 ml of high-titre rat *Salmonella pullorum* antiserum and were killed and their sera tested 24 hr later. The results contained in table 5.1 (Halliday

TABLE 5.1

The entry from the gut to the circulation of agglutinins to *Salmonella pullorum* prepared in the rat. (From Halliday 1955a.)

Concentration quotients	Age in days																							
	1	2	3	4	5	6	7	8	9	10	11	12	13	14	15	16	17	18	19	20	21	22	23	30
$\frac{1}{8}$	2	1	·	·	2	·	·	·	·	·	·	·	·	·	·	·	·	·	·	·	·	·	·	·
$\frac{1}{16}$	·	1	·	2	2	·	2	1	·	·	·	2	·	·	·	·	·	·	·	·	·	·	·	·
$\frac{1}{32}$	·	·	·	·	1	·	·	·	1	·	·	5	·	·	2	1	2	1	·	·	·	·	·	·
$\frac{1}{64}$	·	·	·	·	1	·	1	1	3	·	2	7	1	·	1	1	·	1	2	·	·	·	·	·
$\frac{1}{128}$	·	·	·	·	·	·	·	·	·	·	1	·	·	·	·	·	·	·	4	·	·	·	·	·
$\frac{1}{256}$	·	·	·	·	·	·	·	·	·	·	·	·	·	·	·	·	·	·	1	4	·	·	·	·
$\frac{1}{512}$	·	·	·	·	·	·	·	·	·	·	·	·	·	·	·	·	·	·	·	4	·	·	2	·
$< \frac{1}{512}$	·	·	·	·	·	·	·	·	·	·	·	·	·	·	·	·	·	·	·	1	11	8	2	2

1955a) show clearly that the relative concentrations of antibodies in their sera decline gradually with age from $\frac{1}{8}$ to $\frac{1}{16}$ at birth to $\frac{1}{32}$ to $\frac{1}{64}$ at eighteen days. Over this period the body weight would increase, and hence the plasma volume, by a factor of *c.* $\times$ 4.6 (Trávníčková and Heller 1963) and since the dose was constant the concentration in the serum would be expected to decline by dilution by the same amount provided that the absolute quantity of antibody absorbed remained constant. Since the observed relative concentration on day 1 was $\frac{1}{8}$, a relative concentration of $\frac{1}{37}$ would be expected on day 18 on this assumption, an expectation which agrees remarkably well with the observed $\frac{1}{32}$ to $\frac{1}{64}$. It would appear that over the period the efficiency of absorption of antibody by the intestine as a whole from a constant dose of 0.25 ml of serum does not change, and since the intestine is growing, the efficiency per unit area of the intestine must decline. After day 18 the relative concentration declines rapidly and on and after day 21 no transmission of antibody from the intestine could be observed. Thus the termination of the capacity of the young rat to absorb antibody from serum administered orally occurs suddenly between days 18 and 21. Subsequently (Kelly, unpublished observation; Halliday 1959) similar information was obtained for the mouse, showing that in this species the termination of the transmission of passive immunity occurs equally suddenly and 4 days earlier. We will return later to discuss the mechanism by which this change in the permeability of the gut is brought about.

Antibody appears in the circulation very rapidly after oral administration of immune serum to a young rat (Halliday 1955a). It could be detected in the serum 30 min after oral administration to 12 day old rats and attained a maximum concentration within three hours, remaining at the peak level for 45 hr. Thus the time at which maximum antibody levels in the serum after a single dose can be observed is not at all critical and may be at any interval between 3 hr and 2 days.

5.3. The amount of antibody transmitted from a single oral dose

The relation between the dose of immune serum administered and the relative concentration of antibody attained subsequently in the circulation has been studied also (Halliday 1957b). High titre serum of rats immune to *Salmonella pullorum* was fed in single doses varying from 0.0125 to 0.6 ml to 12 day old rats and after an interval of 24 hr their sera were titrated. The relative

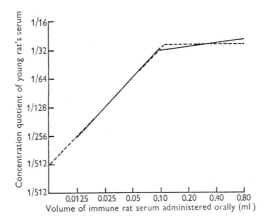

Fig. 5.1. Regression (solid line) of the proportion of antibody transmitted to the circulation from varying doses of homologous antiserum administered by stomach tube to 12-day old rats. The broken line is the theoretical regression if the amount transmitted was directly proportional to the dose up to 0.10 ml and constant thereafter. (After Halliday 1957b.)

concentration of antibody attained was linearly and directly related to the volume of the dose up to 0.1 ml but there was no increase in concentration with larger doses (fig. 5.1). Thus a constant proportion of the immune globulin is transmitted to the circulation in 12 day old rats from doses of up to 0.1 ml when the maximum amount that can be transmitted from a single dose is attained. This amount is such as to produce a mean concentration in the serum of $\frac{1}{32}$ of that in the serum administered. Since the live weights of young rats from this colony are known it can be shown that the mean relative growth rate over the 12 to 13 day period is 8.25% per day. Thus an increase of $\frac{1}{32}$ in live body weight, and hence in accessible fluid volume, would be achieved in approximately 9 hr. Hence the uptake of immune globulin from a single dose of 0.1 ml of serum is sufficient to account for the whole of the growth increment in this fraction of the plasma proteins over this period, assuming a similar concentration to that in the serum administered. Assuming a plasma volume of 1.0 ml at most and since the dose of immune serum was 0.1 ml it would appear that almost $\frac{1}{3}$ of the immune globulin administered was transmitted to the circulation.

It appears, therefore, that only a certain proportion of the γ-globulin in a single dose of serum administered orally, irrespective of the size of the dose up to a certain maximum, which is *c*. 0.1 ml for a 12 day old rat, can be transmitted to the circulation. This fraction for rat serum is nearly 33% for doses below the maximum and declines for doses above the maximum. The problem arises, therefore, as to what happens to the residue of γ-globulin which is not transmitted to the circulation. The use of isotopically labelled γ-globulin has thrown some light on this problem (Brambell, Halliday and Hemmings 1961). Bovine γ-globulin labelled with ^{131}I at a concentration of *c.* 1 % in saline was fed to 14 day old rats in single doses of 0.1 to 0.2 ml and serum samples were obtained at autopsy 4 hr later. The concentration of labelled protein found in the serum was regularly *c.* 0.01 of that administered, since bovine γ-globulin is transmitted less readily than rat γ-globulin. Assuming a total plasma volume of 1.0 ml this represents at most a proportion of 0.10 of the labelled protein in the dose fed. Since between 0.6 and 0.8

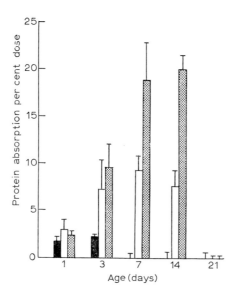

Fig. 5.2. Histograms of the proportions of the doses of labelled albumin (■), transferrin (□) and γ-globulin (▨) transmitted to the circulation after intragastric administration to young rats at different ages. The values at 1 and 3 days are the means of groups of 4, and at 7, 14 and 21 days of groups of 6. The standard error of each mean is indicated. (From Jordan and Morgan 1968).

of the activity of the dose had disappeared from the intestine by absorption it is evident that $\frac{5}{6}$ to $\frac{7}{8}$ of the protein absorbed had been degraded. Cytological evidence to be considered later indicates that this degradation occurs within the endoderm cells.

A recent paper by Jordan and Morgan (1968) has done much to increase our knowledge both of the relative rates of transmission of serum proteins other than γ-globulin and of the changes in the permeability of the gut to these between birth and 21 days. Purified homologous albumin, transferrin and γ-globulin labelled with ^{131}I or ^{125}I were administered in pairs by stomach tube at ages of 1, 3, 7, 14 and 21 days. The doses given in saline solution at a concentration of *c*. 2 mg/ml of each protein were at 1 and 3 days 0.1 ml, at 7 days 0.1–0.2 ml, and at 14 and 21 days 0.1–0.3 ml. The amount of protein bound activity in each fraction of the young rat's serum after four hours was determined and is expressed as a percentage of the activity in the dose in fig. 5.2. All three proteins were transmitted nearly equally readily at 1 day; the percentage of transferrin and γ-globulin had increased considerably but that of albumin had not changed at 3 days; the percentage of γ-globulin continued to increase, that of transferrin showed little change and albumin was not transmitted at 7 and 14 days; transmission of all three had ceased at 21 days. Labelled whole rat serum or milk whey was administered also at these ages and gave a similar picture, though the rates of transmission were less than with the purified fractions. There was a progressive increase in selectivity with age favouring the fractions with the lowest electrophoretic mobility, absorption ceasing first with albumin, then with the α-globulins, while the β- and γ-globulins still showed increasing transmission at 14 days. The authors suggest that the net electric charge on the molecules may be related to the relative selectivity.

5.4. *Termination of the transmission of immunity*

The termination of the capacity to transmit immune globulin from the gut to the circulation occurs comparatively suddenly in the mouse between 14 and 16 days of age and in the rat between 18 and 20 days of age (Halliday 1955a, 1959). The normal 17 day old mouse and the normal 21 day old rat do not transmit detectable quantities. The means by which this change in the permeability of the gut is brought about has attracted a good deal of attention but is still far from clear. Halliday (1956), by fostering experiments, provided convincing evidence that a factor transmitted in the milk is not responsible. He showed that young rats of 6 to 9 days of age could absorb antibody as readily from immune foster mothers that had been lactating for 21 to 25 days whereas young rats of 22 to 23 days of age could not absorb any antibody from immune foster mothers which had been lactating for only

9 to 10 days (see p. 104). Further, young rats reared from birth by successive fostering on normal mothers lactating for less than 16 days failed to absorb antibody when transferred at 22 or 23 days of age to immune foster mothers.

It was thought that the taking of solid food might be the stimulus which brought about termination of transmission. Accordingly Halliday (1956) gave young rats 12 days old five feeds of solid food over 24 hr and administered immune serum by mouth 24 hr after the last feed, testing the sera 24 hr later. All had antibody in the sera at concentrations equal to those of their litter-mate controls which had received no solid food. Clearly solid food did not bring about termination of transmission within the 24-hr period. However, subsequently (Halliday 1959) it was found that the removal of young rats at 16 days of age from their mothers and maintaining them for a period of 48 hr in an incubator on glucose and water did result in premature termination of transmission. It is, therefore, possible that solid food might have this effect after a longer interval than the 24 hr employed in the first experiments.

It had been observed by Moog (1951) that a large increase in the alkaline phosphatase activity of the duodenum of the normal young mouse occurs between 13 and 18 days of age. It was shown subsequently (Moog 1953; Moog and Thomas 1955) that this increase can be brought about prematurely by increasing the level of adrenal steroid hormones in the circulation. The coincidence in time of this phenomenon with the termination of the transmission of immunity in the young mouse suggested that the two might be connected. Investigation of the normal young rat (Halliday 1959) showed that there is an increase in duodenal alkaline phosphatase, similar to that in the mouse, but occurring between 18 and 23 days of age. It was found that administration of large doses of deoxycorticosterone acetate or of cortisone acetate, either parenterally or orally, to young rats brought about both a premature increase in duodenal alkaline phosphatase and termination of transmission of antibodies from the gut to the circulation. The termination of transmission could be effected up to at least 9 days before it would have occurred normally. The reduction in transmission after administration of the hormone was apparent in 24 hr and greatest after 48 hr. Aldosterone had no effect on transmission, even in very large doses. This is remarkable as aldosterone is more active than deoxycorticosterone acetate and cortisone acetate, and whereas it is a normal product of the adrenal of the rat neither of the latter two hormones are produced in significant quantities in this animal. The possibility that the approach of weaning may bring about a state of stress resulting in adrenal secretion and hence in the termination of transmission of immunity, cannot be ignored, but, if so, the actual steroid hormone involved is unknown. It is rendered more plausible by the observation that premature removal and maintenance away from the mother brings about increase in duodenal alkaline phosphatase in mice (Moog 1951) as well as termination of transmission in rats (Halliday 1959). Moreover, the work to be described in the next paragraph might well be capable of a similar interpretation.

Recently it has been discovered (Kyffin 1967) that the transmission of immunity terminates prematurely in runted mice. New-born hybrid C57 BL × A2G mice were injected intravenously with a suspension of the order of 1 million spleen cells from an 8-week-old C57 BL ♂ mouse. This treatment resulted uniformly in runting and death, usually between the ages of 15 and 20 days. Transmission of antibody from the gut to the circulation was normal at 8 days but declined sharply thereafter and had almost completely stopped by 11 days of age, 6 days earlier than in the normal animal. Runting in mice, very similar to that resulting from the graft-against-host reaction, can be produced also by large injections of bacterial antigens at birth. This form of runting, also, is accompanied by a premature termination of transmission of immunity (Kyffin, personal communication).

It is evident that much remains to be done before the mechanism whereby the termination of transmission of immunity is effected in the normal young rat or mouse is fully understood and the problem of whether or not it is causally linked with conditions of stress can be solved. Apart from its intrinsic interest, the solution of this problem could have important bearings on intestinal permeability in domestic animals and man.

5.5. *Transmission from the gut of heterologous antibodies*

Antibodies produced in species other than the rat can be transmitted from the gut to the circulation of suckling rats. Haemolytic disease was produced in rats under 22 days of age by Bessis and Freixa (1947a, b) by the oral administration of rabbit anti-rat red cell serum. The clinical picture was similar to that resulting from intraperitoneal injection of the antiserum and it was evident that it resulted from antibody reaching the circulation. Subsequently Morris (1958, 1961) studied the haemolytic disease produced in suckling mice by the oral administration of either rabbit anti-mouse red cell or anti-mouse leucocyte sera. Thus in both young rats and young mice rabbit antibodies are transmitted from the gut to the circulation. It is interesting that if the intestinal endodermal cells which transmitted the antibodies possessed any antigens in common with the red cells or the leucocytes these did not absorb out the antibodies and prevent their transmission, since the damage resulting from both these sera was vascular.

Comparing the transmission in young rats of antibodies from sera prepared in several species (Halliday 1955a) striking differences were found. Antibodies from mouse antisera to *Salmonella pullorum* were transmitted nearly as readily as those from rat antisera to *Salmonella pullorum* or as rat incomplete agglutinins to sheep red cells. Antibodies from rabbit antisera to *Brucella abortus* were transmitted also, but only at a relative concentration (C.Q.) of $c. \frac{1}{8}$ that of the rat antibodies. Antibodies from bovine and fowl antisera to *Brucella abortus*, however, were not transmitted in detectable quantities. The amount of antibody reaching the circulation of 12-day-old rats from a single dose of immune rabbit anti-sheep red cell serum increased with the size of the dose up to the maximum of 0.6 ml which could be given (Halliday 1957b). The relation of concentration to volume of dose was linear and can be expressed by the regression $y = -1.52 + 0.820\,x$, where $y =$ the number of the concentration quotient in the series $\frac{1}{512}, \frac{1}{256}, \frac{1}{128}, \frac{1}{64}$, and $x =$ the number of the dose in the doubling series beginning 0.0125, 0.025, . . ., 0.40. The slope of this regression is significantly less than that for the direct relation of concentration to volume showing that the proportion of antibody transmitted to the circulation declines with increasing dose, so that a concentration quotient of $c. \frac{1}{64}$ could be obtained with a dose of 0.6 ml.

In the young mouse it was found (Hemmings and Morris 1959) that the antibodies from the serum of guineapigs hyperimmune to *Salmonella pullorum* were transmitted only about half as readily, and those from hyperimmune rabbit anti-sheep red cell serum only about one quarter as readily, as those from hyperimmune mouse anti-*Salmonella pullorum* serum.

It was shown subsequently (Halliday and Kekwick 1960) that the amount of antibody transmitted to the circulation by the gut of the young rat depends to a large extent on whether it has been produced early in the immune response or after hyperimmunization and also on the nature of the antigen used. Thus, mother rats actively immunized to *Salmonella pullorum* transmitted a much smaller proportion of antibody to their young shortly after an initial immunization than when they were hyperimmune. This was not due to a difference in the proportion of circulating antibody secreted in the milk, as in both cases the titre of the milk whey approximated to that of the maternal serum. It was shown directly by oral administration of immune serum that it was a difference in the proportion of antibody transmitted to the circulation by the gut of the young rat. If the serum administered was taken shortly after a primary immunization a much lower relative concentration was attained in the young rat's serum than when hyperimmune serum was used, even when this was diluted with non-immune serum to a titre corresponding to that of the primarily immune serum. However, antibodies from the serum of rats hyperimmunized to *Brucella abortus* were not transmitted from the gut to the circulation of young rats as readily as those from hyperimmune anti-*Salmonella pullorum* serum, the concentration quotients being about two dilutions lower and approximating to those from primarily immune anti-*Salmonella pullorum* sera. Aqueous-ethyl ether fractionation of the immune sera indicated that this difference was related to the distribution of the antibody between the various γ-globulin fractions, the first formed antibody to *Salmonella*, and much of the antibody to *Brucella*, even in hyperimmune sera, separating mainly with the β-globulins and being, in the light of subsequent knowledge, presumably mainly macroglobulin (γM), whereas most of the antibody in hyperimmune anti-*Salmonella* sera was in the fraction containing the 7S γ-globulin (γG). Thus, these results are consistent with the subsequent finding that macroglobulin antibodies are not transmitted by the gut of the young rat and that γG antibodies are transmitted.

These authors (Halliday and Kekwick 1960) also prepared sera hyperimmune to *Salmonella pullorum* in a variety of other rodents, mouse, vole, wood-mouse, cotton-rat, hamster and guineapig, as well as in rabbits and found that after oral administration to young rats the antibodies were transmitted at rates that did not differ significantly, within the experimental limits, from those of the antibodies from hyperimmune rat anti-*Salmonella* sera. The antibodies from hyperimmune anti-*Brucella abortus* sera prepared in rabbits and guineapigs were transmitted at much lower rates, approximating to those from hyperimmune rat anti-*Brucella* sera, although there was some indication that the rabbit antibodies were being transmitted more readily than the rat or guineapig antibodies. Diphtheria antitoxin prepared in rabbits was transmitted more than twice as readily as diphtheria or tetanus antitoxin prepared in rats, while the rates for cotton-rat and mouse diphtheria antitoxins fell in between (Halliday and Oakley, unpublished, quoted by Halliday and Kekwick 1960). It has been shown also (Halliday 1968) that only 7S antibody to *B. abortus* from rabbit, rat, sheep and bovine immune sera are transmitted by the young rat, and those from rabbit antisera more readily than the other sera, even than the homologous serum.

5.6. *Alteration of heterologous antibodies during transmission*

Bangham and Terry (1957a) fed ^{131}I-labelled whole serum proteins to young rats 7, 14 and 21 days of age and estimated the proportion of the dose in the circulation after 3 hr. Rat, rabbit and monkey serum proteins were used. Very little albumin reached the circulation, being in the vicinity of 0.1% of the dose, irrespective of age or species of origin. Significant amounts of globulins were transmitted to the circulation at 7 and 14 days of age, the average for rat globulin being 7.5%, for rabbit globulin 2.3% and for monkey globulin 3.1%, whereas at 21 days less than 0.5% of the globulin from any of these species was transmitted. Thus transmission was clearly selective both as between albumin and globulin and between homologous and heterologous globulins. These authors (Bangham and Terry 1957b) also found that the survival time in the circulation of the homologous globulin transmitted from the gut of the young rat approximated to that of γ-globulin in adult rats and that the survival times of the heterologous globulins in the circulations of the young rats was at least as long. Thus the globulin had not been denatured during transmission from the gut.

Nevertheless, there is evidence that some change may take place in the γ-globulin during transmission by the gut of the young rat. High titre bovine anti-*Brucella* serum was given orally to young rats of 10 to 15 days of age in single doses varying from 0.1 ml to 0.8 ml, the maximum that could be accommodated, but agglutinins could not be detected in their sera after 24 hr even at relative concentrations of $\frac{1}{512}$ (Brambell, Halliday and Hemmings 1961). However, when ^{131}I-labelled bovine γ-globulin was fed to 14 day old rats in single doses of 0.2 ml of a *c.* 1% solution the protein bound activity in their sera after 4 hr was approximately 1% of that in the solution administered. Most of the labelled protein in the young rats serum was electrophoretically indistinguishable from the γ-globulin administered and was precipitable by an immune rabbit anti-bovine γ-globulin serum. The sera of these young rats containing the labelled bovine γ-globulin that had been transmitted from the gut was administered orally to a second series of 14-day old rats. The labelled bovine γ-globulin, that had already been transmitted from the gut to the circulation once, was transmitted more than twice as readily the second time. This difference was highly significant. The experiment was controlled by administering young rat serum to which labelled bovine γ-globulin had been added at a concentration similar to that in the sera administered to the second series when it was found that the amount transmitted was at a level somewhat lower than in the first series, thus tending to increase the significance of the difference from the second series. Clearly the difference could not be accounted for either by the concentration of the albelled bovine globulin or the medium in which it was administered. The possibility that less acceptable molecules of bovine γ-globulin were removed in the circulation of the young rat after transmission from the gut was examined. Labelled bovine γ-globulin was injected intravenously into young rats and their sera harvested after 24 hr and administered orally to 14-day old rats, but the amount transmitted to the circulation was no greater than in the other controls. Clearly the labelled bovine γ-globulin that has been transmitted from the gut to the circulation of one young rat is transmitted more readily a second time by another young rat, and many times more readily than anti-*Brucella* agglutinins. This increased acceptability for transmission might be due either to selective transmission of more acceptable molecules from a heterologous population or to alteration of the molecules so as to make them more acceptable during transmission. It was not possible to distinguish between these possibilities with the evidence available from these experiments but further light has been thrown on the problem subsequently which tends to show that both suppositions may turn out to be correct.

Rabbit anti-*Brucella abortus* serum was administered orally in single doses of 0.01 ml/g body weight to 12-day old rats and 11-day old mice and their sera tested after 4 hr (Morris 1963a). The rabbit serum used had a saline and a Coombs test titre of $\frac{1}{4096}$ and it was therefore impossible to determine if incomplete agglutinins were present as these did not exceed the complete agglutinins. No complete agglutinins could be detected in the young rats sera at concentrations of $\frac{1}{1024}$ (C.Q.) of the serum administered, whereas incomplete agglutinins, as determined by the Coombs test, were present at a C.Q. of $\frac{1}{64}$.

This phenomenon was pursued (Morris 1965) in an effort to determine whether the incomplete antibody had resulted from (1) dissociation of 19S complete antibody into 7S incomplete antibody, (2) transformation of 7S antibody from complete to incomplete antibody, (3) selection of incomplete in preference to complete antibody. Three sera of rabbits immunized to

Brucella abortus were selected, one of which had been immunized over a long period of 8 months and two of which had been immunized over a short period of 24 days. Electrophoretic and chromatographic fractionation studies of these showed that almost all the antibody activity of the former one was in the 7S γ_2 fraction (γG), whereas much, but not all, the activity in the latter two was in the 18S γ_1 fraction (γM). It was shown by administration of the separated macroglobulin fraction that the γM antibody is not transmitted from the gut to the circulation of the young rat. This conclusion agrees with the results of Hemmings (unpublished) which showed that ^{131}I-labelled rabbit macroglobulin is not transmitted by the gut of the young rat. All the antibody transmitted was in the γG fraction and only incomplete antibody could be detected in the sera of the young rats although in the immune sera administered incomplete antibody, if present, was at a lower titre and masked by complete antibody. Quantitative considerations showed that the complete antibody was changed to incomplete during transmission. This change was brought about during transmission through the gut and did not occur after reaching the circulation of the young rat. Further evidence that this transformation had occurred was provided by the observation that the incomplete antibody in the serum of the young rats could be partly reconverted to complete antibody by the comparatively mild treatment of gel-filtration on a column of Sephadex G-200. Nevertheless, there was evidence that selection of 7S antibody was operating also because the transmissions from the three immune sera used were significantly different at C.Q.'s of $\frac{1}{21}$, $\frac{1}{64}$ and $\frac{1}{80}$ respectively.

A similar study (Morris 1967) was carried out with an immune bovine anti-*Brucella* serum, in which it was shown by electrophoresis, gel-filtration and chromatography that 60 to 70% of the antibody activity was in the γM, most of the remainder of the activity in the fast γG and less than 5% of the activity in the slow γG. The slow γG was itself complex, with a main component and a still slower minor component. The γM agglutinins were not transmitted by the gut to the circulation of 12-day old rats in detectable amounts, very little of the fast γG agglutinins was transmitted, but the slow γG agglutinins were transmitted readily. Only incomplete agglutinins were detected in the sera of the young rats, but it was not possible to determine whether this was due to the exclusion of complete agglutinins or to their alteration in transit to incomplete agglutinins. Thus, there was selection as between the fast and slow components of the γG and possibly between the main and minor components of the slow γG.

5.7. Interference

The selective nature of the transmission of immunity is a property that must be accounted for in any satisfactory theory of the cellular processes involved. Another phenomenon of equal significance in this context was discovered by Morris (1956) and has been called interference. I. G. Morris (1957), worked with the experimental induction of haemolytic disease in young mice by administration orally of rabbit anti-mouse red cell serum. He found that dilution of the minimum lethal dose with saline had no effect. Admixture of the immune rabbit serum with non-immune rabbit serum, on the other hand, had a simple dilution effect such that the lethal dose of a 1:1 mixture was double the volume of that of the unmixed immune serum alone. Presumably the non-immune γ-globulin was being transmitted from the gut to the circulation as readily as the immune globulin. The antiserum employed was of very high titre, agglutinating mouse red cells at a dilution of $\frac{1}{81,920}$. As little as 0.2 μl/g of this serum injected intraperitoneally was lethal to 7 day old mice. It was found that the antibody from an oral dose of approximately 1.0 μl/g of this serum was necessary to produce the same effect, so that intraperitoneal injection was *c.* 5 times as efficient as oral administration. Dilution of the immune rabbit serum with non-immune sera from certain other species also decreased the amount of rabbit antibody transmitted from the gut to the circulation of the young mouse, but to a lesser extent than with rabbit serum (fig. 5.3). The relative efficiency of the various non-immune sera in decreasing the transmission of the rabbit antibodies to the circulation was found to be: rabbit, 1; guinea-pig or human, $\frac{1}{3}$; bovine, $\frac{1}{12}$; sheep, hamster, rat or mouse $< \frac{1}{25}$. These differences were too great to be accounted for by variations in the globulin content of the sera.

A similar phenomenon is demonstrable in the young rat (Halliday 1957b). The addition of non-immune rat serum to 0.01 ml of immune rat anti-*Salmonella pullorum* serum had no effect on the titres attained in the sera of 12 day old rats receiving the mixture orally until the volume of the dose reached 0.16 ml, thereafter, for larger volumes it had a simple dilution effect. The addition of non-immune sera of certain other species to the immune rat serum had a marked effect in reducing the entry of the rat antibodies, even at low dilutions; for example, admixture of an equal quantity of rabbit serum with the immune rat serum significantly reduced the transmission of antibodies. Human, monkey, bovine and guineapig sera had similar effects to rabbit serum; hamster and mouse sera had much smaller effects and sheep

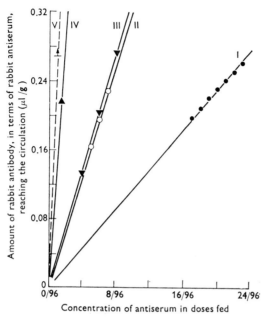

Fig. 5.3. Diagram showing the effects of the presence of heterologous sera on the transmission of rabbit antibodies by the gut of the young mouse. The heterologous sera were I rabbit, II guineapig, III human, IV bovine, V mouse, rat, hamster or sheep. (From Morris, I. G. 1957.)

serum had little, if any, effect. Similarly, the transmission of antibodies from immune rabbit serum is interfered with by dilution with non-immune rabbit or guineapig sera, but is not interfered with by sheep, rat, mouse or hamster sera.

It is evident that the sera of several species are capable of interfering with the transmission of antibodies from the gut to the circulation both in the young rat and the young mouse. There is also a remarkable correspondence in the effectiveness of the serum of a given species in both these animals, since rat, mouse, hamster and sheep sera do not appear to interfere significantly in either the rat or the mouse, while rabbit, guineapig, human and bovine sera, in that order, are the most effective in the mouse and these four, together with monkey serum, all appear to be equally effective in the rat. Further, interference may occur with the transmission of either homologous or heterologous antibodies.

The next problem was to determine which fractions of the serum were responsible for interference (Brambell, Halliday and Morris 1958). Accordingly 12-day old rats were fed by stomach tube with 0.24 ml of immune rat serum diluted with 7 volumes of (a) non-immune rat serum, (b) human serum, (c) 1% solution of human γ-globulin, (d) 10% solution of human albumin; or with (a) non-immune rat serum, (b) bovine serum, (c) 2% solution of bovine γ-globulin, (d) 10% solution of bovine albumin. In each series the γ-globulin fraction was found to be rather more active than the whole serum, whereas the albumin fraction had no effect. Thus the whole of the interference produced by the serum can be accounted for by the γ-globulin fraction alone. Solutions of human γ-globulin at concentrations of 0.2% or less were not effective. It was found that interference resulted when the dose of human γ-globulin was given up to 4 hr before the dose of immune serum, but declined as the interval increased and was not apparent after longer intervals. Similar experiments were performed on 7-day old mice, using immune rabbit serum alone or mixed with an equal volume of (a) normal rabbit serum, (b) human serum, (c) 1% human γ-globulin, (d) 4% human albumin. It was found that the human albumin had no significant effect, that the human γ-globulin produced as much interference as the whole serum, but the non-immune rabbit serum was more effective than either. Subsequently, Morris (1963b) showed that the whole of the interference produced by rabbit serum on the transmission of guineapig antibodies in mice could be reproduced by the γ-globulin fraction alone. Thus, in both species it is the γ-globulin fraction of serum which is responsible for interference.

Since γ-globulin is the effective component of serum in producing interference with the transmission of immunity in rats and mice, it was of interest to determine which part of the γ-globulin molecule was responsible. Morris (1963b) compared the effects of the papain fragments of rabbit γ-globulin with that of whole rabbit γ-globulin on the transmission of guineapig antibodies in young mice. He found that the Fab pieces produced no detectable interference, whereas the Fc piece was 3.5 times more effective than the intact molecule. Thus the capacity to interfere with the transmission of another γ-globulin resides in the same part of the molecule as is involved in the transmission of that molecule, and which is also the part which is responsible for most of the antigenic activity of the whole molecule in another species.

5.8. *The relation between selective transmission and interference*

Clearly, selective transmission of γ-globulins by the endoderm cells must involve some mechanism whereby there is recognition of the differences between the molecules, such as might be provided by specific receptors. Interference by one γ-globulin with the transmission of another is difficult to account for except as competition for receptor sites. These considerations led to the suggestion that specific receptors on or in the cells were responsible for both these phenomena of transmission (Brambell, Halliday and Morris 1958). Not only is the same part of the γ-globulin molecule responsible both for transmission and for interference but there is evidence of a quantitative relationship between these two activities.

Morris (1964), working with mice, found that the relationship of the concentration of γ-globulin (y) attained in the serum of the young animal to the dose (x), administered orally, was in the form of a rectangular hyperbola and could be represented empirically by the formula:

$$\frac{a}{y} - \frac{b}{x} = 1 \tag{1}$$

where a and b are constants. The value of y approaches a theoretical maximum $y_{max} = a$ when x becomes very large. For any given dose (x) the proportion of y_{max} attained in the serum will depend inversely on the magnitude of b. The values of b for the γ-globulins tested decline in the order rat > bovine > guineapig > rabbit. This is the order also of the extent to which the transmission of these γ-globulins is interfered with by any other γ-globulin and is the inverse of the order in which they themselves interfere with the transmission of another γ-globulin. Thus the higher the value of b the less it interferes with the transmission of other γ-globulins but the more readily other γ-globulins interfere with its transmission.

Assuming that attachment to receptors is involved in transmission, then the reaction should be capable of representation by the equation appropriate to an enzyme/substrate reaction, as:

$$A + R \underset{k_1}{\overset{k_2}{\rightleftharpoons}} AR \overset{k_3}{\rightarrow} R + A^1, \tag{2}$$

where R = receptor, A = γ-globulin entering the absorptive cells, and A^1 = γ-globulin leaving the absorptive cells for the circulation.

Provided the receptors are on or in the absorptive cells, whether it is a single phase or a heterogenous system the Briggs–Haldane treatment is appropriate, yielding the equation:

$$v = k_3 [R_t] \left(\frac{[A]}{[A] + K} \right), \tag{3}$$

where v is the rate of transmission of A; $[R_t]$ is the total concentration of receptors; k_1, k_2 and k_3 are reaction rates and $K = (k_1 + k_3/k_2)$. The rate of transmission of γ-globulin A in the presence of another competing γ-globulin B will be:

$$v_A = k_{3A} [R_t] \left(\frac{[A]}{[A] + K_A + (K_A/K_B) [B]} \right). \tag{4}$$

It is evident that the higher the value of K for any given γ-globulin the less it will interfere with the transmission of other γ-globulins but the more readily it will be interfered with itself. This theoretical treatment is consistent with the empirical equation (1) provided that x (= the size of dose) is proportional to $[A]$ (= the γ-globulin entering the cells), and (2) y (= the concentration attained in the serum) is proportional to v (= the rate of transmission). Since eq. (1) was derived from the results of experiments in which the dose/g body weight was of constant volume and uptake by the cells is pinocytotic, the first condition would appear to be met. Since the maximum concentration resulting from any given dose, irrespective of the amount or the specificity of the γ-globulin in it, is attained within 2 hr, it would appear that v is proportional to y. Hence the conclusions that can be drawn from the values of b with reference to interference are equally applicable to the values of K.

5.9. *In vitro studies of transmission*

Although the young rat is so convenient for experiments *in vivo* on the transmission of immunity there are certain disadvantages inherent in experiments on the intact animal. Some parameters cannot be determined and others can only be estimated within wide limits. Although the concentration of antibody or of γ-globulin in the dose administered can be accurately determined it may be very different to that pertaining at the surface of the absorptive epithelium. Moreover the absolute amount transmitted to the circulation is difficult to estimate accurately because the concentration attained in the serum depends on both input and output from the circulation, on the total fluid volume and on the rate of exchange between the intra-vascular and extravascular compartments, all of which are difficult to esti-mate accurately. The total absorptive area of the gut cannot be estimated with sufficient precision to be meaningful and the rate of disappearance of the dose from the gut lumen is difficult to determine. Many of these dis-abilities could be overcome if transmission could be studied *in vitro* as well as *in vivo*. Accordingly efforts were made to develop suitable techniques to this end (Bamford 1965, 1966). The everted intestinal sac technique of Wilson and Wiseman (1954) appeared the most promising as it had been widely used for studies on the adult rat intestine. The method involves turning the small intestine inside out, cutting it into convenient lengths, the ends of which are ligatured to form sacs containing a suitable amount of physiological medium and incubating it in a larger volume of medium suit-ably gassed. Eversion results in the villi diverging on the periphery of the sac, instead of being crushed together in the lumen as they would have been otherwise. This spreading of the villi facilitates adequate oxygenation of the tissues and absorption. The fluid surrounding the sac is called the mucosal fluid and that within the sac the serosal fluid. Both can be measured accurately at the beginning and end of an experiment and the dry weight of the sac gives a good estimate of the amount of tissue involved. Transmission from the larger volume of mucosal fluid to the smaller volume of serosal fluid ensures that the concentration of the former remains relatively constant throughout an experiment. The small size and extreme delicacy of the intes-tine of the 18-day old rat presented special problems of treatment and mani-pulation but once these were overcome the technique proved very satis-factory for the ileum, though the jejunum was found to be less amenable. Viability of the tissue was tested by the consistent oxygen consumption, the transport of L-histidine from the mucosal to the serosal surface against a concentration gradient and the histology of the tissue at the end of the experiment. Sacs which had decreased in volume during the experiment were discarded as possibly leaking. One hour was chosen for the duration of the experiments, as well within the period of viability of the sacs.

Both antibodies to *Salmonella pullorum* and ^{131}I-labelled γ-globulins were transported from the mucosal to the serosal fluid in significant amounts. The oxygen consumption of the tissue was increased significantly when either whole serum or γ-globulin was added to the mucosal fluid. There was also a significant increase in the non-protein-bound radioactivity in the tissue and in both the mucosal and serosal fluids when ^{131}I-labelled γ-globulin was used, indicating proteolysis of some of the protein. This proteolysis appeared to occur in the tissues, because there was no increase in the non-protein bound activity when the mucosal fluid alone, at the end of the experiment, was incubated for a further hour.

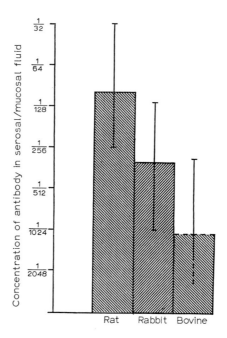

Fig. 5.4. Histogram of the concentrations of antibody in the serosal fluids of inverted ileal sacs of 18-day old rats relative to those in the mucosal fluid after one hour's exposure to rat, rabbit or bovine antisera in the mucosal fluid. (Data from Bamford 1966.)

Antibodies to *Salmonella pullorum* were transmitted from the mucosal to the serosal fluid from immune rat, rabbit and bovine sera (fig. 5.4). The rat antibodies attained titres in the serosal fluid of from $\frac{1}{32}$ to $\frac{1}{256}$ of those in the mucosal fluid, the rabbit antibodies of from $\frac{1}{128}$ to $\frac{1}{1024}$, and of 18 experiments with bovine sera, six had relative titres of $\frac{1}{320}$ to $\frac{1}{640}$ and 12 were negative. The results strongly suggest that the homologous antibodies are transmitted more readily than either of the heterologous antibodies, and that the rabbit antibodies are transmitted more readily than the bovine.

Experiments with ^{131}I-labelled rat, rabbit and bovine γ-globulins showed that all three were transmitted to the serosal fluid in appreciable quantities, but that the rat γ-globulin was transmitted at more than twice the rate of either of the others. The bovine γ-globulin was transmitted slightly, but scarcely significantly, faster than the rabbit γ-globulin.

It is apparent that, whether antibodies or isotopically labelled γ-globulins are used, transmission is selective *in vitro* as *in vivo*.

5.10. *The development of the gastro-intestinal tract*

Transmission of immunity after birth by way of the neonatal gut involves transport of the immune globulin across the gut wall from the lumen to the circulation without loss of its immunological activity. To achieve this the immune globulin must reach the site of transport without such denaturation or degradation as would inactivate it immunologically. The main site of transport in the rat and mouse is certainly the small intestine; there is clear experimental evidence of transport in the ileum (Bamford 1966), and the cytological evidence supports this finding and suggests that the jejunum is also involved (Clark 1959; Kraehenbuhl, Gloor and Blanc 1967). There is no evidence that transport occurs in the stomach or duodenum, but the possibility has not been formally excluded. The problems arise, therefore, as to how immune globulins taken by mouth by the suckling rat or mouse traverse the stomach and duodenum without being digested, and as to whether the subsequent loss of the capacity to acquire passive immunity by mouth is due to their being digested before reaching the small intestine, or to the loss of the capacity to transport them by the small intestine, or to both these changes. Morphological and biochemical studies of the development of the gut have thrown some light on these problems, as well as on the cellular processes involved in transport.

The development of the gastro-intestinal tract of the rat was studied by Kammeraad (1942), who was able to distinguish both chief and parietal cells in the gastric glands one day after birth. These glands increase in length rapidly during the first 15 days of age and the distribution of the chief and parietal cells by the twenty-fifth day is typical of the adult, a finding in agreement with that of Hill (1956). Although pepsinogen granules are present in small numbers one day after birth they are not numerous until after the 15th day, but are present in significant quantities by the 25th day of age. This observation is in agreement with the findings of Boass and Wilson (1963), who measured the pepsinogen content of homogenates of rat

stomachs at intervals from 4 days before birth to adult life. They found that
the content increased very gradually from about 5% at birth to about 15%
of the adult level at 17 days of age, when a very rapid increase to near adult

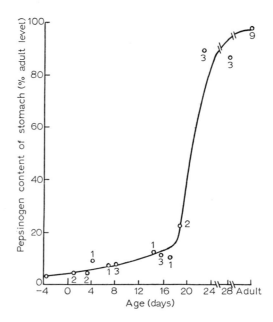

Fig. 5.5. Diagram of the pepsinogen content of the stomach of rats at various ages
expressed as a percentage of that of the adult. The numbers adjoining the points indicate
the number of determinations on which each is based. (From Boass and Wilson 1963.)

levels at 22 days of age occurred (fig. 5.5). Mosinger, Placer and Koldovsky
(1959) found that the peptic activity of the stomach of the young rat was
at a very low level at birth and at 8 days of age, but that it had risen
enormously by 21 days of age; similarly tryptic activity of the intestine
and pancreas showed a substantial increase at 21 days of age as compared
to 8 days of age or at birth. Similarly, it has been shown (Manville and
Lloyd 1932) that the acidity of the rat stomach at full term is about *p*H
6.6, that this rises very rapidly after birth to a mean of *c.* *p*H 5.4, about
which it fluctuates, possibly even declining slightly, until 16 or 17 days of
age when it rises rapidly to the adult value of *p*H 4.6 by 21 days of age. Hill
(1956) found the stomach contents of rats at 20 hr of age to be *p*H 5.0–6.0
and that it subsequently remained at about *p*H 4.0 until 18 days of age,

but that by 25 days of age it had fallen to *p*H 3.0. Thus the evidence from all these sources suggests that the onset of effective gastric digestion in the rat coincides closely with the time when the transmission of passive immunity terminates.

It is interesting that small, but detectable, amounts of intrinsic factor were found in the stomachs of foetal and new-born rats and that the amounts increased rapidly in the second and third weeks of life to reach adult levels about 21 days of age (Boass and Wilson 1963). Nevertheless *in vitro* experiments with intestinal segments or sacs showed that the new-born rat is capable of absorbing vitamin B_{12} without intrinsic factor, but that this capacity declines rapidly to very low levels during the first and second weeks, when it is replaced by an intrinsic factor dependent mechanism. Gallagher (1969) found that ^{57}Co-cyanocobalamin (vitamin B_{12}) and radioactive colloidal gold were absorbed readily by 9–11-day old rats after intragastric administration, at a time when the production of gastric intrinsic factor is deficient. Doses of vitamin ranging from 1 mμg to 1 mg were absorbed with equal facility, and with an efficiency of *c.* 90%. A decrease in absorption was apparent on the 16th day of age and it had virtually ceased at 30 days. The site of absorption was the distal jejunum and the proximal ileum. Absorption was markedly decreased in 14-day old rats which had been injected with 1 mg of cortisone at 9 days of age.

Mackenzie, Donaldson, Kopp and Trier (1968) found that antiserum specific for the mucopolysaccharide coat of the brush border of the small intestinal cells of the adult hamster inhibited the uptake of the intrinsic-factor–B_{12} complex. The antibody did not react directly either with the complex or with the intrinsic factor alone. The inhibitory factor was absorbed out of the antiserum by the brush border of the distal, but not of the proximal, half of the small intestine. The antiserum did not inhibit disaccharidase activity nor impair glucose transport by inverted intestinal sacs. This suggested that the antibody competes with the IF–B_{12} complex for receptors in the surface of the microvilli of the cells of the adult hamster ileum.

5.11. The structure of the absorptive cells

The early development of the absorptive cells of the small intestine of the rat has been investigated recently by both light and electron microscopy (Shaw Dunn 1967). The intestine grows rapidly in 13 to 18 day foetuses and, at the end of this period, localised areas of intense epithelial proliferation develop and are invaded by cores of connective tissue to give rise to the rudiments of the villi. The absorptive cells become increasingly differentiated from 18 days to full term and their free surfaces become clothed with microvilli. These microvilli are somewhat shorter and thicker than in the adult and the cells have a well developed terminal web (Kraehenbuhl, Gloor and Blanc 1966). Smooth endoplasmic reticulum is abundant and rough endoplasmic reticulum is equally apparent. Vacuoles are not numerous. Pinocytosis begins in the cells at the apices of the villi at 20 days and is well marked at 22 days (Hayward 1967). Goblet cells can be identified first in the duodenum at 20 days (Kammeraad 1942). They differentiate rapidly and, although most numerous in the duodenum, are found throughout the intestine of the new-born animal.

After birth the absorptive cells show all the characters associated with active pinocytosis. Caveoli, communicating with the intestinal lumen, can be observed forming between the bases of the microvilli. Beneath these the apical cytoplasm is crowded with channels and vacuoles and the terminal web appears to be disrupted by them. Wissig and Graney (1968) observe that the pinocytotic invaginations or caveoli and the apical vacuoles or cisternae show on the luminal surfaces of their bounding membranes an ordered array of minute discrete plaques with a dense particle *c.* 70 Å in diameter centered over each. These particles are arranged in a two-dimensional square lattice with centre-to-centre spacing of *c.* 120 Å (plate 5.1). The vacuoles or phagosomes increase in size the further they are from the apical surface (Kraehenbuhl, Gloor and Blanc 1966). These vacuoles often contain a dense material and they appear to discharge into a single large

---

Plate 5.1. A. Electronmicrograph of part of the apical surface of an ileal cell of a 14-day old suckling rat. The apical network of tubules and vesicles can be seen to open to the exterior at two points between the bases of the microvilli. The interconnecting nature of the network can be seen on the left. The myelin figure in the network on the right is believed to be a fixation artefact. × 22,500.   B. Electronmicrograph of a part of the apical network of tubules and vesicles in the ileal cells of a 14-day old suckling rat. Where the plane of section is normal to the membrane limiting these channels, as indicated by the arrows, it can be seen to consist of a conventional 3-layered unit membrane approximately 75 Å thick bearing on its luminal surface an array of small particles each 60–80 Å in diameter spaced at 120 Å centre to centre. At these points the outer leaflet of the unit membrane appears to be interrupted or 'hyphenated' in a regular manner, each 'hyphen' bearing one particle. These appearances cannot be seen in thicker or oblique sections of the membrane. × 160,000. (From Wissig and Graney 1968.)

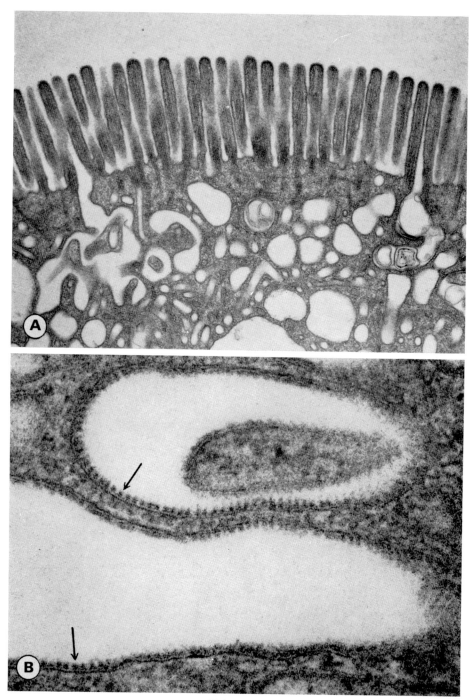

PLATE 5.1

vacuole which occupies much of the cell and is immediately apical to the nucleus, which it may equal or exceed in size (Graney 1968; Wissig and Graney 1968). Cornell and Padykula (1969) have shown that this large supranuclear vesicle is absent before the first feed and appears soon after the initial ingestion of milk. Initially the Golgi complex is supranuclear and central but the development of the large vesicle displaces it to the side. At the level of the apical pole of the nucleus and lateral to the large vacuole the parallel membranes and small vesicles of the Golgi apparatus are seen. According to Kraehenbuhl et al. (1966, 1967) these small vesicles are filled with dense material and can be observed in communication with the large vacuole. They appear to link it with the intercellular space, which contains a similar material. The channels and vacuoles in the apical cytoplasm decrease after the 10th day and have disappeared by the 20th day, when pinocytosis appears to have ceased.

The absorptive cells of the small intestine are formed in the crypts, migrate slowly up the sides and are ultimately shed from the tips of the villi. By pulse labelling with tritiated thymidine (Koldovsky, Sunshine and Kretchmer 1966) it was estimated that in the adult rat the cells took approximately 48 hr to migrate from the crypt to the tip of the villus but that in the suckling rat they took 4 to 5 times as long. It follows that any materials absorbed by these cells that are not transmitted to the tissues will ultimately be returned to the lumen. Since the transmission of immunity is a rapid process, measurable in minutes, as compared to the life of the cells, measurable in days, the rejection of cells from the villi can have little effect on the process, except in so far as the liberation of enzymes from the disintegrating cells might affect unabsorbed protein in the lumen.

Lymphocytes are normally present in the intestinal epithelium. According to Meader and Landers (1967) the majority are in the basal region of the epithelium, below the level of the epithelial cell nuclei and situated between the cells. They migrate through the basement membrane into the epithelium and back again, and no evidence was obtained of their movement towards the free surface of the epithelium or of their escape into the intestinal lumen.

5.12. *The distribution of enzymes in the cells*

The enzyme alkaline phosphatase is present throughout the small intestine of the rat and mouse and is localised mainly in the brush border regions of the absorptive cells. The changes in the alkaline phosphatase activity

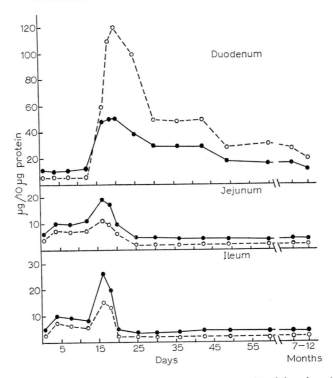

Fig. 5.6. Diagram of the activity of alkaline phosphatase on phenylphosphate (○---○) and on β-glycerophosphate (●——●) in three regions of the intestines of mice at various ages from birth to one year. (From Moog 1961.)

of the tissues of the duodenum, jejunum and ileum of the mouse have been studied by Moog (1961) (fig. 5.6). The enzyme is present at a low level in the duodenum at birth, the activity on the substrate phenylphosphate being less than that on β-glycerophosphate, and remains nearly constant until the 12th day. At this time the activity increases sharply to reach a peak on the 20th day, by which time the phenylphosphate activity is more than double the β-glycerophosphate activity. Thereafter the activity on both substrates declines but remains throughout life much higher than in the other regions and the phenylphosphate activity continues to exceed the β-glycerophosphate activity. The changes in activity in the jejunum and ileum resemble each other; in both the activity rises during the first four days after birth and then remains relatively constant until the 12th day, when a sharp rise starts, reaching a peak on the 16th day and then declining to the low adult level between days 20 and 25. The β-glycerophosphate activity exceeds the phenylphosphate activity throughout in both the jejunum and ileum, unlike the duodenum. It will be seen that the peak of activity coincides in time remarkably closely with the termination of the transmission of passive immunity.

The distribution of enzymes in the intestinal brush border has been studied by tris-disruption and density-gradient fractionation (Eichholz 1967). Most of the activity was in the principal membrane fraction and none in the fraction composed of the cores of the microvilli. All the alkaline phosphatase was in the membrane fraction, as well as maltase, invertase, lactase, isomaltase, trehelase, leucyl naphthylamide hydrolase and ATPase. Lactase and some ATPase were present in other fractions.

Both alkaline phosphatase and acid phosphatase occur in the apical cytoplasm and in the large vesicles of the absorptive cells of the ileum (Vacek 1964; Jeal 1965; Shervey 1966). The presence of alkaline phosphatase in the region that is crowded with pinocytotic vesicles and channels and in the large vesicle suggests their origin from the apical cell membrane, with which this enzyme is generally associated and the occurrence of acid phosphatase would justify their identification with phagolysosomes. Cornell and Padykula (1969) found that the large vesicle and the smaller denser ones adjacent to it and which appear to discharge into it are rich in hydrolytic enzymes, acid phosphatase, ATPase, thiamine pyrophosphate, alkaline phosphatase and esterase. They consider that these vesicles are part of the well developed phago-lysosomal system of the cells. The large vesicles, because of their cytochemical similarities, have been compared to the 'meconium corpuscles' of the foetal human intestine (Shervey 1966). Non-specific esterase is present in the cytoplasm (Vacek 1964; Shervey 1966; Jeal 1965) but is absent from the brush border and from the large vesicle and nucleus (Jeal 1965). Leucine and alanine aminopeptidases and succinic dehydrogenase are present also in the apical cytoplasm of the absorptive cells (Jeal 1965). Williams and Beck (1969) studied the lysosomal enzyme activity of the small intestinal cells of rats and other animals during the pinocytotic phase and came to the conclusion that 'the neonatal ileum is a physiologically separate organ, differing in many respects from the adult. Protein and other macromolecular complexes are digested intracellularly in this part of the gut until "closure", when the adult role is assumed, with the bulk of digestion taking place extracellularly.' Nordström, Koldovský and Dahlqvist (1969) found that the neutral β-galactosidase (lactase) activity in the jejunum and ileum of rats of all ages was greatest at the tips of the villi. Acid β-galactosidase and acid phosphatase activity in the ileum of the 12-day old rat, unlike the adult, also was greatest at the tips of the villi.

5.13. *Evidence of pinocytotic absorption*

The absorption by pinocytosis of bovine γ-globulin and of albumin was demonstrated in the mouse by Clark (1959). Using the fluorescent antibody technique he was able to demonstrate the pinocytotic absorption of these bovine proteins by the cells of the jejunum and ileum, but not of the duodenum, in suckling mice up to 18 days of age, but not thereafter. Specific fluorescence could be detected in the apical region, and in the mesenteric lymph node and even in the lacteals of the villi, indicating transport via the lymphatic drainage. Using colloidal gold or saccharated iron oxide it was possible to demonstrate the uptake of these into the apical vesicles and the large vesicle. Lecce (1966), using fluorescein-labelled γ-globulin, demonstrated the pinocytotic absorption *in vitro* of the protein by the cells of the jejunum of the 5-day old mouse, but not by those of the adult mouse. The absorption of ferritin in the jejunum of the suckling rat has been studied with the electron microscope by Kraehenbuhl, Gloor and Blanc (1967). It was taken up by the caveoli between the bases of the microvilli, appeared in the vesicles and channels of the apical cytoplasm, and discharged into the large vesicle, as has been shown also very clearly by Graney (1968) (plate 5.2). The ferritin was found to pass from this in very small vesicles into the Golgi complex, situated between the large vesicle and the nucleus. From the Golgi complex the ferritin appeared to be set free in the cytoplasm and to pass from it into the adjoining intercellular space (fig. 5.7).

Experiments with ferritin, colloidal gold, saccharated iron oxide and other radio-opaque materials are all open to the objection that these substances may be treated by the cells in a different way to the special manner with which they deal with the transmission of immune globulins, and that

---

Plate 5.2. Electronmicrograph of part of an ileal cell of a 15-day old rat $1\frac{1}{2}$ hr after oral administration of ferritin. Ferritin can be seen in the tubules (T) of the apical system, and in the large supranuclear vesicle or cisterna (C). Three tubules are connected with this vesicle. The intestinal lumen is towards the top of the figure. × 117,000. (From Graney 1968.)

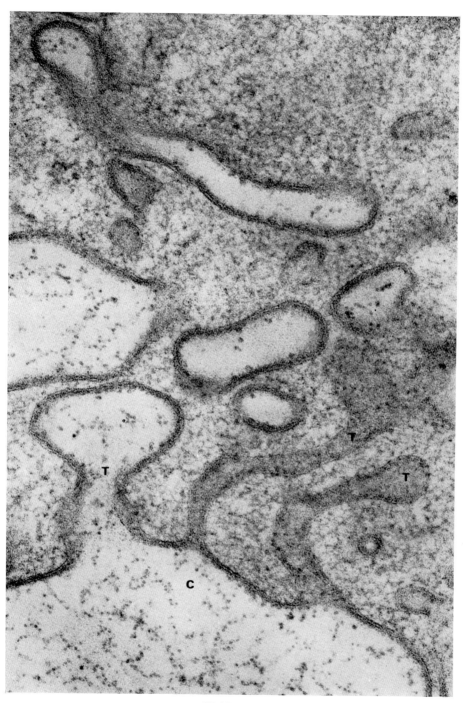

PLATE 5.2

these substances may follow a different route within the cells. Some method of tracing the immune globulins themselves within the cells is required, but even such a method would be suspect if it were achieved by attaching to them labels, such as fluorescein or ferritin, which might alter their acceptability to the cells. An interesting attempt in this direction has been described in a preliminary note by Anderson (1964). Young rats were given rat anti-ferritin serum orally and killed at varying intervals, when frozen sections were made of jejunal tissue after brief formalin fixation. These sections were soaked in ferritin for 30 min, washed, fixed in OsO_4, embedded and cut for electron microscopy. Ferritin, presumably reacted with antibody, was found in vesicles within and between the epithelial cells, as well as in the basement membrane and occasionally in the lacteals. It was evenly distributed throughout the contents of the small apical vesicles, but mainly aggregated at the walls of the large perinuclear vesicles. It exhibited an even more marked peripheral distribution in the extracellular vesicles. It is to be hoped that a full account of this work will appear.

Although pinocytosis appears to be reduced to a very low level after the termination of the transmission of immunity, the difference may be of degree rather than absolute. By injecting ferritin into isolated loops of intestine of adult hamsters Bockman and Winborn (1966) were able to demonstrate pinocytosis on a small scale. When the hamsters had been immunized previously by injection of the horse ferritin, absorption was much more active. In the electron microscope the ferritin could be seen densely packed in a few small vesicles in the apical cytoplasm and in the Golgi complex of the absorptive cells, as well as in macrophages, fibrocytes and endothelial cells of the lamina propria. Pinocytotic vesicles and channels were never plentiful in the apical cytoplasm, as they are in the suckling, nor was a large vesicle present in the cell. Similarly, in adult rats, Sanders and Ashworth (1961) demonstrated pinocytosis by the jejunal cells of polystyrene latex particles of 2200 Å size when these were given by stomach tube as an emulsion with food. The particles could be identified in vesicles within the cells, in the intercellular spaces, in the lamina propria and in the lymphatics.

5.14. *Transmission from the maternal circulation to the milk*

Transmission of passive immunity after birth involves the secretion of all the antibodies that are to be transmitted in the colostrum or in the milk, or in both. In rats and mice antibodies continue to be secreted in the milk

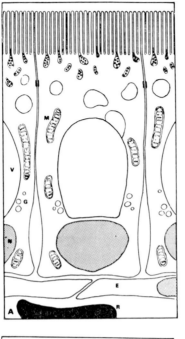

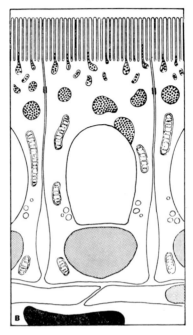

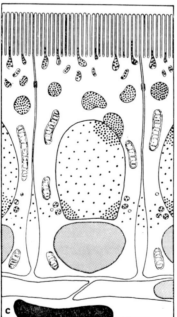

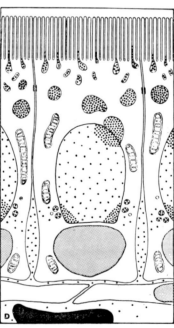

Fig.
5.7

throughout lactation. The way in which maternal immunity is transmitted to the milk should be of no less interest than the way in which it is transmitted from the gut to the circulation of the suckling, but, unfortunately, we know much less about this first stage of the process. It is surprising that although so much attention has been paid to the physiology and biochemistry of milk production comparatively little has been paid to the immunology. Consequently, it is still difficult to answer such questions as whether any immune globulins produced by the mother and capable of being absorbed by the suckling are excluded from the mammary secretions or whether any immune globulins present in the mammary secretions are not transmitted by the gut of the suckling. In the main it is information concerning the secretion of immunoglobulins in the milk rather than concerning the transmission of these from the gut of the suckling that is lacking to answer these questions adequately. However, some information is available for rats.

The origin of the albumin, transferrin and γ-globulin in the milk was studied by injecting these proteins isotopically labelled into rats on the 2nd, 9th and 17th days of lactation (Jordan and Morgan 1967). The maternal serum changed very little throughout lactation in the concentrations and rates of turnover of these proteins. In the milk whey the concentrations of albumin and γ-globulin remained constant but that of transferrin increased greatly as lactation proceeded. The ratio of whey protein-bound radioactivity to maternal serum activity was constant throughout lactation for all three proteins, implying that the rates of transmission from the maternal serum to the milk were constant, but the ratio was highest for albumin and lowest for transferrin, implying that the γ-globulin was transmitted to the milk less readily than the albumin and more readily than the transferrin (fig. 5.8). Since the transferrin is believed to be a much smaller molecule than the γ-globulin, it is evident that transmission of serum proteins from the serum to the milk is selective. The specific activity of the whey albumin

---

Fig. 5.7. Diagrammatic representation of the successive stages in the absorption of ferritin by the jejunal cells of the young rat. A shows the ferritin after 2 min being absorbed by pinocytosis. B shows the larger vacuoles becoming charged with ferritin after 5 min and in C these are discharging into the large supranuclear vesicle and are passing from it to the Golgi apparatus in small vesicles after 20 min. It is released from the Golgi apparatus into the cytoplasm and is discharged into the intercellular spaces from where it reaches the capillaries after 40 min, as in D. E = vascular endothelium, G = Golgi apparatus, M = mitochondria, N = nucleus, R = erythrocyte, V = large supranuclear vesicle. (After Kraehenbuhl, Gloor and Blanc 1966.)

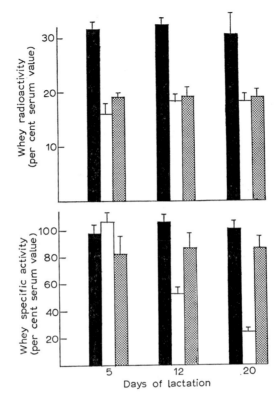

Fig. 5.8. Histograms of the protein-bound radioactivity of the whey and of the specific activities of the whey proteins three days after intravenous injection of radioiodine-labelled albumin (■), transferrin (□) and γ-globulin (▨) into rats at different times of lactation. The results are expressed as percentages of the serum values at the times when the milk was collected. Each is the mean of the values for 4 animals and the standard error of each mean is indicated. (From Jordan and Morgan 1967.)

was 100%, and that of the γ-globulin 85%, of that of the serum albumin and serum γ-globulin respectively, so that whereas all the albumin in the whey appeared to be derived from the circulation, a small but significant proportion of the whey γ-globulin appeared to be synthesized locally in the mammary gland and secreted in the milk without being liberated into the general circulation. The specific activity of the whey transferrin fell from 100% of that of the serum at the beginning of lactation to 25% at the end, so that a steadily increasing amount of this protein, amounting finally to 75%, must be synthesized in the mammary gland. It had been shown previously (Laurell and Morgan 1965) that serum macroglobulins and lipoproteins are absent from the whey. Unfortunately there is no evidence concerning the γA-globulin, which from our knowledge of other species one might expect to be present in relatively high concentration. About one third of the protein in milk whey, or approximately one tenth of the total protein of rat milk, was derived directly from the circulation.

The transmission of active immunity to *Brucella abortus* from the circulation to the milk in the rat has been studied by Biswas (1961). The killed antigen was injected subcutaneously in the neck region of pregnant rats near full term and paired samples of serum and milk whey were collected at intervals during the following lactation. The same animals were reimmunized near full term in the succeeding pregnancy and similar samples taken. During the first lactation both the serum and milk whey titres were on average $\frac{1}{80}$ to $\frac{1}{160}$, but during the second lactation whereas the average serum titre was one dilution higher, the average milk whey titre was one dilution lower. This is a surprising result and difficult to account for, since it might have been expected that macroglobulin antibody, which is presumably not excreted in the milk, would constitute a greater proportion of the total serum antibody after primary immunization than after secondary immunization, and hence that the ratio of antibody in the milk to that in the serum would be lower in the first lactation than in the second, the opposite of what was observed. Unfortunately, only complete agglutinins were measured and the possibility that a transformation from complete to incomplete agglutinins may occur during transmission from the circulation to the milk, such as occurs with heterologous *Brucella* agglutinins during transmission from the gut to the circulation (Morris 1965, 1967), cannot be excluded.

5.15. *Changes in the serum proteins of the foetus and newborn*

How far the transmission of passive immunity overlaps with, and possibly affects, the development of active immunity by the young animal is a problem which requires much further experimental investigation for its solution. First, it is necessary to consider the information that has been obtained concerning the relative contributions which passively acquired and autogenous components make to the serum proteins of the young rat at successive stages of development.

Although maternal albumin, as well as globulin, is passively transferred to the foetus and suckling in significant amounts, synthesis of albumin and of at least some globulin components of serum, if not γ-globulin, is proceeding in the young animal, even during foetal life. It has been shown (Kelleher, Kenyon and Villee 1963) by injection of ^{14}C-labelled amino-acids into 20 to 22 day foetal rats that both albumin and some globulins are being synthesized at this stage of development, although there is no evidence to suggest the synthesis of γ-globulin.

Heim (1961), using paper electrophoresis, claimed that a fast albumin component was present in the near full-term rat foetus, and possibly a component in the β-region, which were absent at later stages. In contrast, using free boundary electrophoresis Halliday and Kekwick (1957) found a fast albumin component in sera of rats of all ages from 12 to 90 days. A component peculiar to full-term foetuses with the mobility of an α_1-globulin, and which was not detectable in the maternal serum, was noted by Kelleher and Villee (1962) using immunoelectrophoresis. This component was demonstrable with rabbit antisera to normal adult rat serum, and hence must have shared antigenicity with adult serum proteins. However, Boffa et al. (1965) claim that the macroglobulins of the foetal and new-born rat are mainly α_2M-globulins, which are absent from normal adult rat sera, together with only very small quantities of α_1M-globulins, although it is to these that the αM-globulins of the mother belong. During the first 15 days after birth the α_2M-globulins gradually disappear and are replaced by α_1M-globulins in the neonatal rat. This suggested that the α_2M-macroglobulin is synthesized by the near full-term foetus. It is possible that this serum protein is the same as a slow α_2-globulin identified by starch gel electrophoresis (Beaton et al. 1961) which is absent from normal rat serum but appears in that of pregnant animals at about midgestation and disappears again after parturition. This component is conspicuous in the sera of young rats at birth but decreases thereafter and has disappeared by 3 weeks of age. Halliday and Kekwick (1957) also identified both α_1- and α_2-globulins, the latter being the more plentiful, in the sera of rats from 12 to 90 days of age. In view of these conflicting results it is scarcely possible to establish the autogenous synthesis of specific serum proteins in foetal and neonatal rats on qualitative differences in them alone.

Quantitative and immunological evidence provides a somewhat clearer picture regarding the immunoglobulins. It has been shown that the total serum protein concentration of the young rat rises fairly steadily from *c.* 38 mg/ml at 12 days of age to *c.* 60 mg/ml at 70 days, most of this increase being due to albumin. During this period the γ-globulin (γG) level fell sharply, both relatively and absolutely from 11% (5 mg/ml) at 18 days, when the transmission of maternal γ-globulin is ceasing, to 1.8% (0.9 mg/ml) at 24 days and thereafter rose steadily to adult levels, presumably due to autogenous synthesis. Thus, by 24 days of age the rate of synthesis of γ-globulin by the young rat must be sufficient to replace the loss of γ-globulin, whether autogenous or passively acquired, and to provide for the growth increment and the gradual increase in concentration towards the adult level. The changes in the γM-globulin are more difficult to elucidate, since the technique employed would have resulted in these being included in the β-globulins. The β-globulins showed an initial rapid rise from 13.4% (5.1 mg/ml) at 12 days to 17.4% (8.1 mg/ml) at 24 days, followed by a fall to 10.0% (5.2 mg/ml) at 40 days, when a gradual rise to the adult level of 11.3% (6.5 mg/ml) began. The reasons for the fall are obscure but since maternal macroglobulin is not transmitted the γM-component at least must be presumed to be autogenous.

Plasma and blood volumes of young rats from birth to 30 days of age have been measured by the dye (T–1824) dilution technique (Trávníčková and Heller 1963). Expressed as a percentage of body weight, both decline from birth to 20 days of age, the plasma volume from 5.84 ml/100 g to 5.24 ml/100 g.

5.16. *The age of development of active immunity*

Rats given a single injection of killed *Salmonella pullorum* antigen at 11 days of age produced circulating antibody by 14 days of age, whether they were or were not allowed to continue suckling their non-immune mothers in the interval. Hence the antibody produced was synthesized by the young animals (Halliday 1957a). Subsequently, it was shown that injection of killed *Brucella abortus* antigen at ages from birth to 4 days resulted in the appearance of circulating antibody in a few individuals at 10 days of age and thereafter in an increasing proportion until all had antibody by 15 days. The age at which antibody appeared was unaffected by the stage from birth to 4 days at which the antigen was injected. Antibody appeared more rapidly after immunizing injection with increasing age and by 16 days was almost as rapid as in the adult. The titre of antibody produced also increased rapidly with age at injection during the first month of life (Halliday 1964). Further work with injection of killed *Brucella abortus* antigen at birth showed that in a few instances circulating antibody appeared at 7 days of age and consistently by 10 days of age (Hervey 1966). Even prenatal injection of the antigen did not result in the production of antibody before 8 or 9 days of age. Hervey's results confirm those of Halliday and show that circulating bacterio-agglutinins do not appear consistently in young rats before about 10 days of age, irrespective of how early the antigenic stimulus is administered. Hervey (1966) suggests that the long delay between antigenic stimulation and the appearance of detectable circulating antibody may be due, at least in part, to slow clearance of the antigen leaving sufficient in the circulation to absorb out the antibody at first. Although bacterioagglutinins can be produced relatively early in life by young rats, during the period when the transmission of maternal passive immunity to other antigens is proceeding actively, this cannot be taken to mean that they are immunologically mature. The capacity to produce circulating precipitins to soluble antigens appears to develop very much later (Broughton, personal communication). This difference may be due to bacterioagglutinins when first produced in response to a primary immunization in rats being predominantly or exclusively in the γM-globulin fraction, especially when the antigen used is *Brucella*. Halliday (1957a) found that injection of *Salmonella pullorum* antigen at 10 and 15 days of age resulted in increasing quantities of antibody at 18, 21 and 24 days of age. At 24 days the antibody was found to be concentrated in the fractions which must have contained most of the γM-globulin, with very little in the γG-globulin fraction. Thus at the time when passive immunity acquired from the mothers is rapidly declining the development of active immunity is predominantly due to synthesis of macroglobulin antibodies. Thus it appears that the antibodies synthesized by very young rats are in a different globulin fraction to those acquired from the mother. Hence the very low level of γG-globulin concentration (0.9 mg/ml) in the serum of normal 24 day old rats is to be interpreted as due to the decline of that passively acquired before active production is well under way. Nevertheless, antigenic stimulation at 10 and 15 days of age does result in increased production of γG-globulin raising the minimum concentration at 24 days of age to 2.9 mg/ml (Halliday 1957a). At this time, however, the production of γM-globulin may be much more considerable (see p. 139). Kerman, Segre and Myers (1967, personal communication) found that the newborn young of female mice immunologically paralyzed to pneumococcal polysaccharide type III were immunologically paralyzed or were immunized by doses of the antigen in each case about $\frac{1}{10}$ the size of those necessary to induce a similar stage in the newborn young of normal mice. This difference was attributed to the absence of natural antibody of maternal origin in the young of the paralyzed mothers, an interpretation supported by the fact that difference from the controls declined gradually with age and could be eliminated by the administration of either the purified specific antibody to the polysaccharide antigen or normal γG-globulin, but not by γG-globulin that had first been adsorbed with the antigen.

The presence of passively acquired maternal antibody can interfere so long as it persists with the active production of antibody to the specific antigen. Halliday (1968) has shown that anti-*B. abortus* agglutinins of maternal origin, even at very low concentrations, can significantly inhibit the active production of agglutinins in young rats, but the effect is transient because of the decline in the passive immunity and the increasing potential for active immunity.

It is interesting that homologous skin grafts, and even heterologous ones such as chick skin, on new-born rats are stated (Steinmuller 1961) to heal into place and acquire a good blood supply within 3 days and persist for a further 5 to 10 days before they are rejected.

CHAPTER 6

Transmission of immunity in the guineapig, cat, dog and hedgehog

6.1. Introduction

There are a very few mammals, other than those to which separate chapters are being devoted, about which we have some knowledge of the manner in which passive immunity is transmitted from mother to young. The differences between them are such as to require separate treatment but their inclusion together in this chapter is on grounds of convenience rather than resemblance. Chief amongst these is the guineapig, then there are the dog and the cat about which information is curiously incomplete considering their availability, and the hedgehog concerning which all our knowledge derives from the work of Dr. B. Morris at Nottingham, despite the difficulties of the material.

6.2. Transmission of passive immunity in the guineapig

6.2.1. Development of the foetal membranes and placentation

The guineapig is remarkable in that it has a very long gestation period of 68 days for so small an animal and the young are born in a correspondingly advanced stage of development. Transmission of immunity takes place before birth and the route of transmission has been investigated experimentally. Therefore it is necessary to consider the manner of its early development and the arrangement of its foetal membranes. The excellent review of the embryological literature by Amoroso (1952) has been drawn on freely.

The fertilized egg reaches the uterus between the 3rd and 4th day and by the 6th day it has become lodged in the antimesometrial extremity of the slit-like lumen, apparently attaching itself to the uterine epithelium by processes of the trophoblast of the abembryonic pole which perforate the zona. The zona disappears on the 6th day and the blastocyst erodes and penetrates the uterine epithelium while it is still very small, only about $\frac{1}{10}$ mm in diameter. The process of implantation has been described in detail by Sansom and Hill (1931). The blastocyst lengthens as it implants in the meso-metrial/antimesometrial axis of the uterus, the embryonic knob or inner cell mass being at the antimesometrial end of the cylinder and the träger or ectoplacental cone of trophoblast at the mesometrial end. The endoderm differentiates as a covering of the antimesometrial hemisphere of the inner cell mass and extends to the base of the ectoplacental cone as a tube en-closing a cavity, which will become the exocoel. This tube of endoderm forms the splanchnic wall of the yolk-sac but an outer or bilaminar wall is not formed, the endoderm not extending to form a lining to the parietal trophoblast. The parietal trophoblast itself, after invading and destroying the adjacent decidual tissue, ceases by the 8th day to form a continuous layer and the splanchnic endoderm is left freely exposed in a cavity in the decidua. The amnion develops as a closed cavity from the beginning in the inner cell mass. As the blastocyst develops and expands the mucosa covering it bulges into the uterine cavity and by the tenth day is pushed against and fuses with its antimesometrial wall, obliterating the lumen of the uterus at this level. The mesoderm has extended and lined the exocoel and by the 13th day the anlage of the allantois grows out from the hinder end of the embryo as a solid stalk projecting into the exocoel. It enlarges and extends across the exocoel and becomes applied to the base of the ectoplacental cone, the trophoblast of which deeply invades the mesometrial mucosa, to form the allantochorionic placenta by the 20th day. Meanwhile, by the 15th day a uterine lumen has been established antimesometrially and the tissues between it and the implantation cavity break down, exposing the splanchnic endoderm in the uterine cavity. Thus, an arrangement of the embryonic membranes, broadly similar to that in the rat or the mouse, is brought about but in a rather different manner. The chief difference is that the yolk-sac splanchnopleur does not closely invest the allantoic stalk but is attached near the margin of the placenta. Consequently only the sides of the placenta are covered with endoderm and crypts of Duval are not formed. The placenta itself is of the haemochorial type resembling that of the rat or the mouse, but it is divided into lobules by spongy syncytial tropho-blast in which only maternal blood circulates, the trophoblastic tubules invested with foetal capillaries being confined to the lobules. The disc-shaped placenta is very concave on its foetal surface and the central region, lying deeper than the rest, is known as the sub-placenta and has a structure somewhat different from the other lobules, the functional significance of which is not understood.

6.2.2. *Transmission of homologous antibodies from mother to young*

Much of the earlier work on the transmission of immunity was on guineapigs and before the turn of the century it was known that it occurred before birth. There was also evidence that it did not occur after birth. Widal and Sicard (1897) actively immunized two guineapigs with *Salmonella typhi*, one immediately and the other three days after parturition. Another guineapig was passively immunized over 20 days with a total of 50 ml of immune serum with a titre of $\frac{1}{43,000}$ and had a titre in the circulation of $\frac{1}{800}$. The young were reared entirely on their mother's milk and on weaning at 24 days of age they had no trace of agglutinins in their sera. Their mother's milk never had a titre of more than $\frac{1}{10}$ to $\frac{1}{30}$. Staübli (1903) found that typhoid agglutinins, whether actively produced or passively acquired, were transmitted from mother to foetus. The longer the interval between immunization of the mother and parturition the higher was the agglutinin titre of the foetal serum and the more nearly it approached to that of the maternal serum. He noted that there was little variation in agglutinin levels between siblings. Anderson (1906) showed that the offspring of guineapigs immunized against diphtheria with a mixture of toxin and horse antitoxin had antitoxin in their sera and were anaphylactically sensitive to horse serum, hence sensitizing antibody also had been transmitted. Ratner, Jackson and Gruehl (1927b) also sensitized guineapigs to horse serum by injection and found that sensitivity was transmitted to their offspring before birth but not after birth (1927a). The sensitivity passively acquired persisted for about $2\frac{1}{2}$ months, in some degree occasionally up to 4 months. Subsequently Ratner and Gruehl (1929) sensitized guineapigs by inhalation to horse dander dust and showed that their newborn young exhibited respiratory anaphylaxis when exposed to the dust. Schneider and Szathmary (1940) found that the newborn young which had received diphtheria antitoxins from their mothers had titres equal to or higher than those of the maternal serum. The titre of the colostrum was substantially lower than that of the maternal serum and no transmission took place after birth. Jo (1953) actively immunized guineapigs with *Reckettsiae typhi* or *R. prowazeki* before and during gestation or passively during gestation with guineapig or rabbit antisera. Cross-nursing experiments, in which the newborn young of immunized and normal guineapigs were exchanged, were performed. The complement fixing antibodies were transmitted to the young before birth but not via the colostrum and milk after birth. The antibody was demonstrated also in the foetal amniotic fluid in one pregnant guineapig which had a high level of immunity. Barnes (1959), in a more detailed study, found that pregnant guineapigs which had been actively immunized before pregnancy and had a stable titre of diphtheria antitoxin transmitted the antibody to their foetuses from the 35th day of gestation onwards. The foetal serum titre rose from nil at 30 days to equality with the maternal serum titre at about 52 days and to *c.* 2.6 times the maternal serum titre at 60 days, falling slightly to 2.3 times at

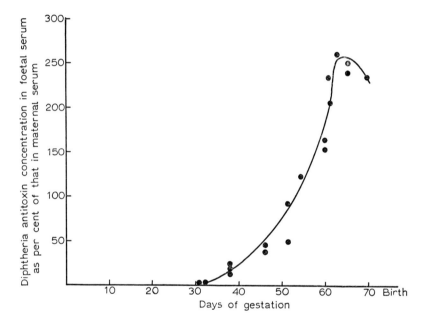

Fig. 6.1. The concentrations of diphtheria antitoxin in the sera of the foetuses of guineapigs, actively immunized before pregnancy, expressed as percentages of the concentrations in the maternal sera. (From Barnes 1959.)

parturition (fig. 6.1). A small amount of antitoxin was present also in the exocoelomic and amniotic fluids and in the stomach contents. Washings of the uterine lumen contained antitoxin. Injection of guineapig diphtheria antitoxic serum, with or without refined horse tetanus antitoxin, into the uterine lumina of guineapigs pregnant for 44, 55 and 63 days resulted in transmission of antitoxin to the foetal serum, amniotic fluid and stomach contents. Antitoxin from guineapig serum administered by stomach tube to 50–64 day foetuses was not transmitted to their circulations. The vitelline circulations of the yolk-sacs of some foetuses were ligatured, others in the same uteri being left as controls, and the uterine and body-wall incisions were then sutured. The mother was passively immunized by intracardiac injection of homologous serum. In seven experiments none of the foetuses with ligated vitelline vessels had detectable amounts of antitoxin in their sera after 24 hr, whereas all the control foetuses with intact vitelline circulations had antitoxin in their sera.

Leissring and Anderson (1961a) actively immunized guineapigs from the beginning of gestation to *B. abortus* and used a modified Coombs test that should detect incomplete as well as complete antibodies. They found, like Barnes, that antibodies could be detected first in the foetuses at 35 days of gestation. The C.Q., or concentration relative to that in the maternal circulation, increased with gestational age and reached $\frac{1}{2}$ to $\frac{1}{1}$ by 50 days, remaining at this level to full term. Pregnant guineapigs also were passively immunized with guineapig anti-*Brucella* serum from 45 days of gestation onwards and the foetal sera were tested after an interval of 24 hr. Antibody was present in the foetal sera in all cases and at C.Q.'s of $\frac{1}{1}$ from 60 days of gestation to birth. A single experiment at 60 days in which the foetal serum was harvested after only 2 hr showed a C.Q. of $\frac{1}{1}$ even after this short period of exposure. The maternal sera from the active immunization experiment were used for the passive immunization. It is puzzling that as none of these exceeded $\frac{1}{2560}$ and although large doses of 5–14 ml were used, titres of $\frac{1}{2560}$ were attained by passive immunization in 4 cases, a level which allows for no dilution in the circulation and extravascular fluid of the recipient. Some experiments were performed in which the uterus was opened and the conceptuses exposed in the peritoneal cavity with (a) the foetal membranes opened but otherwise complete, or (b) the vitelline vessels ligated and the yolk-sac removed, or (c) the vitelline vessels ligated, the yolk-sac removed and the mouth and nose ligated, or (d) the foetal membranes opened but otherwise complete and the mouth and nose ligated. The body wall incision was sutured, 5 ml of immune serum was injected into the peritoneal cavity and the serum of the foetuses harvested after they had been exposed to the immune serum for 2 hr. Those with yolk-sacs (a) all had antibody in their sera but the titres tended to be lower after 50 days gestation than before. Those without yolk-sacs (b) had very variable titres but these tended to be lower as compared to those of foetuses with yolk-sacs. Ligation of the mouth and nose before 50 days gestation tended to lower the titre still more and after 50 days no antibody was detected in most cases. These results were taken to suggest that the yolk-sac was the principal route of transmission up to 40 days gestation and that the foetal gut was the principal route after 50 days gestation. The exocoelomic and amniotic fluids and stomach contents were said to have a small amount of antibody in them from 35 days, but it is not clear whether this was after active or passive immunization or both. Since the number of experiments was small and the results somewhat conflicting, confirmation is required before the foetal gut can be accepted as a principal route of transmission in the guineapig. These authors (Leissring and Anderson 1961b) also fed by stomach tube guineapigs at ages ranging from 0 to to 7 days with either 1 or 2 ml of guineapig anti-*Brucella abortus* serum and determined the titres of their sera after 24 hr by both the direct agglutination method and by a modified Coombs test for both agglutinating and incomplete antibodies. They obtained C.Q.'s of complete agglutinins from birth to 1 day of $\frac{1}{2}$, falling to below the limit of sensitivity of $\frac{1}{128}$ at ages over 3 days. The Coombs test gave C.Q.'s of equality from birth to 1 day old, thereafter varying from $\frac{1}{2}$ to $\frac{1}{8}$ up to 7 days of age, beyond which age the tests were not continued. Levels such as these seem almost incredible as the serum volume alone of the newborn guineapig is likely to have equalled or exceeded the maximum dose of 2 ml and excluding the probability of equilibration with the extravascular compartment it would require complete efficiency of absorption of all the antibody in the largest dose of 2 ml and its total retention in the circulation to attain a C.Q. of $\frac{1}{1}$. Moreover the results are out of line with those of many other workers using well-tried and reliable techniques.

   Thorell (1962) immunized female guineapigs to insulin before mating them. Their sera had sufficient antibody for 1 ml to bind 50% or 0.1 mg insulin-[131]I. The foetal sera near term were even more active and bound 100% undiluted, and 50% at $\frac{1}{4}$ dilution. Block, Ovary, Kourilsky and Benacerraf (1963) showed that guineapigs immunized with 2,4-dinitrofluorobenzene-conjugated bovine γ-globulin or albumin produced both $7S\gamma_1$ and $7S\gamma_2$ antibodies. The $7S\gamma_1$ antibody sensitized guineapigs for passive systemic or cutaneous anaphylaxis, but the $7S\gamma_2$ antibodies did not do so. The $7S\gamma_2$ antibodies fixed complement *in vitro* and lysed in the presence of complement red cells coated with antigen, whereas the $7S\gamma_1$ antibodies did not do so. Both antibodies were transmitted equally readily from both actively and passively immunized pregnant guineapigs to their foetuses. Both γ_1- and γ_2-globulins could be detected in the milk but only the skin-sensitizing antibodies could be shown to be present, as the complement fixing antibodies could not be tested for technical reasons.

Al-Najdi (1965) carried out a careful investigation of transmission in guineapigs. She found that both diphtheria and tetanus antitoxins were transferred from actively immunized mothers to their young at closely similar rates. The C.Q. of the foetal serum increased from 0.025 at 30 days gestation to 0.67 at 60 days and to 2.95 at full term for diphtheria antitoxin, and from 0.51 at 60 days to 2.11 at full term for tetanus antitoxin. Thus the C.Q. increased rapidly during the last week of gestation. The C.Q. of amniotic fluid increased from about 0.00022 at 30 days to 0.0043 at 60 days and the amount of antitoxin in the stomach contents did not exceed that of the corresponding amniotic fluid. Antitoxin from immune serum injected into the uterine cavity at 41 to 56 days of gestation entered the foetal circulation and the amniotic fluid, but the concentration in the amniotic fluid was very much less than in the serum.

6.2.3. Transmission of heterologous antibodies from mother to young

The transmission of antitoxins prepared in guineapigs and in horses was examined by Hartley (1948, 1951). Three forms of each were compared, natural serum, ammonium sulphate concentrated, and pepsin-refined antitoxin. The natural guineapig antitoxin, whether from whole serum or concentrated, was transmitted readily and attained concentrations in the sera of the newborn young exceeding those in the maternal sera by as much as twice when the interval between injection and parturition was more than 1 day. Natural horse antitoxin was transmitted also but less readily than guineapig. Pepsin-refined guineapig antitoxin was not transmitted at detectable levels and pepsin-refined horse antitoxin was transmitted only at very low levels. Barnes (1959) compared the transmission of guineapig diphtheria antitoxin with refined horse tetanus antitoxin by injecting both together into the uterine lumen of guineapigs late in gestation. She found that both antitoxins reached the amniotic fluid and foetal stomach contents at approximately equal, but low, levels; the guineapig antitoxin reached the foetal serum 20 times more readily than the horse antitoxin. Al-Najdi (1965) studied the transmission after intravenous injection from the maternal circulation to the foetal circulation of rabbit, human, horse and of refined horse antitoxins at various stages of gestation. Rabbit and human antitoxins were transmitted in significant amounts, but horse antitoxin, whether crude or refined, only in trace amounts. The concentrations attained in the amniotic fluid were very low. Both human tetanus antitoxin and guineapig diphtheria antitoxin were used in one experiment and the homologous antitoxin was transferred slightly more than twice as readily as the heterologous antitoxin. Homologous and various heterologous antitoxins were injected into the uterine lumen at 41–56 days of gestation. The guineapig antitoxin entered the foetal circulation from the uterine lumen more readily than human or rabbit antitoxins and much more readily than crude or refined horse antitoxin or cow antitoxin. The concentrations of antitoxins attained in the amniotic fluid were much lower than those in the foetal sera, but homologous and heterologous antitoxins entered the amniotic fluid at almost similar rates. The concentrations of antitoxins, whether homologous or heterologous, in the stomach contents did not exceed those in the corresponding amniotic fluids. Pepsin-refined homologous antitoxin injected into the uterine lumen on the 45th day of gestation could not be detected in the foetal circulation at the lowest level tested though it, and all the heterologous antitoxins, entered the maternal circulation at approximately the same rate as natural guineapig antitoxin.

6.2.4. *Transmission of other serum proteins from mother to young*

The transmission of horse serum proteins in guineapigs 40–50 days pregnant was studied by Nattan-Larrier and Richard (1929). They used a test involving complement fixation by rabbit anti-horse antibody which they found had a sensitivity for a $1/10^6$ dilution of horse serum. The horse serum was injected either intracardially or subcutaneously and the foetal sera were harvested after intervals of from 10 min to 72 hr. They found that the heterologous protein was transmitted in very small amounts and very slowly. Kulangara and Schechtman (1963) injected human albumin, bovine albumin and human γ-globulin into pregnant guineapigs and found that after 24 hr all three were present in the foetal sera in relatively large amounts, but only traces were found in the exocoelomic and amniotic fluids.

Dancis and Shafran (1958), using guineapig serum proteins isotopically labelled, either *in vivo* with ^{35}S or *in vitro* with ^{131}I, showed that other plasma proteins as well as γ-globulin are transferred from mother to foetus in large amounts during the last two weeks of gestation. Incorporation of radioactivity into foetal tissues when *in vivo* ^{35}S-labelled proteins were used suggested considerable degradation and reutilization by the foetus. Further experiments with similarly labelled chicken plasma proteins injected into the mother confirmed that a large proportion of the radioactivity reaching the foetal serum was no longer borne by intact protein precipitable by anti-chicken serum, though some of it was precipitable. Injection of ^{35}S-methionine into the near-term foetus showed that it could synthesize all the electrophoretically recognisable plasma proteins except γ-globulin and injection into the mother showed that this amino acid was transferred to the foetus.

Thorbecke (1964) investigated the age of guineapigs at which the synthesis of immune globulins began. He used the incorporation of ^{14}C-labelled amino acids in these globulins by spleen and mesenteric lymph nodes of foetuses and young animals. The fractions were identified and their activity determined by autoradiography of immunoelectrophoretograms. He found that synthesis of γM-globulin could be demonstrated in the foetal spleen and in spleen and lymph nodes of newborn animals. Synthesis of γ_2G-globulin began 2 weeks after birth and that of γ_1G-globulin not until 1 month after birth. Manzallo and Martino (1963) found that young guineapigs responded to immunization with diphtheria toxoid at 10 days of age, and that at 15 days of age they responded as well as adults. They claimed that the presence of antitoxin passively acquired from the mother did not prevent immunization.

6.2.5. Changes in the yolk-sac and alimentary canal

An account of the structure of the yolk-sac under the electron microscope, including the brush border of microvilli and the apical canalliculi of the endoderm cells is given by Dempsey (1953). Anderson and Leissring (1961) examined the histological and histochemical changes in the foetal yolk-sac and in the foetal and neonatal intestine of the guineapig. They found that the yolk-sac appeared to become less active after 50 days gestation, with reduction of glycogen content and of alkaline phosphatase activity as well as of the ability to absorb fluorescent-labelled serum proteins. The intestine, on the other hand, showed marked increase in development from 50 days gestation, with the appearance of alkaline phosphatase and of uptake of fluorescent-labelled serum proteins. They considered that these findings supported their contention that transmission of immunity after 50 days gestation is by way of the intestine rather than the yolk-sac. Very different conclusions can be drawn from the work of Hill (1956) who examined the stomachs of foetuses from 47 days of gestation and of newborn young up to 1 day old. He found that the gastric glands were well-defined in late foetal life and that by 1 hr after birth the gastric mucosa closely resembled that of the adult. Numerous parietal cells were present and moderate numbers of pepsinogen granules were to be found in the peptic cells. The stomach contents of foetuses of 47–55 days gestation was at pH 7.0–8.0 but at 68 days gestation this had changed to pH 4.0 and in all the newborn young it was at pH 1.0–2.0, whether milk clot was present or absent. He noted that protein globules were not seen in the small intestine of the young guineapig after ingestion of colostrum. These results suggest that immune globulins would be unlikely to reach the small intestine of the newborn guineapig un-degraded. They are in striking contrast to those with rats in which the gastric glands were very poorly developed at birth and were not fully developed, nor did the stomach contents fall below pH 4.0, until after 18 days of age.

6.2.6. Conclusions

It is clear that transmission of a wide variety of antibodies occurs before birth in guineapigs and that the level of antitoxins in the serum of the newborn young of actively immune mothers is normally at least double that in the maternal serum. There is satisfactory evidence that transmission *in utero* occurs by way of the yolk-sac and vitelline circulation but the evidence that transmission occurs also by way of the foetal gut is unconvincing at present. It is apparent that transmission is highly selective both as between homologous and various heterologous antibodies and as between the various serum proteins. Evidently removal of the Fc-part of the molecule of homologous γ-globulin by pepsin-refining renders it unacceptable for transmission. The evidence of transmission after birth is conflicting, but that which is the more convincing and is advanced by most workers indicates that it does not occur at a significant level and this conclusion is in accord with what is known of the low level of antibody in the mammary secretions and with gastric pH levels. It would be particularly interesting to know if γ-globulins from different species, or Fc-fragments, can interfere with the transmission of other γ-globulins from the uterine lumen to the foetal circulation, as knowledge of this phenomenon is confined at present to the rat and the mouse.

6.3. *Transmission of passive immunity in the cat and the dog*

The cat and the dog can be considered together conveniently because from what little is known of the process in these two species it would appear that it is essentially similar and takes place to a small but definite extent before birth and mainly during a short period after birth. Such information as is available concerning transmission before birth provides no clue as to the precise route, so that only a short account of the development and arrangement of the foetal membranes and placenta is required as it throws no light on this problem at present but might serve to encourage its investigation.

6.3.1. *Development of the foetal membranes and placentation*

A good description of the embryology of the dog and the cat has been provided by Amoroso (1952), and as these species resemble each other fairly closely in their development they can be considered together in this respect, as well as concerning transmission. Gestation lasts 60–63 days in the cat and 58–63 days in the dog. The eggs take about 6 days to traverse the Fallopian tubes and reach the uterus. The eggs, after becoming spaced out in the uterus, enlarge considerably, like those of the rabbit, and become orientated with their embryonic plates more or less antimesometrial and exposed at the surface. Implantation is central and begins about the 13–14th day in the cat and the 16–17th day in the dog. At first the wall of the blastocyst as it begins to implant consists of the bilaminar wall of the yolk-sac composed of endoderm and trophoblast. The yolk-sac cavity is large. The amnion arises by fold formation, as in the rabbit. The chorionic trophoblast adheres to the uterine mucosa over a transverse area forming a band or zone around the blastocyst which will become the placenta. The uterine epithelium and that of the glands over this area degenerate to form a symplasma and the trophoblast invades and destroys this and the connective tissue immediately underlying it, so that the maternal vascular endothelium of the capillaries comes to be in direct contact with the trophoblast. Meanwhile, the extension of the mesoderm and coelom is proceeding and gradually transforming the bilaminar wall of the yolk-sac first into a trilaminar wall which then becomes progressively split by the exocoel into chorion and yolk-sac splanchnopleur. The whole of the yolk-sac wall becomes very vascular and at first the placental region is supplied by this vitelline circulation. Meanwhile the allantois grows out from the embryo into the exocoel and makes contact with the chorion by the 18–20th day, finally expanding to completely fill the exocoel and envelop the amnion, thereby providing both the chorion and amnion

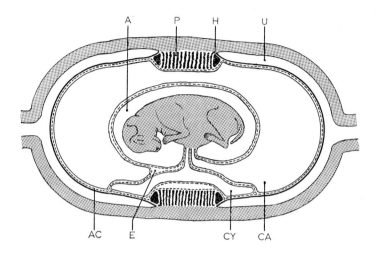

Fig. 6.2. Diagram of the final arrangement of the foetal membranes of the dog shown in longitudinal section of the uterus. A, amniotic cavity; AC, allantochorion; CA, cavity of allantois; CY, cavity of yolk-sac; E, exocoel; H, haematoma at the margin of the zonary placenta; P, encircling the conceptus; U, uterine lumen. (Modified after Amoroso 1952.)

with an allantoic vasculature (fig. 6.2). By the 21–24th day the yolk-sac has been separated from the chorion, except where it remains permanently attached at its tip, and the allantoic vasculature has replaced the vitelline as the supply to the zonary placenta. The allantochorionic placental labyrinth, when fully developed, occupies two-thirds or more of the thickness of the placenta and consists of lamellae arranged more or less vertically to the surface. These lamellae enclose the maternal capillaries which are surrounded and enclosed by the syncytial and cellular trophoblast, the foetal capillaries being situated in the loose mesenchyme between the lamellae. The zonary placenta thus is of the endotheliochorial type in which the maternal vascular endothelium persists as the only maternal tissue intervening between the maternal blood and the foetal trophoblast which envelops the maternal vessels. Maternal blood is extravasated, however, at the edge of the placenta and forms the two marginal haematomas on each side of it, which are so characteristic of these animals.

The allantochorionic placenta is fully established by about the end of the fourth week. It is clear from this description that prior to implantation materials could reach the yolk-sac cavity by traversing the bilaminar wall. In the early stages of placentation it is the yolk-sac which provides the vasculature and at this stage it would appear to be still an important absorptive organ. What functions it may continue to perform after the placenta has been provided with an allantoic circulation is an open question, but although the yolk-sac becomes relatively reduced in size it retains its rich vasculature and persists to full term as a wrinkled sac still attached by its tip to the chorion and enclosed in the umbilical cord. Thus, it is not possible to define the probable route of transmission of passive immunity before birth in these animals on the morphological evidence and an experimental approach to this interesting problem is clearly indicated.

6.3.2. Transmission of immunity in the cat

In 1897 Widal and Sicard injected a cat 3 days after parturition with 4 ml of a broth culture of *Salmonella*. Agglutinins appeared in the milk after 3 days and the titre of the milk rose to $\frac{1}{400}$ by 10 days after inoculation, when the serum titre was $\frac{1}{3,000}$. Another cat immediately after parturition was given 10 ml of donkey serum with a titre of $\frac{1}{43,000}$, and this dose was repeated every 2 days until it had received 50 ml. Its serum did not exceed a titre of $\frac{1}{1,200}$ and its milk of $\frac{1}{150}$. The kittens of both these cats were maintained exclusively on their mother's milk but did not acquire any agglutinins in their sera. Two young cats, respectively 1 month and 6 weeks old, were fed exclusively on goat's milk with a titre of $\frac{1}{300}$ to $\frac{1}{400}$ for 6 weeks but did not have any agglutinins in their sera. It was concluded that transmission did not occur after birth, whereas the failure of the kittens to exhibit transmission was clearly due to their not receiving the immunity sufficiently soon after birth. Harding, Bruner and Bryant (1961) immunized three cats during the last $\frac{1}{3}$ of gestation with *Salmonella montevideo*. Their serum titres at parturition were *c.* $\frac{1}{3,000}$, and the colostral titre was $\frac{1}{400}$, falling after 24 hr to $\frac{1}{200}$ and after 1 week to $\frac{1}{20}$ in the milk. The kittens at birth had serum titres of *c.* $\frac{1}{200}$ before suckling but these rose to $\frac{1}{1,000}$ after suckling and remained at this level for a week before falling gradually to $\frac{1}{20}$ by 1 month after birth. Kulangara and Schechtman (1963) intravenously injected pregnant cats in the last week of gestation with human or bovine serum albumin or human γ-globulin and tested the foetal fluids for these proteins 24 hr later. Both albumins passed to the foetal sera in large amounts, the human at $\frac{1}{4}$ to $\frac{1}{2}$ of the concentration attained in the maternal serum and the bovine at $\frac{1}{32}$, whereas the γ-globulin was transmitted in significant but much smaller amounts. The albumins were found also, according to the authors, in large amounts in the exocoelomic and amniotic fluids and stomach contents, but the γ-globulin only in trace amounts in these fluids. It seems probable that the authors mistook the plentiful allantoic fluid for exocoelomic fluid, which would scarcely exist at so late a stage.

Coles (1957) observed that the high γ-globulin level in the serum of 2-day old kittens declined to a minimum at 21 days of age and rose progressively after 5–6 weeks of age. Albumin, α- and β-globulins in the serum showed little change with age. The total serum protein was minimal at 4 days old at a level of 3.8 g/100 ml and increased steadily thereafter.

Comline, Pomeroy and Titchen (1953) found globules 0.5–10 μ in diameter, that stained with iron haematoxylin or azocarmine, in the endoderm cells of the small intestines of newborn kittens 6–18 hr after ingestion of colostrum. Similar material was present in the lacteals 15–18 hr after suckling. This material was absent from the cells and the lacteals of newborn kittens which had not suckled. Large vacuoles were present also in the cells of near term foetuses and of newborn young whether or not they had suckled.

6.3.3. Transmission of immunity in the dog

Mason, Dalling and Gordon (1930) injected subcutaneously 14,000 units of horse diphtheria antitoxin into a bitch that had no natural antitoxin in its serum 4 days before parturition. It is not stated whether this was natural or refined horse antitoxin. At parturition the bitch's serum had $<5 >3$ units/ml and her milk 2 units/ml. One pup, which may have suckled before it was observed, had no antitoxin in its serum at first but after 24 hr it had $<5 >2$ units/ml. Another pup was given by mouth 5 ml of horse serum containing 16,000 units of tetanus antitoxin and after 24 hr it had $<2 >0.2$ units/ml. It was concluded that heterologous antitoxin in the circulation of a bitch is secreted in the colostrum and that it can be absorbed by the newborn pup either from colostrum or from serum. Schneider and Szathmary (1939b) immunized three pregnant bitches with both *Salmonella typhi* cultures and diphtheria toxoid, one so late that antibody had not been formed at parturition, one in which parturition occurred while the titre was still rising. Two of the bitches had natural anti-*Escherichia coli* agglutinins in their sera. Two litters were bred from each of these bitches. The antibody levels were determined in the maternal serum and colostrum at parturition and in the milk later, and in the sera of the pups before and after suckling and at intervals after birth. The antibody titres of all three anti-bodies in the colostra tended to be 5–10 times those in the maternal sera, but the levels fell rapidly with suckling to levels much less than those of the sera. The newborn young before suckling had titres of anti-*E. coli* aggluti-nins *c.* $\frac{1}{5}$ of those of the maternal sera, but the relative titres of the anti-*Salmonella* agglutinins tended to be lower and those of the antitoxin were less than $\frac{1}{50}$. After suckling the titres of all three antibodies in the pups sera rose rapidly to levels of $\frac{1}{2}$ to equality of those in the maternal sera in most cases. Carmichael, Robson and Barnes (1962) found that puppies get most of their passive immunity to infectious canine hepatitis by way of the colostrum after birth, maximum titres not being attained until 3 days old. The puppies serum titre was related to the maternal serum titre as:

$$\log_{10} \text{(titre of puppy serum)} = 0.92 \log_{10} \text{(maternal serum titre)} - 0.16.$$

The half-life of the antibody in the circulation of the puppies was 8.6 days. Puppies without antibody could be actively immunized to the live virus at any age. Gillette and Filkins (1966) fed puppies deprived of colostrum at various intervals after birth with dog serum hyperimmune to *Salmonella pullorum* and tested their sera at intervals thereafter. Absorption of anti-body was optimal at *c.* 8 hr old, was almost complete by 15 hr old and had ceased by 24 hr old (fig. 6.3). They estimated that by 15 hr after feeding $\frac{2}{3}$ of the antibody in the dose of 3 ml/100 g body weight of immune serum had been transmitted to the puppies circulation. Bitches passively immunized with the serum up to 24 hr before parturition did not transmit antibody to the foetal serum at the detectable level of 3% of the antibody in the dose. Injection of the bitches with ACTH or hydrocortisone 24 hr before parturi-tion significantly reduced the absorption of antibodies from serum by the newborn puppies, but injection of the puppies themselves with hydrocor-tisone, progesterone or an adrenal inhibitor shortly before feeding them with the immune serum did not have a significant effect on absorption. Filkins and Gillette (1966) kept puppies from birth (a) on the bitch, or (b) on a balanced protein diet, or (c) on sucrose saline, or (d) without food and water. Each was given 3 ml/100 g of hyperimmune dog anti-*Salmonella pullorum* serum by stomach tube at birth or at least 4 hr after the last feed and its serum titre determined 12–15 hr later. The diet did not affect signi-

ficantly the titres of their sera but those on the natural diet ceased to absorb
antibody at 24 hr old whereas those on the sucrose diet continued to do so

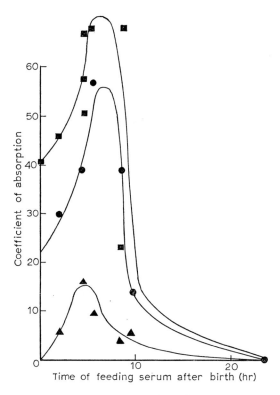

Fig. 6.3. Diagram of the effect of delaying feeding of hyperimmune homologous serum
to puppies at various times after birth. The coefficient of absorption is the percentage in
the circulation of antibody in the dose administered. It was determined at intervals of
5 (▲), 10 (●) and 15 (▆) hr after administration, absorption being practically complete at
15 hr. Maximum transmission resulted from feeding the immune serum about 8 hr after
birth. (From Gillette and Filkins 1966.)

up to 36 hr old; none continued longer (fig. 6.4). The use of fluorescent-
labelled globulin showed that absorption took place primarily in the jejunum
and ileum. The fluorescence was in the cells 1–2 hr after feeding and it was
sub-mucosal 3–4 hr after feeding. It was detectable up to 24 hr of age in the
puppies on the natural diet and up to 28 hr of age in those on the artificial
diets, but not thereafter.

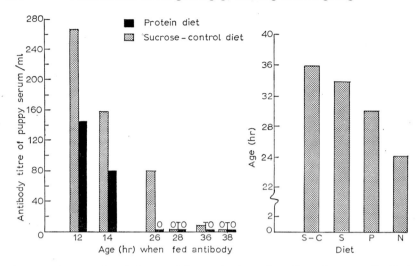

Fig. 6.4. Diagrams of the influence of diet on the absorption of homologous antibodies by newborn puppies. The diagram on the left compares the absorption in puppies fed on a milk-substitute diet containing protein with that in puppies fed on sucrose–saline. The diagram on the right compares the periods during which absorption continues in puppies fed on these diets and in those starved or naturally reared on the bitch. (From Filkins and Gillette 1966.)

McCance, Hutchinson, Dean and Jones (1949) found an enormous cholinesterase activity in the colostrum of bitches. Puppies that suckled showed a large rise in serum cholinesterase during the first three days whereas those fed on evaporated cow's milk showed no corresponding rise. This was considered evidence of the passive transmission of the enzyme. However, subsequent work on the rat suggests that the increase in cholinesterase may have been autogenous in the puppies, as it is in rats.

Whipple, Hill, Terry, Lucas and Yuile (1955) administered to pregnant bitches dog plasma proteins labelled *in vivo* with [14]C. After intravenous administration relatively little of the activity was transferred to the foetuses but when given orally relatively large quantities were transferred promptly. Plasma proteins labelled with ^{131}I were not transferred. It was estimated that not more than 200–300 mg/day of maternal plasma protein or its derivatives reaches each foetus, but the quantities of dietary protein that do so after digestion are very much larger.

6.3.4. Conclusions

It is clear from these results that both in the cat and the dog there is a significant transmission of passive immunity before birth but that the transmission after birth is greater. It is also apparent that transmission after birth is intense and short lasting, having ceased by 1 or 2 days of age. The colostrum, as in other animals in which transmission after birth is very limited in duration, concentrates antibodies to several times the maternal serum concentration and many times that of the subsequent milk. Heterologous, as well as homologous serum proteins are transmitted from the maternal circulation to that of the offspring both before and after birth, but the evidence is insufficient to determine if transmission is selective. Haemolytic disease of the newborn in dogs will be considered subsequently (pp. 294–295).

6.4. Transmission of passive immunity in the hedgehog

The hedgehog is the only wild animal of which we have any substantial knowledge of the transmission of immunity. Dr. Brinley Morris and his associates at Nottingham have shown how it is possible to obtain a large amount of information concerning transmission from a somewhat intractable and difficult animal. Practically all of the few species mentioned in this book have enhanced significantly our knowledge of this process and it is probable that work on a few other species, preferably of groups not so far represented, would be worth while. The hedgehog provides an example of how this can be done.

6.4.1. Development of the foetal membranes and placentation

The development of the foetal membranes and placenta of the hedgehog has received comparatively little attention since the appearance of the classical paper by Hubrecht (1889), which is still the authority. The blastocyst implants excentrically and antimesometrially while it is still small. The uterine lumen is roughly T-shaped, the cleft-like stem of the T being directed antimesometrially and the blastocyst lodges in the tip of this. The uterine decidual tissues close over it to form the decidua capsularis, which separates the implanting blastocyst from the mesometrial portion of the uterine lumen that persists throughout pregnancy. Consequent on this early implantation while the blastocyst is still small, the amnion is formed by cavitation from a closed cavity which appears in the inner cell mass. The yolk-sac cavity is lined by endoderm throughout which together with the overlying trophoblast forms the bilaminar omphalopleur. The implanted blastocyst is orientated with the embryonic region antimesometrial and the yolk-sac with its covering of decidua capsularis mesometrial. Once implanted, the blastocyst enlarges rapidly. The trophoblast, which is thickest antimesometrially, grows into the gland mouths and invades the maternal tissues, especially antimesometrially and laterally. The uterine epithelium breaks down and disappears. The endothelial cells of the mucosal blood vessels enlarge and give rise to a trophospongia, with the maternal blood in the lacunae, and which, after a time, is difficult to distinguish from the invading syncytiotrophoblast. Meanwhile the mesoderm and exocoel extend, separating the amnion and the upper hemisphere of the yolk-sac from the chorion (fig. 6.5). The mesoderm extends beyond the equator, forming a

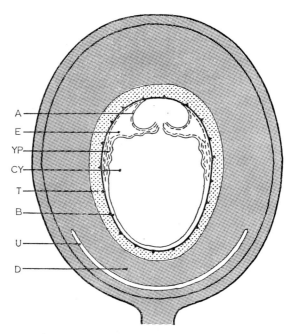

Fig. 6.5. Diagram of a transverse section of a conceptus of the hedgehog showing the arrangement of the embryonic membranes at an early stage of development. A, amnion; B, bilaminar omphalopleur; CY, cavity of yolk-sac; D, decidua capsularis; E, exocoel; T, trophospongia; U, uterine lumen; YP, yolk-sac placenta. (After Morris, B. 1957.)

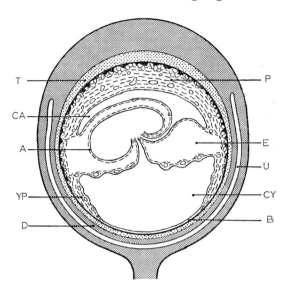

Fig. 6.6. Diagram of a transverse section of a conceptus of the hedgehog showing the final arrangement of the embryonic membranes. CA, cavity of allantois; P, allanto-chorionic placenta; other key letters as in fig. 6.5. (After Morris 1953.)

band of vascular trilaminar omphalopleur encircling the blastocyst and leaving only the lower third of the yolk-sac wall bilaminar (Morris 1953). This region remains bilaminar and persists to term (fig. 6.6). The band of trilaminar omphalopleur is the first region to become vascularised by the vitelline vessels and gives rise to a true yolk-sac placenta. The maternal blood in the lacunae of the trophospongium and syncytiotrophoblast is only separated from the foetal in this region by a thin layer of trophoblast and the foetal capillary walls, so that the placenta is haemochorial. The allantois grows out from the embryo into the exocoel and makes contact with the chorion antimesometrially, thus vascularising and transforming it into an allantochorionic placenta. The extension laterally of the vascular splanchnic mesoderm of the allantois gradually takes over from the vitelline circulation the vascularising of the whole placental region. The growth of the foetus in its amnion presses on and inverts the splanchnic wall of the yolk-sac so that its cavity comes to be crescentic, but it persists as a sizeable structure to term, although once the allantochorionic placenta is formed it would appear to be less important as an absorptive organ. A Reichert's membrane is formed between the trophoblast and the somatic mesoderm of the chorion (Morris 1957). At first thin, this membrane soon thickens and it persists to term. The duration of pregnancy is between 35 and 39 days (Morris 1961a). Morris (1961b) suggests that the yolk-sac has the morphological appearance of being an important absorptive organ up to about the 7-mm stage but that it subsequently retrogresses and appears to be less active and that in consequence the allantochorionic placenta is the more probable route of transmission before birth.

6.4.2. Transmission of immunity

Morris (1959, 1960) immunized hedgehogs before and during pregnancy with *Brucella abortus* killed antigen and obtained titres in their sera of $\frac{1}{160}$ to $\frac{1}{1280}$, and in their milk of from $\frac{1}{4}$ to 4 times those in the corresponding serum. The newborn young of these animals had no agglutinins at detectable levels in their sera before suckling, but after suckling agglutinins were present at titres of $\frac{1}{10}$ to $\frac{1}{40}$, a maximum C.Q. of $\frac{1}{32}$. These titres persisted almost unchanged until weaning at 39 days of age, but had disappeared by 66 days. Subsequently (Morris 1961b) female hedgehogs were hyperimmunized with *Salmonella pullorum* killed antigen before pregnancy and developed agglutinin titres of $\frac{1}{5120}$ to $\frac{1}{20,480}$. The young of these animals were born with circulating agglutinins at C.Q. of $\frac{1}{8}$ to $\frac{1}{32}$ and after suckling at 4–6 days of age had a C.Q. of $\frac{1}{2}$. There was no fall in the serum titre of suckling young at 30 days of age, but by 40 days of age the titre had fallen to $\frac{1}{4}$ to $\frac{1}{2}$ of its previous level. Young hedgehogs have an average birth weight of 15 g and at 27–30 days of age weighed 170–178 g, an increase of about 12 times the birth weight; that the antibody titre remained constant while the fluid volume increased in this proportion clearly implied continued uptake of antibody from the milk. The antibody titre of the milk shortly after parturition was $\frac{1}{2}$ that of the maternal serum and it remained at this level throughout lactation. The 7 day old young of a non-immune mother produced anti-*Brucella* agglutinins 5 days after a single subcutaneous injection of the antigen. At 3 weeks of age their capacity for the active production of agglutinins had improved considerably.

   Suspecting that this striking difference between the transmission of homologous agglutinins to *Brucella* and to *Salmonella* might be due to differences in their distribution among the immune globulins Morris and Baldwin (1962) set out to explore this problem by electrophoretic fractionation in starch gel. Sera arising from a single injection of antigen and from hyperimmunization with *Brucella abortus* and also with *Salmonella pullorum* were fractionated and compared. Anti-*Brucella* agglutinins arising from a single injection were found to be distributed with 80% of the activity in the β-region and even after hyperimmunization were still predominantly (62%) in this region. Anti-*Salmonella* agglutinins arising from a single injection were fairly evenly distributed between the β- and the γ-regions and after hyperimmunization 80% of the activity was in the γ-region.

The next step was to compare the transmission of homologous with heterologous antibodies (Morris 1963). Anti-*Salmonella* and anti-*Brucella* sera prepared in hedgehog, guineapig, rabbit, rat and ox were used. Young hedgehogs 4–4$\frac{1}{2}$ days old and one hour after having been removed from their mother were given by stomach tube a dose of 0.4 ml of immune serum and their serum was sampled 3 hr later. Hedgehog anti-*Salmonella* agglutinins were transmitted more readily than the heterologous antibodies, and rabbit and guineapig agglutinins more readily than rat or bovine. Hedgehog, rabbit, rat and bovine anti-*Brucella* agglutinins were all transmitted much less readily than the anti-*Salmonella* agglutinins from these species. Anti-*Brucella* agglutinins even from high titre bovine sera were almost completely excluded and no significant amount of antibody was transmitted from the rabbit or rat anti-*Brucella* sera, the titres of which unfortunately were not high, though adequate to have shown transmission had they been anti-*Salmonella* sera. Both the anti-*Salmonella* and the anti-*Brucella* agglutinins from guineapig sera were transmitted at about the same rate.

Morris and Steel (1964) found that the capacity of young hedgehogs to absorb anti-*Salmonella* agglutinins from high titre hedgehog serum administered orally did not decline between 30 and 41 days of age, but only slight absorption occurred at 45 days of age and none at 50 and 54 days. Young hedgehogs began to take solid food at 25 days old and continued to suckle for a further 15 days. The amount of alkaline phosphatase in the hedgehog duodenum declines during the first 30 days. A transient increase occurs towards the end of this time, followed by a decline to adult levels. More of the enzyme appears to be present in the ileum than in the duodenum. Cortisone acetate administered orally or intraperitoneally to suckling hedgehogs had little effect either on the capacity to absorb antibody or on the amount of alkaline phosphatase in the duodenum.

It has been shown by Morris and Steel (1967) that peptic cells are present at the bases of the gastric glands in the stomachs of newborn hedgehogs but that oxyntic cells are far less numerous than peptic cells throughout the suckling period. Pepsin is present in the fundic mucosa in considerable amounts at 9 days of age and at near adult levels by 4 weeks of age. The gastric *p*H is near neutrality at birth and declines gradually to between 3.0 and 4.0 during the 4th and 5th weeks. It appears to be the hydrogen ion concentration, not lack of enzyme, which delays the onset of peptic digestion. It was suggested that it is changes in digestive enzyme activity rather than in the absorptive capacity of the intestinal epithelium which leads to the cessation in the transmission of passive immunity.

6.4.3. Conclusions

It is clear from this account that in the hedgehog some transmission of passive immunity occurs before birth but that most occurs after birth. The hedgehog resembles the rat and the mouse in these respects. Transmission of immunity after birth in the hedgehog is uniquely prolonged for 40 days, apparently continuing even after weaning had begun and as long as suckling continued. The maintenance of high antibody titres in the milk throughout lactation is consistent with this prolonged transmission. Evidently transmission both before and after birth is selective. The striking difference in the transmission of anti-*Brucella* and of anti-*Salmonella* agglutinins, both from homologous and most heterologous sera, suggest that γM-globulins are not transmitted either before or after birth. The differences in the transmission of antibodies to the same antigen produced in different species is also clear, but as in other species it is not possible to determine how far this is due to the specific characters of the γ-globulins or to differences in the distribution of the antibody activity between the γ-globulin fractions. It would be interesting to know if any of the passively acquired antibody of the young animal is mercaptoethanol sensitive. It would also be interesting to discover whether γA-globulin is plentiful in the milk and if a pepsin inhibitor is present.

6.5. Transmission of passive immunity in marsupials

Immunoglobulins are not detectable by immunoelectrophoresis in the amniotic fluid, yolk-sac fluid or in the serum of the embryo or precolostral newborn quokka, *Setonix* (Waring, personal communication). They are present in the serum of postcolostral pouch young at 24 hr old. Antibodies to bacteriophage ΦX 174 and to *Salmonella adelaide* are transmitted with the milk throughout the 180 days of pouch life, but cease when the young leave the pouch although they continue to suckle. Publication of these results will be awaited with great interest as they provide the first information concerning transmission of immunity in marsupials.

It has been shown recently (Kalmutz 1962) that the pouch young of the Virginian opossum are capable of active immunization from an early age. Bacteriophage was used as antigen and the young were injected at 11 or 22 days of age. Accelerated elimination of the antigen began within a few days and antibody was present soon after the disappearance of the antigen. These pouch young are poikilothermic for about 65 days and cannot be weaned until 80–90 days of age, so that they displayed active immunity at a very early stage of their development.

CHAPTER 7

Transmission of immunity in the pig and the horse

7.1. The pig

7.1.1. The placenta and foetal membranes

Transmission before birth in the pig is absent or insignificant, so no detailed account of the embryonic membranes and placenta is required, but a brief outline, based on the account given by Amoroso (1952) appears desirable for comparison with those of animals in which transmission before birth is significant.

The developing blastocyst in the pig traverses the Fallopian tubes and reaches the uterus about $3\frac{1}{2}$ days after ovulation. During the succeeding week the blastocysts remain free in the uterine cavity, becoming spaced out and undergoing an extraordinarily rapid elongation to form long fusiform tubes, the ends of which overlap those of the neighbouring blastocysts. The embryonic disc is placed near the middle of each and the amnion is formed by folds. The yolk-sac endoderm at this stage occupies most of the space within the trophoblast and is in contact with the chorion. By the 11th day the trophoblast is beginning to be in close contact with the uterine epithelium and the rapid expansion of the middle part of the fusiform blastocyst results in its filling and expanding the uterine cavity to form a chamber around it, a process which corresponds to implantation although no fusion of the trophoblast with the maternal tissues takes place. This process is complete by the 24th day. Meanwhile the allantois has grown out from the hinder end of the embryo as a vesicle which rapidly expands on each side of the embryonic region to nearly fill the exocoel. It presses the amniotic vesicle against the inner surface of the chorion, to which the amnion adheres and forms a circular area of amniochorion. It envelops and adheres to the rest of the amnion to form an allantoamnion and it fuses with the inner surface of the chorion everywhere else except at the extreme tips of the fusiform membranes, displacing the yolk-sac from its contact with the chorion in doing so. Thus the yolk-sac is isolated from the chorion at an early stage and shrinks to a rudiment which disappears completely before full term. The whole extent of the outer enveloping membrane, except for the extreme tips of the chorion and the circular area of amniochorion above the embryo, is converted into allantochorion and is vascularised by the allantoic vessels. The exocoel is almost entirely obliterated and only the allantoic and amniotic cavities remain as large containers of extra-embryonic fluids. The composition and origin of these fluids has been investigated by McCance and Dickerson (1957). Longitudinal folds in the allantochorion fit in between corresponding folds in the uterine epithelium resulting in close apposition of the two, and giving the appearance in cross section of interlocking villi. Later, numerous very small secondary folds on these primary ones result in still more complex interlocking. Many small specialised areas called areolae are developed over the openings of the uterine glands and appear to be concerned with the absorption of the uterine milk secreted by these glands. Throughout, the uterine epithelium persists and there is no invasion of the maternal tissues by the trophoblast. Consequently the placenta is of the simplest mammalian type and is said to be epitheliochorial. It is also diffuse since it extends over the whole surface of contact of maternal and foetal tissues.

7.1.2. Transmission before birth

The young pig acquires all, or almost all, its passive immunity from the mother after birth. It has a very low concentration of γ-globulin in its serum at birth and this amount may well be produced by active synthesis rather than passive transmission (Sterzl, Kostka, Mandel, Riha and Holub 1960). Such evidence as there is at present of transmission of immunity before birth is not very convincing. Many authors have failed to find antibodies in the blood of the newborn young of immune sows before they have suckled. Antibodies were absent from the sera at birth of the piglets of sows immune to *Brucella abortus* or to *B. melitensis* (Hoerlein 1952, 1957); nor were antibodies found in the sera, even after concentration, of the newborn young of sows immune to *B. suis* (Sterzl et al. 1960). Moreover, maternal isohaemagglutinins to foetal red cell antigens could not be detected by the Coombs test on the red cells of young at birth, which rapidly developed haemolytic

disease after they had suckled (Andresen and Baker 1963). Young and
Underdahl (1949, 1950) examined the sera of 50 piglets of sows with high
haemagglutination-inhibition titres for swine influenza virus and failed
to find any in 37, and only very low titres in the remaining 13, which they
attributed to non-specific reactions. They also failed to find neutralizing
antibodies against this virus in the sera of the newborn young. Similarly,
the newborn young of sows immune to *Salmonella pullorum* had sera from
which antibodies were virtually absent, the very low positive reactions
observed being attributed to non-specific reactions (Miller, Harmon, Ullrey,
Schmidt, Luecke and Hoefer 1962). Antitoxins provide the only clear evidence of transmission before birth, but this rests on only two litters (Myers
and Segre 1963). One pregnant sow was actively immunized with a mixture
of diphtheria and tetanus toxoids administered 23 and 9 days before the
young were delivered by hysterotomy. At the time of operation she had
antitoxin titres of $\frac{1}{320}$ for diphtheria, and $\frac{1}{1280}$ for tetanus toxoids. The sera
of the young were pooled but antitoxins could not be demonstrated in the
whole pooled serum. The crude immune globulin fraction was separated
by cold ethanol precipitation, freeze-dried and reconstituted in buffered
saline at a 10-fold concentration. This concentrated globulin preparation
had antitoxin titres of $\frac{1}{64}$ for diphtheria and $\frac{1}{128}$ for tetanus toxoids. To exclude
the possibility of active immunization of the foetuses by transmission
of the toxoids, another pregnant sow was passively immunized, 2 days
before the young were obtained by hysterotomy, by intravenous injection
of 100 ml of a concentrated solution of immune pig γ-globulin containing
approximately 2,000,000 haemagglutination units of diphtheria and
33,500,000 haemagglutination units of tetanus antitoxins. At the time of
hysterotomy her serum had antitoxin titres of $\frac{1}{320}$ for diphtheria and $\frac{1}{5120}$ for
tetanus toxoids. The whole pooled serum of the young appeared to have
no detectable antitoxins but the γ-globulin in 10-fold concentration had
titres of $\frac{1}{128}$ for diphtheria and $\frac{1}{1024}$ for tetanus toxoids. The amounts of
antitoxins observed in the concentrated γ-globulin fractions of the pooled
sera in both these experiments were such that they should have been detectable at a 10-fold dilution, as they were in the whole sera. The authors
suggest that a haemagglutination inhibitor in the whole sera that was removed
by fractionation might account for this anomaly. It will be seen that the
titre of the foetal serum relative to that of the maternal serum of the actively
immunized sow was $\frac{1}{50}$ for diphtheria antitoxin and $\frac{1}{100}$ for tetanus antitoxin.
At relative concentrations of this order it should be possible to detect other

antibodies, as well as antitoxins, in the sera at birth of the offspring of hyper-immunized sows and it is hard to account for the failure of other authors to do so. Clearly further work is desirable before it can be concluded that transmission before birth occurs in this species.

7.1.3. Transmission of antibodies after birth

It has been known for a long time (see Edsall 1956) that the offspring born and reared by immune sows are themselves immune, but that they ultimately lose this immunity. The first attempt to verify this experimentally appears to have been that of McArthur (1919), who vaccinated against hog cholera sows that had not been previously vaccinated and had not been exposed to the disease, so far as was known. Most of these sows were parous and pregnant at the time of vaccination. Subsequent immunity of the sows and their offspring was tested by exposure to infected pigs or by exposure to the virus. It was shown in this way that the offspring of the immunized sows had a high degree of immunity while suckling, which was gradually lost after weaning. Nelson (1932) immunized sows by intradermal injection of vaccinia virus and showed that piglets from these sows when suckled did not respond to vaccination with the virus whereas their hand-fed litter mates did, thus clearly establishing that the immunity was transmitted after birth. He showed (Nelson 1934) that a sow, once immunized, continued to transmit immunity to her suckled offspring for six successive litters. The passively acquired immunity began to decline during the second month and was negligible by the end of the third month. Vaccination of the suckling young of immune sows was ineffective in producing an active immunity.

It has been mentioned already that Young and Underdahl (1949, 1950) failed to find haemagglutination-inhibition antibodies in 37 and only trace amounts, probably ascribable to non-specific reactions, in a further 13 young pigs at birth of sows immune to swine influenza virus. However, antibody was detected in the sera in 30 min of beginning to suckle, had attained significant titres within 1 hr and had reached near maximum levels within 6 hr and remained at this level up to 72 hr and thereafter declining gradually (fig. 7.1). The titres attained in the piglets' sera was approximately three times that of the dam's serum. The transmission after birth of antibodies by sows immunized to sheep-red-cells, *Brucella abortus* (Hoerlein 1957) and *B. melitensis* (Hoerlein 1952) also occurs, the titres attained in the sera of the piglets being half that of the mother's colostrum. Nordbring and

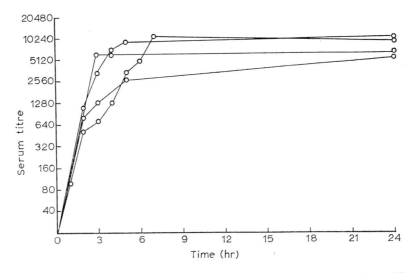

Fig. 7.1. The rate of appearance of haemagglutination-inhibition antibodies in the suckling piglets of sows actively immunized for swine influenza virus. (From Young and Underdahl 1949.)

Olsson (1957) demonstrated the transmission to the young after birth of paratyphoid H agglutinins by sows immunized by vaccination. They showed that after suckling the titre of the piglets' sera equalled or exceeded, by up to four times, that of the mother's serum. Subsequently these authors (1958b) demonstrated the passage of these antibodies from known quantities of colostrum administered orally to newborn piglets, the titres attained in their sera after 16 hr varying from $\frac{1}{2}$ to $\frac{1}{16}$ of that of the colostrum. Serum from sows immunized to *Escherichia coli* was administered orally to piglets of non-immune mothers (Speer, Brown, Quinn and Catron 1959). The piglets were given a dose of 40 ml/kg body weight of this high titre serum immediately after birth and their sera sampled 12 hr later, the piglets being allowed to suckle their mothers normally in the interval. All had high titres varying from 2 to $\frac{1}{16}$ that of the colostrum administered. The transmission after birth of antibodies to *Salmonella pullorum* (Miller, Harmon, Ullrey, Schmidt, Luecke and Hoefer 1962) and to swine erysipelas (Wellmann, Schwietzer and Liebke 1961; Wellmann and Engel 1963) from actively immune sows has been shown to occur. It appears that all kinds of homologous antibodies investigated, covering a wide variety, are transmitted from mother to young after birth in pigs.

Perry and Watson (1967a) gave a single dose of salted-out anti-*S. pullorum* antibody in 10 ml of distilled water to 245 young piglets at ages ranging from 1 to 24 hr after birth. Five concentrations of antibody in the dose ranging from $\frac{1}{1280}$ to $\frac{1}{20,480}$ were used. The piglets were allowed to suckle normally so that only those dosed at birth had not received colostrum previous to the dose. Their blood was sampled 12 hr after the dose was given. They came from 26 litters sired by 10 boars. The efficiency of transmission to the piglet's serum was calculated as: (observed titre/maximum possible titre) × 100, by assuming the blood volume to be 7.4 ml/100 g live weight and that all the antibody in the dose might be transmitted. The results classified according to the titre of the dose and the age when administered

TABLE 7.1

Antibody absorbed by piglets in each dosage class. (After Perry and Watson 1967a.)

Titre of dose	No. of litters	No. of piglets	Efficiency of absorption (%)
20,480	1	10	1.7
10,240	3	31	2.3
5,120	9	92	13.8
2,560	10	87	13.1
1,280	3	25	12.3
	26	245	

TABLE 7.2

The effect of time of dosage on efficiency of antibody absorption. (After Perry and Watson 1967a.)

Time of dosage after birth (hr)	No. of litters	No. of piglets	Efficiency of absorption (%)
1–6	11	103	10.8
7–12	8	77	14.5
13–18	4	39	11.4
19–24	3	26	5.4
	26	245	

are given in tables 7.1 and 7.2, respectively. It is interesting that, although the numbers are small, the efficiency of absorption should appear to fall off so much with the higher concentrations of antibody in the dose. The efficiency of absorption also declines from at least 18 hr after birth. Analysis of variance showed that the age when dosed contributed 25% of the total variance, the titre of the dose 13% and the sire 6%. Three quarters of the remainder of the variance was between litters and only one quarter within litters. Thus most of the variation was between litters and attributable to maternal effects associated with the colostrum. Further analysis of these maternal influences was effected (Perry and Watson 1967b) by immunizing 16 sows in late pregnancy with *S. pullorum* antigen. 12 hr after birth the sera of the 173 piglets born were determined and compared to those of their mothers' serum, to which they were positively related. The titres of the colostral samples showed marked variations both between different teats of the same sow and between different sows. The colostral titres were not related to those of the sera of either the sows or the piglets. Those piglets with high serum titres at 12 hr after birth displayed better growth rates and a

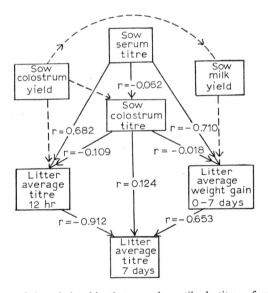

Fig. 7.2. Diagram of the relationships between the antibody titres of sow and suckling piglets sera and litter weight gain from birth to 7 days of age. The significance levels of the given correlation coefficients are $r \geq 0.400$, $P = 0.10$; $r \geq 0.468$, $P = 0.05$; $r \geq 0.589$, $P = 0.01$; $r \geq 0.708$, $P = 0.001$. (From Perry and Watson 1967b.)

lower mortality than those with low serum titres. The relationship between the various factors is shown diagrammatically in fig. 7.2. These authors (Perry and Watson 1967c) have shown also, by isotopic-labelled pig serum administered to newborn pigs which were then allowed to suckle, that 7S γG-globulin is transmitted preferentially to albumin, and albumin preferentially to 19S γM-globulin.

7.1.4. Transmission of homologous γ-globulins

The rapid transmission of immunity as soon as the young piglets suckle an immune mother is paralleled by the changes in the serum proteins. Earle (1935) was the first to show an increase in total globulins after suckling of six times that at birth, most of the increase being in euglobulin. Jakobsen and Moustgaard (1950), using sodium sulphate fractional precipitation, confirmed the rapid increase in total serum proteins after suckling, most of the increase being attributable to euglobulin which was absent at birth but was as much as 30 to 40% of the total protein a few hours after suckling. This was confirmed by free boundary electrophoresis (veronal buffer, *p*H 8.6) in a further paper (Rook, Moustgaard and Jakobsen 1951). These authors could not detect any γ-globulin in the serum at birth, but during the first few hours after suckling it constituted up to 40% of the total serum proteins. A correspondingly sharp, but smaller, rise in the β-globulin to nearly 20% of the total serum proteins occurred at the same time. In the light of modern knowledge the apparent increase in the β-globulins may have been due largely to the faster migrating γ-globulin components. At the same time, Foster, Friedell, Catron and Dieckmann (1951) found a similar sharp rise in total serum proteins during the first day from 25 mg/ml to 61 mg/ml accompanied by a corresponding rise in the γ-globulin from 1.3 mg/ml to 20.3 mg/ml. The relative concentration of γ-globulin at 24 hr was 24 to 40%.

Nordbring and Olsson (1957), using micro-Keldahl estimations of total proteins and paper electrophoresis for estimation of the components, examined the sera of piglets suckled naturally by their mothers. They found in the cord blood 17.6 mg/ml of total serum proteins, 3.9 mg/ml of β-globulin and 1.4 mg/ml of γ-globulin. At 4 hr the total protein was 36 mg/ml and the combined β+γ-globulins 21.2 mg/ml; the latter accounting for most of the increase in total proteins. The total proteins had risen further to 55.3 mg/ml by 12 hr and the combined β+γ-globulins to 37.3 mg/ml, at which level they remained until 24 hr and thereafter declined very gradually. Subsequently, these authors (Nordbring and Olsson 1958a) administered known quantities of pig colostrum orally to newborn pigs. They gave 130 to 135 ml of colostrum in all in five feeds during the first 12 hr to each little pig. The cord sera of these pigs had 15.2 mg/ml of total proteins, including 2.35 mg/ml of β-globulin and 1.6 mg/ml of γ-globulin. At 16 hr, 4 hr after the last feed, the mean total protein was 37.3 mg/ml and the combined $\beta+\gamma$-globulins 20.2 mg/ml. It was estimated that the increase in the $\beta+\gamma$-globulins accounted for 15.5 to 18.7% of these proteins in the dose administered. Similarly, 75 ml of pig serum was given in five feeds during the first 12 hr to other young pigs (Nordbring and Olsson 1958b). The mean values for the cord sera were 19.1 mg/ml total proteins, 2.5 mg/ml β-globulin and 1.8 mg/ml γ-globulin. At 16 hr the mean values were 25.2 mg/ml total proteins, 3.8 mg/ml β-globulin and 4.5 mg/ml γ-globulin. It was estimated that the increase in the $\beta+\gamma$-globulins represented approximately 8.3% of those in the serum administered; a rather lower efficiency of absorption than with colostrum.

Rutqvist (1958), using paper electrophoresis, was unable to detect any γ-globulin in foetal or newborn pig sera, but large amounts appeared shortly after suckling. Using similar methods Lecce and Matrone (1960) noted the absence of γ-globulin in the serum of newborn pigs, but after suckling for 48 hr there was 12 mg/ml of β-globulin and 32 mg/ml of γ-globulin.

The blood volume and plasma protein composition of young pigs was measured by Ramirez, Miller, Ullrey and Hoefer (1963). It can be calculated from their data that the plasma volume at birth was 5.5% of body weight, at 6 hr it was 6.5% and at 12 hr it was 6.9%. The total plasma protein was 24 mg/ml at birth, 39 mg/ml at 6 hr and 53 mg/ml at 12 hr. At birth the β-globulin was 3.1 mg/ml and the γ-globulin 2.1 mg/ml; at 6 hr the β-globulin was 12.8 mg/ml and the γ-globulin 12.9 mg/ml and at 12 hr the β-globulin was 14.8 mg/ml and the γ-globulin 22.4 mg/ml.

Kim, Bradley and Watson (1966) found that the sera of newborn miniature pigs obtained germfree by hysterectomy at 3 to 5 days before full term were devoid of $\gamma_1 A$-, $19S\gamma_1$- and $7S\gamma_2$-globulins, but contained γM-globulin. They calculated that the sensitive methods of immunoelectrophoresis on concentrated fractions of the piglets sera would have revealed as little as 0.25 μg/ml. When the piglets were obtained from sows hyperimmunized to the actinophage, antibody could not be detected in their sera either by immunoelectrophoresis of 20 times concentrated fractions or by phage neutralization assay. It was calculated that a concentration of $\frac{1}{2} \times 10^7$ of that in the sows serum would have been detectable.

Pierce and Smith (1967a), using sensitive methods of quantitative immunodiffusion and ultracentrifugation found that the sera of newborn piglets before suckling contained very low levels of γG-globulin, only 1 to 4 mg/100 ml. This amount, however, is very much more than Kim et al. (1966) found in their slightly premature miniature pigs. Porter (1969) found that precolostral piglet serum was almost entirely deficient in immunoglobulins but a component sharing antigenic determinants with γG-globulin was present in concentrations less than 50 μg/ml. These results are consistent with the failure of Rutqvist (1958) and of Lecce and Matrone (1960) to detect any γG-globulin by the less sensitive method of paper electrophoresis but they are clearly inconsistent with those of Nordbring and Olsson (1957, 1958a, b) and of Foster et al. (1951), who found 1.3 to 1.8 mg/ml in cord blood and of Ramirez et al. (1963), who found 2.1 mg/ml at birth. In view of the methods employed much more reliance can be placed on the lower estimates. Porter (1969) found that γG-, γA- and γM-globulins were all transmitted from the colostrum to the serum of suckling piglets. The post-colostral serum concentrations of γG- and γM-globulins of piglets were similar to those of adults, but γA-globulin concentrations generally exceeded those in adults, sometimes by as much as 3–4 times. It has been shown by McCance and Widdowson (1959) that the effect of the absorption of colostral globulin over 24 hr on newborn piglets is to increase the plasma volume by 30% and the globulin concentration of the plasma from 0.93 to 3.58 g/100 ml.

7.1.5. Termination of transmission

Transmission of passive immunity declines very rapidly after birth in the normal suckling piglet and effectively ceases at about the end of the first day. Nordbring and Olsson (1958a) gave known amounts of immune pig colostrum to piglets not allowed to suckle their dams. Each piglet was given 125 to 135 ml in five feeds extending over 10 to 12 hr starting at various ages from birth to 72 hr. Their sera were tested 4 to 6 hr after the last feed. At birth 17% of the globulin in the dose was transmitted but at 72 hr only 4% was transmitted. It must be noted, however, that these piglets were not fed except with the immune colostrum. Speer, Brown, Quinn and Catron (1959) gave immune pig colostrum to young pigs that were allowed to suckle their non-immune dams normally. The colostrum administered was from pigs actively immunized to *Escherichia coli* and had a titre of $\frac{1}{10,240}$ or $\frac{1}{20,480}$. It was given in single doses of 40 ml/kg body weight to each young pig, the serum of which was tested 12 hr afterwards. Eight litters were used and one piglet from each was dosed at birth, another at 6 hr, and another at each 6-hr interval up to 36 hr. The titre attained in the piglets sera declined logarithmically with the time of administration of the dose from birth to zero at 24 hr. Confirmatory results were obtained by Miller, Harmon, Ullrey, Schmidt, Luecke and Hoefer (1962) who hyperimmunized a pregnant sow to *Salmonella pullorum*. Her colostrum had a titre of $\frac{1}{2560}$. At birth and at each 6-hr interval thereafter a piglet from a litter born at the same time to a non-immune sow was exchanged with one of hers. The serum of each piglet was tested after it had been suckling the immune sow for 6 hr. The titres of the piglets sera declined logarithmically with the time of suckling after birth and had ceased to be significant at 24 hr (fig.7.3).

Sows immune to swine erysipelas were used by Wellmann, Liebke and

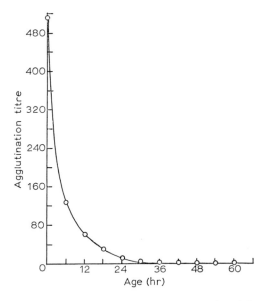

Fig. 7.3. Antibody titres of the sera of suckling piglets transferred from a non-immune sow to a foster-mother actively immunized to *S. pullorum* at various ages. The amount of antibody transmitted decreases logarithmically with time and is not detectable when the piglets are more than 24 hr old when fostered. (From Miller et al. 1962.)

Engel (1962; Wellmann and Engel 1963). Piglets suckling these sows acquired antibody rapidly on the first day and at a decreased rate on the second
day but even at 48 hr complete protection against the disease was acquired.
A minor amount could be detected both serologically and by the infection
test even at 120 hr. Long, Ullrey and Miller (1964b) found that piglets
deprived of colostrum and maintained on glucose diets were still able to absorb γ-globulin at two weeks of age. Payne and Marsh (1962) also found that
starved piglets or those given only water were still able to absorb γ-globulin
at 106 hr, the latest age tested, whereas those suckled or fed on modified
cow's milk did not do so after 12 hr. They stated that the amount of γ-
globulin absorbed by a newborn piglet from whole colostrum is directly
proportional to the amount taken up to a maximum of 60 ml.

Lecce and Morgan (1962), using the transmission of polyvinylpyrrolidone
(PVP) from the gut to the circulation as an indicator of the capacity to
transmit γ-globulin, found that this substance was transmitted readily for
20 hr, and that a minority of piglets transmitted it up to 36 to 48 hr if they
were allowed to suckle, but if they were starved it was transmitted readily
up to 62 to 86 hr. The quantity of colostrum consumed appeared to be the
determining factor in bringing about cessation of transmission. Young pigs
were fed with varying quantities of cow's colostrum up to 20 hr and tested
with PVP at 24 hr. All five piglets given 80 ml of colostrum transmitted the
PVP, four of the five given 200 to 300 ml did so but only one of six given
400 to 500 ml and none of the five given 750 ml.

7.1.6. Characteristics of colostrum

Recently Lecce, Morgan and Matrone (1964) have claimed that there is a
heat-stable, low molecular weight, factor in the protein and fat-free fraction
of colostrum or milk which is responsible for bringing about the termination
of transmission. This factor was present in dialyzates of cow's colostrum
and of non-fat dried milk solids as well as in boiled, and essentially fat and
protein free, cow's colostral whey. Solutions of egg albumen, pig albumin,
or pig γ-globulin, did not bring about termination of transmission, nor did
synthetic solutions of milk salts, vitamins or sugars. If these results can be
confirmed it would be of great interest, especially if it could be determined
whether the factor has its effect by stimulating digestion of the γ-globulin
before reaching the absorptive region of the intestine or directly on the
cells ingesting the γ-globulin.

Earle (1935) gives the composition of sow colostrum before suckling in terms of nitrogen determinations of the sodium sulphate precipitated fractions as:

Casein	12.34 mg/ml
Albumin	4.57 mg/ml
Pseudoglobulin	5.41 mg/ml
Euglobulin	16.80 mg/ml
Total protein N	39.12 mg/ml
Non-protein N	2.42 mg/ml

Foster, Friedell, Catron and Dieckmann (1951) find only about 80 mg/ml of total proteins in the colostral whey at the time of farrowing, or about half the amount found by Earle. They state that about 70% of the whey protein is γ-globulin, but that during the first 24 hr there is a marked drop both in total protein concentration and in the proportion of γ-globulin in it. Morgan and Lecce (1964) in a thorough examination of the changes in the sow's mammary secretions throughout lactation, record a total protein concentration at farrowing of 180 mg/ml in the colostrum, of which about 150 mg/ml are whey proteins. The whey proteins include 39% of γ-globulin. On suckling the total protein concentration drops precipitately in the first day or two to about 50 mg/ml and the proportion of γ-globulin in the whey proteins falls to about 20%. By mid-lactation the whey proteins constitute only about 30% of the total protein. Thus the actual concentration of γ-globulin falls from 60 mg/ml in the colostrum at farrowing to 3 mg/ml in the milk during mid-lactation and most of this change is brought about in the first two or three days. These authors found an immunoelectrophoretic identity of all the whey proteins with the maternal serum proteins, with the exception of a prealbumin in the whey of which they could find no trace in the serum (fig. 7.4).

Porter (1969) found that γM-, γA- and γG-globulins were all present in colostrum and accounted for 63.6 $\pm$ 8.6% of the whey proteins. The distribution in the whey was γG 79.7 $\pm$ 16.9%, γM 6.27 $\pm$ 2.35% and γA 14.05 $\pm$ 7.35%, the concentrations of γG and γM being 2–3 times those in serum but the γA 3–11 times greater than those in serum. An S17.8 component antigenically identical with γG-globulin is present in colostrum and the γA-globulin appeared on gel filtration to have a wide range of molecular sizes. Long, Ullrey and Miller (1964a) found that the alkaline phosphatase activity in the colostrum at farrowing was significantly reduced

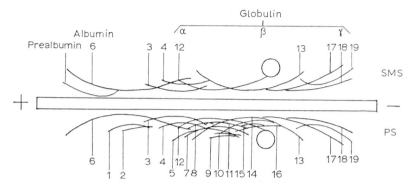

Fig. 7.4. Diagrammatic comparison of the immunoelectropherograms of sow's whey and pig serum, showing that the prealbumin was the only component of the whey proteins absent from the serum. (From Morgan and Lecce 1964.)

after 24 hr suckling, but that little change occurred subsequently during lactation.

Antibody content of the colostrum parallels that of γ-globulin. Young and Underdahl (1950) found both neutralizing and haemagglutination-inhibition antibodies to swine influenza virus at high titre in the colostrum but the titres dropped considerably during the first 4 weeks. Wellmann, Liebke and Engel (1962) state that the erysipelas antibody titre of immune sows as a rule is higher in the colostrum than in the serum, but there are some exceptions. The titre starts to decline during the first day after farrowing and continues to do so during subsequent days, but some antibody is present even at 8 weeks.

7.1.7. *Colostral trypsin inhibitor*

It was discovered by Laskowski and Laskowski (1951) that a trypsin inhibitor is present in large amounts in bovine colostrum, and in much smaller amounts in human colostrum. The bovine colostral trypsin inhibitor was purified and a crystalline compound with trypsin was obtained which was inactive. When this was split into its two components, both were found to be active, the one as enzyme and the other as inhibitor. The inhibitor was obtained in this way in crystalline form and was found to be 2 to 3 times as potent as soya bean inhibitor. Subsequently Laskowski, Kassell and Hagerty (1957) prepared crystalline trypsin inhibitor from swine colostrum in which it is present in large quantities. 1 ml of first-day swine colostrum inhibits approximately 2 mg of crystalline trypsin. Sow colostrum has 6 to 7 times the inhibitory activity of cow colostrum and 67 times that of human colostrum. The activity is greatest at the time of farrowing and falls off

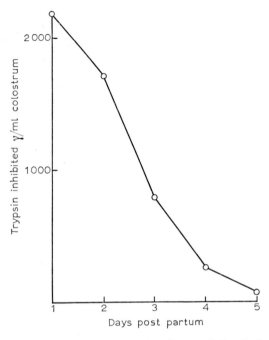

Fig. 7.5. The content of trypsin inhibitor in sow's colostrum during the first five days after parturition. (From Laskowski et al. 1957.)

rapidly during the succeeding five days to very low values (fig. 7.5). The crystalline swine inhibitor has an activity of 5,600 units/E by one method, and 4,500 units/E by another; bovine inhibitor 4,600 units/E, pancreatic inhibitor 2,780 units/E and soya bean inhibitor 1,100 units/E. One unit/E is that amount of inhibitor in 1 ml of a solution of optical density 1 at 280 mμ which will inhibit 1 μg of trypsin. The inhibitor appears to be a protein, from its ultraviolet absorption curve, probably of small size. It is very resistant to digestion with pepsin, unlike soya bean inhibitor.

The trypsin inhibitory properties of colostrum may play an important part in ensuring that the immune globulin reaches the absorptive region of the small intestine without being degraded by the digestive enzymes of the stomach and duodenum. Although enzyme activity of the gut is low at birth it may not be negligible from this point of view. Hartman, Hays, Baker, Neagle and Catron (1961) found that in piglets proteinase activities of the stomach tissues were low during the first 2 weeks, but later increased rapidly with age. Pancreatic proteinase activities also increased with age.

Barrick, Matrone and Osborne (1954) gave pig or bovine γ-globulin with and without soya bean inhibitor to newborn pigs and found that very little of the γ-globulin was absorbed whether or not the inhibitor was present. This may have been due to destruction of the inhibitor by pepsin (Laskowski, Kassell and Hagerty 1957). They found also that little γ-globulin was absorbed by piglets from bovine colostrum, though it was freely absorbed from swine colostrum. Nordbring and Olsson (1958a, b) found a small, probably significant, increase in the absorption of γ-globulin from swine colostrum or from swine serum when purified bovine colostral trypsin inhibitor was administered with it. Hardy (1965) examined the absorption by the newborn piglet of isotopically labelled γ-globulin and found that it was increased by bovine colostral trypsin inhibitor. Sow, ewe and goat colostrum also accelerated the absorption of the labelled γ-globulin. Bovine colostral whey was much less effective in the pig, although it is extremely active in promoting absorption in the calf. Nevertheless, Chamberlain, Perry and Jones (1965) on the supposition that the decline in colostral trypsin inhibitor with suckling might be responsible for the termination of the transmission of immune globulins, failed to demonstrate transmission of isotopically labelled γ-globulin in 3-day old piglets even when this was administered with trypsin inhibitor. Hourly doses of trypsin inhibitor, prepared from pig colostrum, were given from 74 to 92 hr after birth, and the γ-globulin was given at 80 hr. The total amount of trypsin inhibitor given was 14.4×10^6 units, the equivalent of 1 litre of colostrum and sufficient to inactivate over 2 g of crystalline trypsin.

7.1.8. Transmission of heterologous immune globulins

The question of whether transmission of protein in the newborn pig is selective or not is still somewhat open, certainly it is not highly selective as in the rabbit, rat, mouse or man. Yet many observations have been made on the transmission of heterologous antibodies and γ-globulins, as well as on serum albumin and other substances. Barrick, Matrone and Osborne

(1954), as referred to above, failed to obtain significant transmission of γ-globulin from swine serum or from bovine serum or colostrum. It is difficult to see why they failed, as many subsequent workers have observed the transmission of a wide variety of proteins. Olsson (1959a), for example, found that large amounts of antibody and of γ-globulin from bovine colostrum were transmitted during the first 12 hr after birth. About 11% of the H-agglutinins to *S. paratyphi* A and 17% of the γ-globulin in the dose was found in the serum. The bovine immune globulins of bovine colostrum appeared to be absorbed as readily as those from pig colostrum. Similarly (1959b) agglutinins to *S. cholerae suis* and γ-globulin from immune horse serum were absorbed as readily as those from immune pig serum. The mean amounts of the various protein fractions of the horse serum, relative to the quantities in the dose, that were transmitted to the circulation were, agglutinins 11.7%, $\beta + \gamma$-globulins 8.7%, albumin and α_1-globulin 3.5%. This would appear to show that the immune globulins were transmitted more readily than the other fractions.

Lecce, Matrone and Morgan (1961), on the other hand, found that albumin and globulins from different species, proteins from cow's milk and colostrum and even egg albumin were transmitted equally readily during the first 36 hr. Payne and Marsh (1962) also observed the non-selective transmission of heterologous globulins.

Locke, Segre and Myers (1964) found that diphtheria and tetanus antitoxins of low molecular weight (6.6S) were readily absorbed from purified sheep γ-globulin solutions whereas the antibodies of high molecular weight (18S) were absorbed poorly or not at all. Hardy (1965) observed that isotopically labelled bovine γ-globulin was absorbed as readily as pig γ-globulin.

Pierce and Smith (1967a) fed by stomach tube separately either pig or bovine colostrum in single doses of 2.1 ml/100 g body weight each containing 6.4 g γG-globulin/100 ml to newborn pigs and found that the mean amount of γG-globulin appearing in the serum after 5 hr was about 400 mg/100 ml irrespective of whether it was homologous or heterologous (fig. 7.6). There was, however, considerable individual variation in the piglets. The serological method of determination employed did not permit of distinguishing intact from fragmented globulin. When a similar dose of bovine colostrum contained in addition to 6.4 g/100 ml of bovine γG-globulin an equal amount of pig γG-globulin, the total amount of the two γG-globulins in the serum after 5 hr was considerably less, being 187 mg/100 ml, but of this amount 64% was pig and 36% bovine. Thus the pig γG-globulin was transmitted

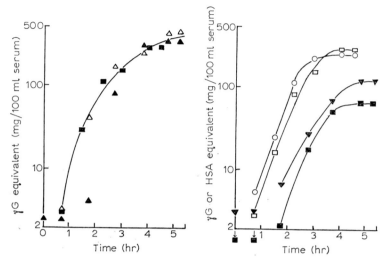

Fig. 7.6. The diagram on the left shows the amounts of γG-globulin (intact and frag-mented) in the sera of newborn piglets that had received dialysed or native pig colostrum or dialysed bovine colostrum, each containing 6.4 g γG/100 ml, in doses of 2.1 ml/100 g body weight as soon as possible after birth. Dialysed pig colostral γG-globulin ▲; native pig colostral γG-globulin △; dialysed bovine colostral γG-globulin ■. The diagram on the right shows the amounts reaching the sera of piglets of human serum albumin and bovine γG-globulin when fed with dialysed bovine colostrum containing 6.3% (w/v) HSA and 6.4% (w/v) bovine colostral γG-globulin, and also those for pig serum γG-globulin and bovine colostral γG-globulin when both were present at concentrations of 6.4 g/100 ml in dialysed bovine colostrum. HSA ○; bovine colostral γG-globulin □; pig serum γG-globulin ▼; bovine colostral γG-globulin ■. The HSA and bovine γG attained similar levels after 4–5 hr, but the pig γG attained values nearly twice those of the bovine γG in the same dose. (From Pierce and Smith 1967a.)

preferentially and nearly twice as readily as the bovine when both were presented together. When a similar dose of bovine colostrum containing 6.4 g/100 ml of bovine γG-globulin and 6.3 g/100 ml of human serum albu-min was fed both the γG-globulin and the albumin were transmitted in equal amounts but the total of the two was 520 mg/100 ml.

Some of the γG-globulin transmitted to the circulation from bovine colostrum was in a fragmented form which the serological method of deter-mination did not permit of distinguishing from the intact globulin. Ultra-centrifugal examination showed that up to 50% of the γG-globulin in the serum might be fragmented. The presence of fragments was confirmed by

double immunodiffusion. Evidence was obtained that fragments were already
present in the dose when it had reached the first third of the intestine and
before it was absorbed. There was evidence also of elimination of fragments
from the circulation by the kidneys and these appeared in the urine.

Bovine γG-globulin was given in doses varying in quantity from 0.32 to
3.95 g in uniform volume of 2.1 ml/100 g body weight of bovine colostrum.
The concentration found in the serum after 4 hr depended on, but was not
directly proportional to the amount in the dose. Only about 1% of the
protein was transmitted to the circulation from a dose of 0.5 g, 5% from
1 g, 10% from 2 g and 11% from 4 g when the efficiency of transmission

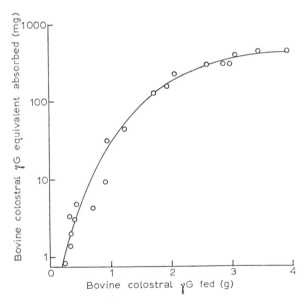

Fig. 7.7. Diagram of the relation between the total amount of bovine colostral γG-
globulin fed to newborn piglets and the amounts of γG-globulin (intact or fragmented)
in the serum $3\frac{1}{2}$ to $4\frac{1}{2}$ hr later. (From Pierce and Smith 1967a.)

was near a maximum (fig. 7.7). Thus even at maximum transmission about
90% of the dose fed remained unaccounted for. None of the γ-globulin was
detectable in the serum after 30 min, but was present by 1 hr after doses
of 1 g or more.

7.1.9. *Transmission of other proteins*

It is evident that soluble proteins other than immune globulins can be transmitted from the gut to the circulation and it is therefore of interest to know if such proteins, as have recognisable biological activity, can be transmitted, as are antibodies, without loss of their biological activity. These fall into two groups: enzymes and protein hormones. Balconi and Lecce (1966) investigated the transmission in the unborn piglet of homologous lactic dehydrogenase isoenzymes (LDH). These are found in five electrophoretically distinguishable forms in the tissues, but the relative quantities of each form vary with the tissue. Pig skeletal muscle is especially rich in LDH_5, heart muscle in LDH_1, and liver almost equally rich in LDH_1, LDH_2 and LDH_3. Accordingly homogenates of these tissues were fed to newborn pigs and the quantities and distribution of the isoenzymes in the sera compared with those of controls. Evidence was obtained of the passage of all the isoenzymes, but it was not possible to determine if the different forms were transmitted equally readily.

There is also evidence of the transmission of the hormone insulin by the gut of the newborn piglet. Asplund, Grummer and Phillips (1962) fed 400 units of insulin or of protamine-zinc insulin to newborn piglets and found a pronounced hypoglycaemia after 3 hr provided that the insulin was given in the first 24 hr after birth.

It was discovered by Lecce, Matrone and Morgan (1961) that polyvinyl-pyrrolidone is transmitted from the gut to the circulation of newborn piglets as well as proteins. This substance is a synthetic, high-molecular weight blood plasma extender. Consequently it is not liable to be affected by digestive enzymes, which enabled Lecce and Morgan (1962) subsequently to exploit its use as an inert marker for studying the effects of feeding proteins on the time of cessation of transmission, as has been mentioned previously. Hardy (1965) studied the transmission of radio-iodinated polyvinylpyrrolidone (^{131}I-PVP) when administered in colostrum. He found that when high molecular weight (mean 160,000 mol wt) PVP was given in sow colostrum a much higher concentration (20 to 25%) was recovered from the serum than with any protein, and that the concentration bore a constant inverse relationship to the fraction of the dose remaining in the gut. When low molecular weight PVP (mean 40,000 mol wt) was used, much less was recovered from the serum and little remained in the gut, resembling the behaviour of protein. It is suggested that this was due to the smaller molecules being more readily dispersed in the body and excreted by the kidneys, and that fragments of protein might be expected to behave similarly.

7.1.10. *Transmission in vitro*

Some use has been made of *in vitro* preparations to study transmission in the gut of the newborn piglet. Lecce (1966) used slices of inverted neonatal intestine in balanced salt solution and found that these still absorbed fluo-rescein-labelled γ-globulin after 4 to 6 hr. Uptake could be discerned within 15 min and was oxygen- and sodium-dependent. It was reversibly inhibited by metabolic antagonists such as iodoacetate, arsenate, fluoride, 4,6-dini-tro-*o*-cresol and phlorrhizin. Smith and Pierce (1966), in the same year, introduced the use of the inverted intestinal sac technique for this purpose. They (Pierce and Smith 1966, 1967b) studied first the release of protein from sacs into the serosal fluid, using the intestines of newborn pigs that had been fed dialysed bovine colostrum and preparing the sacs 90 min later. These were incubated at 37 °C for 2 hr in bicarbonate saline gassed with 95% O_2 + 5% CO_2. The maximum transfer observed was in sacs from the middle region of the intestine and was 2.2 mg/g intestine/hr. Further experiments were performed with sacs from unfed newborn pigs incubated in dialysed bovine colostrum. Again maximal transfer was observed in sacs from the middle region of the intestine and was 45 μg/g intestine/hr. This was about 50 times less than when the protein had already been absorbed before the sacs were made, when the colostrum contained the same amount (9.7 g/100 ml) of immune lactoglobulin. The amount of γG-globulin transferred was dependent on the concentration in the colostrum to which the mucosal surface of the sac was exposed. In some experiments human serum albumin was added in equal quantity by weight (5.2 g/100 ml) to the γG-globulin in the dialysed bovine colostrum to which the mucosal surface of the sacs was exposed, the albumin was transferred to the mucosal surface more readily than the globulin, and it reduced the transfer of the globulin by the middle segments of the intestine significantly. About twenty molecules of albumin were transferred for every one of globulin. As mentioned previously (pp. 182-3, fig. 7.6), when human serum albumin in bovine colostrum was administered *in vivo* no such effects were observed, both the albumin and globulin being transmitted equally readily and no apparent interference of the albumin with the transmission of the globulin being observed. In these experiments no break down of the protein occurred when the sacs were exposed to the protein *in vitro*, but when they were prepared from the intestines of animals previously fed with the colostrum, break down products were apparent.

Smith and Pierce (1967) also investigated the effects of certain amino acids on the transport of γG-globulin by inverted sacs of newborn piglets intestines *in vitro*. They found that the mean transfer of control sacs in dialysed bovine colostrum was: immune lactoglobulin 61.6 μg/g/hr; fluid 0.5 ml/g/hr; glucose 1.9 mg/g/hr. An amino acid to be tested was added to the colostrum at a concentration of 10 mmoles/l. L-alanine had no effect, L-leucine inhibited protein, fluid and glucose transport and L-methionine inhibited protein transport but had no other effect. The D-isomeres of these amino acids had no effect. They consider that these results suggest that a mechanism of facilitated diffusion may be involved in protein transport. Recently Smith, Witty and Brown (1968) have found that poly-L-arginine increases the rate of globulin transport in inverted sacs of newborn pig intestine, whereas poly-L-glutamic acid has no such effect.

Bovine albumin transport has also been studied (Brown, Smith and Witty 1968) both before and immediately after birth with everted intestinal sacs *in vitro*. The foetal intestine up to five weeks before term transports albumin readily, reaching a maximum of *c.* 400 μg/g intestine/hr, at two weeks before term, but the rate of transport falls at birth to about half this level and then returns to it. No digestion of the albumin was found with sacs of foetal or newborn intestine but partial digestion was apparent when the intestine was from piglets 1 day or more old. The presence of albumin stimulated the transfer across the intestine of water and sodium, but not glucose, and the transmural potential difference was lowered with sacs of foetal or newborn intestine but this effect of albumin disappeared during the first two days of age when partial digestion of the albumin became apparent. Both the total and ouabain-sensitive adenosine triphosphatase activities of the mucosa fell during the first two days of life. It was suggested that the movement of sodium into the cells down its concentration gradient may provide energy for the transfer of albumin.

7.1.11. Structure of the intestinal epithelium

Comline, Pomeroy and Titchen (1953) give a brief account of the changes in the intestinal epithelial cells of newborn piglets associated with the absorption of colostral globulins. Globules 0.5 to 10 μ in diam that stained like colostral globulin with iron haematoxylin or azocarmine were present in the cells 6–18 hr after ingestion of colostrum but were absent when colostrum was withheld. At first (6–8 hr) these globules were apical and the nuclei basal but later (15–18 hr) the positions were reversed. Similar globules appeared in the lacteals, especially late in this period. Vacuoles also were present in the cells of late foetuses and of both suckled and unsuckled young.

A more recent account of the structure of the newborn pig intestine has been provided by Sibalin and Björkman (1966), using light and electron microscopy. Unfortunately, the region examined was the proximal part of the jejunum, whereas probably protein transmission is most active in the ileum. The absorptive epithelium of the villi is simple columnar, with a few scattered goblet cells and chromaffine cells. The epithelial cells had regular brush borders of microvilli and ovoid nuclei placed centrally. Mitochondria were numerous in both the apical and basal cytoplasm. The Golgi complex was at the apical pole of the nucleus and rough endoplasmic reticulum occupied most of the cytoplasm. Apically, the cells were closely linked by numerous desmosomes. Caveoli were present on the free surface between the bases of the microvilli and also between the numerous processes in the intercellular spaces. The surfaces of the caveoli and of the microvilli were covered with a fuzzy substance.

In the newborn fasting pig a few caveoli and vesicles in the apical cytoplasm were present and there was little dilation of the intercellular spaces. In the newborn pig fed with colostrum there was a dramatic increase in vesicles and vacuoles in the apical and basal parts of the cells. These were loaded with foamy material, which appeared to be colostrum, and this substance was present also in the intercellular spaces, which were dilated. The Golgi vesicles were dilated with a moderately dense substance and caveoli were numerous on the surfaces bordering the intercellular spaces. After two days there was a marked decrease in the size and the number of vacuoles and vesicles and the intercellular spaces had become narrower. Thus, the period of very active pinocytotic absorption by the cells corresponded with

---

Plate 7.1. A. Electron micrograph of a jejunal cell from the midportion of a villus of a newborn, unfed pig. The apical vacuoles (av) during their formation produce indentations of the nucleus. The cell membranes of the lateral surfaces of these cells are extensively folded (if) and the Golgi apparatus (G) is subnuclear in position. × 4,250.   B. Part of the apical surface of such a cell showing the microvilli (M) and the apical tubules (at) and vacuoles (av), which are well developed. × 26,000.   C. Higher magnification of a similar region showing spine-like structures (s) on the inner component of the trilaminar membrane of caveoli, tubules (at) and vacuoles (av). × 62,000. (From Staley, Wynn Jones and Marshall 1968.)

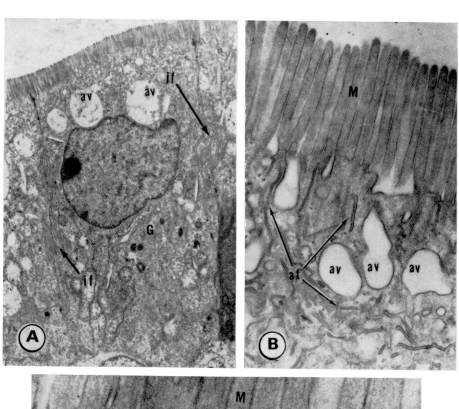

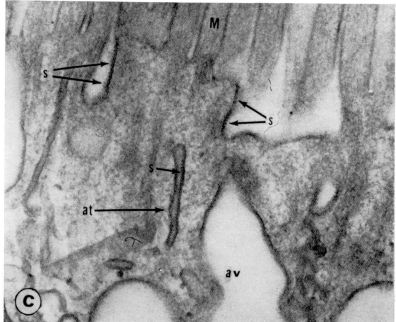

PLATE 7.1

that when transmission occurs and declines at the same time. Staley, Wynn Jones and Marshall (1968) in an electronmicroscopic study of the absorptive cells of newborn and three-week old piglets found that in the former the fuzzy layer on the microvilli was poorly developed, apical tubules and pinocytotic vesicles were numerous and the Golgi was basal to the nucleus. Spinous processes lined the apical tubules (plate 7.1). No appreciable change took place in the first 42 hr if the piglets remained unfed but after feeding the apical tubular system disappeared. Staley, Jones and Corley (1969) subsequently studied the fine structure of the duodenal cells of the newborn pig. At birth these cells resembled those of the adult but on receiving colostrum they rapidly developed an apical tubular system and large protein and lipid filled vacuoles. The protein accumulated in bulb-like enlargements of the ends of the tubules which became detached as vacuoles that passed through the cytoplasm. The appearance after 16 hr suggested that the protein passed through the cisternae of the Golgi apparatus and was discharged into the intercellular spaces. The lipid appeared to be contained in separate vacuoles to the protein and to be discharged in the intercellular spaces and through the basal membrane. The cells in 48-hr old pigs, after transmission of immunity had ceased, had lost these characteristics and returned to a condition resembling those of the adult.

Alkaline phosphatase in the intestine of the newborn pig is located mainly in the brush borders of the epithelial cells at the tips of the villi (Long, Ullrey and Miller 1964a). Phosphatase activity was greatest in the proximal and middle regions of the small intestine in newborn pigs, with less in the duodenum, distal small intestine and colon. After the pigs had suckled for 24 hr the distribution of activity was uniform from the duodenum to the colon and was significantly lower than in pigs of the same age that had been deprived of colostrum. These authors (Long et al. 1964b) also fed γ-globulin labelled with fluorescein isothiocyanate by stomach tube to newborn pigs and observed fluorescence within the epithelial cells after an interval of 6 hr. Pigs deprived of colostrum and sustained on glucose exhibited uptake of the fluorescent γ-globulin when this was administered at 2 weeks of age.

7.1.12. The decline in passive immunity and development of active immunity in young pigs

The problem of the manner in which passive immunity is gradually replaced by active immunity in the young pig is one of great importance for pig husbandry. It has immediate bearing on the development of resistance to disease, whether induced by natural exposure to infection or by artificial immunization, in the young pig. The changes in the γ-globulin content of the serum can provide an overall picture of the decline of passively acquired globulin and its replacement by synthesis.

Jakobsen and Moustgaard (1950) and Rook, Moustgaard and Jakobsen (1951) investigated the serum proteins of normal pigs from birth to maturity by sodium sulphate precipitation and by free boundary electrophoresis

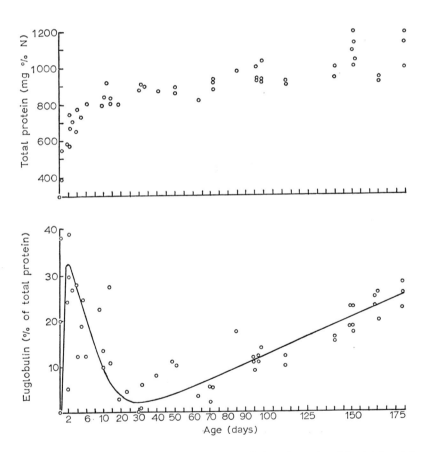

Fig. 7.8. Diagram of the variations with age from birth to 6 months of the total protein and euglobulin content of pig sera. (From Rook, Moustgaard and Jakobsen 1951.)

respectively. They observed that the euglobulin content rose steeply from nil at birth to a maximum of 30 to 40% of the total serum proteins after suckling and then fell off steeply to a minimum of about 5% between 20 to 30 days of age, thereafter rising gradually to the adult level of about 25% at 6 months (fig. 7.8). Foster et al. (1951), also using free boundary electrophoresis, obtained similar results confirming that the γ-globulin level falls to a minimum at 3 weeks of age.

Using paper electrophoresis Nordbring and Olsson (1957) found that the γ-globulin concentration in the serum fell to a minimum at about 4 weeks of age and thereafter increased gradually. Rutqvist (1958), using this method, likewise observed a decrease in γ-globulin to a minimum of 5 or 6% of the total serum proteins at 4 weeks of age and a steady increase thereafter. Lecce and Matrone (1960), also using paper electrophoresis, observed a γ-globulin concentration of 32 mg/ml at 2 days of age falling to 6 mg/ml at 14 days of age, but they did not follow the changes further. Ramirez et al. (1963) similarly observed a fall in the γ-globulin concentration from a maximum of 42% of the total plasma proteins at 12 hr to 13% at 2 weeks of age and 7% at 5 weeks of age. Estimations were not made between 2 and 5 weeks of age, so that the minimum probably was not observed. It is clear from these results that the minimum concentration of γ-globulin that is attained between 3 and 4 weeks of age represents the point at which wastage of the passively acquired γ-globulin is exceeded by synthesis. This conclusion is born out by the decline in passive immunity. Nordbring and Olsson (1957) observed that the antibody titres of the sera of piglets, born and suckled by sows that had been immunized with paratyphoid A vaccine, fell continuously after the initial rise on the first day. They were no longer detectable at 4 weeks of age in one litter that had an average titre of $\frac{1}{160}$ at 12 hr of age, but in another litter that had titres of $\frac{1}{1280}$ to $\frac{1}{2560}$ at 12 hr of age they had only fallen to $\frac{1}{160}$ to $\frac{1}{320}$ at 6 weeks of age. Brown, Speer, Quinn, Hays and Catron (1961) found that piglets farrowed and suckled by sows hyperimmunized with *Serratia marcescens* had an average antibody titre against this antigen of $\frac{1}{930}$ at one day old, $\frac{1}{330}$ at one week old and $\frac{1}{100}$ at two weeks old but were still detectable at 6 weeks old.

A study of the isoantigens of pig serum (Pickup 1968) also throws light on the persistance of maternal serum proteins and the appearance of autogenous proteins. Using nine isoantibodies produced in pigs by the injection of homologous serum proteins, four of the isoantigens were identified as β-globulins and three as γ-globulins; two being unidentified. The three γ-globulin isoantigens were detected in colostrum but three of the β-globulin isoantigens were not. These three β-globulin isoantigens were present and one of the γ-globulin isoantigens was sometimes present in the precolostral piglet serum, presumable being autogenous, while the other two γ-globulin isoantigens were absent. The γ-globulin isoantigens of the colostrum showed a characteristic rise in the piglets serum after suckling. The isoantigens of maternal origin were no longer detectable at 8 weeks of age, but the young pigs had produced detectable levels of their own isoantigens by 14 days of age.

The age at which young pigs can be actively immunized is broadly consonant with this interpretation also, though a number of contributory factors result in considerable variation. Hoerlein (1957) inoculated young pigs intravenously at 3 to 8 weeks of age and again 3 weeks after the first injection with one of four antigens; either killed *Brucella abortus*, or sheep red cells, or bovine serum or egg albumin. The pigs were allowed to suckle normally or else were reared without colostrum. The pigs were from sows that either had been actively immunized to the first two mentioned antigens during pregnancy or were non-immune. Piglets under the age of 8 weeks that had been deprived of colostrum did not produce antibody in measurable quantity, except to sheep red cells, whereas those that had received colostrum from a non-immune dam did produce antibody at 3 weeks old and the responce increased up to 6 weeks old. Antibody production was interfered with between 3 and 6 weeks of age in the piglets that had received immune colostrum. Anaphylactic shock following the second injection of antigen was not apparent in the piglets deprived of colostrum but was severe in the colostrum-fed piglets, as it was also after the first injection in those that had received immune colostrum.

Sterzl et al. (1960) found that piglets given a large immunizing dose of *B. suis* antigen at birth or when prematurely delivered by Caesarean section produced antibody at 3 weeks of age. Some piglets reared without colostrum and that had acquired heavy intestinal infections of *Escherichia coli* even produced demonstrable antibody on the 14th day of life.

Harmon et al. (1959) and Miller et al. (1962) injected piglets at ages ranging from birth to 6 weeks with *Salmonella pullorum* antigen and found that there was little or no antibody production until 3 weeks of age. Thereafter the response increased with age and that at 6 weeks was 20 times greater than that at 3 weeks. Miller et al. (1962) found that piglets, that had been injected at 2 weeks of age and twice subsequently on alternate days with human type B red cells, after an interval of 10 days produced much more

antibody if they had continued to suckle the sow than if they had been weaned at 4 days of age and reared from then on either a complete synthetic
milk diet or a commercial milk replacer. Brown et al. (1961) injected
piglets with *Serratia marcescens* antigen at 15, 18 and 22 days of age, an
antigen which is not found in the body and to which the mother would
never have been exposed. The piglets had produced antibody at 3 weeks of
age, but the titre declined rapidly after 24 days of age. These authors also
claimed that piglets can produce antibodies actively in the presence of
colostrum-acquired antibodies to the same antigens. The sows had been
actively immunized to *Escherichia coli* and *Candida albicans* and the piglets,
which were allowed to suckle, were injected with these antigens beginning
at 1 week old; after the passive antibody level had declined to a minimum
between 3 and 4 weeks old a small rise in titre at five weeks was interpreted as due to active synthesis.

Piglets appear to be capable of producing actively anti-viral antibodies
very early. Piglets suckling the mother and inoculated 6 to 12 hr after birth
with 1 ml of lapinized swine cholera virus showed resistance to the disease,
which declined rapidly with age (Weide, Sanger and Làgacé 1962). Serum
neutralizing antibodies could be detected at 7 days of age and reached peak
levels 3 weeks after inoculation with enterovirus at 1 to 5 days of age (Kelly
1964). Vaccination at birth of piglets with a highly attenuated live swine
virus resulted in resistance to challenge in as little as 9 days and for as long
as 3 months, provided the piglets were deprived of colostrum. Piglets that
had gained passive antibodies by suckling showed little or no resistance as a
result of vaccination and were susceptible to virus at 3 months old. The
authors considered that passively acquired colostral antibodies are more
important than age in preventing an active immune response (Aiken and
Blore 1964). Newborn germ-free piglets were given an injection of phage
(1 i.p. 10^{12} MSP-8) and showed measurable phage neutralizing activity at
48 hr old, which had increased > 80,000 at 73 hr old (Kim, Bradley and
Watson 1964). The primary response was a 19S immunoglobulin. Conventional piglets also developed 19S antibody to the phage which was followed
in 10 days by a rapid synthesis of 7S immunoglobulin.

Segre and Kaeberle (1962) immunized specific pathogen-free piglets at
3 weeks old with combined diphtheria and tetanus toxoids. Those fed
colostrum responded strongly and within a week to both antigens; those
deprived of colostrum responded later and much less strongly to tetanus and
did not respond significantly to diphtheria. However, when a minute amount

of pig serum hyperimmune to diphtheria and tetanus (1 ml of $\frac{1}{10,000}$ dilution) was added to the combined toxoids injected into the colostrum-deprived piglets the response to both antigens was intermediate between that of the colostrum-fed and colostrum-deprived groups receiving toxoid only. Removal of the antitoxins from the hyperimmune serum before adding it to the toxoid resulted in loss of its stimulating effect. These results were interpreted as implying that a trace of the specific antibody is necessary for response to an antigen and that such a trace of tetanus antitoxin, but not of diphtheria antitoxin, would be present in normal colostrum, whereas both antitoxins were present in the hyperimmune serum. To test this hypothesis further Myers and Segre (1963) injected the combined toxoid either at birth or at 3 weeks of age into piglets of hyperimmunized and of non-immune sows. The piglets of the immune sow that were inoculated at birth showed a significantly greater response to both antigens than did those of the non-immune sow, but although tetanus antitoxin was apparent at 1 week old,

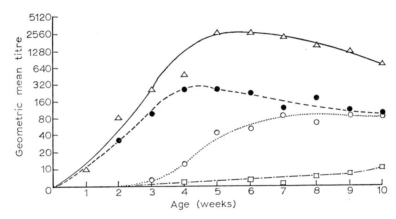

Fig. 7.9. Diagram of antibody production of colostrum deprived piglets born to actively immunized or non-immune sows injected with diphtheria and tetanus toxoids at 1 day of age. Tetanus antitoxin in the sera of piglets from immunized (△) and non-immune (●) sows. Diphtheria antitoxin in the sera of piglets from immunized (○) and non-immune (□) sows. (From Myers and Segre 1963.)

the diphtheria antitoxin was not apparent until 4 weeks old (fig. 7.9). When the inoculation was at 3 weeks of age there was no significant difference in response between the piglets of the immune and non-immune sows, presumably because the passively acquired antibody had disappeared. Subsequently, Locke, Segre and Myers (1964) found that administration orally and intraperitoneally of 750 mg of purified 6.6S sheep γ-globulin to newborn pigs did not result in the production of antibodies to sheep γ-globulin, but intraperitoneal administration of a similar amount of crude sheep γ-globulin, containing both 6.6S and 18S fractions, did result in the production of anti-sheep-globulin antibodies. Toxoid together with dilute 6.6S sheep antitoxin injected intraperitoneally into 3-week old piglets induced the production of large quantities of tetanus and diphtheria antitoxins. Toxoid with dilute 18S sheep antitoxin under the same conditions failed to stimulate the production of diphtheria antitoxin but did result in high titres of tetanus antitoxin. Kaeberle (1968) found that colostrum-fed piglets did not produce antibody in response to tetanus toxoid injections. Colostrum-fed pigs responded better to antigens than colostrum-deprived pigs and the response was enhanced by the presence of a small amount of specific antibody. Colostrum-fed pigs showed a higher rate of increase in complement titres, serum lysozyme activity and in bactericidal activity than did colostrum-deprived pigs. It was concluded that passive immunity derived from colostrum may inhibit the development of active immunity for the first 3 weeks of life but its presence at low levels thereafter enhances the production of antibody.

Kim, Bradley and Watson (1966) injected 2×10^{12} MSP-2 actinophage intraperitoneally into germ-free, colostrum-deprived miniature piglets within 5 hr of obtaining them by hysterectomy 3 to 5 days before full term. No antibody was detectable in their sera at 36 hr, but at 48 hr antibody was detectable and increased until 72 hr, the limit of their survival. At birth no immunoglobulin was detectable in their sera by very sensitive methods and the antibody they synthesized was a 19S immunoglobulin, antigenically identical to the 7S γG-globulin and distinct from the γM-macroglobulin. Piglets given a single injection of the phage at 1 month old showed an antibody response identical to that of the adult sow.

Binns (1968) injected foetal and neonatal pigs with *Salmonella* flagellar antigen. Injection at 2 weeks of age resulted in the appearance of antibody in 5 days that reached a peak titre at 9 days after injection and then declined until 3 weeks after injection when it began to rise to a second peak at 5 weeks after injection. No mercaptoethanol-resistant antibody was present during the first peak, but it was present during the second peak. Injection of newborn piglets had similar results. Foetal piglets injected 8 to 35 days before birth had agglutinins in their sera at birth and when injected again at 10 days of age they gave a secondary type response and had both mercaptoethanol-sensitive and -resistant antibodies. Foetal piglets injected 55 days before birth did not produce antibody and a subsequent injection after birth gave a primary type response.

Tissue transplantation immunity can be developed very early in life also. Binns (1967) injected pig foetuses *in utero* at 60, 80 or 104 days of gestation with bone marrow or lymphoid cells from unrelated or distantly related pigs and grafted skin from the donors of the cells on to them at 10 to 12 days of age. They found that a high degree of immunological tolerance to the skin grafts had been induced by the injections at 60 days of gestation. Injections after 80 days of gestation resulted in sensitization and quicker rejection of the skin grafts than in controls. All the injections into the foetuses resulted in immunoglobulin production detectable by immunoelectrophoresis of the sera of the piglets at birth and before they had suckled.

It would appear that although the young pig can produce antibody during the first week in response to a powerful antigenic stimulus at birth, three weeks old is a more normal time for active immunization and the capacity to respond immunologically increases until at least 6 weeks old. Apparently the receipt of colostrum by the young pig is important for the development of active immunity. It may be that the presence in colostrum and passive transmission of traces of specific antibody may play an important part in the response to those antigens to which pigs are normally exposed, but it seems certain that passive immunity to a specific antigen in greater than trace amounts interferes with active immunization so long as it persists.

7.2. The horse

7.2.1. Introduction

The literature on the transmission of passive immunity in the horse is surprisingly small but such information as is available suggests that the process is similar to that in the pig. Haemolytic disease of the newborn occurs naturally in thoroughbred horses and also in mules, and much of the literature is devoted to this aspect of transmission. It will be referred to here only briefly since a separate chapter is being devoted to a comparative treatment of this disorder.

7.2.2. The placenta and foetal membranes

Development of the embryonic membranes in the horse is broadly similar

to that in the pig, but proceeds more slowly. At first the yolk-sac is large
and joined to the chorion over its abembryonic hemisphere to form the
bilaminar omphalopleur. The amniotic folds appear about the 18th day
and close about the 21st day. Later, about the 10th week, the amniotic
ectoderm gives rise to glycogen-rich thickenings, called the amniotic pustules.
The allantois has appeared by the time the amniotic folds have closed and
by the 28th day it completely surrounds the amnion, isolating it from the
chorion. The extension of the allantois reduces the attachment of the yolk-
sac to the chorion (bilaminar omphalopleur) to a small area, which persists,
unlike that in the pig. The possibility of transference of materials from the
uterine lumen across the bilaminar omphalopleur to the yolk-sac cavity at
later stages is, thus, not excluded, though the relatively small size of this
area and of the yolk-sac itself renders its significance doubtful. Beginning
about the 6th week the allantois everywhere fuses with the chorion to form
an allantochorion, except for this small area of yolk-sac attachment and the
extremities of the fusiform chorionic vesicle. Short, simple villi fitting into
corresponding crypts in the mucosa develop on the equator of the allantochorion. Later these are developed over the whole surface of the allantochorion and tend to be arranged in circular groups around the openings of
the uterine glands. The villi of the mature placenta are long and branched.
During midpregnancy structures called endometrial cups are formed in the
uterine mucosa in a semicircular area overlying the region where the foetal
umbilical cord joins the allantochorion. Numerous enlarged glands discharge into these cups which become filled with a lake of secretion and
cellular debris, rich in gonadotrophine, between it and the allantochorion.
It will be noted that, as in the pig, the trophoblast does not invade the maternal tissues and the uterine epithelium persists intact, so that the placenta
is epitheliochorial and diffuse.

7.2.3. *Transmission of immunity*

Horses are particularly good producers of antitoxins and, as tests for these
are very sensitive, conditions are favourable for the study of the transmission
of passive immunity. Ransom (1900) appears to have been the first to describe a case in which a mare was immunized with tetanus toxin, the treatment
beginning when she was 2 months pregnant. The foal's serum was sampled
within 8 hr of birth and was found to have an antitoxic titre $\frac{1}{5}$ of that of the
mother's serum, at which level it remained approximately constant. The

milk was tested 3 days after parturition and had a titre $\frac{1}{40}$ that of the mother's serum. Bardelli (1930) hyperimmunized a mare during the last four months of pregnancy to tetanus and found at the time of birth an antitoxic titre of $\frac{1}{300,000}$ in her serum and $\frac{1}{400,000}$ in her colostrum, but the serum of the foal was negative. Five days later the titre of the colostrum had fallen to $\frac{1}{100,000}$ and the foal's serum had a titre of $\frac{1}{60,000}$, at which it remained for the first month. At the end of the second month the foal's serum titre had fallen to $\frac{1}{8,000}$ and at five months to $\frac{1}{1,000}$, thereafter falling gradually to nil at 17 months. The milk remained at a titre of $\frac{1}{1,000}$ from the first month until the foal was weaned at five months. Mason, Dalling and Gordon (1930) record the case of a mare with a 'natural' diphtheria antitoxic titre in her serum of 1.25 units/ml. She gave birth to a foal which had no detectable diphtheria antitoxin in its serum at birth. The foal at birth was given a dose of 50 ml sheep anti-lamb-dysentery serum, containing 14,000 units of antitoxin, and 50 ml horse anti-tetanus serum containing 90,000 units of antitoxin. Antitoxin was present in the foal's circulation 3 hr later and within 24 hr had attained titres of 0.5 units of lamb dysentery antitoxin and 3 units of tetanus antitoxin. Thus both the homologous and heterologous antitoxins were transmitted approximately equally readily. Alexander and Mason (1941) observed that the foals of dams immune to horsesickness had no antibodies to this virus at birth but in less than 30 hr after suckling they had titres at least as high as their dams. The titre of the foal's serum therafter declined gradually, the duration of its persistance being proportional to the initial titre attained, but usually persisted for approximately 6 months. This passive immunity gave protection against the virulent virus for 157 days but not for 239 days. While antibodies were demonstrable in the serum, and for an indefinite period thereafter, vaccination against horsesickness had no immunizing effect. Polson (1943) states that Alexander and Polson (unpublished) had found subsequently that a foal of an immune dam fostered for its first feed on a susceptible dam and then returned to its own immune dam was fully susceptible to horsesickness, whereas a foal of a susceptible dam fostered for its first feed on an immune dam and then returned to its own dam was resistant to artificial infection. Lemétayer, Nicol, Jacob, Girard and Corvazier (1946a, b), using mares hyperimmunized to tetanus, always found antitoxin in the sera of the newborn foals, provided the maternal serum concentration exceeded 1 unit. They found that transmission after birth is much greater. Antitoxin was present in the colostrum at birth, though the concentration was variable, but the titre fell rapidly thereafter. The foals

serum, after the first suckling, attained a concentration of antitoxin approximately the same as that in the maternal serum, provided none of the
colostrum had been lost. Bruner, Edwards and Doll (1948) were unable
to detect any transmission of immunity before birth and maintain that it
occurs entirely by way of the colostrum. Initially the antibody concentration
of the colostrum was higher than that of the maternal serum, but with
suckling by a vigorous foal the concentration fell within the first 12 hr to less
than 5 % of the initial value and remained at this level in the milk for several
weeks. They found that a 5-day old foal did not absorb any antibodies from
colostrum.

7.2.4. Haemolytic disease of the newborn

Haemolytic disease of the newborn is brought about by immunization of
the mother to antigens of the offspring inherited from the father and borne
mainly on the red blood cells. The maternal antibodies transmitted to the
circulation of the offspring result in agglutination and lysis of the blood
corpuscles, with consequent anaemia, jaundice and uraemia, that may be
fatal. The subject will be dealt with in more detail later but it is necessary
to mention here that study of the disease in horses has provided evidence
concerning transmission that confirms the conclusions outlined above.
Susceptible foals are born unaffected but rapidly develop the disease after
having ingested the maternal colostrum. Susceptible foals remain healthy
if they are fostered on a mare that is not immune to their sire. After being
fostered for a few days they can be returned to their own mother without
harmful effects. Thus it is apparent that no significant amount of antibody
reaches them before birth, but that it does so rapidly after birth by way of the
colostrum. Evidently their capacity to absorb antibody from the gut is
lost if they are allowed to suckle a foster mother for a short period, after
which the antibody in the maternal milk has no appreciable effect upon them.

7.2.5. Changes in the serum proteins

There is little information concerning the changes in the serum proteins of
the newborn foal. Earle (1935), using sodium sulphate fractional precipitation
and nitrogen determinations, found that euglobulin was absent or present
in at most very small quantities and pseudoglobulin I in only small quantities
at birth. After ingestion of colostrum there was an increase in euglobulin

and a very marked increase in pseudoglobulin I, as well as an increase in total globulins. Polson (1943), using electrophoresis, found a complete absence of γ-globulin and only traces of β-globulin at birth, with relatively low total serum proteins. At five days of age after suckling there are traces of γ-globulin, a tremendous increase in β-globulins, little change in the α-globulins and a decrease in albumin, the total serum protein having increased by more than 40%. Thereafter the γ-globulin content of the serum rises gradually.

CHAPTER 8

Transmission of immunity in the ruminants

8.1. Introduction

The ruminants are a compact group so far as transmission of immunity is concerned, since information is available for three species only. Most of the considerable literature relates to the cow, some to the sheep and a small part only to the goat. The only significant transmission of immunity in all three occurs during a brief interval after birth by way of the colostrum and neonatal gut. All three appear to resemble each other in these processes sufficiently closely for it to be convenient to deal with them together.

The development of the foetal membranes is similar (see Amoroso 1952; Chang 1952) to that in the pig, as is their final arrangement, except that the placenta is more complex and its attachment to the uterine tissues more intimate. The number of young born is small, usually one, sometimes two or even three, and consequently the conceptus occupies the whole or a large part of the uterine cavity and separate chambers are not formed around each, as in the pig. Fusion of the allantochorions and anastomoses of the blood vessels occurs commonly when twins are present in cattle and sometimes in goats and sheep (Steven 1968). It results in vascular exchange between the co-twins. The ruminants have specialised regions of the uterine mucosa, where placental attachment occurs, called caruncles. These are circular or oval thickenings, free from glands and regularly arranged in rows. They are present at all times but enlarge during pregnancy. There are 160–180 caruncles in the uteri of a goat, 88–96 in sheep and 70–120 in cows. Those of sheep and goats are concave on their free surfaces, whereas those of cows are convex. The foetal trophoblast of the allantochorion, where it is in contact with a caruncle, thickens and gives rise to allantochorionic villi which grow into the caruncle, the uterine epithelium of which degenerates so that the foetal villi are lodged in crypts in the sub-epithelial connective tissue, which is very vascular. These tufts of villi are called cotyledons and, with their corresponding caruncles, form placentomes. Cotyledons are formed only in connection with caruncles but some caruncles may not be occupied by cotyledons. The cotyledons are scattered over the surface of the allantochorion, the intervening regions of which remain smooth and unattached, though closely applied, to the uterine tissues. However, the uterine epithelium in contact with the smooth allantochorion degenerates also, except around the mouths of the uterine glands. Thus the placenta of the ruminant is cotyledonary in form and syndesmochorial in structure; since the chorionic trophoblast is in direct contact with the uterine sub-epithelial connective tissue and there is one less layer of tissue, the uterine epithelium, intervening between the maternal and foetal circulations than in the epitheliochorial placentae of horses and pigs.

8.2. *Transmission of antibodies before birth*

All the evidence available suggests that transmission of immunity does not occur before birth in any of the three ruminants examined, the goat, the sheep and the cow. Famulener (1912) could find no appreciable amounts of haemolysins in the sera of the newborn kids, of goats that had been actively immunized to sheep red cells, before suckling. Reymann (1920) confirmed that goats, immune to *Escherichia coli*, typhoid, rabbit-red cells and horse red cells, did not transmit agglutinins to their kids before suckling. McAlpine and Rettger (1925) found that calves before suckling are always negative for both agglutination and complement fixation tests for *Brucella abortus*, regardless of whether or not their mothers are positive reactors. McDiarmid (1946) confirmed that heifers, exposed to virulent infections of *B. abortus*, did not transmit agglutinins in demonstrable amounts to the sera of their calves until after these had suckled. Mason, Dalling and Gordon (1930) failed to find antitoxin in the serum of a calf at birth of a cow immunized to diphtheria toxin. Kerr and Robertson (1946) found that neither the antibodies to *Trichomonas foetus* induced by active immunization nor the natural agglutinins normally present in adult bovine serum, and which are specific for this protozoan parasite, were transmitted before birth to the calves. Brown (1958a) could detect no antibodies in the sera of calves from cows immune to rinderpest before they had suckled.

Graves (1963) showed that cows vaccinated against the virus of foot-and-mouth disease did not transmit neutralizing antibodies to their calves before suckling. Thus it appears that bovine antibodies to a variety of antigens, bacterial, protozoan, virus and foreign red cells, are not transmitted from the cow to her calf before suckling. Further, heterologous serum albumin does not appear to be transmitted to the serum of the foetal calf either from the circulation or from the uterine lumen of the mother. Kulangara and Schechtman (1963) injected human serum albumin intravenously into three cows near full term, respectively 18, 63 and 96 hr before parturition. The quantities injected were sufficient to produce concentrations of *c.* 0.5 to 2.0 mg/ml in the maternal serum at parturition and the sensitivity of the antiserum used was sufficient to detect 1 µg/ml of the albumin, yet the sera of the calves before suckling were negative. These authors also injected into the uterine lumen of another pregnant cow, 70 hr before parturition, 120 ml of human serum albumin solution containing 16.8 g of albumin. Although the albumin was present in significant quantity in the maternal serum at parturition, it could not be detected in the serum of the calf. Mason, Dalling and Gordon (1930) could find no trace of lamb dysentry antitoxin in the sera of the lambs before suckling of ewes that had been hyperimmunized to the formalized toxin. Horse diphtheria antitoxin (112,000 units), injected intravenously into a pregnant ewe 10 days before lambing, was not detectable in the sera of the lambs at birth, despite the sensitivity of the test for this antibody. Oxer (1936) also failed to find antitoxin in the sera of lambs before suckling of ewes which had been prophylactically vaccinated against entero-toxaemia. Schneider and Szathmary (1939a) could find no significant amounts of agglutinins or of antitoxins in the sera of lambs before suckling of ewes immunized during pregnancy to both typhoid bacteria and diphtheria toxoid. Cummings and Bellville (1963) immunized ewes to *Salmonella pullorum* but failed to demonstrate any transfer of antibodies from mother to foetus.

8.3. *Transmission of antibodies after birth*

Famulener (1912) actively immunized pregnant goats with sheep red cells and found that their kids after taking colostrum rapidly acquired a relatively high antibody titre in their serum. Reymann (1920) found that antibodies to *Escherichia coli*, typhoid, rabbit and horse red cells, are transmitted to kids with the colostrum. Maximum titres were found in the sera of the kids as early as 11 hr after birth. Sometimes the titre of the kid's serum exceeded that of the mother's serum, but rarely exceeded that of the colostrum, which was normally higher than that of the maternal serum.

Mason, Dalling and Gordon (1930) observed the transmission, by way of the colostrum, to newborn lambs of the antitoxins to lamb dysentry and to tetanus toxoid. Tetanus antitoxin, administered passively to a pregnant ewe 10 days before parturition, was detectable in the lamb's serum within $\frac{1}{2}$ hr of oral administration of her colostrum. Maximum titres were attained in the lamb's serum between 12 and 24 hr after taking the colostrum. Oxer (1936) found that the titres of the sera of lambs, after suckling ewes pro-phylactically vaccinated against entero-toxaemia, often equalled or exceeded those of the maternal sera. However, Schneider and Szathmary (1939a), observing the colostral transmission of antibodies to *E. coli*, typhoid and diphtheria toxoid to lambs, found that the titres attained by the lambs sera tended to be somewhat lower than those of their dams. McCarthy and Mc-Dougall (1949, 1953) state that when ewes were immunized during the second half of pregnancy to *Salmonella typhosa* H antigen, the maximum titres attained in the sera of the lambs equalled those of the maternal sera in most cases but seldom were as high as those of the colostrum.

Orcutt and Howe (1922) showed that the calves of cows immune to *Brucella abortus* had detectable antibody in their blood as early as 2 hr after taking colostrum and that the titre continued to rise until after at least 18 hr. McAlpine and Rettger (1925) and McDiarmid (1946) confirmed that antibodies to *B. abortus* appeared in the calf's serum within 2 hr of suckling and increased up to 24 hr, thereafter declining gradually over the first 6 months or so, depending on the titre of the colostrum taken. Thorp and Graham (1933) also observed the transmission of *Brucella* agglutinins to the calves of cows of infected herds. Diphtheria and tetanus antitoxins and antibodies to *Hemophilus pertussis*, vaccinia, rabies, rinderpest, foot-and-mouth disease, *Escherichia coli*, *Trichomonas foetus* and *Salmonella* are all transmitted to calves by way of the colostrum (Smith and Holm 1948; Kerr and Robertson 1946, 1954; Brown 1958a; Williams 1961; Graves 1963; Schoenaers and Kaeckenbeeck 1964; Valette 1967; Royal, Robinson and Duganzich 1968). Brown (1958a) found the mean half-life of maternally derived antibodies to rinderpest in calves to be 36.7 days and the extinction point 10.9 months.

Kerr and Robertson (1946, 1954) found that naturally occurring, specific agglutinins for *T. foetus* are transmitted by way of the colostrum to the suckling calf. The titre of these antibodies in the calf's serum is nearly always less than in adult serum. These antibodies do not sensitize the skin of the calf and they disappear from the circulation between the 17th and 55th days. Cows, actively immunized to *T. foetus*, produce colostrum with a high titre, sometimes higher than that of the serum. The suckling calf rapidly acquires a serum titre of these antibodies approximating to that of the colostral whey. For example, 2 hr after the first feed a calf had a titre practically equal to that of the whey. The peak titre usually is reached after 12 to 16 hr. The titre declines gradually to its lowest level, below that of the normal adult, by the 4th month. The passively acquired immune antibody, unlike the normal antibody, becomes fixed by the skin after 10 days or more and a positive reaction to intradermal injection of the antigen can be obtained then. The skin test remained positive up to $3\frac{1}{2}$ months but it was negative at 7 months. Antibody was absorbed also when immune serum was given as a first feed, but the titre attained in the calf's serum was not as high as that of the serum fed and the skin was not sensitized. However, Connan (1968) failed to demonstrate transmission of antibodies to gastro-intestinal nematodes.

8.4. *Transmission of homologous γ-globulins after birth*

Interpretation of the fairly extensive literature on the transmission of γ-globulins in ruminants, that has appeared during the last thirty years, is complicated by the rapid advances in the techniques of identification and separation of the various components. This period spans the time from when identification was dependent on salt fractionation, and the immune globulins were recognised as euglobulin and pseudoglobulin 1, through that in which free-boundary electrophoresis was regarded as the essential criterion, to the present time, when gel immunoelectrophoresis and column chromatography have provided much more powerful tools that have enabled several distinct species of γ-globulin to be identified. Since most of the literature relates to the cow, it is convenient to dispose of that relating to the goat and the sheep first.

Earle (1935) showed that newborn kids and lambs before suckling had very low levels of euglobulin and of pseudoglobulin 1 in their blood and that these proteins increased rapidly during the first day after suckling and then decreased gradually. Hansen and Phillips (1949) also observed a striking increase in the γ-globulin component of the serum of newborn kids, following ingestion of colostrum. Deutsch and Smith (1957) found an

increase in total serum proteins in kids of from 4.95% at birth to 5.25% at
12 hr of age, following suckling, with an accompanying rise in the 6.5S
γ-globulins from 0 to 14.5% of the total serum proteins. Charlwood and
Thomson (1948) used free-boundary electrophoresis on sheep sera and on
lamb sera before suckling and after suckling at 24 hr of age. The lamb sera
contained a higher percentage of α-globulins than did adult sheep sera but the
β-globulins, though present in the adult, were scarcely distinguishable in the
lamb sera. The γ-globulins were almost entirely absent from the sera of
lambs at birth, but at 24 hr they showed a very large increase with a serum
content higher than that of the adult. McCarthy and McDougall (1949) as
a rule could find no immune globulin in the sera of lambs before suckling,
though occasional lambs had traces. After suckling there was a rapid increase
in serum γ-globulin which later declined gradually in amount; though even
at 5 weeks of age it was still higher than at birth, although appreciably
lower than in the serum of the dam. Similarly, Ullrey, Long, Miller and
Vincent (1962) noted a rapid increase in the total serum protein concentration and in the percentage of γ-globulin in the sera of lambs after the consumption of colostrum.

Regarding cattle, Howe (1921, 1924) and Orcutt and Howe (1922) found
that the amounts of euglobulin and of pseudoglobulin 1 in the serum of the
newborn calf were negligible before suckling but that they rose rapidly
after suckling and reached peak values at about 1 day. Smith and Little
(1922a, b) showed that the large increase in neonatal mortality in calves,
resulting from withholding colostrum from them, could be reduced by the
oral and intravenous administration of adult serum. San Clemente and
Huddleson (1943) examined the sera of newborn calves before and after
the ingestion of colostrum. They found that, before ingestion of colostrum,
the outstanding characteristic of the serum was the extremely high concentration of α-globulin and the almost or complete absence of γ-globulin.
Within 4 hr of ingesting colostrum the γ-globulin might account for about
15 per cent of the total protein, or if the cow was infected with *Brucella*,
as much as 30 or 40 per cent. Jameson, Alvarez-Tostado and Sortor (1942)
state that there is no γ-globulin and only small amounts of β-globulin in
the sera of newborn calves before suckling but that, after suckling, γ-globulins appear and both β- and γ-globulins increase rapidly in the sera. Hansen
and Phillips (1947) observed in calves which had ingested colostrum or
colostral pseudoglobulin an immediate increase in serum γ-globulins during
the first 24 hr of life. Subsequently, these authors (Hansen and Phillips 1949)

claimed that the serum of the newborn calf contained a small amount of proteins, immunologically similar to the immune proteins of colostrum. Smith (1948) and Smith and Holm (1948) found that the serum of the calf did not contain any electrophoretically slow-moving globulins at birth but that two days after birth 44% of the total serum protein was colostral globulin. This immune globulin decreased to about half its initial concentration in 20 days but some persisted for many months. Polson (1952) agreed that the calf at the time of birth has no γ-globulins in its serum, though they are present at high concentration within a few hours of the first feed of colostrum. Deutsch and Smith (1957), after giving a feed of 2,500 ml of colostrum to a newborn calf, observed an increase during the first 12 hr of from 4.46 to 5.45% of total serum proteins, mainly due to the 6.5S γ-globulins increasing from 0 to 20% of the total serum proteins.

Bangham, Ingram, Roy, Shillam and Terry (1958) fed newborn calves with either ^{131}I-labelled whole bovine serum, or ^{131}I-labelled bovine colostral whey, in warm milk and subsequently determined the activities of the various serum protein fractions after separation by column electrophoresis (fig. 8.1). They came to the conclusion that the several labelled proteins in the serum or colostrum administered were transmitted by the gut to the

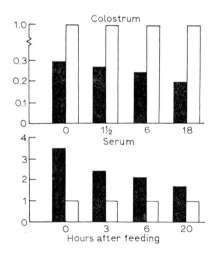

Fig. 8.1. Histograms of the changes in the relative concentrations of ^{131}I-labelled albumin (■) and globulins (□) in the circulations of two calves fed with labelled bovine colostral or serum proteins. The ratio at 0 hr is as in the preparations fed. (From Morris 1968, after Bangham et al. 1958.)

circulation with equal facility. Subsequently the proportions of the various labelled proteins in the circulation changed gradually, due to differential rates of equilibration with the extravascular fluid. Pierce and Feinstein (1965) confirmed that, when whole bovine serum is fed to the newborn calf, the fast and slow components of γG are transmitted to the circulation approximately equally readily, although the slow component is normally deficient in colostrum. Graves (1963) showed, by the sensitive method of immunoelectrophoresis, that calves were born with no γ-globulin in their sera but that it was already present 2 hr after they had ingested colostrum.

Much research has been carried out at the Institute of Animal Physiology, Cambridge, on the identification and characterisation of the immune globulins of bovine serum and colostrum. This work extends over a long period with the consequent employment of increasingly sophisticated methods. Pierce (1955a) identified electrophoretically in precolostral calf serum albumin, two major components similar to the α- and β-globulins of adult serum and a minor component, comprising 1.4% of the total serum protein, which was not fibrinogen and which had a mobility similar to γ_1-globulin. It was suggested that it was either autogenous or passively acquired before birth. During the first day after suckling there was a rapid increase of γ-globulin to 30% of the serum proteins. Johnson and Pierce (1959), in further electrophoretic and ultracentrifugal studies, could not find any γ-globulin sedimenting at 6.5–7.0S in precolostral calf serum. In postcolostral calf serum there was a rise in total proteins, of which up to 51.6% was immune lactoglobulin sedimenting at 6.0–6.5S, but no such component occurred in precolostral sera. The electrophoretic and ultracentrifugal characteristics of this globulin had not been significantly altered by transmission. Milstein and Feinstein (1968a, b) state that there are two principal varieties of γG in bovine serum, a fast and a slow $\gamma_1 G$ and $\gamma_2 G$, of which only the $\gamma_1 G$ is concentrated in colostrum and is the sole source of the passive immunity transferred to the calf. This component activates complement and fixes in skin, whereas $\gamma_2 G$ does neither. This finding is the reverse of that noted by Morris (1967) on the transmission of bovine immunoglobulins in the young rat, where the fast γG component is scarcely transmitted at all and almost all the passive immunity is derived from the slower components, but whereas in the cow the selection occurs in the mammary gland and not by the gut of the calf, in the rat it is the gut which is selective and little is known about selection by the mammary gland. The transfer of colostral immunoglobulins has been studied quantitatively by Klaus, Bennett and Jones (1969) who found that γM- and γG-globulins were absorbed equally well by the newborn calf. However, these authors claim that there is considerable individual variation and that 3 out of 10 calves remained virtually agammaglobulinae-mic despite the ingestion of colostrum.

8.5. *Termination of the transmission of passive immunity*

The capacity of the gut of the newborn ruminant to transmit immunoglo-bulins from the lumen to the circulation is of short duration, persisting for only a few hours from birth under normal circumstances of suckling. The ruminants in this respect resemble the pig and the horse and differ from rats and mice in which transmission continues almost throughout lactation. Corresponding with the brevity of the process in ruminants it is extremely rapid and intense while it lasts. Much work has been directed to determining the duration of transmission and to attempts to hasten or postpone its termination, often referred to as cut-off or closure.

Mason, Dalling and Gordon (1930) found that antitoxin in the colostrum, which is readily transmitted by the newborn lamb, is not transmitted by the four-day old lamb which had received several feeds of colostrum during the first three days. McCarthy and McDougall (1949), by delaying the in-gestion of colostrum by lambs, found that the transmission of immune globulins still occurred at 29 hr, but did not occur 48 hr or more after birth. Lecce and Morgan (1962) found that lambs kept without food for 24 or 48 hr, could still transmit PVP, bovine colostral proteins and hens egg proteins to the serum at these ages, whereas lambs fed bovine colostrum from birth were unable to transmit PVP or egg proteins at 24 hr old. This cut-off was not due to the presence of food in the gut at the time these foreign substances were administered, because a lamb that was suckled for 5 days from birth and then starved for 2 days could not transmit PVP when 7 days old.

Howe (1921) showed that although there was a large increase in the γ-globulins of the serum of a calf that received a first feed of colostrum at 5 hr after birth, there was only a very small increase in those of a calf that had been fed with milk at 5 hr after birth and then colostrum at 21 hr after birth. It was shown also that a calf got little γ-globulin from suckling a cow which had been milked until near the time of parturition and had not been dried off before the colostrum formed. Mason, Dalling and Gordon (1930) allowed a calf to suckle normally for the first 12 hr and then gave it a feed of 150 ml of mixed sheep and horse antisera containing 28,000 units of lamb dysentery antitoxin and 160,000 units of tetanus antitoxin. Both antitoxins were present in the calf's serum after 12 hr but attained only very low levels compared to the serum administered. Hansen and Phillips (1947) found that, if colostrum or colostral globulin were withheld from calves until after 24 hr from birth, no measurable increase in serum γ-globulin occurred. Deutsch and Smith (1957) state that the gut of the newborn calf or kid loses its permeability to large molecules during the first 24–30 hr of life. They attempted unsuccessfully to prolong the period of permeability by maintaining calves on orally administered sugar solution or by intravenous transfusion for 36–40 hr, and then at 48 hr giving a feed of 2500 ml of colostrum. Also they failed to prolong transmission in milk-fed calves by treatment with steroid hormones, including diethylstilboestrol, progesterone, cortisone and with ACTH. Neither feeding on a mixture of milk and amniotic fluid nor inhibition of gastric digestion with aluminium hydroxide gel had any effect on prolonging transmission. Smith and Erwin (1959) maintained calves on milk and at 6, or 18, or 48–60 hr after birth introduced colostrum directly into the duodenum, behind a ligature. Those receiving the colostrum at 6 or at 18 hr rapidly transmitted γ-globulin to the circulation but none was transmitted by those receiving the colostrum at 48–60 hr (fig. 8.2). Graves (1963) found that antibodies to foot-and-mouth disease were not transferred by vaccinated cows to their calves, if these had been fed first with skim-milk or bovine serum. Smith, Reed and Erwin (1964), after injecting bovine γ-globulin into the amniotic fluid during the 6th, 7th and 8th months of gestation, were unable to find any evidence of absorption by the foetal calf gut. Calves delivered 2–3 weeks prematurely and maintained on milk and aminosol–dextrose for 38 hr thereafter were unable to absorb γ-globulin from colostrum, although calves that received colostrum immediately after premature delivery did so readily. Injection of somatotrophin intramuscularly at birth in full-term calves did not affect the transmission of γ-globulin from colostrum at 15 hr of age. Schoenaers and Kaeckenbeeck (1964) maintained calves for the first 1–4 hr on cow's milk, or egg albumin solution, or glucose solution, and administered 600 ml of immune colostrum 4–8 hr later. They found that the capacity of these calves to transmit the antibodies to their circulations was not reduced, as compared to that of calves receiving the same amount of the same colostrum as a first feed within the first 8 hr after birth. Calves maintained on glucose solution, and nothing else, for 2–3 days absorbed antibodies from colostrum

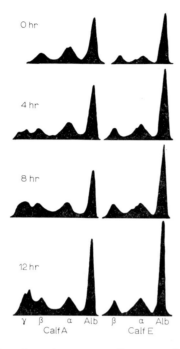

Fig. 8.2. Electrophoretic patterns (on paper, sodium veronal buffer, *p*H 8.6, $I = 0.075$, 16 hr) of the serum before and at 4, 8 and 12 hr after the introduction of colostrum into the duodenum of each of two calves. The duodenum was isolated from the rest of the gut by ligatures above and below the point where the colostrum was introduced. The colostrum was administered to Calf A at 6 hr old and to Calf E at 48–60 hr old. (After Smith and Erwin 1959.)

administered at the end of this period equally as well as those that received it at birth. It was concluded that the prior ingestion of milk, egg albumin or glucose solutions, does not reduce the capacity of the newborn calf to absorb antibodies from colostrum, but that maintenance exclusively on glucose solution does result in prolongation by up to 2–3 days of the capacity to absorb antibodies. Valette (1967) claimed that all calves, given antiserum by mouth up to the fourth day, but not on the fifth day of age, showed significant rises in serum antibody levels. Kruse (1969) found that the proportion of the γ-globulin received in the colostrum that was transmitted to the circulation of the calf was determined by the age at first feeding and decreased linearly by about half between 2 and 24 hr of age. It was unaffected by the quantity or concentration of γ-globulin in the colostrum.

8.6. *The immune globulins of colostrum*

Since the gut of the newborn ruminant appears to transmit proteins in solution non-selectively, it follows that the normal young animal receives into its circulation all those that occur in colostrum. These include maternal serum proteins secreted by the mammary gland and others which are synthesized in the gland. Transmission of immunity in these animals depends, therefore, on the particular components of the immune globulins which are transferred from the circulation to the colostrum and of any that may be locally synthesized by the lymphoid tissues of the mammary glands. A great amount of work over a long period has been devoted to these problems and, in consequence, our knowledge of ruminant, or more particularly bovine, colostrum is more extensive than that of any other species, with the possible exception of man.

Crowther and Raistrick (1916) distinguished caseinogen, lactalbumin and lactoglobulin, in both bovine colostrum and milk. They considered that the lactoglobulin was probably identical with the serum globulin, but the lactalbumin was very different from serum albumin. They noted that the protein content of the mammary secretion declined rapidly with milking over the first few days, but this decline was much greater in globulin than in albumin and was least in caseinogen. Wells and Osborne (1921) distinguished caseinogen, lactalbumin, lactoglobulin and an alcohol soluble protein in cow's milk and showed, by anaphylactic tests, that these four protein components were distinct. The globulin component alone sensitized guineapigs to injections of bovine serum and alone produced an anaphylactic reaction in guineapigs that had been previously sensitized with bovine serum, thus supporting Crowther and Raistrick's (1916) contention of the identity of the globulin fractions of mammary secretions and of serum. Smith (1946a) showed electrophoretically that immune lactoglobulin is the predominant protein in bovine colostrum. He considered that the immune lactoglobulin, although equivalent to serum globulin in guineapig anaphylactic tests, is not identical. Subsequently (Smith 1948), he showed that the protein concentration of colostrum within a few hours of parturition was as high as 15–26%, or 2–3 times the concentration in plasma. The immune globulins constituted 50–60% of the total colostral proteins, and 85–90% of the total colostral whey proteins. Polson (1952), in free boundary electrophoretic studies of bovine serum and colostrum, noted the absence of albumin and a high concentration of both γ_1- and γ_2-globulins in colostrum.

However, his figures suggest that there is a much higher proportion of γ_1- to γ_2-globulin in colostrum than in serum, and that the γ_2-globulin of colostrum has a higher mobility than that of serum, though he considers this difference in mobility insignificant.

Askonas, Campbell, Humphrey and Work (1954), using antibody to type III pneumococcus and isotopic labelling with ^{35}S-methionin, showed that immune globulin passes from the blood to the milk or colostrum without degradation and resynthesis. Blakemore and Garner (1956) likewise showed that homologous bovine γ-globulin, isotopically labelled with ^{131}I, after injection into the circulation, appears in the precolostrum within 22 hr and is concentrated there at least 13 times. Later, Garner and Crawley (1958) found that ^{131}I-labelled bovine γ-globulin intravenously injected into a cow in late pregnancy was concentrated by the mammary gland 2–3 times, but that this did not occur when it was injected into a cow 5 months pregnant. Secretion into the precolostrum ceased abruptly at parturition. Larson (1958) found that, as parturition approached, the serum proteins in the lacteal secretions increased relatively to the specific proteins synthesized in the mammary glands. All the major blood protein components were detectable in colostrum but the very large increase was in the β_2- and γ_1-globulins. Johnson and Pierce (1959) found that immune lactoglobulin constituted nearly half of the total colostral protein and consisted mainly of a component sedimenting in the ultracentrifuge at 6.4S, together with a small proportion of macroglobulin sedimenting at 18S. Murphy, Aalund, Osebold and Carroll (1964), using the techniques of immunoelectrophoresis, anion exchange chromatography and double diffusion antigenic analysis, were unable to find any qualitative differences between the γ-globulin components of bovine lacteal secretion and serum, although they did find large quantitative differences. Pierce and Feinstein (1965) were able to identify three immune globulin components both in serum and colostrum, using biophysical and immunological techniques, but these were in very different proportions in the two fluids.

There is no doubt that the concentration of immune globulins in the colostrum exceeds that in the serum, whereas the concentration in the milk is very low in comparison. Reymann (1920) observed that the antibody titre of the colostrum was higher than that of the serum in immune cows. Minett (1937) found that the concentration of staphylococcal antitoxin in the colostrum equalled or exceeded that in the blood in normal cows, whereas the concentration in milk whey was only $\frac{1}{40}$ to $\frac{1}{80}$ of that in the serum. Miller and Heishman (1943) also found considerable amounts of staphylococcal antitoxin in the colostrum of cows that had the antitoxin in their blood. In a few cases the colostral concentration exceeded that of the blood by 4–6 times, whereas little or none was found in the milk. Dixon, Weigle and Vazquez (1961) state that the udder of the cow continually incorporates serum proteins into its secretions. During colostrum formation γ-globulin is concentrated over 100 times more than serum albumin, and at parturition its concentration in the colostrum is 5 times that in serum, whereas albumin is only $\frac{1}{25}$ that in serum.

Larson and Kendall (1957) found that the serum protein concentration of pregnant cows increased from about 14 weeks before parturition, to a maximum at 4 weeks before, and then declined by 10–30% to a minimum at parturition. This decline was due to a loss of immune β_2- and γ_1-globulins and of some α-globulins, whereas the levels of albumin, β_1- and γ_2-globulins did not change. The decline in serum proteins corresponded with the time of colostral formation. Larson (1958) estimated that the amounts of β_2- and γ_1-globulins leaving the blood corresponded with the amounts appearing in the lacteal secretions. Dixon, Weigle and Vazquez (1961) estimated that γ-globulin constituted 78% of the total whey proteins of colostrum and amounted to 100 mg/ml. The amount present in the colostrum at parturition approximately equalled the amount that disappeared from the circulation during colostrum formation, indicating transmission. The cessation of γ-globulin secretion by the udder during the early part of the dry period is reflected by the development of a hypergammaglobulinaemia in the circulation, and the removal of γ-globulin from the circulation by the udder, during colostrum formation, results in an antepartum hypogammaglobuli-naemia. The loss of γ-globulin from the circulation to the udder amounts to about 10% of the total γ-globulin turnover during most of lactation but it may exceed catabolic loss during the latter part of colostrum formation. The normal half-life of bovine γ-globulin in the circulation is about 10 days.

There is clear evidence of the selective secretion and concentration in the colostrum, not only of immune globulins in preference to other serum proteins but also of some components of the immune globulins in preference to others. Smith (1946a, 1948) appears to have been the first to recognise that the lactoglobulin of colostrum was not identical with serum globulin in electrophoretic mobility and other properties, although admitting their equivalence in guineapig anaphylactic tests. Polson (1952), however, claimed that both γ_1- and γ_2-globulins of serum are secreted in colostrum, although

his electrophoretic diagrams permit of the conclusion that the slower components are, at least relatively, deficient compared to the faster. Murphy,
Aalund, Osebold and Carroll (1964) found that fast 7S γ-globulin (γ_1G) was
selectively concentrated in colostrum, whereas the slow 7S component

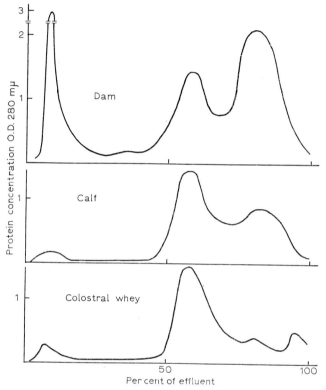

Fig. 8.3. Anion exchange chromatograms of maternal and calf sera and of colostrum from
another dam for comparison. The slow 7S γ_1G-globulin peak predominates in the dam's
serum, but is only just discernable in the calf's serum and colostrum, whereas the fast
γ_2G-globulin peak is dominant in both the calf's serum and colostrum. (From Murphy,
Aalund, Osebold and Carroll 1964.)

(γ_2G) was virtually completely absent (fig. 8.3). They state also that both
γA-globulin and γM-globulin were present in colostrum but at lower concentrations than in serum. Pierce and Feinstein (1965) distinguished three
components of different electrophoretic mobilities in both serum and colostrum. The two faster components in each were antigenically similar and

probably identical, but the fastest was present in colostrum in high concentration and in serum at low concentration. The slowest component was present in serum at high concentrations but was present as only a very minor component in colostrum. Milstein and Feinstein (1968a, b) identify, by studies of the amino acid sequences of the heavy chains, the electrophoretically faster component of both serum and colostrum as $\gamma_1 G$, and the slowest component as $\gamma_2 G$. The $\gamma_1 G$-globulin activates complement, sensitizes skin and is concentrated in colostrum, whereas $\gamma_2 G$-globulin does none of these things. Thus the $\gamma_1 G$-globulin is the source of passive immunity transferred to the calf. Milstein and Feinstein also state that the C-terminal ends of the heavy chains of these two varieties of γG-globulin are very similar in amino acid sequence, differing only in one threonine residue in the $\gamma_1 G$ being replaced by methionine in the $\gamma_2 G$-globulin. This part of the heavy chain resembles very closely the octadecapeptides of rabbit, human and horse γ-globulins, especially the last named. Beale, Feinstein and Hobart (1968) have shown that although the light chains appear similar in the two, the arrangement of the interchain disulphide bridges linking them to the heavy chains is different. Feinstein and Hobart (personal communication) have repeated on sheep the work done by Pierce and Feinstein (1965) on cows, and have obtained similar results. Specific antisera for sheep $\gamma_1 G$ or $\gamma_2 G$ cross react with the corresponding bovine proteins and complement fixation is restricted to sheep $\gamma_1 G$, as with the bovine globulin. Jonas (1969) records γM-antibody activity in presuckling sheep colostrum. Stone and Gitter (1969) also find that the major component of bovine immune globulin transferred from mother to calf is γG-globulin, but that the γG-globulins of colostrum and of calf serum have a slightly different electrophoretic mobility to that of maternal serum. They identified γM- and γA-globulin in colostral whey but found no evidence of albumin.

Most of the immune globulin in colostrum of a normal animal is certainly derived from the circulation but the problem remains as to whether there is any local production in the mammary gland of antibody that is secreted into the colostrum. Minett (1937) observed that with staphylococcal infections of the udder the amount of antitoxin in the colostral whey rose, but this increase was attributed, probably correctly, to an increased permeability of the inflamed gland to serum antibody rather than to local production. Miller and Heishman (1943) noted that in cows with circulating staphylococcal antitoxin there was variation in the quantities in the colostrum between quarters of the udder. There were large amounts in the colostrum when there was an udder infection. Lascelles, Outteridge and Mackenzie (1966) tackled this problem experimentally by infusing killed *Salmonella typhi* 'O' bacteria into one side, and killed *Brucella abortus* bacteria into the other side of the udder of pregnant ewes, about 1 month before parturition. The antibody titres of the colostrum from both sides were higher than those of the serum, but the concentration of each specific antibody usually was higher in the colostrum of the side that had received the infusion of the corresponding antigen than in that of the other side, indicating that both local synthesis and active transfer from the circulation were occurring (fig. 8.4). During the first week of lactation there was a rapid fall in the titres of the milk but the differences between the two sides in the concentrations

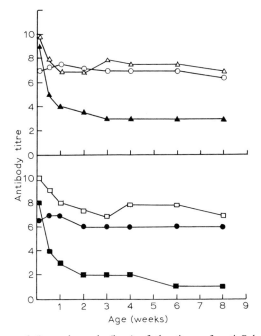

Fig. 8.4. Diagrams of the reciprocals ($\log_2$) of the titres of anti-*Salmonella* and anti-*Brucella* antibodies in plasma and in milk whey from both sides of the udder of a lactating ewe. The udder had been infused some weeks before parturition on the one side with killed *S. typhi* 'O' antigen and on the other side with killed *B. abortus* antigen. Anti-*Salmonella* titres of the plasma (○) and of the whey on the *Salmonella*-infused side (△) and on the *Brucella*-infused side (▲). Anti-*Brucella* titres of the plasma (●) and of the whey on the *Salmonella*-infused side (■) and on the *Brucella*-infused side (□). (From Lascelles, Outteridge and Mackenzie 1966.)

of the respective antibodies persisted, indicating that most of the milk antibody was of local origin.

8.7. *Other colostral protein components*

Colostrum has been shown to contain protein of small molecular size. Smith (1946b) states that about 6% of the colostral pseudoglobulin is of small molecular size, sedimenting in the ultracentrifuge at 2–3S. Johnson and Pierce (1959) observed that about 22% of the colostral whey proteins sediment at 3S or less, and undoubtedly contain α- and β-lactoglobulins. Balfour and Comline (1962) observed that ^{131}I-labelled bovine serum γ-globulin, introduced into the duodenum of the newborn calf, was transmitted to the lymph rapidly and in large quantities when administered in colostral whey but that very little was transmitted when administered in saline containing sodium, potassium, magnesium and calcium chlorides at

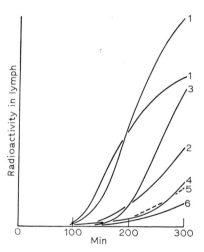

Fig. 8.5. Diagram of the recovery after 1–2 hours of radioactive protein in the thoracic duct lymph of calves given ^{131}I-labelled bovine γ-globulin directly into the duodenum. The labelled protein was given in 1, colostral whey filtrate containing small protein accelerator; 2, colostral whey filtrate without small protein accelerator; 3, small protein accelerator, inorganic phosphates and glucose-6-phosphate; 4, small protein accelerator and glucose-6-phosphate; 5, small protein accelerator and inorganic phosphate; and 6, small protein accelerator. (From Morris 1968, after Balfour and Comline 1962.)

cationic concentrations similar to those in whey (fig. 8.5). This was found to be due to the presence of a protein fraction, probably of low molecular weight, that was not heat-coagulable at pH 5.4 and that required the presence of inorganic phosphate or of glucose-6-phosphate to be active. Some of this activity was present also in milk whey but not in adult serum.

Bovine colostrum also contains large amounts of trypsin inhibitor. This was prepared as an inactive crystalline complex with trypsin, both components of which, when the complex was split, were active. The inhibitor itself was prepared in crystalline form, after separating it from the split complex, and had an activity 2–3 times greater than that of soya bean inhibitor.

8.8. *The cytology of the alveolar cells of the mammary gland*

Dixon, Weigle and Vazquez (1961), using the fluorescent antibody technique, observed that the connective tissue stroma of the bovine udder contains at all times considerable amounts of serum proteins, albumin and γ-globulin. The interstitial fluid of the stroma increases greatly during colostrum formation. At this time the acinar cells enlarge, develop secretory vacuoles and become loaded with large amounts of γ-globulin, but with little or no albumin. They concluded that the acinar epithelium of the udder transports serum proteins, particularly γ-globulin, from the circulation to the lacteal secretions. Few plasma cells could be found in the glandular tissues and they considered that little or no formation of γ-globulin occurs at any time in the normal udder. During colostrum formation the acinar epithelium of the udder functions primarily as a transporter of serum proteins, largely γ-globulin, while in lactation it acts primarily as a protein producer. Feldman (1961) states that during colostrum formation the alveolar cells, including the nuclei, are enlarged to about twice the size of those of the dry udder. The cytoplasm appears active and its texture is denser than that of the cytoplasm of the dry-phase cells. The Golgi element is somewhat enlarged and often may be seen on both sides of the nucleus. The vacuoles of the Golgi element are increased in number, distended, and generally of the same diameter. The amount of γ-globulin transported from the circulation to the acinar lumen was estimated to be 15% of the weight of the alveolar epithelium. The fluorescent antibody method revealed the γ-globulin as rounded or oval masses, usually in the supranuclear portions of the cells. Fluorescence was absent or faint in the rest of the cytoplasm. The contents of the alveolar lumen were densely and homogenously fluorescent. The Golgi element was the only constant organ comparable in size to the γ-globulin masses that could be seen with the electron microscope. It was concluded that 'the dynamic process whereby gamma globulin is selectively removed from the blood and transported through the cytoplasm to the Golgi element and from the Golgi element to the acinar lumen remains undisclosed'.

8.9. *Transmission of heterologous immune globulins and other substances*

There is no doubt that heterologous serum proteins in the maternal circulation can be transmitted to the colostrum in ruminants. Dixon, Weigle and Vazquez (1961) found that heterologous γ-globulin is concentrated in bovine colostrum to a degree similar to homologous γ-globulin. Two cows were given intravenously 500 ml of human plasma each, respectively 2 and 1 week before parturition; the first concentrated the human γ-globulin 300 times, and the second 100 times, more than the human albumin. Kulangara and Schechtman (1963) likewise observed the passage to the colostrum, after an interval of 18 hr, of human albumin injected intravenously into a pregnant cow, but they failed to observe it in another cow in which the interval was 96 hr. Mason, Dalling and Gordon (1930) demonstrated the passage of horse diphtheria antitoxin into the colostrum of a pregnant sheep injected intravenously with it 10 days before lambing.

There is also evidence that other soluble proteins, as well as serum proteins, reaching the intestine of the newborn ruminant are transmitted to the circulation indiscriminately. Mason et al. (1930) showed that both horse tetanus antitoxin and horse diphtheria antitoxin are transmitted readily from the gut to the circulation of the newborn lamb. Approximately $\frac{1}{8}$ of the dose administered orally reached the circulation in one lamb. Transmission of these heterologous antitoxins did not appear to be at significantly different rates to the homologous antitoxins. These authors also demonstrated the transmission of antitoxins prepared in sheep and horse from the gut to the circulation of a newborn suckling calf. Hansen and Phillips (1949) fed newborn kids *ad libitum* with goat, or cow, or pig, colostrum and found that in each case, the γ-globulin was present in the circulation in large quantities after 24 hr (fig. 8.6). The γ-globulins appeared to be unaltered by transmission, as the bovine γ-globulin retained its slightly greater electrophoretic mobility as compared to that of the goat and the pig. Deutsch and

Smith (1957) demonstrated that goat γ-globulin, human γ_2-globulin, ovalbumin and conalbumin, are all transmitted to the circulation of the newborn

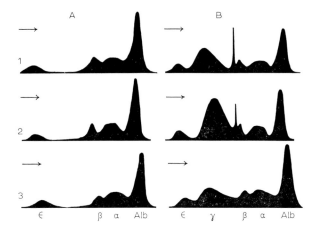

Fig. 8.6. Electrophoretic patterns (barbiturate-citrate buffer, pH 8.6, $I = 0.088$) of newborn goat serum before (A) and 24 hr after (B) ingestion of 1, goat; 2, bovine; and 3, pig
colostrum. (From Hansen and Phillips 1949.)

calf when administered orally in bovine colostrum. Balfour and Comline
(1959) injected into the duodenum of newborn calves 2 % solutions of either
bovine or human serum albumin or of dextran with a mean mol wt of 40,000
or 100,000 and observed their appearance in lymph from the cannulated
lymphatic duct. All were transmitted to the lymph and the transmission
of the dextran was accelerated when it was administered in an ultrafiltrate
of colostrum. Pierce (1961a) showed the passage of gelatin from the gut
to the circulation of newborn calves after oral administration, in either
boiled milk or saline. Lecce and Morgan (1962) found that lambs, kept
without food for 24 or 48 hr from birth, could still transmit at these ages
PVP, bovine colostral proteins and hen's egg proteins, to the serum. Calves
fed on bovine colostrum from birth were unable to transmit either PVP or
egg proteins at 24 hr old. A lamb that had suckled for five days from birth
and was then starved for 2 days could not transmit PVP when 7 days old.
Pierce, Risdall and Shaw (1964) observed that bovine insulin, orally administered to calves less than 24 hr old, was transmitted to the circulation in a
biologically active form and could produce a severe hypoglycaemia.

8.10. Transport of globulin from the intestine to the circulation

It has been shown by Comline, Roberts and Titchen (1951b) that in newborn calves and kids, the absorption of colostral globulin takes place entirely in the small intestine and that none is absorbed from the abomasum or large intestine, when these have been isolated by ligatures from the small intestine. Antibody globulin in colostral whey, introduced into the duodenum at 6 to 27 hr after birth, appears in the lymph after 1–2 hr. It was shown by cannulation of the intestinal lymphatic duct and the thoracic duct, that the transport of the absorbed globulin to the circulation is entirely lymphatic and that none enters the foetal circulation directly. This is in contrast to results with the smaller molecules of serum albumin, of which a considerable proportion is transported by the blood, although the major part is lymph borne (Balfour and Comline 1959), and to those with the still smaller molecules of insulin, of which the major part appears to be transported by the blood and only a minor part by the lymph (Pierce, Risdall and Shaw 1964).

8.11. Changes in the digestive tract associated with transmission

There is evidence that the absence of proteolytic activity in the digestive tract of the newborn ruminant may facilitate the colostral proteins reaching the small intestine without degradation, and to this end the colostral trypsin inhibitor may contribute, and that absorption is affected by the epithelial cells of both jejunum and ileum. Comline, Roberts and Titchen (1951a) examined the cytology of the small intestine of calves, from 3–24 hr after birth, that had received colostral whey by duodenal cannula and of others which had not received it. They examined also the cells of calves 63–65 hr old. The epithelial cells of the younger calves contained lightly stained homogenous bodies. The epithelial cells of the jejunum and ileum when absorption was taking place contained globules with similar staining properties to the whey in the lumen. These globules varied in size and position within the cells. Discrete globules up to 2μ diam were present in the cytoplasm immediately within the free borders of some cells, together with either one or two large globules up to 10μ diam or several smaller ones $2–6 \mu$ diam. Sometimes material staining like the whey could be seen in the lacteals. Very few globules could be seen within cells when the whey was administered

63–65 hr after birth, in contrast to the appearance when absorption was taking place, after administration of the whey during the first day. Hill (1956) examined the histology of the abomasum and of the small intestine of foetal and newborn lambs, as well as the hydrogen ion concentration and proteolytic activity of the abomasal contents. At birth peptic cells containing pepsinogen granules were numerous and well defined in the abomasal mucosa but parietal cells were very few in number. During the first three days of life there was a progressive increase in the number of parietal cells and, by the end of this period, the appearance of the gastric glands resembled that of the adult. During this period the hydrogen ion concentration of the abomasal contents changed from pH 7.0 to pH 3.0

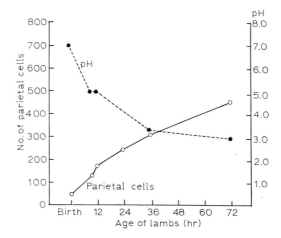

Fig. 8.7. Diagram of the changes with age of the pH of the contents of, and of the number of parietal cells in, the abomasa of 6 young lambs. (From Hill 1956.)

(fig. 8.7). The clotting activity of the contents was considerably greater than that of adult gastric juice but the proteolytic activity, when adjusted to pH 2.1, was considerably less than that of the adult. Thus, although pepsinogen was present in the peptic cells and the activity at pH 2.1 of the abomasal contents showed that pepsin was present in the lumen, the paucity of parietal cells capable of secreting hydrochloric acid, and the consequent near neutral pH, would have prevented proteolysis occurring during the period when immunity is transmitted. It was observed that the epithelial cells of the jejunal villi of newborn lambs which had not received colostrum, were devoid of protein globules but that at $9\frac{1}{2}$–12 hr old, after receiving colostrum, these cells contained numerous globules. The globules were less numerous in the cells at 24 hr old, were scarce and largely replaced by pale-staining 'ghosts' at 36 hr old, and were absent at 72 hr old. Hill and Hardy (1956) also record large numbers of globules of varying sizes from 2.5–15 μ diam. in the intestinal epithelial cells of lambs and kids up to 36 hr old, which were absent from the cells in older animals. These globules were present throughout each cell but the majority were infranuclear in position, as the nucleus was close to the free border. The material in these globules was identified as muco- or glyco-protein by its reaction with a variety of histochemical reagents. The colostral whey in the lumen stained similarly, as also did material in the lacteals of the villi. Huber, Jacobson, Allen and Hartman (1961) examined the digestive enzyme activity in the young calf and found that pancreatic amylase, lipase and protease activities were lowest during the first day, increased during the first week and changed little thereafter. Intestinal lactase activity was highest during the first day and decreased thereafter. Intestinal maltase activity was low, as compared to lactase and did not change with age, and intestinal sucrase activity was not detectable.

8.12. *Proteinuria of the newborn*

Newborn ruminants receiving colostrum display an intense but transient proteinuria, as is generally well known and the physiological basis of which has been the subject of much research. Howe (1924) showed that the ingestion of colostrum by the newborn calf is followed by a marked proteinuria, which does not appear if colostrum is withheld. This proteinuria was transient and did not continue beyond the first few days though the rise in serum globulin, consequent on the ingestion of colostrum, remained. Smith and Little (1924) also observed this phenomenon and showed that the feeding of colostrum was responsible for the proteinuria, which develops soon after birth and disappears after the third day. They found that the urine of bovine foetuses and of unfed calves did not contain appreciable protein. The time of appearance and the quantity of protein in the urine was related to the time and amount of colostrum fed. Deutsch and Smith (1957) confirmed the occurrence of proteinuria in calves after feeding colostrum. They found that the principal protein component in the urine up to 10 hr after feeding was β-lactoglobulin which, in the ultracentrifuge, sedimented at 2.75S. It could be prepared in crystalline form from the urine.

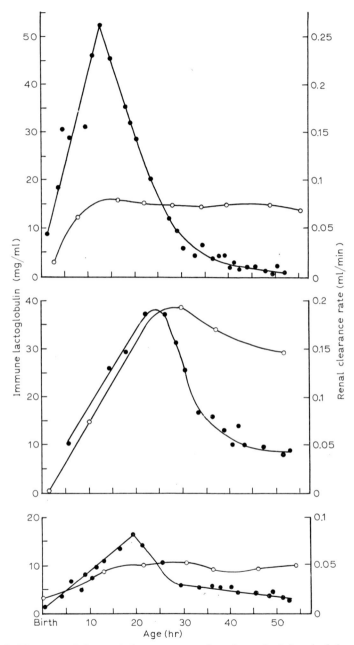

Fig. 8.8. Diagrams of the renal clearance rates of total protein (●) and of the concentrations of immunoglobulin in the sera (○) of three newborn calves fed on colostrum. (From Pierce 1959.)

Small amounts of a protein with an electrophoretic mobility similar to γ-globulin and sedimenting at 6.4S, and still smaller amounts sedimenting at 12.5S, were found in the urine 48 hr after feeding, when much of the β-lactoglobulin had been eliminated. Pierce (1959) noted proteinuria during the first 30–40 hr of life in calves fed colostrum (fig. 8.8) and its absence in calves fed on boiled milk. The proteinuria increased up to 17–26 hr after birth and rapidly declined thereafter to minimal levels at 40 hr. Thus the peak level coincided with the cessation of transmission of colostral proteins. There were at least six components in the urine proteins, of which two had mobilities faster than serum albumin and which constituted more than half of the total protein. Pierce and Johnson (1960) found that precolostral calf and adult bovine urines had less than 0.2 g/100 ml of protein, while post-colostral calf urine had up to 2.0 g/100 ml of protein. During proteinuria the excess protein had a wide range of electrophoretic mobilities, including components faster than serum albumin. The latter resembled β-lactoglobulin and lactalbumin of colostrum in its slow ultracentrifugal sedimentation. Antibody activity could be detected in the urine of calves of immune mothers and also protein with the electrophoretic mobility, but not the sedimentation behaviour, of γ-globulin, indicating the presence of fragments of immune globulins. All these small molecular weight colostral proteins, although detectable in the lymph from the intestine, were cleared from the circulation by the kidneys so quickly that they were not detectable in the blood. Pierce (1961a) subsequently showed that newborn calves, fed on gelatin in glucose–saline, developed a proteinuria in which frequently over 50% of the urinary protein was gelatin. Calves fed on sterilized milk or glucose–saline and injected intravenously with gelatin, developed a proteinuria, even if they were too old to transmit proteins from the gut. Thus it appears that the termination of proteinuria in the normal young animal is due to no more colostral proteins of small molecular weight reaching the circulation from the gut rather than to any change in the kidneys, which remain permeable to protein molecules of an appropriately small size. Molecules of a size up to and including β-lactoglobulin and gelatin, both with molecular weights of *c.* 40,000, continue to be excreted, while glomerular filtration retains molecules such as serum albumin, with a molecular weight of *c.* 70,000, and apparently the foetal serum protein fetuin, with a molecular weight of *c.* 50,000, as well as all the immune globulins. For example, Pierce, Risdall and Shaw (1964) showed that insulin, presumably in the form of a hexamer with a molecular weight of *c.* 36,000, administered orally to the newborn calf and resulting in a very high blood insulin level and severe hypoglycaemia, appeared in the urine. Elegant proof that most of the urinary protein of the newborn calf is maternal β-lactoglobulin was provided by Pierce (1960). He confirmed the existence of two electrophoretically distinct β-lactoglobulins, A and B, in bovine colostra. These are genetically determined and either one or both may be present in the colostrum of a particular cow. Three calves were fed with colostra respectively containing AB, A or B β-lactoglobulins. The protein appearing in their urines corresponded electrophoretically with that in the colostrum fed. A similar proteinuria occurs in the newborn lamb. McCarthy and McDougall (1949) observed a strong, but transient, proteinuria in lambs suckling immune ewes during the first day or two after birth. The protein present in the urine included globulin and showed an appreciable antibody titre.

8.13. *The decline of passive immunity and development of active immunity*

The normal young ruminant that has taken colostrum and acquired its maximum concentration of maternal immune globulin by the second day, enters upon a period when the decline in the passively acquired globulin overlaps the rise in autogenous γ-globulin and tends to obscure it (fig. 8.9). Consequently, a point is reached some time after birth when the γ-globulin concentration is at a minimum and the loss of passively acquired γ-globulin is equalled by the production of autogenous γ-globulin. Determination of the rate of disappearance of the one is complicated by the rate of appearance of the other. Considerable breed differences also are encountered (Tennant, Harrold, Reina-Guerra and Laben 1969). Young ruminants reared without colostrum over the first few days and therefore without passively acquired γ-globulin, provide material in which the appearance of autogenous γ-globulin can be followed without such complication, but the possibility should be borne in mind that the rate of synthesis of autogenous γ-globulin might be affected by the initial agammaglobulinaemic state as compared to the normal animal. Another method of following the production of immune globulin is by examining the production of antibody in response to active immunization with various antigens but, in this case, there is a probability that early exposure to antigenic stimuli may expedite the onset of, and perhaps accelerate, the synthesis of γ-globulin as compared to the normal animal. It is as well to bear these considerations in mind in considering the

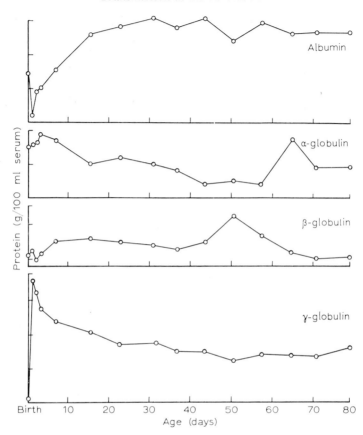

Fig. 8.9. Diagrams of the changes with age from birth to 80 days of the electrophoretic components of the serum of a colostral fed calf. (From Pierce 1955a.)

evidence available on the decline of passive immunity and the development of active immunity. This is a subject of practical importance in determining the duration of protection from disease provided by passive immunity, as well as the stage at which active immunity can be induced effectively. The time at which active immunity can be induced may be affected also by the presence in the circulation of passively acquired antibody to the particular antigen employed. There is also the possibility of the induction of a state of partial or complete tolerance resulting from very early exposure to antigen.

Hansen and Phillips (1947) found that when calves were raised without access to colostrum, the various blood serum protein fractions did not approach normal values until the animals were about 8 weeks of age. During this period there was a gradual increase in the serum γ-globulins and a concurrent decrease in the serum α-globulins in the blood of these calves. Smith (1948) noted that the globulin acquired from the colostrum decreased steadily in calves from 2 days of age, reaching about half its initial maximum concentration after 20 days, but that some persisted for many months. Electrophoretically slow moving globulin was hardly detectable in the blood of the newborn calf, and even after 4 months it had not reached the normal adult level. Smith and Holm (1948) observed that slow-moving γ-globulin does not appear until some time after birth and then gradually increases in concentration. These authors examined the rate of disappearance of diphtheria antitoxin and of antibodies to *Hemophilus pertussis* and vaccinia, passively acquired from the mother, in the colostrum and found the time taken to decline to $\frac{1}{2}$ the initial value to be *c.* 16 days for the antitoxin and *c.* 50 days for the other two antibodies. Electrophoretic estimation of the decline in immune globulin concentration gave a half-life of about 20 days. Macdougall and Mulligan (1969) determined the half-life of $\gamma_1 G$ in the newborn calf and found it to be 18 days, a catabolic rate corresponding to the degradation of 6% of the intravascular pool each 24 hr and an extravascular to intravascular distribution of 1.2 to 1.

Kerr and Robertson (1954), studying immunity to the common protozoan parasite of cattle, *Trichomonas foetus*, found that adult animals, without being immunized or suffering from the disease, had a natural agglutinin to this organism at a titre of $\frac{1}{48}$ to $\frac{1}{96}$. This 'natural' antibody was passively transmitted with the colostrum to the calf, in the circulation of which it declined gradually and disappeared from the 17th to the 55th day. Autogenous antibody began to appear by the 35th–60th day and was fully established by the 63rd–113th day. The induced antibody, transmitted by actively hyperimmunized cows to their calves, declined logarithmically with a half-life of 14–20 days and, in one animal, of 57 days. Injection of *T. foetus* antigen into young calves up to 4 weeks old induced no antibody. When the dose given at this early age was small, the animal did produce antibody in response to another dose at a later age, but when the initial dose was large, the capacity to respond to a subsequent injection of the same antigen, but not of other antigens, was seriously impaired, evidently due to a state of tolerance. Pierce (1955a,b), in electrophoretic and serological studies, confirmed these findings concerning the colostral transmission of natural and induced agglutinins to *T. foetus*, their subsequent logarithmic elimination from the circulation of the calf, and the production by the calf of natural agglutinins between the 30th and 60th day. He showed further that the autogenous production of γ-globulin by the calf begins soon after birth, although calves could not be actively immunized to this antigen at that stage. Using colostrum deprived calves it was possible to distinguish autogenous γ_1- and γ_2-globulin components by the 10th day, at which time the γ_1-globulin was the greater, but by the 30th day the γ_2-globulin exceeded the γ_1-globulin component and a small γ_3-globulin component could be distinguished. Subsequently Johnson and Pierce (1959), in an electrophoretic and ultra-centrifugal study, largely confirmed these results showing, in colostrum deprived calves, a steady rise in γ-globulin concentration from a very low level during the first week to a near adult level by 60 days, together with a concurrent rise in albumin levels. The α-globulin, after an initial rise during the first week, fell to a very low minimum at 60 days, while the β-globulin level remained relatively constant after the first week. Finally, Pierce (1961b) provided further evidence of the synthesis of γ-globulins in colostrum depri-

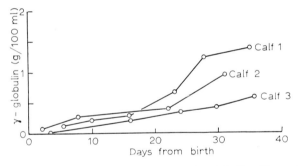

Fig. 8.10. Diagram of the changes in concentration of γ-globulin with age in the sera of three calves deprived of colostrum, showing the onset of autogenous synthesis. Electrophoretic determinations (phosphate buffer, pH 8.0, $I = 0.2$). (From Pierce 1961b.)

ved calves from the end of the first week (fig. 8.10). The antigenic effect of heterologous serum proteins absorbed by the newborn after oral administration was shown by giving hyperimmune equine diphtheria antitoxic serum in maternal colostrum to a newborn calf and testing subsequently for antitoxin and for equine protein in the serum, as well as for anti-equine-serum-protein antibody. Anti-equine antibody was produced by the 16th day and had reached a titre of $\frac{1}{50}$ by the 23rd day. At 74 days, when neither antitoxin or equine protein could be detected in the circulation, the calf showed skin sensitivity in response to intradermal injection of equine serum protein. It was given then an intramuscular injection of equine serum to which it showed a clear anamnestic response with a titre of $\frac{1}{16,000}$.

The newly born lamb can respond to immunization with the toxoids of *Clostridium welchii* (Batty, Thomson and Hepple 1954) or diphtheria (Barr, Glenny, Hignett, Randall and Thomson 1952). The newborn calf can respond to tissue transplants (Billingham and Lampkin 1957) and to rinderpest vaccine (Brown 1958b). The latter author found that a passive immunity tends to prevent an active response to rinderpest vaccine. Williams (1961) observed that in calves rabies antibody, passively acquired from their vaccinated dams, persists for 12–14 weeks after birth. Calves with measurable passive immunity did not respond to vaccination whereas those without measurable passive immunity did respond. Similarly, Graves (1963) found that a passively immune calf, of a cow vaccinated for foot-and-mouth disease, did not itself respond to vaccination until its circulating passive antibody had fallen to a low level, whereas a calf of the same age born to a non-immune dam, did respond to vaccination by the production of neutralizing antibody.

Thus it appears that the young ruminant at birth has already a considerable measure of immunological competence and can react by the production of antibody to stimulation by a variety of antigens, provided that it does not receive passive immunity to these. The very small amount of immune globulin present in the serum before receiving colostral globulin, may be due to lack of antigenic stimuli *in utero* rather than to incapacity to respond to these. This is borne out by clear evidence that the foetal ruminant can respond to appropriate antigenic stimulation from a comparatively early stage of development.

Richardson, Beck and Clark (1968) found that foetal lambs injected *in utero* with 10^{10} killed *Brucella* 4–10 days before birth produced agglutinins reaching titres of $\frac{1}{320}$ to $\frac{1}{640}$ at 15–17 days after injection. The levels of antibody produced were as high as those of adults, whereas newborn lambs given a similar injection produced much lower levels, presumably because of maternal antibody passively acquired after birth.

Osburn and Hoskins (1969) found that foetal lambs produced both γM and γG antibodies to *B. ovis* after viable antigen had been injected into the placental cavities at various stages of gestation. Complement fixing antibodies appeared first at 91 days gestation. The first antibodies to appear were γM, precipitating antibodies were found 81 days after inoculation but haemagglutinating antibodies were not observed. Complement fixation occurred with both γM and γG antibodies.

Schinckel and Ferguson (1953) performed skin autografts and homografts on foetal lambs between the ages of 80 and 117 days and found that the homografts were actively rejected by the foetal lambs at 110–117 days of age. Visual and histological examination showed that the characteristic features of a homograft rejection reaction were present, as did also the more rapid rejection of second-set homografts from the original donor. Even homografts from the dam were rejected, showing that the reaction was foetal and not maternal in origin. Silverstein, Prendergast and Kraner (1964) confirmed their results and showed that orthotopic skin homografts are rejected by the foetal lamb at any time after the 77th day. Prior to the 77th day of gestation the grafts remained in place, without eliciting any detectable immunological response but, once competence to reject the graft is achieved, rejection occurs as rapidly as in the adult. Rejection is not accompanied either by the formation of plasma cells or the production of immunoglobulins. Silverstein, Uhr, Kraner and Lukes (1963) showed that foetal lambs are able to form large amounts of specific antibody, in response to suitable antigenic stimuli, as early as the 66th to 70th day of the 150 day gestation period. They responded earliest and with the highest titres to bacteriophage ΦX, horse ferritin was slightly less effective and ovalbumin was a weak antigen, in the earlier stages especially. Diphtheria toxoid, *Salmonella typhosa* and BCG, were antigenically ineffective at any time in foetal, or early neonatal, life. The quantity of antibody found 10 days after immunization with bacteriophage did not differ significantly in foetuses inoculated at 60–120 days of gestation. The earliest produced anti-phage antibody was 2-mercaptoethanol sensitive, and presumably macroglobulin, and 7S γG-globulin antibodies were only produced by older foetuses after longer lasting stimuli.

Bovine foetuses also are capable of immunological responses. Fennestad and Borg-Petersen (1957, 1958, 1962) infected bovine foetuses with living, attenuated, strains of *Leptospira saxkoebing* by injecting them into a placental cotyledon at laparotomy at ages varying from the 110th to 223rd day of the 280 day gestation period. Three foetuses, aged 132–168 days when inoculated, had produced specific agglutinins at titres of $\frac{1}{1,000}$ to $\frac{1}{10,000}$ when tested 32–62 days later and all three showed symptoms of infection. Mature plasma cells were present in the two older foetuses at 230 and 190 days of age respectively, and immature plasma cells in the younger foetus at 164 days of age. Plasma cells were not found in normal foetuses up to 8 months of age. Foetuses infected earlier than the 132nd day of age did not survive.

CHAPTER 9

Transmission of immunity in man and in the monkey

9.1. Introduction

It would not be possible in a book of this size, to review the whole of the extensive literature on transmission of immunity in man and its consequences. A large section of the literature is concerned with comparisons of the antibody concentrations in the cord blood of newborn infants with that of their mothers, much of it old and repetitive, of which adequate reviews exist. Another large section is concerned with haemolytic disease of the newborn, a large subject in itself dealt with in many recent publications, both text-books and reviews. Consequently, a treatment of the subject somewhat different to that in the chapters preceding appears necessary. In this chapter no attempt will be made to provide a comprehensive review of all the papers on transmission of antibodies and only the more significant ones will be mentioned, but the same general approach will be followed as with other species. The following chapter will be concerned with a comparative review of haemolytic disease in man and other animals.

9.2. The foetal membranes and placenta

The development and final arrangement of the placenta and foetal membranes of monkeys and man are broadly similar to each other but differ in many important respects, affecting possible routes of transmission of immunity, from all those animals that have been considered in previous chapters. There is scarcely a vestige of an allantoic cavity; the yolk-sac is rudimentary; and the exocoel is obliterated by the expansion of the amniotic cavity at an early stage; the later conceptus is bounded throughout by the conjoined allantochorion and amnion; the discoid allantochorionic placenta is haemochorial but of the lacunar type, very different from that of the rabbit. There is no possibility, therefore, that transmission of immunity could take place by way of the vascular splanchnic wall of the yolk-sac, as it does in the fowl, the rabbit, the guineapig and the rat, and other routes have to be considered.

The median uterus in higher primates is attached marginally by the broad ligaments, which correspond to the two mesometria of bicornuate forms, and the two Fallopian tubes open into its anterior lateral extremities. Thus the median sagittal plane may be regarded as corresponding to the antimesometrial region of bicornuate uteri and it is in this region, either in the dorsal or ventral wall of the uterus, that implantation occurs normally. It takes place early while the blastocyst is still very small, before it has undergone significant expansion, in both monkey and man. The details of implantation, however, differ in the two, and must be considered separately, although the final arrangement of the embryonic membranes is essentially similar. This account is based on those by Boyd and Hamilton and by Amoroso in Marshall's Physiology of Reproduction (1952) and owes much to the distinguished series of papers from the Carnegie Institution of Washington, Department of Embryology, by Hartman, Hertig, Heuser, Streeter and others and to the review of primate development by Hill (1932).

The egg of the macaque reaches the uterus at the 16-cell stage, 96 hr after ovulation (Lewis and Hartman 1933). The zona pellucida becomes detached early on the 9th day and the blastocyst then begins to implant. It becomes attached superficially to the uterine epithelium by the trophoblast covering the embryonic primordium and invasion of the maternal tissues by this trophoblast ensues. By the end of the 10th day the trophoblast has differentiated into an inner cellular cytotrophoblast and an outer syncytiotrophoblast, which invades and destroys the uterine epithelium, connective tissue and vascular endothelium in its path, so opening up the maternal blood vessels and coming into direct contact with the blood. At the end of the 10th day a secondary site of attachment develops at the abembryonic pole. During the 15th to 17th days the cytotrophoblast proliferates to form columns covered with syncytiotrophoblast, which are the rudiments of the villi and into which vascular mesenchyme grows later. The mature placental arrangement is attained by the 35th day of the 164-day gestation period. It should be noted that attachment to the uterine tissues is confined to the embryonic pole, which will become the primary placenta, and a little later the abembryonic pole, which will become the secondary placenta. Elsewhere the surface of the blastocyst is exposed to the uterine lumen, so that no decidua capsularis, like that of the human embryo, is formed (Heuser and Streeter 1941).

The human embryo implants even earlier than that of the macaque. It attaches on the 6th day by the trophoblast of the embryonic pole (Hertig and Rock 1945). At $7\frac{1}{2}$ days this thick disc of trophoblast has already differentiated into an inner cytotrophoblast, immediately over the embryonic primordium and an outer syncytiotrophoblast, derived from the cytotrophoblast (Tighe, Garrod and Curran 1967) which has penetrated the uterine epithelium and invaded the connective tissue stroma. At this stage the abembryonal hemisphere of the blastocyst is still thin-walled and exposed to the uterine lumen, but very soon afterwards the blastocyst has buried itself completely in the mucosa. Between the 10th and 15th day the perforation through which the blastocyst entered the mucosa is closed by a fibrin clot and the uterine epithelium has proliferated and grown over it, completely enclosing the blastocyst. Thus implantation is interstitial, not superficial as in the macaque. Blood lacunae are already present in the area of trophoblastic invasion by the 9th day. The syncytiotrophoblast is not uniformly thick but projects as primitive syncytial villi over the whole surface. The cytotrophoblast then proliferates and grows out as columns of cells into the syncytium to form the primary chorionic villi about the 12th to 13th day, and very soon after the mesenchyme grows into these and converts them into secondary villi. Blood vessels form in these mesenchymal cores of the villi. In the macaque the villi are formed only over the two areas of attachment, which will become the placentae, but in the human embryo, they are formed over the whole surface of the blastocyst, though they are better developed on the deeper situated embryonic pole. In both monkey and man the villi become much branched, like trees. Some of the villi hang free in the lacunae of maternal blood, others become attached to the maternal decidual tissue beyond the lacunae. The cytotrophoblast of their anchored tips proliferates and spreads laterally to form the trophoblastic shell, the outer surface of which constitutes the boundary between the foetal and maternal parts of the placenta. As the human conceptus expands, the uterine tissues separating it from the uterine lumen become progressively stretched and thin and the blood supply to this region of decidua capsularis correspondingly reduced. The chorionic villi over this region become compressed and reduced to give rise to the chorion laeve or smooth membrane, while those villi on the deeper side meet the decidua basalis and constitute the definitive disc-shaped placenta. The lacunae surrounding the placental villi become continuous. The maternal arterial blood is delivered into this placental lacuna by coiled maternal arteries, which pass obliquely through the basal plate and open into the intervillous space by narrow nozzles; from these the blood comes in spurts. The blood is drained away from the placental margin by a plexus of veins. The foetal blood is brought to the tips of the branches of the villi by foetal arteries which break up in capillaries; through these the blood flows back to the foetal veins. The definitive condition of the circulation in the human placenta is attained by the second month. The circulation of the human placenta has been described in detail and compared with that of the macaque, which is essentially similar (Ramsey and Harris 1966; Harris and Ramsey 1966). The area of close proximity of maternal and foetal circulations in the human placenta is very great and has been estimated to be as much as 10–13 m^2 (Christoffersen 1934). The cytotrophoblast of the villi (Langhan's layer) is temporary and largely disappears early in pregnancy, so that the maternal and foetal bloods are then separated by the foetal endothelium, by a delicate network of reticular fibrils representing the mesenchyme, and by the attenuated syncytiotrophoblast.

The mesoderm in the early blastocyst differentiates when the endoderm has spread only partly around the interior of the blastocyst cavity. Thus a yolk-sac is formed which has a roof of endoderm and a lower, or abembryonic, hemisphere bounded by mesoderm, the surface of which is differentiated as Hensen's membrane. Between this primitive yolk-sac and the chorion is a cavity containing an open meshwork of mesenchymal strands. Later the abembryonic hemisphere of the yolk-sac, composed of Hensen's membrane, is separated off and disappears, leaving the now closed endodermal vesicle of the true yolk-sac completely isolated from the chorion by the mesoderm and the exocoel which have extended around it. Thus although blood islands develop in the splanchnic mesoderm covering the yolk-sac and it becomes vascularized, it is at no stage so placed as to constitute an organ capable of absorbing materials directly from the exterior and it remains small and rudimentary throughout development.

The amnion arises at about $7\frac{1}{2}$ days in the human embryo as a cavity or cavities between the trophoblast and the embryonic ectoderm. The embryonic ectoderm grows up around this cavity, which is separated soon from the chorion by the extension, between it and the trophoblast, of mesoderm and coelom. At one point, posterior to the em-

bryonic plate, the embryonic mesoderm retains continuity with the mesoderm of the chorion, forming the body stalk. At a later stage a short endodermal diverticulum of the hind-gut region extends into the base of this
body stalk and represents all that is formed of an allantois. With the development of the vascular system, blood vessels extend through the body stalk to
vascularize the placenta and the whole of the chorion, which can be termed
allantochorion by homology with other mammals.

Early in development, while the foetus is still small, the amnion expands
until it fills and occludes the whole of the exocoel. Its outer surface is closely
applied to the whole of the inner surface of the chorion, closely investing
the body stalk, which becomes the umbilical cord, as well as the foetal
surface of the placenta and of the chorion laeve. Thus the only extraembryonic cavity in the later conceptus is the amniotic cavity. The enlargement
of this cavity results in the conceptus filling and expanding the uterine cavity.
Thus the chorion laeve and, in man but not in the macaque, the decidua
capsularis becomes closely opposed to the wall of the uterus. This results
in the disappearance in man of the decidua capsularis and the fusion of the
chorion laeve with the decidua vera of the uterine wall in both man and
monkey; thus bringing the chorion laeve once again into contact with vascularized maternal tissues (fig. 9.1) (Strauss 1967). Hence the definitive
arrangement of the foetal membranes shown in fig. 9.2 is achieved.

It will be apparent from this account that exchange of substances between
mother and foetus must take place across the chorion, which forms the
boundary between maternal and foetal tissues at all points. Thus, there is no
entry to the foetus except by traversing the chorionic trophoblast, either
within the placenta or of the chorion laeve. The obvious direct route from
the maternal to the foetal circulation is from the maternal blood in the
placental lacunae, across the trophoblast covering the villi, to the rich network of foetal capillaries beneath. There can be no reasonable doubt that
the bulk of the transfer from mother to foetus, and *vice versa*, takes place
by this route. However, the possibility exists that some transfer might
occur by way of the amniotic fluid, which is swallowed by the foetus as
soon as movements begin, and from which substances could be absorbed
by the foetal gut and transmitted to the foetal circulation. This possible
route for the transmission of immunity has the attraction that it involves absorption by the endoderm, as occurs, so far as is known, in all other groups
of animals. Substances might reach the amniotic fluid either from the maternal blood in the lacunae, across the chorionic plate of the placenta and its

covering of amnion, or from the blood in the vessels of the decidua lateralis, across the intervening decidual tissues, the remains of the uterine lumen and the chorion laeve with its lining of amnion. The proteins of the amniotic fluid and the experimental evidence bearing on the route of transmission will be dealt with in later sections, but the morphological details of the membranes concerned will be considered here.

The most authoritative account of the structure of the trophoblast of the human and monkey placentas, as it can be seen with the light-microscope, is provided by Wislocki and Bennett (1943). The outer surface of the placental trophoblast was found to vary from a brush border to one consisting of irregular streamers of cytoplasm. A variety of vacuoles occur in the syncytium which appear to be taking in fluid from the intervillous space or the decidua. It was found that the trophoblast of the rhesus monkey did not phagocytose particles of Indian ink and on this evidence it was thought

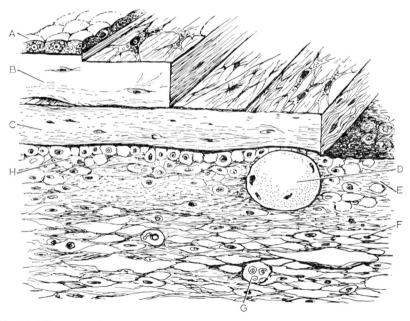

Fig. 9.1. Diagrammatic representation of the structure of the chorioamnion and decidua lateralis of a human conceptus in late pregnancy. A, amniotic epithelium; B, amniotic mesoderm; C, chorionic mesoderm; D, remnant of villus; E, compact zone of decidua; F, spongy zone of decidua; G, capillary; H, trophoblast. (From Strauss 1967, redrawn from Schmidt 1956.)

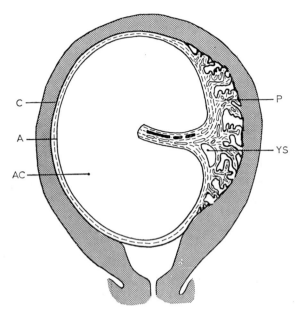

C —

P

A —

YS

AC —

Fig. 9.2. Diagram of the final arrangement of the embryonic membranes in the human uterus. A, amnion; AC, amniotic cavity; C, chorion; P, placenta; YS, remnant of yolk-sac. (After Mossman 1937.)

that phagocytosis did not play an important part in placental transfer. These authors say that, 'the placental barrier (syncytium) exercises selective and regulatory functions of a complex nature. These involve the selective entry of substances into the syncytium, their regulation in the cytoplasm and the control of their egress from its inner surface in the case of substances

Plate 9.1. A. Electronmicrograph of the trophoblast of a human chorionic villus during the last trimester of pregnancy. A capillary (K) with its endothelium (E) touching the basal membrane (B). The plasmodiotrophoblast (P) is clothed with microvilli, between the bases of which caveoli are present and the peripheral cytoplasm is full of pinocytotic vesicles. The surface of the plasmodium adjoining the basal membranes is much folded, as can be seen on the right of the picture, but the cells of the cytotrophoblast (C) have smooth surfaces resting on the membrane, as can be seen on the left. × 12,000.   B. The microvilli covering the plasmodiotrophoblast of a ripe placenta at a higher magnification. Caveoli between the bases of the microvilli and pinocytotic vesicles in the peripheral cytoplasm are evident. M, mitochondria; N, nucleus; O, osmiophil granule. × 24,500. (From Strauss 1967, after Strauss, Goldenberg, Hirota and Okudaira 1965.)

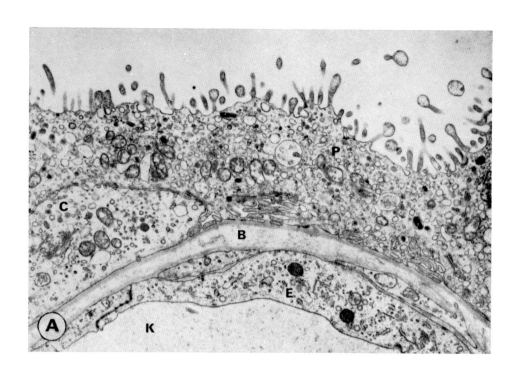

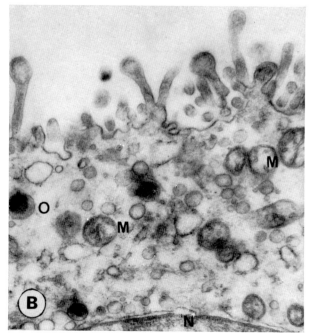

PLATE 9.1

coming from the mother, and in the opposite sense for excretory products of the fetus. In addition to these functions, it is becoming apparent that certain substances including a variety of enzymes, as well as hormones, are actually formed in the syncytial cytoplasm. Some of these may be retained in the cytoplasm to exercise certain functions there, while others may be excreted into the maternal and fetal blood streams.'

A review of the literature and an excellent account of electron-microscopic structure of the placenta and membranes in man is provided by Strauss (1967). It is shown that the syncytial trophoblast of the ripe placenta is covered with microvilli, some of which are club-shaped, and that active pinocytosis with the formation of caveoli is taking place between the bases of the microvilli (plate 9.1). The peripheral cytoplasm is filled with vesicles or cisternae, mitochondria and various granules. The basal surface of the syncytium, where it adjoins the basement membrane without the intervention of cytotrophoblast cells, is provided with many finger-like processes, less regularly arranged than the microvilli, on the free surface. The endothelium of the foetal capillaries is in direct contact in places with the inner surface of the basement membrane, which is all that intervenes between them and the syncytium. A still more recent account of the fine structure of the tropho- blast from 10 to 40 weeks gestation has been provided by Tighe, Garrod and Curran (1967). The microvilli, covering the surface of the syncytium, were longer at 10 weeks than at term. Caveoli at the bases of the microvilli indicate active pinocytosis. The superficial cytoplasm contains an abundance of rough endoplasmic reticulum, the channels in which are dilated into cisternae. Free ribosomes are present as well in the cytoplasm and there is an abundance of mitochondria, lysosomes and small vacuoles. Other organelles include large multivesicular bodies and phagosomes, in the deeper part of the syncytium, and autophagous vacuoles. The surface of the microvilli is covered with a fuzzy coat, or glycocalyx, of acid mucopolysac- charide, and this occurs also within the small vacuoles, lysosomes and the multivesiculate bodies. This substance was digested by hyaluronidase, and was taken to be chondroitin sulphate A or C, or hyaluronic acid, or a combi- nation of these. Boyd, Hamilton and Boyd (1968) give an even fuller des- cription of the syncytial surface. A well-developed brush border of microvilli can be present close to regions with a smooth surface, even on one and the same villus. They note, also, the formation of caveoli between the bases of the microvilli and the presence of a glycocalyx on the microvilli; this can be seen lining the caveoli in their illustrations. The reactions of the glycocalyx to treatment with diastase and PAS staining suggests its mucopolysac-charide nature. The peripheral cytoplasm in the photographs appears full of vacuoles and cisternae.

It is apparent from these accounts that the syncytial trophoblast of the placental villi of the human placenta up to term presents the appearance of an actively absorptive membrane. Indeed, allowing for the difference be-tween a syncytium and a cellular epithelium, its cytology under the electron microscope bears a very striking resemblance to that presented by the endo-derm of the foetal rabbit yolk-sac or of the neonatal mouse or rat intestine. It is easy to imagine, on the basis of their fine structure, that essentially similar processes of pinocytotic absorption are proceeding actively in all these membranes.

Comparatively little attention has been paid to the structure of the chorion laeve, but the most complete account is provided by Bourne (1962). The amniotic epithelium is a thin layer of cuboidal cells, forming an epithelium on the inner surface of the chorion laeve resting on a thin basement membra-ne. Beneath this is the thicker layer of amniotic mesoderm, in contact with a similar layer of chorionic mesoderm, bounded by another thin basement membrane on which rests the chorionic trophoblast cells. The trophoblast is in intimate direct contact with the uterine decidua. The total thickness of the chorion laeve when in place in the uterus, measured from the photograph given by Strauss (1967, Abb. 56) is *c.* 0.1 mm. The fine structure of the full-term human amnion, stripped from the chorion, has been described by Bourne and Lacy (1960). These authors found that the surface of the amnio-tic epithelium was covered with a brush border of microvilli. The inter-cellular spaces were enlarged in many places into cavities, with irregular microvillous-like processes of the cells extending into them, and into which fine channels in the cytoplasm opened. The basal borders of the cells, next to the basement membrane, were similar to the lateral borders, with spaces between the cells and the membrane into which villous-like processes ex-tended. Vacuoles were present in the cytoplasm of the cells, but were not numerous.

9.3. *The transmission of antibodies*

The large literature of the transmission of antibodies from mother to infant in man has been well reviewed by Edsall (1956), Vahlquist (1952, 1958) and Freda (1962) and the full bibliographies in these papers, especially the last named, will serve to supplement the references mentioned herein. Most of the literature is concerned with the transmission of either naturally occurring antibodies or active immunity. Unfortunately very little can be identified as relating to passive immunization of the mother with heterologous antibodies. More information might have been expected, and would be of great interest, on the transmission of both pepsin-refined and unrefined equine diphtheria or tetanus antitoxins which must have been administered therapeutically to women in late pregnancy on many occasions.

Much of the literature does relate to homologous antitoxins, either naturally or actively acquired, and is particularly useful because of the precision with which antitoxin levels can be determined. The earliest record of antibody in cord blood appears to be that of Fischl and Von Wunscheim (1895) who found diphtheria antitoxin in a number of instances. Polano (1904) observed that the infants of mothers who had diphtheria antitoxin in their blood, whether natural or due to active or passive immunization, had antitoxin in their sera at birth. Unfortunately no information is given as to the nature of the passive immunization. Ten Broeck and Bauer (1923) compared the antitoxin levels in the maternal and cord sera in six confinements, in which the women were carriers of tetanus bacilli, and found that these were approximately the same in most cases. Ruh and McClelland (1923) performed Schick tests on 100 mothers and newborn infants and found that these were positive in both in 20, negative in both in 75, positive in the mother and negative in the infant in 4, and negative in the mother and positive in the infant in 1. Thus apparent failure of the transmission of immunity occurred in only 1 %. Magara (1936) immunized 21 women during pregnancy with diphtheria 'anatoxin' and found antitoxin in the cord blood in all cases, usually at an equal concentration to that in the maternal blood but varying from 0.5 to 2.0 times. Liebling and Schmitz (1943) examined the levels of diphtheria antitoxin in the maternal and infant sera of both non-immunized and immunized mothers, all of whom had been subjected to Schick tests. Antitoxin was present in the sera of all infants of Schick negative mothers, whether immunized or not, at levels at least equalling, and often exceeding, those of the mothers. Antitoxin was absent from the sera of all infants of non-immunized Schick positive mothers, but was present in the sera of some immunized Schick positive mothers. In most cases the infant level was higher than that of the mother, and it was less in only one instance. Vignes, Richou and Ramon (1948) examined the concentrations of naturally occurring antitoxins to both diphtheria and staphylococcus toxins in the bloods of 72 Parisian women and the cord bloods of their infants. Almost all had staphylococcal antitoxins and most had diphtheria antitoxins. The cord blood concentrations of both antitoxins were approximately equal to the maternal concentrations, or were distinctly higher in about one third of the cases. Barr, Glenny and Randall (1949) found that the diphtheria antitoxin content of the cord blood was appreciably higher than the maternal blood and in most cases more than 50% higher. Bryce and Burnet (1932) and Lichty, Katsampes and Baum (1943) examined the staphylococcal antitoxin content, and Plummer (1938) and Gordon and Janney (1941) the streptococcal antitoxin content of paired samples of maternal and cord bloods and found that in the majority the concentrations were equal, in a considerable minority the infant concentrations were higher, and only in a very few lower, than the maternal concentrations. Murray, Calman and Lepine (1950), however, found that the levels of staphylococcal antitoxins in the cord blood were higher than in the mothers' blood in the great majority of cases (fig. 9.3). Lichty, Katsampes and Baum (1943) also examined in the sample the transmission of agglutinins to the capsular antigen of virulent

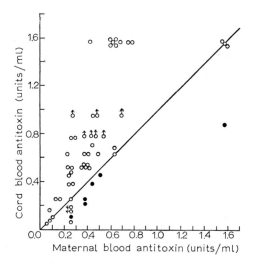

Fig. 9.3. Diagram of the relations between antistaphylococcal haemolysin levels of 56 pairs of maternal and cord bloods. Solid circles denote cases in which the antitoxin level was higher in the infant's peripheral blood than in the mother's. Arrows indicate the direction in which the points would have moved had an end point been reached in those particular cases. (From Murray, Calman and Lepine 1950.)

staphylococci and found that it occurred less readily and more erratically than with the antitoxins; the titres in the infants being less than the mothers in 16, equal in 30 and greater in only 4 sera. Florman, Schick and Scalettar (1951) found that the levels of streptococcal agglutinins in cord blood were in most cases about one quarter of those of the mother. Neter, Rajnovich and Gorzynski (1960) found that staphylococcal antibodies of the Rantz type in the cord blood tended to be equal or less than in the maternal blood and only rarely greater. Vahlquist, Lagercrantz and Nordbring (1950) found that the close correspondence of maternal and infant titres of antistreptolysins and antistaphylolysins at term is established in the second half of pregnancy. Foetuses of 16–22 weeks gestation showed consistently lower values for both these antibodies than their mothers but premature infants of 30–39 weeks gestation had antistreptolysin titres corresponding closely to those of their mothers, though the relative values for antistaphylolysins were not quite so good. Adamson, Löfgren and Malmnäs (1951) found no difference between the cord and maternal blood in the levels of antistaphylolysins and of antistreptolysins, but Murray and Calman (1953) and Stück, Natzschka and Wiesener (1957) observed that antistreptolysins were higher as a rule, often considerably higher, and only very rarely less, in the cord blood than in the mother's blood.

Osborn, Dancis and Rosenberg (1952) compared the titres of diphtheria antitoxin in the cord blood of 56 premature infants with those of their mothers, who had not been actively or passively immunized. They found a significant correlation between the maternal/infant ratio and birth weight, the small infants (under 1200 g) having much less antitoxin proportionately than the larger ones. Thirty-five of the babies, including 13 under 990 g, had a lower concentration than their mothers, 14 had an equal concentration and only 7 had a higher concentration. The regression line for the data was

$$y = 0.199 - 0.00318\,(x - 1452),$$

where $y = (\log_{10}$ maternal titre $- \log_{10}$ infant cord titre), and $x = $ birth weight in g. Toivanen, Mäntyjärvi and Hirvonen (1968) examined the levels of mercaptoethanol treated antistreptolysin-O and antistaphylolysin-α as well as of several antiviral antibodies, in foetuses and their mothers at various stages of gestation. They found no antibody in foetuses of 125–150 mm crown–rump length, some in foetuses of 155–215 mm in which the maternal concentration was high, more frequently in foetuses of 230–380

mm, and the same or a higher level than in the mothers in foetuses of 390 mm
or more. The cord sera of full-term infants had levels significantly higher
than the mothers for 7 of the 12 antibodies studied.

Chesney (1945) records two cases in which the mothers were passively
immunized with horse diphtheria antitoxin shortly before delivery. Mother
A was given 24,000 units intravenously and 24,000 units intramuscularly
4 days before, and a further 32,000 units 3 days before delivery. She was
believed to have had 2 units ml in her circulation at the time of delivery of
twins, but the cord blood had only 0.01 units/ml. Mother B was given 20,000
units intravenously and 20,000 units intramuscularly a few hours before
delivery, at which time she had 5.0 units/ml in her circulation. The infant's
cord blood had only 0.001 units/ml. Clearly the transmission of refined
horse antitoxin near term is not rapid.

Wasz-Höckert, Wager, Hautala and Widholm (1956) describe a series of
six infants born with oesophageal atresia in which the diphtheria antitoxin
levels of the mothers' and infants' sera were determined. In two no antitoxin
was present in mother or infant, but in the other four the levels of the infants
were equal to those of the mothers. Of six normal infants whose mothers
had antitoxin in their sera, four had higher levels than the mothers and two
had equal levels. This has been regarded as evidence against transmission by
way of the foetal gut.

Cohen and Scadron (1943) found that antibodies to pertussis were transmitted from vaccinated mothers to their infants almost quantitatively.
Kendrick, Thompson and Eldering (1945) observed that opsonins to *Bordetella
pertussis* were transmitted by both vaccinated and non-vaccinated mothers
to their infants, but the babies tended to have lower levels than their mothers.
Miller, Faber, Ryan, Silverberg and Lew (1949) examined the pertussis
agglutinin levels of mothers, who had neither been vaccinated nor contracted
pertussis during pregnancy, and of their infants and found that the levels largely corresponded within the margin of error, but there was a tendency for
the maternal titres to be the higher. Cohen, Schneck and Dubow (1951)
immunized women in the last trimester of pregnancy against pertussis
and found corresponding levels of agglutinins in the paired sera.

Timmerman (1931) studied the transmission of both the 'H' and 'O'
agglutinins to *Salmonella typhi* in a sample of 59 paired maternal and infant
sera. Forty-four mothers had 'H' agglutinins which were present in the sera
of 28 of the offspring at levels from $\frac{1}{8}$ to equality with, but never above, the
maternal levels. Forty-three of the mothers had 'O' agglutinins, but these

were present in the serum of only one of the infants. Clearly the 'H' agglutinins are transmitted more readily than the 'O' agglutinins.

Antibodies against the enteric group of organisms were always present in massive amounts in the maternal sera examined by Toomey (1934), whereas the cord sera of the infants contained these antibodies at low titres, usually not exceeding $\frac{1}{40}$, but occasionally reaching $\frac{1}{80}$. He claimed to find a marked increase in the infants' titres at ten days of age and attributed this to absorption from the milk. Schneider and Papp (1938), on the other hand, found that the newborn infants before they had suckled had serum titres almost the same as those of their mothers and they found no evidence of a rise in the infants' titres after suckling. When anti-*coli* horse serum with a titre of $\frac{1}{50,000}$ was injected intramuscularly into women near full term, who were not already immune to *Escherichia coli*, the antibodies did not appear in the sera of the newborn infants, although they did appear in the colostrum. Yeivin, Salzberger and Olitzki (1956) examined maternal and infant cord sera for antibodies to two types of *E. coli* and to four types of *Shigella* and found that the infants sera always had much less antibody than the maternal sera. Sussman (1961) examined the anti-*coli* content of 27 pairs of maternal and cord sera and found antibodies in all the maternal sera but in only five of the cord sera, three of which showed a rise in titre by the third day. It appears from these results that the antibodies to the common enteric pathogens are transmitted from mother to foetus much less readily than, for example, antitoxins.

Antibodies against virus appear to be readily, if somewhat erratically, transmitted. Aycock and Kramer (1930) examined a sample of 12 paired maternal and cord sera for antibodies to poliomyelitis capable of neutralizing the virus on intracerebral inoculation into monkeys. The sera of ten of the mothers and of their infants neutralized the virus and those of the other two pairs did not. Hale and Lee (1954) found, in a series of 24 paired maternal and cord sera, that fifteen of the mothers and their infants had antibodies to Japanese type B encephalitis, and the other nine had not. The antibody content of the corresponding maternal and cord sera was the same within the limits of experimental error. Lipton and Steigman (1957) determined the titres of antibodies to types I, II and III poliomyelitis virus in the sera of 48 mothers and in the cord sera of their infants. The series included 3 sets of twins and 4 premature babies. There were no significant differences between the maternal and cord sera in 34 instances, but the cord sera had lower values than the maternal sera for at least one type in the remaining 14 instances, including four in which it was lower for two types and two in which it was lower for all three types. These discrepancies were most frequent for type III and least frequent for type I. The twins showed no discrepancies between each other, but one pair had a much lower titre for type III than the mother and another pair had a much lower titre for type I. Gelfand, Strean, Pavilanis and Sternberg (1960) studied the transmission of polio-myelitis antibodies in single and twin births. They found that foetal levels reached maternal levels during the 8th month of gestation and exceeded them by 1.35 to 1.50 times at full term. There was considerable variation in the antibody levels relative to those in the maternal sera for types I, II and III, not only as between those types in one individual but also as between individuals; for example, in one infant the antibody to type I might be more than double that of the mother, and the antibody to type III less than half that of the mother, and in another infant this might be reversed, or antibody to type II might exceed either of the others. There was equally marked varia-tion between non-identical twins, but the variation between identical twins was considerably less. Gelfand, Fox, LeBlanc and Elveback (1960) compared the titres of antibodies to all three types of poliomyelitis in a series of 66 pairs of maternal and cord sera from a district where the disease was endemic. There was very little variation in titre within each pair, but antibody to type III tended to be less readily transmitted than antibodies to types I or II. Kempe and Benenson (1953) compared the haemagglutination-inhibition titres against vaccinia of 182 mothers, who had been vaccinated, with those of their newborn infants and found that the maternal and infant titres corresponded within the margin of error of one dilution in 58%, that the infant titre was significantly higher than the maternal, often much higher, in 39%, and significantly lower in only 3% of infants.

Syphilitic reagins (Wiener and Silverman 1940; Vogt 1954), antibodies to *Rickettsia* (Schubert and Grünberg 1949; Grasset, De Watteville and Wirth 1952), to *Toxoplasma* (Macdonald 1950), to *Plasmodium* (Edozien, Gilles and Udeozo 1962) and to *Histoplasma capsulatum* (Zeidberg, Gass and Hutcheson 1957) have all been shown to be transmitted from mother to foetus, as have also the antibodies to a variety of other microorganisms and viruses (Freda 1962). On the other hand, the skin sensitizing antibodies of human allergy, even when present at high concentrations ($\frac{1}{100}$ to $\frac{1}{1,000}$) in the maternal serum, are not transmitted, although the blocking antibodies in hay-fever patients immunized with pollen are transmitted (Sherman, Hampton and Cooke 1940).

The transmission of anti-leucocyte antibodies and cold agglutinins has been observed in two cases by Hitzig (1959) and of anti-platelet antibodies in a case of congenital thrombocytopenia by Gwynfor Jones, Goldsmith and Anderson (1961). Parker and Beierwaltes (1961) found anti-thyroid antibodies in the infants of eight out of nine women who had demonstrable amounts of the antibody in their circulations at the time of delivery, but the infants appeared not to be adversely affected. Similarly, Beck and Rowell (1963) observed the transmission of anti-nuclear antibody from a mother with systemic lupus erythematosus to her infant, without affecting it adversely. Epp (1962) demonstrated the transmission of penicillin antibodies from mother to infant by means of the Ley method, but antibodies demonstrable by the bis-diazotized benzidine method apparently were not transmitted. Bar-Shany and Herbert (1967) observed the transmission of antibodies to vitamin B_{12} intrinsic factor from a mother, suffering from pernicious anaemia, to her infant at a titre equalling her own and resulting in B_{12} deficiency in the infant.

It is well known that antibodies to the blood group substances are transmitted from mother to foetus, including both naturally occurring isoagglutinins of the ABO-system and immune antibodies to the antigens of other blood group systems. However, the facility with which these antibodies are transmitted varies greatly, some being transmitted at very low levels or not at all and others being readily transmitted and capable of attaining titres in the cord blood comparable to those in the maternal circulation. In general, immune antibodies are transmitted much more readily than the naturally occurring isoantibodies. Moreover, complete agglutinins, detectable by the saline agglutination method, are transmitted at very low levels or not at all, while incomplete agglutinins, detectable only by titration in colloid media or by the indirect Coombs' technique, are readily transmitted. These differences appear to depend largely on the distribution of antibody activity between the various immune globulins, it having been shown by Franklin and Kunkel (1958) that γM-globulin is not transmitted in man and that only 7S γG-globulin is present in cord sera. Since the complete blood group agglutinins are associated with the γM-globulins and the incomplete agglutinins with the γG-globulins, this finding goes a long way towards accounting for the major differences in transmission, but it is believed that there are other factors which may play an important, though possibly less decisive, part in determining the rate of transmission. Since it is blood group antibodies to antigens on the foetal cells which are responsible for haemolytic disease of the newborn a fuller discussion of their transmission will be reserved for the next chapter.

Study of maternal/foetal incompatibility for the genetic Gm characters of the heavy chains of γG-globulin by Fudenberg and Fudenberg (1964) revealed an instance of a Gm(a−) mother of four children, by a Gm(a+) father, who developed anti-Gm(a) antibody during the third trimester of pregnancy with her fourth, and first (a+) child. This was taken as evidence of foetal synthesis of Gm(a+) γG-globulin and of its transplacental leakage. Evidence of transplacental leakage was provided also by the mother's titre of anti-B isoagglutinin increasing sharply at the same time, the foetus being group B. It was suggested that such maternal antibodies to a foetal antigenic γG-globulin being transmitted to the foetus could be important in the aetiology of functional hypogammaglobulinaemia of infancy. Such antibodies were detected in the 7S γ-globulins of two mothers of infants with functional hypogammaglobulinaemia. Märtensson (1962) had shown by DEAE-cellulose chromatography and density gradient ultracentrifugation that anti-Gm(b) antibodies may be in the 7S γG-globulin in one serum, and in the 19S γM-globulin in another serum. The former would be expected to be transmitted to the foetus and the latter would not. It is relevant also that Steinberg and Wilson (1963) had eight human sera lacking a Gm factor which had anti-Gm antibodies in their sera although they had never been transfused. In all eight cases it was found that the mothers had been positive for the Gm factor, the probability of this occurring by chance being 0.00003. It was concluded that the antibodies must have been formed against the passively acquired maternal γ-globulin. The authors never detected these antibodies in cord blood, the earliest they found them being 7 weeks of age.

9.4. The transmission of serum proteins

Information concerning the serum proteins of the human foetus and newborn infant is consistent with what is known of the transmission of antibodies. Earlier work using salting out procedures had established that the concentration of γ-globulin in the cord blood tended to equal or exceed the level in the maternal blood. In 1945 Longsworth, Curtis and Pembroke, using the more adequate method of free boundary electrophoresis, examined ten pairs of maternal and cord bloods in America. They found that both the relative and absolute levels of γ-globulins in the cord sera were higher than those in the maternal sera. The γ-globulin in the cord sera amounted to

15.7% of the total serum proteins as against 9.9% in the maternal sera, or 0.97 g/100 ml as against 0.71 g/100 ml. Subsequent work on the serum proteins up till 1958 has been well reviewed by Kekwick (1959). It is apparent from this review that the levels in sera of newborn Europeans are relatively similar, but slightly higher than are those of newborn Africans, but the African mothers had very high levels of γ-globulins exceeding those of their newborn infants. Wiener, Berger and Lenke (1951), also using electrophoresis, confirmed that the relative concentration of γ-globulin at birth slightly exceeded that of the normal mother. Orlandini, Sass-Kortsak and Ebbs (1955) investigated the levels of γ-globulin in 28 pairs of normal full-term cord and maternal sera, using the salting out technique because of the numbers involved. They found that the mean γ-globulin content of the cord sera was 0.90 ± 0.13 g/100 ml as compared to 0.82 ± 0.18 g/100 ml in the maternal sera, the slight excess in the cord sera being significant at the 5% level. These figures agree well with those of Longsworth et al. (1945). At birth the γ-globulin accounted for 34.5% of the total globulin and 14.5% of the total protein. The corresponding figures from Longsworth's data are 41.2% and 15.7%. Kohler and Farr (1966) compared the γG-globulin concentrations in 46 pairs of normal maternal/cord sera using the technique of precipitation with an antiserum, specific for γG-heavy chains, in agar plates. They found the mean cord concentration to be 1512.5 mg/100 ml (S.D. 323, range 640–2,250) and the mean maternal concentration to be 1260.1 mg/100 ml (S.D. 286, range 600–1875) (fig. 9.4). Thus, the mean concentration in the cord sera significantly exceeded that in the maternal sera ($P < 0.01$).

Franklin and Kunkel (1958) examined the macroglobulin content in maternal and cord sera in the ultracentrifuge and by immunological estimation with specific antisera to 19S γM-globulin, having shown previously (1957) that normal human γ-globulin contains as much as 10% of 19S γM-globulin. Although the maternal sera contained 50–100 mg/100 ml of γM-globulin as estimated in the ultracentrifuge, thirteen of fourteen cord sera had none at the 10 mg/100 ml limit of sensitivity and one had a very small amount. In contrast 19S α_2-globulin was present. Immunological estimation revealed γM-globulin at a level of 2–5 mg/100 ml in most, but not all, cord sera as compared to a maternal level of 35–70 mg/100 ml. This concentration in the cord sera was of the same order as that in the infants of agammaglobulinaemic mothers and $\frac{1}{10}$ to $\frac{1}{20}$ of that in the normal maternal sera. Clearly the transmission of γM-globulin from mother to infant is

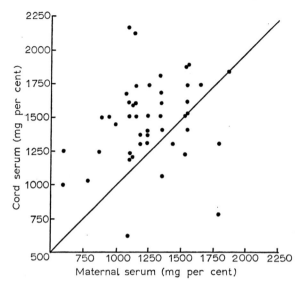

Fig. 9.4. Diagram of the relations between the γG-globulin concentrations of 46 pairs of maternal and cord sera. (From Kohler and Farr 1966.)

at a very low level as compared to 7S γG-globulin, if it occurs at all, for these small amounts might well be autogenous.

Rimington and Bickford (1947) examined the total protein, total globulin and albumin levels of the maternal and cord sera of 30 premature and 8 full-term infants. There was considerable individual variation but linear regressions were fitted to the data of the cord sera and were found to be

$$A = 0.08007T + 0.9536$$

and

$$G = 0.08878T - 1.1837$$

where A = albumin in g/100 ml, G = globulin in g/100 ml and T = length of gestation in weeks. Thus the mean concentration at 20 weeks of albumin was 2.55 g/100 ml and of globulin 0.59 g/100 ml, and at term albumin was 4.16 g/100 ml and globulin 2.37 g/100 ml. These compared with mean maternal serum values for albumin of 3.85 g/100 ml and for globulin of 2.69 g/100 ml. Moore, Du Pan and Buxton (1949) state that the albumin and γ-globulin levels rise rapidly during foetal life with increasing age, while the α- and β-globulins remain at a low level. Kekwick (1959) quotes figures which show a γ-globulin serum content of 0.08 g/100 ml at 4 months of foetal age rising, especially from 7 months, to 1.22 g/100 ml at full term. Gitlin, Kumate, Urrusti and Morales (1964a) found that the concentration of 7S γ_2-globulin in the cord sera was approximately equal to that in the maternal sera at 1.7 g/100 ml. Norton, Kunz and Pratt (1952) examined the serum proteins of 27 premature infants and found a γ-globulin content during the first week of approximately 0.7 g/100 ml, or rather less than that of normal full-term infants, as might be expected.

The transmission from the maternal to the foetal circulation of both γ-globulin and albumin in man and in the rhesus monkey has been demonstrated by isotopic labelling. Du Pan, Scheidegger, Wenger, Koechli and Roux (1959) injected intravenously ^{131}I-labelled human γ-globulin into pregnant women 3–48 hr before parturition. The amount of labelled protein declined rapidly in the maternal circulation over the first 24 hr but that in the cord serum increased with time from $\frac{1}{240}$ of that in the maternal serum after 3 hr to nearly $\frac{1}{6}$ after 48 hr. Dancis (1960) and Dancis, Lind, Oratz, Smolens and Vara (1961) injected intravenously ^{131}I-labelled human serum albumin or γ-globulin into women, about 3 months pregnant, 18–24 hr before Caesarean section for the therapeutic termination of pregnancy. They found in the cord blood with albumin 1.36% of the activity in the maternal serum, and with γ-globulin 2.8%, even at this early stage. Gitlin, Kumate, Urrusti and Morales (1964a, b) injected intravenously into normal women during the last month of pregnancy ^{131}I-labelled 7S γ_2-globulin and found that it was transmitted to the foetal circulation and was present in the cord blood at term. Likewise, Bangham, Hobbs and Terry (1958) and Bangham (1960) labelled whole monkey serum with ^{131}I and injected it intravenously into rhesus monkeys 3–5 weeks before or near full term (6 months). They found that albumin, γ_1- and γ_2-globulins were present in the foetal sera after 8–9 hr, the γ-globulin being transmitted 10–20 times more readily than the albumin; whereas little, if any, α- or β-globulin was transmitted. Quinlivan (1967) confirmed the transmission to the foetal circulation of ^{131}I-labelled homologous γ-globulin injected intravenously into monkeys during the last 4 weeks of gestation.

Moore, Du Pan and Buxton (1949) found that the α- and β-globulins in human foetal sera remained at a low level compared to the maternal sera, and Longsworth, Curtis and Pembroke (1945) found that α_1- and α_2- and, especially, β-globulins were at lower levels in the cord blood of full-term infants than in the maternal sera. In this respect the serum of the newborn infant resembled that of a normal adult in which the levels of α- and β-globulins are lower than in pregnant women during the latter part of gestation.

Dancis, Braverman and Lind (1957) showed by the incorporation of ^{14}C-glycine into tissue slices that the human foetal liver at 3–4 months is capable of synthesizing all the plasma proteins except γ-globulin. Buffe and Burtin (1967) examined the lympho-haematopoietic organs of human foetuses for the presence of immunoglobulins by means of the immuno-fluorescent technique. The only cells giving positive reactions were lymphoplasmacytes. They found γM-globulin in the foetal spleen at the 12th week, γG-globulin after the 20th week and traces of γA-globulin near term. They confirmed that the foetal liver does not synthesize immune globulins. Thus, it appears that although both albumin and γ-globulin are transmitted from the maternal to the foetal circulation, albumin is also being synthesized by the foetus and it is difficult to determine the precise extent of maternal and foetal contributions, whereas the γ-globulin is all or almost all of maternal origin. Both α- and β-globulins are synthesized by the foetus and it is doubtful if there is any significant maternal contribution to them. This is borne out by the observation of Scheinberg, Cook and Murphy (1954) that the concentration of ceruloplasmin, the amount of which rises during pregnancy, in the maternal circulation at term is $8\frac{1}{2}$ times that in the cord-blood, yet the level of non-ceruloplasmin copper is near equality. Ceruloplasmin is an α-globulin with a molecular weight of 150,000 and therefore is a slightly smaller molecule than 7S γ-globulin. Usategui-Gomez, Morgan and Toolan (1966) found that the ceruloplasmin concentration of the maternal serum was about $7\frac{1}{2}$ times that of the infant's serum. Transferrin was at approximately $\frac{1}{3}$ of the maternal concentration in the foetal serum. The relative and absolute concentrations of γG-globulin in the foetal serum slightly exceeded those in the maternal serum, whereas the γM-globulin concentration was less than $\frac{1}{6}$ of the maternal and γA-globulin was absent. Stiehm, Ammann and Cherry (1966) state that the average levels in normal cord serum are: γG, 1031 ± 20 mg/100 ml; γM, 11 ± 5 mg/100 ml; and γA, 2 ± 3 mg/100 ml. However γA-globulin is absent from $\frac{2}{3}$ of the sera. They found that the levels of γM- and γA- in cord sera reflected intra-uterine infections resulting in foetal synthesis, whereas the γG-globulin level reflects that of the maternal serum.

Gitlin and Boesman (1966) followed the changes in α-foetoprotein, albumin and γG-globulin in the foetal serum from $6\frac{1}{2}$ weeks to birth. The α-foetoprotein had a molecular weight similar to albumin and was not found in the maternal serum. It increased in amount in the foetal serum to a maximum at 13 weeks and then declined rapidly to a minimum of less than 2% of the maximum at 34 weeks. It was still detectable in the serum of the newborn infant. The albumin concentration reached a plateau at 22–24 weeks and remained at this level. The γG-globulin concentration was less than 0.2 g/100 ml up to 22 weeks and then increased to the neonatal level by 26 weeks.

9.5. *The leakage of cellular elements across the placenta*

It has been customary to think of the placenta as a perfect barrier between maternal and foetal circulations, allowing the passage of some substances, in one direction or the other, and excluding others. In recent years it has become increasingly apparent, in the human at least, that leakages of blood from one circulation to the other, on a small scale, do occur with sufficient frequency as to be regarded as near normal, and occasionally on a large scale. The active immunization of pregnant Rh-negative women by their Rh-positive foetuses indicated the probability of the leakage of foetal red cells into the maternal circulation and this has been demonstrated as occurring both during gestation and at parturition. Foetal red cells have been demonstrated in the maternal blood in a substantial proportion of pregnancies (Zipursky, Hull, White and Israels 1959; Finn, Clarke, Donohoe, McConnell and Sheppard 1961; Woodrow and Finn 1966), though in the majority the proportion of foetal cells is so small as to be accounted for by a leakage of a very few ml of blood. Leakage can also occur in the other direction, from mother to foetus, and at parturition the passage of platelets and leucocytes has been demonstrated (Desai and Creger 1963).

It might be supposed that the hydrostatic pressures on the two sides of the placental membrane would be in near balance. On this assumption differences in pressure could arise from uterine contraction and relaxation because the pressure on the foetal side would be the sum of the blood pressure exerted by the foetus itself and, since the foetal circulation is a closed system entirely surrounded by the uterus, of that exerted by the uterine musculature. On the other hand, the blood pressure on the maternal side would be augmented by myometrial pressure only in so far as there was resistance to outflow of blood through the placental veins, since it is not a closed system. These theoretical considerations suggest that uterine contractions could result in a rise in the foetal pressure relative to that in the maternal lacunae that might cause rupture of the membrane and spurts of foetal blood into the maternal blood. The powerful contractions during parturition would render leakage at that stage most probable, as indeed seems to be the case according to Woodrow et al. (1965). It .is, perhaps, more difficult to understand how uterine relaxation could result in a sufficient fall in the foetal pressure relative to the maternal to allow leakage in the other direction, from maternal to foetal blood.

9.6. *The proteins of the amniotic fluid*

It has been known for a long time that immune globulins and other proteins occur in human amniotic fluid, but there has been no general agreement as to their origin or as to their route of entry. A good deal of light has been thrown on these problems during the last decade. Steigman and Lipton (1958) found antibody activity against all three serotypes of poliomyelitis virus in the γ-globulin of human full-term amniotic fluid. The level was proportional to that in the maternal serum. A heat-labile inhibitor of the three types of virus also was present. One of six amniotic fluids tested contained enterobacterial haemagglutinins.

Freda (1958) studied the occurrence of maternal A, B and O (H) blood-group antigens in 20 full-term human amniotic fluids. Only when the mother was a secretor, in cases of maternal/foetal heterospecificity, were these to be found in the amniotic fluid and then at a greater concentration than in the serum. They were not found in the cord blood of the infant in these circumstances. Only when the foetus was a secretor, in such cases, could the foetal antigen be found in the amniotic fluid. Thus these substances, despite their large molecular size, do reach the amniotic fluid and, in the case of the maternal antigens at least, they must traverse the amnion. In a subsequent communication, Freda and Carter (1962) state that no significant amounts of isoantibody were found in the amniotic fluid. Abbas and Tovey (1960) studied the proteins of amniotic fluid by means of paper electrophoresis and came to the conclusion that the pattern represented a simple dialysate of the maternal serum, which they were able to reproduce by dialysis of maternal serum across the membrane *in vitro*. They considered that amniotic fluid swallowed by the foetus might provide it with a source of γ-globulin and of antibodies. Garby (1957) had studied *in vitro* in diffusion chambers the permeability of the full-term human amnion, stripped from the chorion. It was found to be permeable to water, sodium, chloride, iodide, creatinine, quinine, iron and albumin, but the differences in the rates of passage of water, creatinine and albumin were much greater than could be accounted for by differences in their mobility in water. Wild (1960), commenting on Abbas and Tovey's results, suggested that the proteins of the amniotic fluid might come from the foetal, rather than the maternal circulation and cites as evidence the occurrence in the fluid of bilirubin in cases of haemolytic disease. He records, also, that in over thirty, but not in all, cases of rhesus disease he found anti-D antibodies in the amniotic fluid. They were generally present when the maternal serum titre was $\frac{1}{128}$ or more, and at titres up to a maximum, in one case, of $\frac{1}{128}$. Wild (1961), in a subsequent paper, provides evidence that the bilirubin probably enters the amniotic fluid bound to albumin and suggests that it originates by passage from the foetal circulation in the umbilical cord. A good discussion of the earlier literature is provided.

Bangham, Hobbs and Tee (1961) found a protein, migrating between the α_1- and α_2-globulins and with a molecular weight of 35,000, in the amniotic fluids of rhesus, vervet and cynomolgous monkeys but not in human amniotic fluid. This protein of the amniotic fluid was not present in either the maternal or the foetal sera. The other serum proteins in the amniotic fluid, with the possible exception of this protein and of traces of foetal albumin, were believed to be derived from, and to return to, the maternal circulation.

Ruoslahti, Tallberg and Seppala (1966) determined the types of Gc-protein in the amniotic fluid and in the maternal and foetal sera in sixteen pregnancies. This is an α_2-serum protein which is present in any individual in one of three commonly occurring genetic types; 1–1, 1–2, and 2–2. In all those cases in which the types of maternal and foetal sera were similar the amniotic fluid type was similar also, but in seven cases in which the maternal and foetal types were dissimilar, the type in the amniotic fluid corresponded to that of the mother, not of the child. Usategui-Gomez and Morgan (1966) obtained similar results in twelve cases, in six of which there was maternal/foetal dissimilarity. Invariably the type of the amniotic fluid corresponded to that of the mother. Clearly this serum protein in the amniotic fluid is of maternal origin. Usategui-Gomez, Morgan and Toolan (1966) also investigated the proteins of this set of samples by disc electrophoresis and immunodiffusion techniques. They found (see table 9.1) that albumin and transferrin were the principal proteins in amniotic fluid, and that γG-globulin, γA-globulin and ceruloplasmin were present in small quantities, but that γM-globulin was absent. Chodirker and Tomasi (1963) estimated that the mean

TABLE 9.1

Comparison of individual protein values in maternal serum, amniotic fluid and foetal serum expressed as percentage of total protein.* (From Usategui-Gomez, Morgan and Toolan 1966.)

	Maternal serum	Amniotic fluid	Foetal serum
Total protein[†]	6.47 ($\pm$ 0.42)	0.22 ($\pm$ 0.05)	6.07 ($\pm$ 0.43)
Transferrin	18.1 ($\pm$ 2.37)	16.9 ($\pm$ 4.27)	6.90 ($\pm$ 1.99)
Ceruloplasmin	0.97 ($\pm$ 0.16)	0.37 ($\pm$ 0.08)	0.14 ($\pm$ 0.02)
Immunoglobulin A	3.04 ($\pm$ 1.06)	0.60 ($\pm$ 0.18)	0.00
Immunoglobulin G	20.2 ($\pm$ 2.49)	7.33 ($\pm$ 2.29)	24.2 ($\pm$ 2.79)
Immunoglobulin M	1.34 ($\pm$ 0.38)	0.00	0.23 ($\pm$ 0.04)
Albumin	42.1 ($\pm$ 3.93)	62.6 ($\pm$ 7.3)	56.0 ($\pm$ 4.82)
β lipoprotein	1.87 ($\pm$ 0.90)	0.00	0.00
α_2 glycoprotein double band	6.40 ($\pm$ 1.64)	0.00	5.80 ($\pm$ 1.56)
Post albumin proteins	8.27 ($\pm$ 1.74)	8.26 ($\pm$ 1.86)	8.17 ($\pm$ 2.14)

*Average of 12 determinations $\pm$ average error.
[†] g protein/100 ml.

content of 4 samples of amniotic fluid was 21 mg/100 ml of γ_2-globulin and 1.6 mg/100 ml of γ_1A-globulin. Gitlin and Boesman (1966) found that the ratio of α-foetoprotein to albumin in the amniotic fluid between the 11th and 13th week of gestation was much higher than in the foetal urine, suggesting another source for some of the albumin.

Usategui-Gomez and Stearns (1969) investigated the anti-D titres of the maternal sera and amniotic fluids at delivery of 33 Rh-sensitized pregnancies. They found antibodies in 27 of the amniotic fluids at varying titres up to equality with, but never exceeding, the maternal serum titre and showing no other correlation with it. These authors claim that the level of antibody reaching the amniotic fluid is the most reliable index of the amount that has reached the foetus and of the severity of the haemolytic disease produced.

These results provide clear evidence of the presence in the amniotic fluid of proteins of both maternal and foetal origin. Clearly the immune globulins are of exclusively maternal origin, but their route of entry to the amniotic fluid could be either direct from the maternal circulation across the chorion, or indirectly from the maternal to the foetal circulation and thence to the amniotic fluid. The ABO blood-group antigens and the Gc-proteins on the other hand, since they were not found in the foetal sera, presumably must have come by the direct route. Bilirubin, α-foetoprotein and probably some of the albumin would appear to have come from the foetus.

9.7. The route of transmission to the foetal circulation

The morphologically possible routes of transmission from the maternal to the foetal circulation in man and monkeys have been discussed already (pp. 238-9, 242). The route via the amniotic fluid and foetal gut had been suggested on several occasions in the older literature as a possible alternative to the placental route, but experimental evidence was lacking. On the basis of findings concerning transmission of immunity in the rabbit, rat and fowl, Brambell, Brierly, Halliday and Hemmings (1954) revived this suggestion. It was argued that since in all of these animals transmission took place by way of the endoderm, either of the foetal yolk-sac or neonatal intestine, and not by way of the haemochorial allantochorionic placenta in the rabbit, it might be by this route also in man. In all these animals endodermal transmission was selective, and transmission in man was also known to be selective. At that time clear evidence of selective transmission of intact protein molecules was generally accepted only in these cases, although we know now that it characterises the transmission of serum proteins across various membranes that are not endodermal, such as the mammary glands. It was suggested that the selective nature of transmission in man might also indicate an endodermal route. Finally, in the rabbit antibodies were transmitted also directly across the chorion and amnion to the amniotic fluid and were swallowed by the foetus and concentrated in the stomach contents, but this transmission was not selective and the antibodies were not absorbed by the foetal gut. It was thought possible, on these comparative grounds, that transmission in man might take place non-selectively across the chorion laeve and amnion into the amniotic fluid and be swallowed by the foetus, transmission across the endoderm of the foetal gut then being selective, as with other endodermal membranes. This suggestion had the merit, at least, of stimulating some experimental investigations of the route of transmission in monkeys and in man, which must be considered here.

Bangham, Hobbs and Terry (1958), and Bangham (1960), studied the transmission of homologous serum proteins labelled with ^{131}I in monkeys 3–5 weeks before and near full term (6 months). The labelled serum, together with ^{51}Cr-labelled red cells, was injected intravenously 8–9 hr before

Caesarean section. Absence of the labelled red cells from the foetal circulation was taken as evidence that contamination with maternal blood had not occurred. Albumin, γ_1- and γ_2-globulins were transmitted to the foetal serum, the γ-globulin being transmitted 10–20 times more readily than the albumin. Little, if any, α- or β-globulin was transmitted. Both albumin and globulin were found in the amniotic fluid, but whereas the fluid contained about twice as much labelled albumin per ml as the foetal serum, the globulin was present only in very small quantities. Thus the total amount of labelled albumin in the fluid was 5–10 times that in the serum. Although these experiments were taken as evidence of direct transmission to the foetal circulation, they do not provide it, because they are compatible with expectation if transmission were via the amniotic fluid; in that event non-selective transmission of maternal serum proteins to the amniotic fluid and selective uptake from there of γ-globulin to the foetal circulation might result in an excess of albumin and a deficiency of γ-globulin in the amniotic fluid, as was observed. However these authors proceeded to more crucial experiments on two monkeys by injecting a similar preparation of labelled serum, the dose containing the same total activity as in the previous experiments, directly into the amniotic cavities. Samples of maternal and foetal sera and of amniotic fluid were collected at Caesarean section 8 and 24 hr later respectively, and amniotic fluid was sampled by aspiration at 3 and 6 hr as well, in the case of the 24-hr experiment. The activity of albumin in the amniotic fluid was about 100 times that after intravenous injection at 8 and 6 hr respectively. It was stated that only very small quantities of labelled proteins were present in the foetal serum, even after 24 hr, and that this showed three apparent radioactive peaks. At 8 hr the duodenal and jejunal contents showed an almost normal pattern of labelled serum proteins at fairly high concentration, hence the injected protein in the amniotic fluid had been swallowed. Thus it appears from these two experiments that some transmission of labelled proteins from the amniotic fluid to the foetal circulation did occur, but at a very low level, whereas, if the foetal gut were the principal route of transmission of γ-globulin, it should have been transmitted in much greater quantity than after intravenous injection into the maternal circulation. These two experiments, such as they are, provide evidence in favour of the placenta being, at least, the principal route of transmission in the monkey.

Quinlivan (1967) injected ^{131}I-labelled homologous γ-globulin intravenously into four monkeys during the last 4 weeks of gestation. The results are summarised in table 9.2. Evidently the amount of labelled γ-globulin

TABLE 9.2

Injection of ^{131}I-labelled homologous γ-globulin during the last 4 weeks of gestation.
(After Quinlivan 1967.)

No. of monkeys	Time after injection (hr)	Percent ^{131}I-labelled γ-globulin per ml recovered		
		Maternal serum	Foetal serum	Amniotic fluid
16	23	0.260	0.010	0.003
8	72	0.140	0.020	0.004
9	116	0.131	0.026	0.009
24	120	0.070	0.027	0.004

in the maternal serum falls and that in the foetal serum rises, with time, whereas that in the amniotic fluid does not show a consistent rise. These results suggest entry and retention of γ-globulin in the foetal blood, with a consequent increase in concentration with time, and a balanced rate of entry and egress from the amniotic fluid, with a consequent relatively constant concentration. They do not provide information concerning the route of entry to either foetal fluid. A further experiment in which labelled γ-globulin was injected into the foetal circulation shows a transfer of the labelled protein to the maternal circulation. A small amount appearing in the amniotic fluid in this experiment could have resulted from leakage and cannot be considered significant.

Some experiments have been performed also on human subjects. Dancis (1960) and Dancis, Lind, Oratz, Smolens and Vara (1961) injected intravenously ^{131}I-labelled human serum albumin or γ-globulin into women about 3 months pregnant and 18 to 24 hr before Caesarean section for the therapeutic termination of pregnancy. Samples of maternal blood, cord blood and amniotic fluid were taken at the time of section. The average activities of the foetal fluids expressed as percentages of that in the maternal serum, were 1.36% for albumin and 2.8% for γ-globulin in the foetal serum, and 0.6% for albumin and 0.5% for γ-globulin in the amniotic fluid. The concentration of labelled albumin in the amniotic fluid was less than in the foetal serum both when the activity was computed as per ml of fluid and when it was computed as per mg of protein. These results seem to indicate clearly direct transmission to the foetal blood rather than indirect by way of the amniotic fluid.

These authors also injected labelled γ-globulin directly into the amniotic fluid in two women about 3 months pregnant and 24 hr before termination of pregnancy. The activity in the foetal serum expressed as a percentage of that in the amniotic fluid was found to be 12.0% and 1.5% in the two experiments respectively. In each of four other women near the end of pregnancy, 5 ml of human serum containing a high titre of tetanus antitoxin was injected into the amniotic fluid 18 to 24 hr before Caesarean section. No antitoxin could be found in the foetal sera at a level of sensitivity of 2.5–10% of that in the amniotic fluid. These experiments show that although there is a passage of γ-globulin from the amniotic fluid to the foetal circulation it is at much too low a level to account for more than a small fraction of the transmission from the maternal to the foetal circulation, the greater part of which must be by way of the placenta.

Gitlin, Kumate, Urrusti and Morales (1964a, b) labelled with ^{131}I human 7S $γ_2$-globulin, its F(=Fc) and S(=Fab) papain hydrolysed fragments, and urinary γ-globulin, which resembles the S fragment and is 1.5S. Normal women received an intravenous injection of one of these during the last month of pregnancy. The concentrations of both labelled and total γ-globulin in maternal and cord sera and in amniotic fluid were determined at the time of delivery. It was found that the concentration in the cord serum relative to that in the maternal serum was approximately the same for the F and S fragments and for urinary γ-globulin and was very much higher than that for the intact γ-globulin. Even after an interval of 13 days from injection the concentration of the labelled $γ_2$-globulin in the cord serum was under 50% of that in the maternal serum, which is surprisingly low, but after 23 days it was 125% of that in the maternal serum. The total 7S $γ_2$-globulin concentration in the cord serum was approximately equal to that in the maternal serum at 1.7 g/100 ml. The concentration of 7S $γ_2$-globulin in the amniotic fluid was 0.19 g/100 ml but there was little or no labelled γ-globulin in it. Thus the specific activity, or counts per mg, of $γ_2$-globulin in the amniotic fluid was lower than that in the cord serum. These results, like those of Dancis et al. (1961), indicate transmission by way of the placenta rather than the amniotic fluid. The increasing concentration with time of the labelled $γ_2$-globulin in the cord serum indicates also that the maternal→foetal rate of transfer must exceed the sum of the rate of catabolism in the foetus plus the foetal→maternal transfer, if there is any.

Puzzling results were obtained by Kulangara, Krishna Menon and Willmott (1965). A solution of bovine serum albumin was injected into the amniotic cavity in three pregnant women between $3\frac{3}{4}$ and 61 hr before delivery, but none could be detected in the foetal serum at birth. However, when the bovine albumin solution was injected into the uterine cavity through the cervix, instead of directly into the amniotic cavity, it was demonstrable at delivery in the amniotic fluid in all cases and in considerably higher concentrations in the cord sera in five out of the six cases.

One other piece of evidence concerning the route of transmission of immunity in man is available. Wasz-Höckert, Wager, Hautala and Widholm (1956) described a series of six infants born with oesophageal atresia, which could not therefore have swallowed amniotic fluid. The diphtheria antitoxin levels in the sera of mothers and infants were determined. Two mothers and infants had no antitoxin, but the other four pairs of sera had antitoxin and the levels in the infants' sera were equal to those in the maternal sera. Of six normal infants, whose mothers had antitoxin in their sera, four had higher levels than their mothers and two had equal levels.

It would appear from these results that the principal route for transmission of immunity in monkeys and in man must be by way of the allantochorionic placenta. It is also apparent that maternal serum proteins do reach the amniotic fluid and that transfer from it to the foetal circulation does occur, but that the quantities passing to the foetal circulation in this way are much too small to account for more than a fraction of the total transmission.

9.8. *The antibodies and serum proteins of colostrum and milk*

Comparatively little attention has been paid to the immunology of human colostrum and milk compared to that which has been paid to bovine lacteal secretions. The information available is scrappy and inconsistent, perhaps partly because colostrum has been sampled in many researches without reference to whether it was taken immediately after parturition and before suckling, or at any time during the first two or three days, when considerable dilution of the initial antibody content may have occurred. Another factor that has lead to discrepancies, particularly with the older work, is lack of information concerning the type of immune globulin carrying the antibody activity. Much more information is required, comparing not only the antibody levels of maternal serum and unsuckled colostrum, but the distribution of activity in each between the various components, γM, γA, $\gamma_1 G$ and $\gamma_2 G$, before a clear picture can be obtained of the immunity of human colostrum and milk. This is a matter which could be of great importance for neonatal health, even if little or no antibody is transmitted to the infant's circulation after birth, through its effect on enteric infections in the alimentary tract.

Kuttner and Ratner (1923) found that human colostrum 48–60 hr *post partum* contains small amounts of diphtheria antitoxin, always less than that in the maternal or cord sera and not detectable in the milk after 60 hr. Vignes, Richou and Ramon (1948) were able to find antitoxin in the milk of only 5 of 38 women with staphylococcal antitoxins, and of only 6 of 35 with diphtheria antitoxins, in their sera. On the other hand, Timmerman (1931) found both typhoid H and O agglutinins in colostrum, sometimes in greater concentration than in the maternal blood. The O agglutinins were concentrated in the colostrum to a greater extent than the H agglutinins. By the 10th day of lactation the O, as well as the H, agglutinins had disappeared from the milk for all practical purposes. Schubert and Grünberg (1949) found that, in women vaccinated for bush typhus, as a rule the quantity of agglutinins in the colostrum exceeded many times that in the blood. It was suggested that the agglutinins were concentrated in the colostrum by water reabsorption. Schneider and Papp (1938) found likewise that anti-*coli* agglutinins were present in the colostrum, always at higher titres than in the serum. Transmission to the colostrum applied not only to actively immunized mothers but also to non-immune mothers passively immunized by intramuscular injection of horse anti-*coli* serum. When the injection was given only a short time before parturition, the amount of the heterologous antibody in the colostrum often exceeded that in the serum. Nordbring (1957a) found that the antistreptolysin and antistaphylolysin titres of the colostrum on the first day were generally considerably lower than those of the maternal serum. The colostral titres decreased rapidly during the first three days and antibody was seldom apparent from the fourth day on. Sussman (1961) examined the anti-*coli* titres of the sera and colostra of 27 mothers, who breast-fed their infants. The samples were tested for haemagglutination with both trypsinated and non-trypsinated group O, Rh+ red cells from a single donor, sensitized with the antigen. All the maternal sera and colostra contained antibodies and in 19 of the 27 the colostral titre on the 1st day was higher than that of the serum. The colostral titre fell rapidly during the next 3–4 days. The highest titre observed in colostrum was $\frac{1}{32,768}$.

The discovery of the occurrence of Rh-antibodies in the colostrum and

milk of women immunized by heterospecific pregnancies was made by
Witebsky, Anderson and Heide (1942). Boorman, Dodd and Gunther (1958)
examined the anti-A and anti-B isoagglutinin content of the serum, colostrum (3rd day) and milk of 97 mothers. The level of anti-B isoagglutinins, for
which there were the most data, in colostrum was on average about double
the maternal serum titre, although there was no clear correlation between the
serum and colostrum titres. The milk titre was correlated with the colostral
titre and tended to be about $\frac{1}{16}$ of it.

Information concerning the immune globulins of human colostrum is
gradually accumulating. Polson (1952), in an electrophoretic study, found
only small quantities of albumin and no γ-globulin in human colostrum.
Lunsford and Deutsch (1957) examined the whey proteins of human milk,
taken one week after parturition, by electrophoretic, ultracentrifugal and
immunochemical techniques. They found that serum albumin constitutes
2.5% of these proteins and that, although γ_2-globulin could not be demonstrated by physical methods, some material, reacting as such immunologically, was present in quantities up to 2.5% of the protein. Gugler and von
Muralt (1959) carried out an immunoelectrophoretic study of human milk
and colostrum and found at least 15 protein components, of which four
were not found in serum. Of the eleven fractions related to blood serum
proteins, five were identified as albumin, β_{1A}-globulin, β_{2A}-globulin, β_2-
macroglobulin and fast migrating γ-globulin. Serum proteins, not present
in milk or colostrum, were tryptophan-containing prealbumin, α_2- and β_1-
lipoproteins, α_2-macroglobulin, siderophilin, fibrinogen and slow migrating
γ-globulin.

Tomasi and Zigelbaum (1963) recorded the occurrence of γ_1A-globulin
in human saliva, colostrum and urine. It sedimented in the ultracentrifuge
in the range 7–11S. Saliva had a γ-globulin/albumin ratio 6 times greater
than serum and most of the globulin was γ_1A. They suggested that this
selective secretion was brought about by a specific transport site on the
γ_1A molecule. Chodirker and Tomasi (1963) determined the quantities in a
variety of human body fluids of γ_1A- and of γ_2-globulin, using two-dimensional gel diffusion. The mean content of 14 serum samples was, γ_2-globulin
1335 mg/100 ml and γ_1A-globulin 178 mg/100 ml compared to the mean
content of 5 samples of colostrum for which the values were γ_2-globulin, no
measurable quantity but qualitatively small traces and γ_1A-globulin, 151
mg/100 ml. Also γ_1M-globulin was present in measurable quantities in
colostrum. Newcomb, Normansell and Stanworth (1968) isolated γA-globu-

lin in a pure state from human colostrum. Its sedimentation in the ultra-centrifuge showed it to be 11.7S, with a molecular weight of about 393,000. Dissociation of the molecules suggested that they were dimers, associated with a secretory piece of about 76,000 mol wt. Free secretory piece also appeared to be present in colostrum. These findings are in good agreement with those of Hurlimann, Waldesbühl and Zuber (1969) on salivary γA-globulin, who found it to sediment at 11.0S with a mol wt of 390,000. It consisted of two molecules of mol wt 170,000, similar to the γA-globulin of ascitic fluid, and a secretory piece of mol wt 50,000. Recently it has been found also (Shim, Kang, Kim, Cho and Lee 1969) that human colostral γA-globulin is resistant to tryptic digestion. It is suggested that although the colostral γA molecules inhibit tryptic digestion of themselves they do not interfere with tryptic digestion of other proteins and that it may be the transport piece which is responsible for this action.

Laskowski and Laskowski (1951) and Laskowski, Kassell and Hagerty (1957) record the occurrence of trypsin inhibitor in human colostrum and state that it disappears by the fifth day. The amount present was only about $\frac{1}{10}$ of that in bovine colostrum and $\frac{1}{67}$ of that in swine colostrum. This means that 1 ml of human colostrum on average would inhibit about 0.03 mg of crystalline trypsin.

These results suggest that there are large differences in the extent to which a given antibody is secreted in the colostrum and milk in man, but that secretion tends to favour antibodies to enteric organisms. Moreover, the amounts of immune globulins in human colostrum are small compared to ungulates, and a large proportion of the immune globulin present may be γA-globulin. It may be that antibodies borne on this fraction of the immune globulins function mainly in the lumen of the alimentary canal, rather than in the circulation. It is also possible that the function of trypsin inhibitor in colostrum could be to favour intra-luminal immunity rather than to contribute to transmission to the circulation. Much more research, with these speculations in mind, might be profitable.

9.9. *Transmission from the neonatal intestine*

The evidence concerning transmission of passive immunity after birth in man is conflicting. Kuttner and Ratner (1923) could find no increase in the antitoxin content of the infants serum after ingestion of colostrum containing diphtheria antitoxin. Conversely, Toomey (1934) claimed that the titres of agglutinins against enteric organisms in the blood of infants at 10 days of age was markedly higher than that of their cord blood, and he attributed this to the colostrum, which had similar titres. Schubert and Grünberg (1949) did not consider that there was any alimentary transmission of agglutinins to bush typhus from mothers vaccinated against this disease. Vahlquist and Högstedt (1949) fed human serum containing diphtheria antitoxin to newborn infants and to older children up to 10 months of age. The newborn infants were given the serum just before normal feeds, beginning from 12–24 hr and continuing until 3–4 days of age. Each infant received 95–210 units of antitoxin. Seven out of thirteen infants showed small increases in serum antitoxin, none of which exceeded 0.3% of the amount in the dose. An unmeasurable trace of antitoxin was demonstrated qualitatively in only 2 out of 14 older children. Moulinier (1953) investigated the possibility of transmission after birth of Rh-antibodies. He found that the Rh incomplete agglutinin titre of human serum was unaffected by incubation for 1 hr at 37 °C with an equal quantity of infant's gastric juices, provided the *p*H level was not lower than 4; at *p*H 3 or below it was almost completely destroyed. A 3-day old Rh-negative infant was given 100 ml of its mother's milk mixed with anti-Rh serum, the mixture having an incomplete titre of $\frac{1}{32}$. Only traces of agglutinin, of doubtful significance, appeared in the infant's serum. A group O infant, at 4 days of age, was given 20 ml of mother's milk mixed with immune anti-A serum, the titre being $\frac{1}{128}$. No antibody was found subsequently in its serum. Another group O infant at 9 days of age was given 150 ml of a similar mixture with a titre of the order of $\frac{1}{50,000}$. The infant's anti-A titre after 12 hr was $\frac{1}{32}$. Finally, infants suffering from haemolytic disease, which had been given partial exchange transfusions, were nursed by their mothers, whose milk had titres of $\frac{1}{2}$ to $\frac{1}{64}$. None exhibited any further adverse effects as compared to similar infants fed artificially. Boorman, Dodd and Gunther (1958) were unable to detect any increase in the anti-A or anti-B titres after birth of the sera of the infants of 97 mothers, with these antibodies in their sera and colostra. Sussman (1961) examined the anti-*coli* haemagglutination titres of the sera, during the first few days, of 27 infants whose mothers all had antibody in their sera and colostra. Of all the infants only three showed a rise of 1 or 2 dilutions on the birth level by the 3rd day and these three were those of the mothers with the three highest colostral titres of $\frac{1}{1024}$, $\frac{1}{2048}$ and $\frac{1}{32,768}$.

Very different are the results reported by Leissring, Anderson and Smith (1962). They administered pooled human serum hyperimmune to *Salmonella typhi* and to tetanus toxin by stomach tube to seven infants, ranging in age from 12 to 124 hr. An initial blood sample was taken from each infant, which was then given 30 ml of the immune serum; 4 hr later a second blood sample was taken and each infant was given 70 ml of the immune serum in 10-ml doses over 2 hr; 9 hr after the last dose a final blood sample was taken. The serum titres were tested for haemagglutination by the indirect method of sensitizing human group O, Rh− red cells with either paratyphoid O-antigen or, after tanning, with tetanus toxoid. The serum was titrated against the sensitized red cells (a) in saline for the typhoid antibodies, (b) in dextran-saline for both antibodies, or, (c) by a modified indirect Coombs' test. All five tests on the sera of all seven infants showed both antibodies to be present in the initial samples and striking increases in the titres of both in the 4-hr samples and again after 15 hr. The age of the infant appeared to have no effect. These results are out of line with those obtained by other workers with the more usual techniques and clearly require confirmation. There are several points that need to be taken into consideration. First, more reliance could be placed on quantitative results obtained by a direct, rather than an indirect method of testing. Secondly, the authors suggest that much of the antibody they found in the sera could be incomplete antibody. This is a possibility, but it does not explain the presence of positive reactions in all infants, for both antibodies, before the immune serum was administered. It is possible also that the methods employed might give reactions with partly hydrolysed immune globulin fragments. Another difficulty is that, in several instances, the final titre attained in the infants serum was only 1 dilution less than that of the serum administered. The weights of the babies are not given but if these are assumed to be around 3.6 kg and the total plasma volume 4.5% of the body weight, or *c.* 160 ml, and since the total volume of immune serum administered was 100 ml, it would involve the presence in the circulation of 80% of the antibody administered, an efficiency of transmission that is difficult to accept.

Not many people have administered heterologous antibodies to infants. Nordbring (1957b) fed sow or cow colostrum containing paratyphoid H agglutinins to nine premature infants but in no case could any antibody be detected in their sera and transmission must have been less than 0.15–0.33% of the amount given. Dixon, Kuhns, Weigle and Taylor (1959) fed 10 newborn infants, 3 children 2–3 months old and 11 medical students, diphtheria antitoxin in cow's milk and serum. The newborn infants had 9,200–18,500 units in 160–325 ml milk and 18–36 ml serum each, the older children had

30,000 units in 550 ml milk and 60 ml serum. In no case was there a significant increase in antitoxin in their sera as determined by rabbit skin neutralization tests and haemagglutination, although amounts over 0.01–0.03% of the antitoxin in the dose would have been detected. Bovine colostrum containing 270 units/ml was fed to 6 one-day old infants and 5 adults, the infants receiving each *c*. 32,000 units and the adults *c*. 215,000 units, but in none was there any increase in serum antitoxin levels. Du Pan, Scheidegger, Wenger, Koechli and Roux (1959) administered ^{131}I-labelled human γ-globulin by mouth to infants 1 day to 2 months old and could find in their sera only very small traces of labelled protein in a few cases but large amounts up to 34% of the dose were recovered from the faeces.

There is no reason to doubt that very small amounts of intact proteins, including immune globulins, may be transmitted from the gut to the circulation of the newborn infant, as they can be in the adult, for it is well known that people can be anaphylactically sensitized, and desensitized, by proteins absorbed by the alimentary tract. Such transmission could be detected if the methods were sufficiently sensitive, and some of the transmissions at trace levels, recorded above, may have been of this order. Transmission of significant passive immunity is of a different order of magnitude and here the results are conflicting, but it is clear that many careful workers, using reliable and sensitive methods, have failed to detect any. Some of the more aberrant positive results, such as those of Leissring et al. (1962) might be accounted for by the transmission of partially degraded polypeptide fragments. These, assuming they were of sufficiently small molecular size, would probably be rapidly eliminated by the kidney and appear in the urine. It is of interest that, in this connection, Pierce (1961c) states that in the human infant up to 200 mg of protein have been found in urine collected after suckling and up to 70 hr of age. This urinary protein shows similarities, in terms of electrophoretic mobility and ultracentrifugal behaviour, with protein, other than immune lactoglobulin, which is present in human milk. Except in such qualified senses, the weight of evidence at present is against the transmission of passive immunity to the circulation of the human infant after birth, though there is a much more credible case for thinking that colostral antibodies may afford protection against enteric infections of the alimentary tract in the human.

9.10. *The replacement of passive by active immunity*

The normal infant is born without active immunity and the passive immunity which it acquires mainly, probably exclusively, before birth begins
to wane from the time of birth. Its resistance to disease during the neonatal
period depends on these two phenomena and their interactions on each
other. Any such interval as there may be, between the decline of passive
immunity below an effective level and the development of a sufficient capacity
for active response to antigenic stimulation, could constitute a period of
special vulnerability. Maternal passive immunity obviously can provide the
infant only with protection against those antigens of which the mother has
had immunological experience and the child may meet with other challenges
before it is, itself, competent to deal with them. During the period of persistence of passive immunity its competence to deal with a specific antigenic
stimulation may be impaired or blocked, by the presence of maternal antibody to the specific antigen, although it may be capable of responding to
other antigens, to which it does not possess residual maternal antibody.
Moreover the risk of a too massive exposure to antigen, that might induce a
state of tolerance, is greater the further the lymphoid system is from achiev-
ing full competence. An excellent review of some of the earlier literature
bearing on this problem is provided by Edsall (1956) but it must be considered here in the light of more recent work. The rate of decline of maternal
passive immunity will be considered first, then the changes in the serum
proteins resulting from the decline of maternal globulin and the synthesis of
autogenous globulin, next the development of immunological competence
and the influence of passive immunity on active immunization.

   The antibody titre of the newborn infant's blood declines rapidly and
exponentially from the time of birth. Wiener (1951) estimated the half-life
of Rh-antibodies acquired from previously sensitized mothers in Rh-negative infants at *c*. 30 days. Stück, Natzschka and Wiesener (1957) estimated
the half-life of antistreptolysins in newborn infants at *c*. 24 days. Gelfand,
Fox, LeBlanc and Elveback (1960) found that the half-life of antibody to
poliomyelitis in newborn infants was *c*. 25 days. Beck and Rowell (1963)
record the rate of decline in titre of passively acquired anti-nuclear antibody
in a newborn infant and found it to be exponential with a half-life of *c*.
17.5 days. This appears to be out of line with the other results quoted above,
but it seems they did not take into account the dilution resulting from growth
increase in volume of plasma. They do not give data of body weight, but

assuming the body had doubled its weight in three months, and hence its fluid volume, thus accounting for a reduction in titre of 1 dilution, then it is apparent from their figure, that the true half-life would have been *c.* 23 days, which is not out of line. Smith (1960b) found that horse tetanus antitoxin, given in large doses of 5 g of γ-globulin each to newborn infants suffering from tetanus, declined exponentially with a half-life of *c.* 20 days. It was still detectable in the serum in one infant after 128 days but not after 150 days. The disappearance of the antitoxin in older infants was more rapid and in some showed an immune phase of accelerated decline. It is interesting that the heterologous γ-globulin did not induce the active production of antibody to horse γ-globulin in any of the younger, and in only some of the older, infants, but it is possible that this was due to the massive dose inducing a state of partial tolerance rather than incompetence to react at so early an age.

It is apparent from these results that the half-life of maternal antibody, passively acquired, in the newborn infant is in the range of 24–30 days and that it is considerably longer than the half-life of immune globulin in the normal adult which is *c.* 18 days. Thus passive immunity in the neonatal period is more persistent and provides protection over a longer period than it would do in adult life.

The changes in the serum proteins after birth bear out the decline in passive immunity. Moore, Du Pan and Buxton (1949) observed that the high γ-globulin level in newborn infants decreases markedly during the first month or two of life whereas all the other serum protein components rise. In an electrophoretic study of the sera of infants from birth to six months of age, Wiener, Berger and Lenke (1951) found that the relative concentration of γ-globulin at birth slightly exceeded that of the normal mother, but the relative concentrations of α- and β-globulins were considerably less. Albumin, as a percentage of total serum protein, remained relatively constant over the first six months, but the α_1-, α_2- and β-globulins rose and the γ-globulin declined to a minimum of 5.8% during the first three months, and then the γ-globulin began to rise slowly and continuously. Norton, Kunz and Pratt (1952) examined the changes in the serum proteins of 27 premature infants. The total serum protein, albumin and γ-globulin declined gradually over the first 5–6 weeks, whereas the α- and β-globulins showed little change. The γ-globulin declined from *c.* 0.7 g/100 ml during the first week to 0.2 g/100 ml at 40 days of age. Orlandini, Sass-Kortsak and Ebbs (1955) also followed the changes in total serum proteins, albumin, total globulins and γ-globulin from birth to 2 years of age in a sample of 150 normal infants (fig. 9.5). The γ-globulin level declined steeply during the first four weeks from a mean of 0.90 g/100 ml at birth to 0.34 g/100 ml and then remained near this level until 3 months of age, when it began to rise gradually to 0.77 g/100 ml at 22 months of age. The decline in concentration of γ-globulin during the first month was exponential, with an apparent mean half-life of 20 days or, in the case of one individual infant followed throughout this period, of 25 days, neither half-life being corrected for growth increment in fluid volume (fig. 9.6). Thus there appeared to be little autogenous γ-globulin produced during this period. Breast feeding, as compared to bottle feeding, did not affect the exponential nature of the decline in concentration of γ-globulin, as it would have done if significant augmentation of the γ-globulin had resulted. Gelfand, Strean, Pavilanis and Sternberg (1960) found that

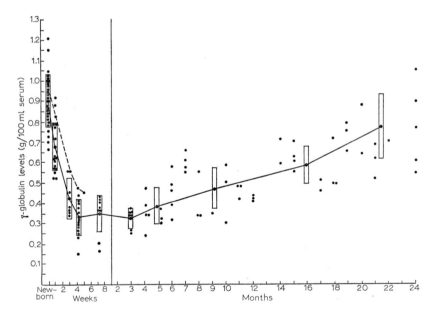

Fig. 9.5. Diagram of the changes in serum γ-globulin levels from birth to 2 years of age. Dots represent individual values and the solid line connects mean values. The bars across the means represent the standard deviation. The dotted line connects the values of the single case followed from birth to 5½ weeks of age. The vertical line indicates the change in the age scale from weeks to months. (From Orlandini, Sass-Kortsak and Ebbs 1955.)

the γ-globulin level in the serum of infants declined from birth to a minimum towards the fourth month and then began to rise again, due to synthesis. Good, Condie and Bridges (1960) found that the γ-globulin levels of new-born infants as a group are slightly higher than those of their mothers at the time of parturition. After birth the γ-globulin level of the infant falls in a logarithmic fashion for a variable period, lasting in most infants between one and three months. The half-life of γ-globulin during this period ranges between 19 and 44 days. Sometime between 3 weeks and 4 months of age, varying greatly from infant to infant, logarithmic decline in γ-globulin concentrations ceases and a brief period of steady state is followed by relatively rapid γ-globulin accumulation. The γM- and γA-globulins are regularly absent from the sera of the newborn and these begin to appear in the circulation in detectable quantities between the second and fourth months of life. The stage at which autogenous γ-globulin becomes appreciable was shown very clearly by two infants of a mother who suffered from agamma-globulinaemia for at least 8 years before the birth of the first and whose γ-globulin level was between 5.6 and 12.8 mg%. The infants' levels at birth

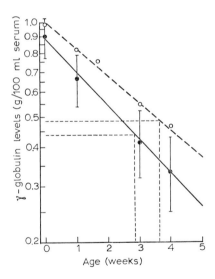

Fig. 9.6. The levels of γ-globulin in the serum during the first 4 weeks of life plotted on a logarithmic scale against age. The solid circles represent the mean values and the lines across them the ranges of the standard deviations. The open circles are the levels in a single individual at different ages. The dotted lines show the half-lives resulting from each curve. (From Orlandini, Sass-Kortsak and Ebbs 1955.)

were similar to their mother's and showed no rise in γ-globulin until 35–42 days of age in the one and 21–28 days of age in the other. Their capacity to form antibodies could be demonstrated only after the levels began to rise.

There is much evidence that the human infant, or even foetus, can produce antibodies at a much earlier developmental stage than that at which antibody production normally starts provided that they are suitably stimulated. Barr, Glenny, Hignett, Randall and Thomson (1952) found that babies produced diphtheria antitoxin titres of the same order, after two injections of 25 Lf of alum precipitated toxoid at an interval of 2 months, whether the first injection was given at 6–10 days of age or at 6 weeks or more. Osborn, Dancis and Julia (1952a) immunized 40 infants from 1 week to 6 months of age with one injection of diphtheria toxoid on alum. The youngest group, under 2 weeks of age at injection, gave a delayed response with significant quantities of antitoxin by 2 months after injection and a further increase subsequently. The time after injection of appearance of the antibody, and the amount produced, improved with age. Twenty seven of these infants were given also, at the same time, a single injection of tetanus toxoid. The production of tetanus antitoxin occurred sooner, and was greater, than that of diphtheria antitoxin, and likewise improved with age at the time of injection. Smith (1960a) injected intradermally over 150 neonatal infants with *Salmonella typhi* vaccine. Over 50% of the infants, who had no passive immunity, had developed titres of $\frac{1}{10}$ to $\frac{1}{5120}$ against the flagellar 'd' antigen at one week of age, and 88% had done so by 14 days of age. No agglutinin against the somatic antigen was detected in 98 infants. The antibody produced was a γ_1-globulin on starch gel electrophoresis and sedimented at *c.* 19S. This antibody was reduced by 2-mercaptoethanol to 7S without loss of activity. No 7S antibody was detected before 21 days of age. Older children produced both 7S and 19S antibody. As mentioned previously (p. 271), Smith (1960b) found that newborn infants given large doses of horse γ-globulin did not become immune to the foreign protein, although some older ones did become immune. Good, Condie and Bridges (1960) were unable to demonstrate the capacity to form antibody by infants lacking γ-globulin from their agammaglobulinaemic mother until autogenous γ-globulin began to appear in their sera. These authors could not find plasma cells in the bone marrow of any newborn child, but they were found in a child with chronic pulmonary disease at 1 month of age and were regularly present in increasing numbers in infants from 3–12 months of age.

Silverstein (1962) observed a consistent pattern of mature plasma cells and plasmacytoid cells associated with the inflammatory lesions in human foetuses, with congenital syphilis, stillborn from the 6th month of gestation onwards. This led Silverstein and Lukes (1962) to point out that human foetuses exposed to congenital infections, such as syphilis or toxoplasmosis, are capable of plasma cell formation and precocious lymphoid development. They suggest that the foetus is immunologically competent, at least during the later stages of gestation, but that this competence is only apparent after stimulation. Thus foetuses with congenital infections show accelerated enlargement of splenic lymphoid nodules and often the development of reaction centres. Van Furth, Schuit and Hijmans (1965) examined 20 foetuses, of from 13 to 31 weeks of age, that were born alive but died soon afterwards, for the formation *in vitro* of immune globulins in spleen cultures, and by immunofluorescent staining of spleen tissue and serum protein analysis. They found that γG- and γM-globulin synthesis starts about the 20th week. Medium and large lymphoid cells and plasma cells gave positive reactions for either γG- or γM-globulin. The ratio of γM to γG production was higher than postnatally. There was no indication of synthesis of γA- or of γD-globulin prenatally. Fudenberg and Fudenberg (1964) and Mårtensson and Fudenberg (1965) found, by means of highly specific typing systems for genetic γ-globulin characters, that the human foetus may be synthesizing small amounts of γG-globulin. Epstein, Fong and Tan (1966) found haemagglutinins specific for Bence-Jones proteins, usually λ-chains and rarely κ-chains, in matched maternal and cord sera. The concentrations in the cord sera exceeded those in the matched maternal sera and sometimes the antibodies were present in the cord sera and absent from the corresponding maternal sera. The antibody was a macroglobulin, as shown by gel filtration chromatography and sensitivity to mercaptoethanol. The antibody was believed to be of foetal origin and no other macroglobulin antibodies, such as were present in the maternal sera, were found in the cord sera. A concentration of 2 μg/ml of λ-chains was found in pooled cord serum, as compared to 8–16 μg/ml in maternal sera. Buffe and Burtin (1967), using immunofluorescent staining, found γM-globulin in the foetal spleen after the 12th week of gestation and γG-globulin after the 20th week. It was only in one large foetus and one infant that γA-globulin was found. These immune globulins were found only in large lymphoplasmacytes, and sometimes in plastocytes, but never in small lymphocytes.

It appears that the normal human infant, sheltered from antigenic stimuli *in utero*, and possibly with stimulation by the common antigens blocked for an interval after birth, by maternal antibodies passively acquired does not produce appreciable quantites of immune globulin until it is some weeks old. Given appropriate antigenic stimulation it is clear that competence can develop precociously and the infant at birth, or even the foetus, can produce antibody and that such antibody probably is exclusively macroglobulin. It is well established that the presence of a sufficient level of passively acquired specific antibody can interfere with active immunization at all ages. There is evidence that in the newborn infant the presence of maternal passive immunity can interfere similarly with active immunization. Osborn, Dancis and Julia (1952b) attempted to quantify this effect. Twenty-three infants, 2 weeks to 6 months old all of whom had measurable levels of maternal diphtheria antitoxins, were each given a single injection of diph-theria toxoid on alum. Those with low levels of passive immunity responded as well, or nearly as well, as those without passive immunity, but antitoxin production was depressed in those with higher levels of passive immunity. It was suggested that active immunization of the neonatal infant depends both upon the potency of the antigen and the level of passive immunity to it. However, Levi, Kravtzov, Levova and Fomenko (1969) found that babies with antibodies in the cord blood responded better to pertussis–diphtheria–tetanus vaccine.

CHAPTER 10

Haemolytic disease of the newborn

10.1. Introduction

The mammalian foetus, having antigens inherited from its father, is of necessity to some degree immunologically incompatible with its mother and the degree of incompatibility is reduced to a minimum when both parents belong to the same highly inbred strain. The possibility exists of an immunological reaction on the part of the mother against foetal antigens which she does not possess or even of the foetus reacting against maternal antigens which it did not happen to inherit through its individual haploid complement of maternal chromosomes. The latter possibility can be conveniently dismissed on the grounds of immaturity of the foetal lymphoid system, although, as has been shown, foetuses of at least some species can react *in utero* to sufficiently strong antigenic stimuli. The reasons why maternal immunological reactions to foetal antigens are not more frequent are obscure. Theoretically, such reactions could be either of the cellular or serological kind. The foetus is, in effect, a homograft in the uterus and a cellular reaction of host against graft tissues, resembling a graft rejection reaction, might be expected; that it does not normally, perhaps ever, occur presents a fascinating immunological and embryological problem that has attracted a great deal of attention but which fortunately falls clearly without the scope of this book. Serological immunity of the mother, resulting in the production of maternal antibodies to foetal antigens is, on the other hand, clearly within the scope. Such reactions occur both in man and other animals and give rise to foetal and neonatal diseases of varying severity and importance when the maternal antibodies are transmitted to offspring possessing the corresponding antigens. It has been realised for a long time that this might happen, but the first clear demonstration of the natural occurrence of such a disease came in 1939/1940 with the discovery of Rhesus disease in man. This discovery led rapidly to an appreciation of its great importance, to the discovery of a number of other similar diseases in man, and of comparable diseases in animals, notably in the horse and the pig. All result from the production of antibodies by the mother to foetal blood cell antigens inherited from the father and on the transmission of these antibodies to the young before or after birth. Most relate to antigens borne by the red blood cells and are grouped under the title of haemolytic disease of the newborn. It is proposed to deal with these diseases comparatively in this chapter in so far as they throw light on the transmission of immunity. Other aspects, such as the genetical, anthropological, forensic and clinical need not concern us except in passing and all have been admirably reviewed in other works. Haemolytic disease of the newborn in man and animals has been treated comparatively by Fulton Roberts (1957). The genetics of the blood groups in man is dealt with in the standard work by Race and Sanger (1968) and the immunological aspects in relation to clinical medicine by Mollison (1967). These have been drawn on liberally in the following pages and we have not attempted to rival the bibliographies contained in them. The distribution of blood groups in man and other animals and their anthropological bearing are treated by Mourant (1954). It will be convenient to consider Rhesus disease in man first, since far the most is known about it, and then to consider other similar human diseases. Afterwards haemolytic disease of the newborn in horses, pigs and other animals will be considered, both those that arise naturally or as a result of medical insults and those that have only been produced experimentally.

10.2. *Rhesus disease in man*

The first significant step in the discovery of haemolytic disease of the newborn in man was taken by Levine and Stetson (1939) when they recorded the case of a woman, who had borne two previous children, giving birth to a stillborn foetus. In consequence of serious haemorrhage she was given blood transfusions from her husband, both donor and recipient being of group O and apparently compatible. A transfusion reaction occurred and it was found that the woman's serum contained an isoagglutinin which agglutinated her husband's red cells and those of 80% of group O donors. The reactions were independent of the M, N and P factors and the isoantibody was as active at 37 °C as at 20 °C. The next step was the announcement by Landsteiner and Wiener (1940) that the sera of rabbits immunized with Rhesus monkey blood agglutinated the corpuscles of 39 of 45 group O donors. The reactions were independent of the M, N and P factors as well as A and B factors. Wiener and Peters (1940) found anti-Rh (Rhesus) antibody, similar to that produced in rabbits, in some human sera from donors who had had transfusion reactions with ABO compatible blood, and Levine and Katzin (1940) found a similar antibody that had resulted from isoimmunization of pregnancy. The following year, Levine, Burnham, Katzin and Vogel (1941) showed that haemolytic disease resulted from Rh blood group incompatibility between mother and child in their famous paper.

Following on the discovery of Rh incompatibility, the 85% of people in the American population whose blood was agglutinated by anti-Rh serum were said to be Rh+, and the remainder Rh−. The Rh antigens, like those of other blood groups, are inherited in a Mendelian manner. It soon became apparent that a number of distinct antigens were involved in the system and that three closely linked pairs of alleles, Dd Cc Ee, now thought to belong to one complex locus or cistron, were necessary to account for them (Race 1944), the dominant D being responsible for the Rh+ antigen. During the quarter of a century which has elapsed since some thirty antigens belonging to the system have been recognised and there is some doubt if so simple a symbolism can continue to be adapted to represent the increasing complexity of their genetics. However, since the great majority of cases of haemolytic disease are due to the offspring inheriting the D antigen from the father, who may have it in double or single dose (DD = homozygote; Dd = heterozygote), while the mother lacks it (dd = homozygote), the simpler notation of Rh+ (= Dd or DD) and Rh− (= dd) is adequate in practice in most cases for serological purposes. It should be added that the Rh genes are inherited independently of the ABO genes and of those of all other known blood groups.

A Rh− woman may become immunized and produce anti-Rh antibodies in one of two ways: either (1) by transfusion with Rh+ blood (or injection with material containing Rh+ red cells); or (2) by pregnancies with Rh+ foetuses. Transfusion is the more effective way. A single transfusion of Rh+ blood stimulates the formation of anti-Rh antibodies in at least 50% of cases (Mollison 1967). Even if antibody is not produced in response to a single transfusion, the subject is usually sensitized and is likely to produce antibody on any subsequent stimulation. An Rh− woman who has had a Rh+ transfusion has about an 80% chance of producing antibody during her first subsequent pregnancy with a Rh + infant. However, some subjects to not produce antibody even after repeated transfusions.

Pregnancies with Rh + foetuses alone, without previous transfusions, can induce the formation of antibodies in Rh − women, although in the majority of cases they fail to do so. It is rare for antibody to be produced during a first such pregnancy, of the order of less than 1 % (Mollison 1967). The probability of antibody being produced for the first time is greatest with the second Rh + pregnancy and declines steeply with subsequent pregnancies. Nevanlinna (1953) points out that as a rule the production of anti-Rh antibody requires a minimum of two antigenic stimuli from Rh + foetuses. He suggests that the first sensitizes, generally without the production of appreciable antibody, and the second results in antibody production. Pregnancy is inefficient in producing sensitization and in the majority of cases fails to do so. Transfusion, on the other hand, is highly efficient and in the majority of cases achieves sensitization on the first occasion and may even result in production of antibody. Once sensitization has occurred, subsequent pregnancy with an Rh + foetus is an efficient means of inducing the formation of antibody and does so in the majority of cases, as witness the 80 % chance of a previously transfused Rh − woman producing antibody with her first subsequent Rh + pregnancy. Sensitization by pregnancy, when it occurs, is most frequent with first Rh + pregnancies, as is shown by the decline in the probability of antibody production from the second Rh + pregnancy onwards.

The commonest time for the appearance of antibody induced by pregnancy is immediately *post partum* and when antibody is already present in the serum it generally shows a rise in titre after delivery, reaching a peak in 1–3 weeks (Mollison 1967). Since the Rh antigens are not present in solution in body fluids, as are the A and B antigens and those of some other blood groups, but are confined to the red cells, it is thought that immunization by pregnancy must involve the passage of foetal corpuscles into the maternal circulation. That the passage of red cells occurs most frequently at parturition is indicated by the rarity of immunization during a first pregnancy and by the post-parturient rise in titre. Such leakages might result from the more violent uterine contractions of labour, as has been suggested (see pp. 255-256), or from trauma at parturition. However, there is reason to believe that passage of foetal red cells into the maternal blood can occur during pregnancy and may be common (see pp. 255-256 and 260). Chown (1954) has recorded a case of massive foetal haemorrhage into the maternal circulation during pregnancy which resulted in 5–10% of the red cells in the maternal blood being of foetal origin, and some foetal red cells frequently can be found in the blood of pregnant women (Woodrow and Finn 1966).

Rh+ red cells of an ABO blood group that is incompatible with the recipient are much less likely to induce Rh− immunization than are Rh+ red cells that are ABO compatible. Thus injections of Rh+ABO incompatible cells induced the production of anti-Rh antibody in only 15% of recipients, whereas similar injections of Rh+ABO compatible cells induced anti-Rh antibodies in nearly 70% of recipients. This effect is apparent also in immunization of pregnancy, for haemolytic disease occurs more often when the parents are ABO compatible than when they are incompatible. ABO incompatibility appears to afford the greatest protection when the recipient is group O and will therefore have isoantibodies to both A and B antigens, as has been shown recently by Ascari, Levine and Pollack (1969) who found that Rh sensitization occurred in 17% of Rh− women with their first Rh+ABO compatible pregnancy, but in only 9–13% of Rh− group O women with their first Rh+ABO incompatible pregnancy. The reasons for the protection afforded by ABO incompatibility are not understood, but the more rapid clearance of the incompatible red cells by the naturally occurring anti-A and anti-B isoantibodies is likely to be involved. This concept has led to work at Liverpool (Woodrow et al. 1965; Clarke et al. 1966; Clarke 1968) which has resulted in an effective method of protecting women against Rh-sensitization by pregnancy. The method consists in administering passively, potent anti-D antibody to a Rh− mother within a few hours of delivery of a first Rh+ABO compatible infant. A high degree of protection against Rh-sensitization is effected by this means.

Natural antibodies produced without apparent stimulation by antigen, such as anti-A and anti-B isoagglutinins which are normally present in the sera of persons lacking the corresponding antigen on their red cells and such as are found with some other blood groups, do not normally occur in the Rh system. Rh antibodies result from stimulation with Rh antigens of persons who lack them and are immune antibodies. The antibody produced by Rh+ cells in Rh− subjects is usually only anti-D although the sensitizing red cells may have borne other Rh antigens which the subject lacked. The Rh antibodies found in pregnant women are anti-D in 95% of cases (Boorman, Dodd and Mollison 1944). Stimulation with Rh antigen generally results in the production of γM-antibodies first, then γG-antibodies as well and finally only γG-antibodies. Anti-Rh serum generally contains antibodies which attach to Rh+ red cells but which do not agglutinate them in a saline medium, in addition to those that do agglutinate in saline. This discovery was made simultaneously and independently by Race (1944) in this country and by Wiener (1944) in America and the antibody has come to be known as 'incomplete'. These incomplete antibodies will agglutinate the red cells if these are suspended in serum or suitable colloidal solutions but the best and most sensitive test for them was devised by Coombs, Mourant and Race (1945) and has become generally known as the Coombs test. The red cells after exposure to serum suspected of containing incomplete antibody are washed and exposed to an anti-human-γ-globulin serum, prepared in a rabbit or other suitable animal, which reacts with any incomplete antibody attached to the red cells and agglutinates them. Antibodies that are γM-globulins usually are of the complete type and agglutinate incompatible red cells in saline whereas γG-antibodies are usually incomplete. Occasionally γA anti-D antibody may be produced and it can be either complete or incomplete. It appears that only γG-globulin is transmitted across the foetal membranes to the human infant *in utero* (see pp. 250-255). Only very small traces of γM-globulin are present in the cord blood (Franklin and Kunkel 1958), and this may well be all autogenous. Since γG anti-Rh antibodies are mostly incomplete it is these which are most frequent in cord blood and are by far the more important in causing haemolytic disease (Wiener 1948).

The severity of Rhesus disease can vary widely with, at the one extreme, slight and transient neonatal symptoms and, at the other extreme, death before or after birth or permanent damage to those that survive. The rate of stillbirth of Rh+ infants, excluding the first, of Rh− mothers with anti-Rh antibodies in their sera is about 29% (Mollison 1967). The overall still-birth rate in pregnancies with Rh antibodies in the sera is *c.* 12%. Intrauter-ine death may occur sometimes before the 20th week but usually takes place in the last trimester. Chown (1955) records a case in which antibody had al-ready reached the foetus at six weeks. Many stillbirths exhibit the condition of hydrops foetalis and are grossly oedematous. Infants born alive may be only moderately anaemic and develop jaundice within a few hours. Jaundice becomes profound in severe cases and the tissues of the brain may become stained with bilirubin and permanently damaged by the condition, known as kernicterus. However, in the first affected infant the disease tends to be less severe than in subsequent ones. The haemolytic process resulting from the reaction of the maternal antibodies with the infant's red cells is maximal at the time of birth, since the transmission of immunity does not continue after birth. Knowledge of the nature and causes of the disease have led to great advances in the prediction of its incidence and severity and in its treatment by postnatal exchange transfusion and intrauterine transfusion, as well as in its prevention, but it is still a serious hazard to infant survival.

Apart from anti-D antibody, antibodies to a number of other blood group antigens have been known to cause haemolytic disease (Race and Sanger 1968). These include other antigens belonging to the Rh group and antigens of the ABO, MNSs, Kell, Duffy, Kidd, Diego and a number of the rare or so-called 'private' groups. The most important are the A and B antigens of the ABO group and as haemolytic disease due to the isoantibodies to these antigens differs in several respects from that resulting from anti-D, it will suffice to consider it.

10.3. ABO haemolytic disease in man

Naturally occurring isoantibodies anti-A and anti-B are normally present in the sera of persons lacking the corresponding antigens, thus group O sera have both antibodies, and group A or group B sera one or the other, both being absent in group AB sera. The antigens occur in solution in body fluids, in most tissues and are borne by the leucocytes and platelets as well as by the red cells. About 80% of the population have the antigens in solution in their saliva, gastric juice and other secretions and are known as secretors. The secretor character is inherited as a Mendelian dominant. These are two respects in which the ABO system differs from the Rh system and they have important bearings on haemolytic disease.

The naturally occurring isoantibodies are usually γM-globulins, which do not reach the foetus. The antibodies formed in response to immunization by transfusion or pregnancy are most often 7S γG-globulins and it is only these which reach the foetus. People of groups A or B form γM-antibodies predominantly, whereas group O people form both γM- and γG-antibodies (Kochwa, Rosenfield, Tallal and Wasserman 1961). The immune 7S γG-antibodies are mainly incomplete agglutinins, but a serum with a potent γG-antibody is almost invariably also haemolytic. Incomplete agglutinins are transmitted readily, whereas complete agglutinins are transmitted at a low rate (Wiener and Sonn 1946; Wiener, Wexler and Hurst 1949), presumably because they tend to be mainly γM-globulins. Haemolysins appear to reach the foetus less readily than incomplete agglutinins but more readily than complete agglutinins (Freda and Carter 1962).

Anti-A antibody titres tend to be higher than those of anti-B, whether in group O sera or in group B as compared to group A sera (De Kromme and Van der Spek 1950; Zeulzer and Kaplan 1954a, b). Anti-A antibodies are transmitted more readily than anti-B antibodies, both as to a higher proportion of cases and at higher titres, but there are individual variations (De Kromme and Van der Spek 1950). The antibodies reach the foetus more readily when the mother is group O than when she is group A or group B, and also more readily when she is subgroup A_2 than when she is subgroup A_1 (Freda and Carter 1962). Maternal anti-A antibody does not react with the corpuscles of subgroup A_2 infants (Zeulzer and Kaplan 1954b), possibly because the antigen on the corpuscles is not sufficiently developed at birth, and in consequence haemolytic disease due to ABO incompatibility is confined to group B and subgroup A_1 infants, subgroup A_2 being spared. The disease is almost confined to the infants of group O mothers, because the production of γG antibody tends to be greater in them.

The A and B antigens can be detected on the red cells of a foetus as early as 5 or 6 weeks (Kemp 1930), but they are not fully developed even at birth. The antigens occur in the foetal tissues as well as on the red cells but it is only when the foetus is a secretor that the antigens are found in the amniotic fluid, foetal membranes and placenta (Freda 1958). AB-sensitization of the mother during pregnancy is almost confined to cases where the infant is a secretor (Wiener, Wexler and Hurst 1949). There is generally a rise in the mother's antibody titre after parturition or sometimes near full term when the infant is incompatible and a secretor.

The proportion of ABO incompatible infants in the population is about 20% but as the disease is almost confined to group A or group B infants of group O mothers it is only about $\frac{3}{4}$ of these, or 15% of all infants, that are at risk. Although antibody may reach the foetus in a large proportion of those at risk the effect in most cases is sub-clinical or only mildly clinical. Cases sufficiently severe to require treatment are only about 1 in 3,000 births, or 10% of the number requiring treatment for Rh-disease (Mollison 1967). It is doubtful if ABO-incompatibility ever causes intrauterine death, but severe cases do occur and can cause kernicterus and neonatal death, though they are very rare. ABO-disease, unlike Rh-disease, may affect the firstborn (Wiener, Wexler and Hurst 1949; Zeulzer and Kaplan 1954c), and often unaffected infants may be born after affected ones (Mollison 1967). Probably, the A and B substances in the tissues of the foetus are mainly responsible for protecting it against the incompatible antibodies (Zeulzer and Kaplan 1954b).

It is not necessary to refer here to the rare cases of haemolytic disease due to other blood group antigens since they do not add significantly to the information concerning transmission of immunity which can be derived from Rh and ABO haemolytic diseases.

It should be mentioned, however, that neonatal ideopathic thrombocytopenia appears to be a disease resembling haemolytic disease in that it is due to the transmission from the mother to the foetus of anti-platelet antibodies. These antibodies when present during pregnancy can result in thrombocytopenia of the mother only, or of both mother and child, or of the child only. Cases are very rare but a good example has been recorded by Gwynfor Jones, Goldsmith and Anderson (1961). The woman had ideopathic thrombocytopenia and had had four pregnancies, in three of which the infants were also affected. Incomplete anti-platelet antibodies were present in the serum of both mother and child but anti-red cell antibodies were absent. The mother's platelet count fell to 12,000–14,000/mm^3 at the end of pregnancy but recovered afterwards to 108,000/mm^3. The infant had a count of 28,000/mm^3 at birth but rose gradually to normal levels later.

10.4. Haemolytic disease in monkeys

Haemolytic disease of the newborn has occurred in the marmoset *Tamarinus nigricollis* in two litters recorded by Gengozian, Lushbaugh, Humason and Kniseley (1965). Twins are normal in the species. In the first case one twin was stillborn and the other survived for 16 days. Both complete and incomplete antibodies reacting with the paternal red cells were present. In the second case the red cells of both twins gave positive reactions with the Coombs test, as did the paternal red cells.

10.5. Haemolytic disease of the newborn in horses and mules

Jaundice of the newborn foal has been known as a serious disease causing heavy losses in mule breeding districts for a very long time but was wrongly attributed to various causes, particularly to infection with *Nuttalia equi*. The true nature of the disease was recognised first by Caroli and Bessis (1947a) in France, who appreciated the similarity to haemolytic disease of the newborn in man. They found none of the signs of chronic infection, the mule foal being born perfectly healthy and vigorous and the symptoms only appearing a few hours after birth. Once a mare had given birth to a mule foal which became jaundiced all her subsequent mule foals became similarly affected, whereas she could be mated to a horse and bear healthy foals. They noted that haematuria was a frequent accompaniment of the disease in mules, although in the human disease this is exceptional. The blood of affected mules displayed intense red cell autoagglutination and spherocytosis. The mare's serum had a raised titre of agglutinins ($\frac{1}{64}$ to $\frac{1}{128}$) for donkey and mule red cells as compared to normal horse serum. Injection of donkey red cells into a normal horse produced a titre of only $\frac{1}{128}$, whereas a similar injection into a mare with affected mule foals produced a titre of $\frac{1}{512,000}$, showing she had been previously immunized by her foals. An affected mare with a serum titre of $\frac{1}{128}$, had a milk titre of $\frac{1}{32}$, whereas antibody could not be detected in the milk of normal mares. Subsequently these authors (1947b) showed that normal mares had only traces of antibody to donkey red cells in their sera, whereas mares that had borne healthy mule foals had distinct titres and those which had borne affected mules had relatively high titres. Bessis and Caroli (1947) also found that the serum of immunized mules contained incomplete agglutinins at titres of $\frac{1}{256}$ to $\frac{1}{4,000}$ when titrated in serum, as compared to complete agglutinin titres of $\frac{1}{16}$ to $\frac{1}{64}$ in saline. Caroli and Bessis (1947c, 1948) state that about 8–10% of the mules bred in Poitou were affected by the disease. They quote evidence that of 44 affected mule foals only three survived. The symptoms appeared very soon after birth, often within hours or a day of birth and only as late as 3 days in less severe cases. These were extreme weakness with shallow and rapid respiration, very accelerated pulse, jaundice of the mucous membranes, haematuria and in many cases haemaglobinuria. Death followed after one or two days prostration and coma. Post mortem showed splenic enlargement, intense capillary engorgement of the liver and pigmentation of all the viscera, but there was no sign of kernicterus, as occurs in the human infant.

Brion (1949) pointed out that neither the means by which the foetal antigens reached the mother nor the route by which the maternal antibodies reached the young were known for certain. He wondered why first mule foals were not affected and why only 5–10% of mares breeding mules became immunized. He suggested that foetal blood could only reach the mother through uterine trauma, possibly occurring at parturition or during gestation through partial placental displacement. He also believed that antibody only exceptionally reached the foetus before birth or at parturition and that the colostrum and first milk were the principal vehicles (Brion and Goret 1949). He found that the titre of the mare's colostrum is higher than that of her serum at first but falls very rapidly. This concentration of antibody in the precolostrum and colostrum as compared to the serum was confirmed by Millot and Gorius (1950), who noted that the extent to which the foal is affected depends on the titre of the colostrum. Both these authors and Bessis and Millot (1949) advocate preventing the foal taking colostrum but allowing it to return to its mother after she has been milked for two or three days. Healthy foals can be reared from affected mares if this is done.

Coombs, Gorius and Bessis (1950) found that the red cells of all affected mules gave positive antiglobulin reactions. Brion (1950) was the first to attempt to produce the disease experimentally. He immunized a mare, pregnant for the first time with a mule, by intravenous injection of donkey blood. At parturition the serum agglutinin titre was $\frac{1}{256}$ and the colostrum $\frac{1}{500,000}$. The vigorous healthy foal was abandoned to its mother. By the afternoon it had become feeble, with pale and jaundiced mucous membranes. At 8 hr after birth the haemocrit had fallen from the initial value of 7,320,000/mm^3 to 1,300,000/mm^3, the urine was wine red and the serum agglutinated at $\frac{1}{128}$. At 13 hr after birth the blood count was down to 1,000,000/mm^3, the heart and respiratory rates were accelerated and the animal was prostrate. It died 20 hr after birth. Post mortem revealed intense general jaundice, blood coloured fluid in the peritoneal and pleural cavities, splenomegaly and haemoglobulinuria, but not haematuria. A similar experiment is recorded by Pigoury and Charny (1951).

The year following the recognition of haemolytic disease in newborn mules, a similar disease was identified in thoroughbred horses simultaneously in America and in England. Bruner, Hull, Edwards and Doll (1948) studied 17 fatal cases, some of which were the first affected foal a mare had produced and others were the second or third from a mare bred to the same stallion. The foals were normal at birth but developed the disease 24–48 hr after birth, dying before the 4th day. Post mortem showed marked general jaundice, severe anaemia with blood counts down to 2–3 × 10^6/mm^3. The mare's serum in six cases examined agglutinated the stallion's corpuscles and those of the only foal that survived, as well as those of about 75% of 80 other horses tested. The sera of 40 other mares failed to agglutinate the red cells of the sires of the affected foals. Bruner, Hull and Doll (1948) reviewed a large number of cases, including one of a mare that had borne by one stallion an affected foal which died and subsequently by another stallion a healthy foal. This mare's serum agglutinated the red cells of the first stallion but not those of the second. The sera of sensitized mares were found to contain haemolysins as well as agglutinins. Five mares were experimentally immunized by repeated injections of the stallions' blood during the last three months of pregnancy. Three of these mares, whose blood groups were evidently compatible with those of the stallions, did not respond and one responded weakly. The fifth responded strongly and had an agglutinin titre in her serum of $\frac{1}{512}$ and in her colostrum of $\frac{1}{1024}$ against the foal's corpuscles. After suckling the foal developed jaundice and anaemia and its corpuscles were agglutinated strongly in its own serum but it recovered slowly from the 3rd day. Its recovery was attributed to the apparent absence from the mare's serum of haemolysins. These authors suggest that the mares become sensitized through the break down and absorption of parts of the placenta, as many placentae at parturition exhibit signs of inflammatory changes, tissue destruction and necrotic areas. Bruner, Edwards and Doll (1948) found that the titre of the colostrum is higher than that of the serum at parturition but that suckling by an active foal reduces it to less than 5% of its initial value in 12 hr, whereas the serum titre remains constant for a long period. At 5 days old a foal was unable to acquire antibody from colostrum.

Coombs, Crowhurst, Day et al. (1948) were the first to observe the disease in England. They found antibodies in the sera, colostra and milk of the dams of icteric foals and demonstrated that the red cells of the foals were sensitized. They considered that more than one antigen-antibody system was involved. Parry, Day and Crowhurst (1949) dealt with the clinical aspects of these cases. Britton (1950) gave the foaling histories of mares bearing icteric foals, showing that these had produced healthy foals before the diseased ones, in three instances by the same incompatible sire. This author successfully reared foals by muzzling and bottle-feeding for 48 hr, while the mares were milked out, and then returning the foals to their mothers. This method is recommended also by Bruner, Doll, Hull and Kinkaid (1950) as a result of feeding foals on immune serum. The foals absorbed the antibodies from the serum until 24 hr old but lost the power to do so between 24 and 36 hr old.

Beijers, Van Loghem and Van der Hart (1950) record a single case of haemolytic disease in a newborn thoroughbred foal in Holland. Both complete and incomplete antibodies were present in the mare's serum and colostrum, the foal's corpuscles were sensitized with incomplete antibodies and antibodies were present in the urine, which displayed haemoglobinuria.

Doll and Hull (1951) and Cronin (1955) give full descriptions of the clinical and post mortem finding with affected foals, but as these closely resemble those already described in affected mules they need not be repeated. Doll and Hull (1951) noticed that vaccination for virus abortion, the vaccine being prepared from foetal horse liver, tended to raise the haemagglutination titres, and some mares, known to be sensitized, showed an increase in antibody titre during gestation of an incompatible foal, whereas others did not, suggesting that foetal antigens do not invariably reach the mother. Doll, Richards, Wallace and Bryans (1952), following up this work, found that although the vaccination sensitizes mares and could cause haemolytic disease, yet natural immunization by pregnancy does occur. When the antibody titre increases during incompatible pregnancy, it does so between the 8th and 10th months. However, no such increase occurred in 39 of 45 incompatible pregnancies of sensitized mares. Cronin (1955) found that the annual incidence of isoimmunization of mares foaling in the Newmarket area is about 1 per cent. One mare in which isoimmunization occurred in a first pregnancy was recorded.

10.6. Haemolytic disease in newborn piglets

Bruner, Brown, Hull and Kinkaid (1949) produced experimentally haemolytic disease of the newborn in pigs by injecting the sow with the red cells of the boar during pregnancy. The piglets were shown to obtain the antibodies from the colostrum; they became anaemic and died. Two-day old piglets could take the colostrum without harm as at that age they did not absorb the antibodies. Kershaw (1950) observed several cases in which sows in good condition produced piglets, apparently healthy at birth, which all died after suckling and generally within 36 hr of birth. Anaemia was evident at post mortem examination, when the findings were similar to those described by Bruner et al. (1949). It was suggested that this was haemolytic disease of the newborn, but serological evidence to support this suggestion was lacking. The disease was first demonstrated as occurring in commercial herds in this country and in Hungary in 1953. Buxton and Brooksbank (1953a, b) showed that losses of piglets soon after birth, that had been occurring in the East Midlands, were due to maternal isoimmunization. Although the piglets appeared healthy at birth, jaundice became apparent at about 48 hr and generally all the pigs in a litter were dead by the 5th day. Post mortem examination revealed congestion and enlargement of spleen and liver, blood stained peritoneal fluid, much darkened urine and general jaundice. The piglets' red cells were invariably agglutinated by anti-pig-globulin serum and incompatibility of the blood of the boar with that of the sow was demonstrable. All the piglets were born to Wessex sows mated to Large White boars. Simultaneously and quite independently Szent-Iványi and Szabo (1953, 1954; Szabo, Szent-Iványi and Szeky 1956) recognised and gave an account of a similar disease in crossbred piglets in Hungary, and Doll and Brown (1954) in America observed the disease in two litters of a Duroc sow, after she had borne four healthy litters. The two affected litters and the three preceding them were all by the same boar. Subsequently the disease was found in Japan, where it presented a similar pattern but occurred in several breed crosses (Mogi, Hosoda and Himeno 1966; Himeno, Nagano, Mori, Mogi and Hosoda 1967, 1968). Buxton, Brooksbank and Coombs (1955) showed that the piglets' red cells were not coated with antibody at birth but positive reactions to the Coombs test were obtained within 6 hr of suckling. The symptoms were those of rapid haemolysis *in vivo*, but lysis of red cells did not occur *in vitro*, even with guineapig complement. In one case the antibody appeared to be incomplete. Although the jaundice in fatal cases was accompanied by diffuse general staining of the brain tissues with bilirubin, as occurs with kernicterus in human infants, it was not determined if this condition in the piglets had neurological sequelae.

Saison, Goodwin and Coombs (1955) found naturally occurring anti-A isoantibodies in the sera of pigs of blood group O. Goodwin and Coombs (1956) found this antibody in the blood of 55 of 59 unvaccinated adult pigs of group O. The antibody level varied widely not only from one individual to another but at different times in the same individual. The antibody was concentrated in the colostrum and reached the piglets in high concentration. However, the A-antigen was found to be absent from the red cells of newborn piglets of group A and only developed during the first month. Consequently, anti-A antibody cannot produce haemolytic disease of the newborn. Moreover, newborn group A piglets, although lacking the antigen on their red cells, have soluble A substance in their saliva and gastric juice which could neutralize the antibody. Goodwin, Heard, Hayward and Fulton Roberts (1956) found that several blood group systems were concerned in haemolytic disease of newborn piglets and that both agglutinating and incomplete antibodies were present in the circulations of affected piglets. These antibodies were not transmitted before birth but appeared as early as $3\frac{1}{2}$ hr after suckling and attained a titre of $\frac{1}{256}$ by 4 hr after birth. The greatest concentrations of antibody were in colostrum, where titres up to $\frac{1}{32,000}$ were found (Goodwin, Hayward, Heard and Fulton Roberts 1955).

Goodwin, Saison and Coombs (1955) discovered that repeated injections of crystal violet swine-fever vaccine produced high titres of isoantibodies in pigs. A large proportion of pigs on farms that had been prophylactically vaccinated had high titres of antibodies in their sera. These antibodies could account for haemolytic disease in piglets whose blood groups were incompatible with those of their mothers. Goodwin and Saison (1957) found that of 32 sows with clinically affected litters 30 had been vaccinated. In 22 sows with litters to which the disease had been fatal, the antibody titre of the serum at farrowing was $\frac{1}{512}$ or more.

Andresen and Baker (1963) obtained a sow that had produced three successive litters with haemolytic disease and which had a strong anti-B_a isoagglutinin in its serum. It was mated to a heterozygous B_a boar and injected with the boar's red cells during each of two pregnancies. Two litters of 7 and 6 respectively were produced, with 3 B(a+) piglets in the first and four in the second, the remaining 6 piglets being B(a−). All the piglets were

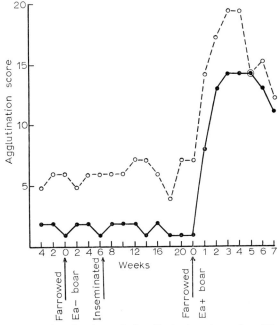

Fig. 10.1. Diagram showing the changes of antibody titres in an A−, E(a−) sow against A−, E(a+) red cells after giving birth to E(a+) piglets. No change occurred at parturition when the piglets were E(a−) or during the subsequent gestation of an E(a+) litter but a steep rise occurred when these were born. (From Linklater 1968.)

born healthy but all the B(a +), and none of the B(a −) piglets developed severe haemolytic disease. Anti-B$_a$ was believed to be the antibody responsible,
as the only other one that appeared to be present was anti-A which cannot
cause the disease. Linklater (1968) records a sow which had anti-E$_a$ isoantibody in its serum after having borne a litter of E(a+) piglets. Mated to
an E(a−) boar no change in titre of the isoantibody was observed but
when mated to an E(a+) boar a steep rise in titre was observed after parturition, reaching a peak at 10–17 days (fig. 10.1). This pig was from a minimal
disease herd and was known not to have had any injection involving red cells,
so that the antibody must have resulted from isoimmunization of pregnancy.

10.7. *Haemolytic disease in newborn rabbits*

The first attempt to produce haemolytic disease experimentally in rabbits
was made by Castle and Keeler, several years before the discovery of haemolytic disease in man. These authors (1933) first identified two isoantigens on
rabbit red blood cells and showed that they were inherited as Mendelian
dominants, the genes responsible being either allelomorphs or closely linked.
They called these antigens H$_1$ and H$_2$, and defined four blood groups according to whether the one, the other or both antigens were present, or both
absent, on the red cells (Keeler and Castle 1933). The H$_2$ antigen was the
stronger of the two. The antigens were detectable already on the red cells of
15 day foetuses and were present at birth, but they were not found in tissues
other than red cells. Keeler and Castle (1934a, b) then immunized doe rabbits,
lacking both H$_1$ and H$_2$ antigens, before and during pregnancy, with blood
containing both these antigens, and mated them with bucks possessing
either the H$_1$ or H$_2$ antigen. All the young produced were incompatible for
either the one or the other antigen. The H$_1$ young were found to have
anti-H$_2$ antibody in their sera but not anti-H$_1$, and *vice versa* for the H$_2$
young. Presumably the incompatible antibody was on the red cells and had
been absorbed out of the sera, yet none of the young showed any apparent
effect; possibly the antibody was not sufficiently potent. The maternal serum
titre declined during the second half of pregnancy and then rose sharply
during the first few days after parturition.

The first claim to have observed the natural occurrence of haemolytic
disease in rabbits came from Nachtsheim and Klein (1948) in Germany.
They recorded the occurrence of oedema and erythroblastosis invariably
resulting in death with newborn rabbits of an inbred colony. All the affected

young were the descendants of one albino buck and both affected and normal young occurred in the same litters. The affected young were born alive but died at, or within a few hours of, birth and they constituted 3% to 24% of the progeny of a doe. Their spleens were enlarged and although they were not jaundiced there was much extramedullary haemopoiesis. At the time it was not possible to continue the work in Berlin and some of the stock was sent to Cambridge, where Heard, Hinde and Mynors (1949) failed to reproduce the phenomenon. These authors then attempted to produce the disease experimentally by immunizing does with the red cells of the buck to which the does were mated subsequently. Some of the does produced both agglutinating and incomplete antibodies. Four immunized does produced seven litters in which the red cells of the young were incompatible and gave positive Coombs tests, yet no clinical symptoms were detectable.

Kellner and Hedal (1952) identified an allelic pair of antigens, G and g, present on the red cells but not in other tissues of rabbits. Rabbits lacking one or other of these antigens could be immunized and produced anti-G or anti-g antibody. Both agglutinating and incomplete antibodies were produced and the antibody was haemolytic and complement fixing. Pregnancy could result in immunization of the doe. Antibody was produced in five of ten does mated to incompatible bucks, three producing anti-G and two anti-g. The antibody affected the foetuses; when the maternal titre was low, the young were born alive but in most cases their red cells were coated, when the maternal titre was high, the foetuses were often stillborn and macerated or else died shortly after birth. Antibody could be found coating the red cells and in the serum of the foetuses. There was oedema, necrosis of the liver and extramedullary haemopoiesis in the affected young. These authors (Kellner and Hedal 1953a, b) found no rabbits lacking both antigens and concluded that they were not the same as the antigens of Keeler and Castle. In most cases the antibodies were detected first 1–2 weeks after parturition. Antibody was often present in the milk of immunized does. A GG doe passively immunized with anti-g serum during pregnancy by a Gg buck produced both Gg and GG young. The red cells of the Gg young gave a positive Coombs test and antibody was absent from their sera, while the GG young had free antibody in their sera but the red cells gave a negative Coombs test.

Anderson (1956) produced two isoantibodies in rabbits by injection of red cells and with these identified four blood groups, AB, A, B and O. Using Kellner and Hedal's sera he identified his A with their g, and his B with their G, and he claimed also that his A was the same as Keeler and

Castle's H_1 and his B as their H_2. Difficulty was experienced in producing high titre sera but these were produced with adjuvant and repeated injections. Matings of 40 immunized does with incompatible bucks produced 77 compatible young, 55 that died *in utero* and were probably erythroblastic and 134 that were shown to be incompatible. Most of the affected young that were born alive were oedemic and those that were grossly oedemic died soon after birth. Anaemic young without gross oedema were feeble but sometimes survived. Most of the incompatible young had red cells which gave a strongly positive Coombs test. Reticulocytosis and spherocytosis was apparent. Compatible young had serum titres of both complete and incomplete antibodies closely similar to the maternal titres. Autopsies of affected young revealed much fluid in the peritoneal and pleural cavities which was generally colourless, but sometimes was yellow or blood stained; also enlargement and congestion of the liver, spleen and lungs, but no noticeable jaundice. Reif, Norris, Mahoney, Klein and McVety (1964) immunized does of type DF or F with A red cells and mated them with A bucks. Oedema was seen in 2 of 23 A-compatible young of these does, which was believed to be due to antibodies to other isoantigens. There were 77 A-incompatible young, of which 32 were dead and 18 were oedematous.

These results are somewhat conflicting but it would appear that it is possible to produce experimentally severe haemolytic disease in rabbits provided sufficiently high titres of isoantibodies are attained and that these are of a kind that is destructive of red cells. Whether severe haemolytic disease can occur naturally, as a result of immunization by pregnancy must remain somewhat doubtful until confirmed.

10.8. Haemolytic disease in dogs

Young, Ervin and Yuile (1949) produced an isoantibody in dogs by trans-fusion which agglutinated and haemolysed the red cells of about two out of every three other dogs. The antibody fixed complement both *in vivo* and *in vitro* and behaved like an incomplete antibody under certain conditions. The antigen responsible was called A. Subsequently three other antigens B, C, and D were identified and it was found that there were at least two variants of A, A_1 and A_2 (Christian, Ervin and Young 1951). Anti-D anti-body occurred naturally, but the antibodies to the other antigens were only observed after transfusion. Swisher and Young (1954) added two more anti-gens, E and F, to the list. Anti-A was a potent haemolysin of A_1 cells both

in vivo and *in vitro*. *In vivo* it produced intravascular haemolysis with complement. Anti-A opsonized both A_1 and A_2 red cells which were then
phagocytosed by fixed macrophages. Anti-B, anti-C and anti-D strongly
agglutinated incompatible red cells at body temperature, but they did not
cause haemolysis *in vivo* or *in vitro* and they did not shorten the survival
time of the cells in the circulation. Incomplete antibody was found after
repeated transfusions.

Young, Ervin, Christian and Davis (1949) immunized an A− bitch by
transfusion of A+ blood and mated her with an A+ dog. She produced
4 A+ and 4 A− pups. The A+ pups all did less well than their siblings,
two were anaemic and one was jaundiced. The red cells of all four A+ pups
gave positives with the Coombs test. The A− pups had antibody in their
sera, but the A+ pups did not, presumably the red cells had absorbed all
the antibody. In a further study Christian, Ervin, Swisher, O'Brien and
Young (1949) found that in immunized bitches the antibody is present in the
colostrum at parturition at high concentration and persists in the milk for
several weeks. Pups that were A+ regularly developed haemolytic anaemia
when allowed to suckle an immunized bitch during the first day after birth,
but did not do so when allowed to suckle only after the second day. Young,
Christian, Ervin, Davis, O'Brien, Swisher and Yuile (1951) found no evidence
of transmission of isoantibodies before birth, none being demonstrable in
the pups' serum at birth. Autopsies of affected pups revealed enlargement of
liver and spleen, bone marrow hyperplasia and extramedullary erythropoie-
sis. The blood showed anaemia, erythroblastosis, reticulocytosis, spherocytosis and osmotic fragility. The bilirubin concentration was only slightly
increased. The red cells gave strong positive reactions with the Coombs test
for as long as 22 days in A_1 pups and 65 days in A_2 pups. The A_2 cells were
only mildly affected although they gave a strong Coombs positive. The
C+ pups of immunized C− bitches showed no signs of haemolytic disease.

10.9. *Haemolytic disease in newborn rats and mice*

Haemolytic disease can be produced readily in newborn rats and mice by
the oral administration of immune sera prepared in other species against
rat or mouse blood. Bessis and Freixa (1947a, b) gave rabbit anti-rat red
cell serum with agglutinin titres of $\frac{1}{1,000}$ to $\frac{1}{4,000}$ to young rats of from 10 to
30 days of age in doses of 0.15–2.00 ml. All young rats less than about 22
days of age given this serum developed jaundice and haemolytic anaemia.

Large doses killed them in 8 hr, producing haemoglobinuria, pallor and congestion of the liver and spleen. Medium doses killed them in 24 hr, producing obvious intense jaundice, slight haemoglobinuria sometimes, anaemic liver and enlarged spleen. Small doses produced severe anaemia and slight jaundice and the survivors were retarded in growth. The symptoms of the disease in the blood were spherocytosis, erythroblastosis, leucocytosis and erythrophagocytosis. Phagocytosis of the red cells occurred intravascularly and was very intense in the spleen, liver and lungs. Intense jaundice accompanied erythrophagocytosis. Brain damage was not observed in any of the rats. Oral administration of the immune serum had no effect on rats more than 22 days old, even when the amount of antibody in the dose was over 20 times, on a weight for weight basis of that invariably fatal for younger rats.

Morris (1958) carried out similar experiments both on mice and on rats. The antisera were prepared in rabbits against rat or mouse red cells. Young mice receiving large doses died quickly, showing pallor only. Jaundice and bilirubinuria were evident with medium doses. Small doses from which some of the animals survived resulted in haemoglobinuria, but only after a comparatively long interval. Young rats on the other hand showed early haemoglobinuria. It was found that if young mice were given injections of guineapig complement at the same time as the oral dose of immune rabbit serum haemoglobinuria developed early, as in the rats, the difference apparently being due to deficiency of complement in the sera of young mice. Morris (1961) subsequently produced a haemolytic disease in young mice by oral administration of an anti-leucocyte-platelet serum prepared in rabbits. The differences between the disease produced by this serum and that produced by the anti-red-cell serum were interesting. Most of the symptoms with the anti-leucocyte-platelet serum were attributable to capillary fragility and thrombocytopenia, aggravated by leucopenia. There was a resemblance to human ideopathic thrombocytopenic purpura. Whereas the anti-red-cell serum resulted in intravascular agglutination and lysis of the corpuscles in the capillaries, the anti-leucocyte-platelet serum resulted in extensive extravasation and destruction of the unagglutinated red cells in the tissues.

Haemolytic disease has not been recognised as naturally occurring in rats or mice and even attempts to produce it by isoimmunization have failed. Mitchison (1953) immunized female mice with incompatible red cells or tumour grafts from another strain. The antibody produced was detectable at high titre only when titrated in serum, resembling incomplete antibody in this respect. The females were crossed with males so as to produce both compatible and incompatible young. Although antibody was present in the maternal serum the incompatible foetal and newborn mice survived and showed no apparent ill effects. It was found that the isoantigens were not developed on the red cells of the mice at birth and only appeared at 8–12 days of age and it was suggested that this may have protected them. Since transmission of immunity in the mouse is known to continue until 16 days of age, this does not appear a sufficient explanation. It was shown by Kaliss and Dagg (1964) that repeated pregnancies of inbred female mice, lacking the strong H-2 tissue antigen, with foetuses inheriting it from the father induced the formation of haemagglutinins and leucoagglutinins. These antibodies were transmitted to the foetuses *in utero* and to the sucklings in the milk but appeared to have no adverse effect upon them (Kaliss 1968).

The production of experimental haemolytic anaemia in rats and mice by the oral administration of heteroagglutinins is surprising, as one might expect that these would react with the tissues through which they must pass before reaching the blood cells. That these antisera prepared in rabbits, for example, are specific for antigens borne on the red cells and not shared by the tissues, suggests that these tissue-specific antigens are more powerful as heteroantigens than species-specific antigens shared by most or all of the cells.

10.10. The absence of haemolytic disease in newborn ruminants

Haemolytic disease has never been proved in ruminants and attempts to produce it have been unsuccessful. Kiddy, Stone, Tyler and Casida (1958) immunized cows with the blood of a bull to which they were subsequently mated. The cows were given booster doses of the bull's red cells during the last six weeks of gestation. The serum and milk whey of six of the cows at parturition reacted strongly with the red cells of their calves and of the bull. The calves' sera after suckling also reacted with the bull's red cells but not with their own cells, showing that free maternal antibody not incompatible with the individual calf's own red cells was present. The calves showed no ill effects and were perfectly normal. It was suggested that antigen in the tissues might have absorbed or neutralized the incompatible antibody and so prevented it reaching the red cells. Tucker (1961) immunized a ewe to the red cells of a ram to which it was then mated. Twin lambs were produced. The ewe's serum and colostrum, with rabbit complement, haemolysed the precolostral red cells of the lambs *in vitro* at $\frac{1}{8,192}$ to $\frac{1}{16,384}$. The postcolostral red cells taken at 24 hr were shown to be sensitized; and antibody reacting with the red cells was present free in the lambs' sera. The lambs showed no ill effects and at 2 months old some of their red cells were labelled with ^{51}Cr and returned to the circulation after incubation with either (a) a $\frac{1}{4}$ dilution of the ewe's serum taken at parturition, or (b) a $\frac{1}{4}$ dilution of its own serum taken at 24 hr old when it had a titre of $\frac{1}{64}$; in both cases the labelled red cells were very rapidly eliminated.

It would seem that much has still to be learned about the factors which determine whether incompatible isoantibodies reacting with red cells *in vivo* will cause their destruction or do no harm.

CHAPTER 11

Conclusions and hypotheses

11.1. Introduction

It remains in this concluding chapter to examine the evidence presented in the preceding pages concerning transmission of immunity in the various species and to consider whether any general principles emerge concerning the mechanism by which transmission is effected. The evidence is voluminous enough to warrant a working hypothesis that might help to direct the lines of future progress. The advances in knowledge of the chemistry of γ-globulins, the improvements in methods of identification and separation of fractions, the refinements of electronmicroscopic techniques and the feasibility of *in vitro* studies of transmission have opened up great possibilities for further progress. The facilities are largely available and the need is for ideas that might direct effort along the most fruitful lines. Some speculation seems justified in the circumstances as a contribution to this need.

11.2. Transmission to the egg in the ovary

Very effective transmission of immunity occurs in birds, though neither the avenue of transmission *in utero* or that by way of mammary secretions is open to them. Maternal circulating antibodies are secreted by way of the ovarian follicle into the yolk of the developing egg, from where they are subsequently absorbed by the endoderm cells of the embryonic yolk-sac and transmitted to the circulation of the chick. Similarly, in the tortoise circulating antibodies are transmitted to the yolk of the egg while it is still in the ovary (Maung 1963). Consequently, it would not be surprising if this were found to be the case also in mammals, though their eggs contain comparatively little yolk, and a hint that this may be so is provided by the observation that labelled serum proteins injected into female rats appear in the cytoplasm of ovarian oocytes, having traversed the wall of the follicle and the zona pellucida (Mancini, Vilar, Heinrich, Davidson and Alvarez 1963). Clearly the amount of antibody that could reach the mammalian embryo in this way would be insignificant in relation to the bulk of the foetus at term for conferring postnatal immunity, but theoretically such antibodies of maternal origin, if directed against spermatozoal antigens, could conceivably affect fertilization and early development.

11.3. *Transmission to the circulation of the young*

Transmission of immunity before birth in the rabbit, rat and guineapig occurs by way of the uterine lumen and the foetal yolk-sac. This appears to be the only route of transmission in the rabbit, probably the only route in the guineapig, and at least the principal, if not the only, route before birth in the rat. The route of transmission before birth in the mouse is not known but on account of its similarity to the rat in other respects it is probable that it resembles it in this also. The yolk-sac of these animals is morphologically the homologue of the yolk-sac of the bird or reptile and its endodermal lining is exposed to the uterine fluid as is that of the bird to the yolk. So far as the foetal tissues are concerned the route of transmission is strictly comparable to that in the bird. The routes of transmission of immunity before birth in the dog, cat and hedgehog are unknown, and the differences in structure of their foetal membranes are such that speculation is not warranted beyond the clear necessity for passage across the chorionic trophoblast. Transmission of immunity in monkeys and man on the evidence available appears to be mainly by way of the allantochorionic placenta, though it is possible that some maternal antibody might reach the foetus by way of the amniotic cavity and the foetal gut. Both these routes involve passage across the foetal chorionic trophoblast. Transmission after birth in all mammals in which it occurs involves secretion in the colostrum and milk and absorption by the endoderm of the neonatal gut. Thus in all those animals in which the route of transmission is known the effective absorptive organ is the endoderm of the foetal yolk-sac or neonatal gut with the exception of the primates.

The colostrum of those species in which transmission occurs after birth is characterized by its high content of immunoglobulins, in contrast to that of those in which such transmission does not occur. When transmission continues for a long period after birth the milk also has a high immunoglobulin content, but when transmission is confined to a brief neonatal period the initial high colostral content falls very rapidly to a low level in the milk. Most of the immunoglobulins of the lacteal secretions are derived from the circulation but some are locally produced in the mammary glands. The γA-globulin of the lacteal secretions appears to be mainly or entirely produced in the glands and not drawn from the circulation, but whether it accounts for the whole of the locally produced antibody is less clear. The suggestion that the function of this antibody may be to combat enteric pathogens in the lumen of the neonatal gut rather than for transmission to the circulation is attractive. Possibly the trypsin inhibitor of colostrum plays an important part in its survival in the gut, for it is not yet clear that it has much influence on the transmission of immunoglobulins to the circulation.

The greater part of the immunoglobulins, and probably of other serum proteins, absorbed by the endoderm cells, whether of the foetal yolk-sac of the rabbit or the rat or of the neonatal gut of the rat, are degraded within the endoderm cells. Degradation within the cells has been demonstrated *in vivo* and *in vitro*. It is highly probable that similar degradation within the cells of all that moiety of the protein absorbed by the cells and not transmitted to the circulation will be found to occur wherever transmission is selective; there is no other way apparent to account for the disappearance of protein administered and not transmitted as such. Transmission is not selective in the ruminants and almost certainly not in the pig and the horse and it may be that in these animals no degradation of protein accompanies transmission; in the calf it seems that all the small molecular proteins excreted in the urine during the period of transmission were already present as such in the colostrum and further degradation is not necessary to account for them. It is not clear how far the process of degradation within the cells proceeds and there is some evidence that the foetal rabbit yolk-sac releases polypeptides, of sufficient size to be retained by the placenta (Hemmings 1956), as well as small products. Possibly maternal homoreactant which is transmitted to the foetal circulation could play a part in the utilization of such fragments of γ-globulins. However that may be, it is evident that any hypothesis to account for selective transmission must also account for the disposal of the residue absorbed and not transmitted, and of which in at least two species there is clear evidence of intracellular digestion.

The factors which bring about the termination of the transmission of immunity after birth appear complex and are far from being fully understood.

It seems probable that the onset of gastric digestion is an important one and the effect of feeding in hastening closure may operate by stimulating gastric digestion. It is clear that active pinocytosis by the endoderm cells of the small intestine ceases at the same time as transmission, but this could be brought about in a number of ways, for example the presence of intact protein may be necessary to stimulate pinocytosis, or the presence of protein degradation products might inhibit it, or it might be a direct response to hormones. In the rat and the mouse some corticosteroids can bring about premature closure as well as changes in the alkaline phosphatase content of the intestine, but how these phenomena fit into the sequence of events culminating in closure is obscure. The observation that closure does not occur *in vitro* with inverted sacs of rat intestine may prove to be an important clue, and the presence of a factor in bovine colostrum which stimulates transmission may be another. Certainly further work on this problem is required.

11.4. Selective transmission

The selective nature of transmission in so many animals is, perhaps, its most remarkable feature. Transmission is selective before birth in the fowl, rabbit, rat, mouse, guineapig, hedgehog, monkey and man, and after birth in the rat, mouse and hedgehog. Satisfactory evidence of selection either before or after birth is lacking for the cat and the dog. There is much evidence that transmission across the gut of the newborn ungulate is not selective and, as already mentioned, there does not appear to be any degradation of protein in transit in the endoderm cells in these animals. Possibly these pecularities of the ungulates are associated with the intensity and briefness of transmission. It must be remembered, however, that transmission from the maternal circulation to the colostrum is highly selective in the ruminants, as well as in the rat, and quite possibly this will be found to be the case in all mammals.

Selection in all cases operates in favour of homologous γ-globulin as compared to the other proteins of homologous serum, and in most cases in favour of the γ-globulin as compared to the other proteins of an heterologous serum, though in cases of extreme species disparity the rate of transmission of the heterologous γ-globulin may be less than that of the corresponding heterologous albumin. Although in most instances the homologous γ-globulin is transmitted more readily than an heterologous γ-globulin, this is not always the case.

There is clear evidence of selection between the various components of γ-globulin. Whereas γM-globulin is transmitted from mother to foetus in the rabbit, and apparently approximately as readily as 7S γG-globulin, it is not transmitted in young rats, mice, hedgehogs, fowl or man. Similarly γA-globulin is not transmitted in man, but nothing is known about its transmission in other species that show selection. Unfortunately very little is known regarding selection in transmission between the varieties of 7S γG-globulins. There appears to be no difference between the rates of transmission of 7S $γ_1$- and 7S $γ_2$-globulins from mother to foetus in guineapigs. In the young rat and mouse selection appears to operate in favour of the electrophoretically slower components of γG-globulin in rabbit and bovine sera. Again, in ruminants there is marked selection in transmission to the colostrum, the $γ_1$G-globulin being transmitted readily and attaining concentrations many times higher than in the serum, whereas the $γ_2$G-globulin is almost excluded. More information on this problem is highly desirable and might go a long way to clarify the reasons for selection as between antibodies to different antigens prepared in a given species and even as between γ-globulins of different species. It could be of importance also in relating the properties of γ-globulin determining transmission to those determining anaphylactic sensitization, skin fixation and activation of complement. The evidence concerning the transmission of pepsinised or papainised fragments of γ-globulin in rabbits, rats and mice indicates that it is the C-terminal halves of the γ-chains that determine the rates of transmission of the molecules.

It is evident that in most species and probably in all serum albumin is transmitted at the same time as the γ-globulin, though less readily. There is evidence that in the rabbit bovine-serum-albumin is transmitted less readily than rabbit or human serum albumin, but the differences are not large and it appears that serum albumins, unlike γ-globulins, are transmitted at nearly similar rates irrespective of species of origin.

Maternal serum proteins reach the amniotic fluid in the rabbit, guineapig and man and probably in all species in which transmission occurs before birth. Transmission from the maternal circulation to the amniotic fluid is not selective in the rabbit or guineapig, both homologous and heterologous proteins attaining concentrations relative to those in the maternal circulation that are nearly similar. The evidence available suggests that the passage of maternal serum proteins to the amniotic fluid in man may also be non-selective. Thus transmission to the foetal circulation is in striking contrast to that to other foetal fluids in being selective.

11.5. Interference with transmission

The interference of one γ-globulin with the transmission of another has been observed so far only in the rat and the mouse. It is a property of γ-globulin alone, the other serum proteins having no such effect. Further, it is a property of the Fc-piece of the γ-globulin molecule, which has as much or even a greater effect than the whole molecule. The more a particular γ-globulin interferes with the transmission of other γ-globulins, the less its own transmission is interfered with by other γ-globulins. The extent to which various γ-globulins interfere with the transmission of others in the mouse is: rat > bovine > guineapig > rabbit. The rate at which a γ-globulin is transmitted is related, but not simply, to the degree to which it can interfere with the transmission of another γ-globulin.

11.6. Pinocytosis

The endodermal epithelia of the yolk-sacs or neonatal intestines through which transmission occurs in any of these animals and that have been examined under the electron-microscope show remarkable similarities in structure. The free surfaces of the cells in all cases are clothed with a pile of microvilli, between the bases of these caveoli can be seen and the apical cytoplasm is filled with cisternae and vacuoles. The appearance is typical of active pinocytosis and the pinocytotic uptake of substances can be demonstrated readily with proteins and a variety of colloids. Generally the microvilli are clothed and the caveoli, cisternae and many of the vesicles are lined with a glycocalyx. The cytoplasm of the cells is rich in enzymes, including proteolytic enzymes, and lysosomes appear to be plentiful. In the rat the apical cisternae and vacuoles discharge into a large vesicle more deeply situated in the cell near to the nucleus and Golgi elements. Colloidal materials taken up pinocytotically by the cells sometimes can be demonstrated in the intercellular spaces, basement membrane and lymphatics, but the manner of their discharge from the endoderm cells is much less clear than that of their uptake. At the time when transmission across the intestine ceases pinocytosis also appears to stop and the apical cytoplasm of the cells ceases to be crowded with cisternae and vacuoles. It is particularly interesting that the syncytial trophoblast of the human placental villi, through which presumably transmission must occur, shows a remarkably similar appearance, with a brush border of microvilli, caveoli and numerous cisternae and vesicles in the peripheral cytoplasm, giving the familiar appearance of active pinocytosis.

11.7. An hypothetical mechanism of transmission

A satisfactory working hypothesis of the mechanism of transmission of immunity must take into account (a) selection, operating not only between very different molecules, such as albumin and γ-globulin but also between closely similar ones, such as two isologous 7S γG-globulins, (b) interference by one γ-globulin with the transmission of another, (c) both selection and interference being associated with the C-terminal halves of the γ-chains, (d) a substantial part of the protein absorbed being degraded instead of being transmitted, and (e) absorption of protein by pinocytosis being the only demonstrable uptake by the cells. It was suggested (Brambell, Halliday and Morris 1958) that selection can be understood most easily on the assumption of specific receptors in the cells for the γ-globulin molecules that are transmitted and that interference strongly suggests competition for receptors. It was pointed out that entry to the cells was non-selective and probably by pinocytosis. At that time it was thought probable that the protein taken up non-selectively and not transmitted intact to the circulation was broken down in the cells but the evidence for this view was not considered conclusive, nor was it certain that the uptake was always pinocytotic. The evidence that has accumulated since then, and has been reviewed in these pages, justifies the conclusion that the degradation of the protein during transmission occurs within the cells. Work in several laboratories has amply confirmed the pinocytotic absorption of the protein, both by yolk-sac and neonatal intestinal cells. The hypothesis advanced in 1958 has been restated, in the light of these advances (Brambell 1963; Brambell, Hemmings and Morris 1964; Brambell 1966) and is represented in fig. 11.1. It is suggested that the receptors are on the surface of the microvilli and are carried in by the invagination of the caveoli and are to be found in the walls of these and of the pinocytotic phagosomes, that the protein attached to them is ultimately released from the cells intact into the intercellular spaces and so reaches the lymphatic drainage, and that the protein in the phagosomes not so attached is degraded

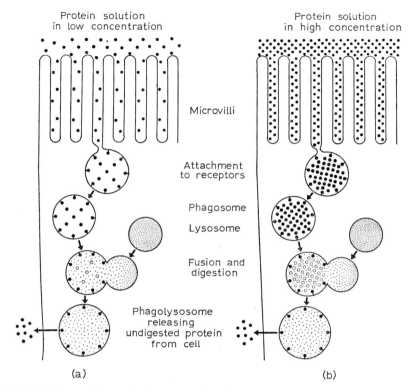

Fig. 11.1. Diagram illustrating the suggested mechanism of γ-globulin transmission by the cell. In (a) the concentration of γ-globulin is only a little more than sufficient to saturate the receptors on the walls of the phagosomes and the proportion of molecules detached and degraded is less than 40%. In (b) the concentration is about four times that in (a) and hence over 80% of the molecules fail to find receptors and are degraded. The amount released from the cell remains constant, irrespective of concentration. (From Brambell 1966.)

by lysosomal enzymes in the vesicles and escapes from the cell by diffusion. This hypothesis has the attraction that it does not involve the assumption of the passage of molecules as large as γ-globulins through the cell membrane but rather their conveyance through the cisternal system of the cell. There is nothing new in the idea of specific receptors for biologically active molecules on cells, nor in pinocytosis and enzymic digestion within cells in phagolysosomes. The only elements of novelty in the hypothesis are that the receptors for γ-globulin are assumed to be in the walls of the phagosomes and to protect the protein attached to them from degradation. No simpler explanation has been advanced so far to account for the transport of intact γ-globulin by cells that are at the same time actively phagocytosing and degrading protein.

On this hypothesis the amount of γ-globulin that can be transmitted intact to the circulation is limited by the population of available receptors. The rate of transmission will depend on the rates of attachment and of release from the receptors. Selective transmission would then depend on one or other or both these rates varying with different kinds of γ-globulins. An alternative, and in some ways more attractive, possibility is that the receptors are not simply of one kind but that there are a population of different receptors and that selection depends on the number of varieties of receptor in this population to which a given type of γ-globulin can attach. Such an arrangement might account for the transport of other proteins, such for example as serum albumin, without having to assume entirely distinct mechanisms for them. Albumin certainly is transmitted at the same time as γ-globulin but at a much lower rate; if this were because it could attach only to a relatively small proportion of the receptors available to γ-globulin the difference in rate would be understandable and the fact that it does not appear to interfere with transmission of γ-globulin to an appreciable extent. It is possible that these receptors could also be those which have been assumed for the transport of amino acids.

The ungulates present a special case because in them all the protein absorbed by the cells of the neonatal gut appears to be transmitted to the circulation non-selectively and without degradation. The further assumption that in these animals no degradation occurs in the phagosomes would be sufficient to adapt the hypothesis to them, and seems obvious since there is no doubt of the presence during transmission of the protein in vesicles in the cells. The process in them is so intense for the brief period to which it is confined that some modification of that employed by other animals might be expected.

This has proved a useful working hypothesis in directing research during the last decade and has stood up well to advances in knowledge over that period. No doubt it will have to be modified and adapted to future advances, if it survives, but it has a good deal of flexibility and, as Morris (1964) has shown, permits of mathematical treatment on the familiar lines of enzyme/substrate reactions. It leaves many questions unanswered of which perhaps the most fundamental and exciting are the nature of the receptors and of the groupings on the Fc-piece of the γ-globulin molecule which attach to them.

The glycocalyx of the ileal cells of the young rat is an obvious candidate for investigation in the search for receptors.

11.8. Anaphylaxis

The behaviour of γ-globulins during transmission of immunity resembles that in anaphylactic sensitization to a remarkable extent. Some account must be given of the nature of anaphylaxis before considering these resemblances. Anaphylactic reactions have been observed in a variety of mammals and in birds and probably occur in all warm-blooded vertebrates, although they are much more readily elicited in some species than in others. The classical material, and certainly the experimental animal of choice, is the guineapig. Typically, if a few micrograms of ovalbumin or bovine serum albumin are injected into a guineapig followed after an interval of at least a week by a further intravenous injection of a few milligrams of the same antigen the animal will suffer severe anaphylactic shock and probably will die within a few minutes. Death results from suffocation due to acute bronchial spasm brought about by contraction of the smooth musculature of the bronchioles which is particularly well developed in this species. If the animal survives it will generally return to normal in a few hours and is then insensitive to further injections of the antigen for a time, but sensitivity will gradually return. This is systemic or general anaphylaxis, actively induced. It is believed to be due to the production of antibodies, in response to the small initial or sensitizing injection of antigen, which are fixed by the cells. The second or shocking injection of antigen must be large enough to neutralize any free antibody present in the circulation and to reach and react with the antibody fixed by the cells. The reaction with this fixed antibody so affects the cells concerned that histamine and other active substances are released by them and bring about the contraction of the smooth muscle. After anaphylaxis the animal remains insensitive until all free antigen has been eliminated from the system and more antibody has been produced and fixed by the cells.

Anaphylactic sensitization can be passively induced by injection of a small quantity of immune guineapig serum and allowing a few hours for the antibody to be fixed by the cells and removed from the circulation before giving the shocking dose of antigen. Passive anaphylaxis can be demonstrated locally in the skin, as well as systemically, if a very small quantity of the sensitizing antibody is injected intradermally and the shocking dose a few hours later intravenously when a weal or Arthrus reaction will develop gradually around the site of the sensitizing injection.

Anaphylactic reactions can be brought about *in vitro* with tissues excised from animals systemically sensitized either actively or passively. Excised tissues also can be sensitized *in vitro* by exposing them to suitable antibodies. The tissues most used are strips of smooth muscle from the uterus or intestine, chopped lung or mesentery of the gut. Strips of sensitized smooth muscle contract on exposure to the antigen. This Schultz-Dale reaction (Schultz 1910; Dale 1913) can be conveniently recorded on a kymograph and is very sensitive. Sensitized chopped lung releases histamine on exposure to antigen and under standard conditions can give quantitative results (Mongar and Schild 1957). Sensitized mesentery on exposure to antigen displays degranulation of the mast cells which can be observed microscopically (Humphrey and Mota 1959b).

All that has been said relates to direct anaphylaxis in which the cells have been sensitized by fixing antibody which then reacts with free antigen. Reversed anaphylaxis can be affected by sensitizing the cells with γ-globulin and then exposing them to an antibody to the γ-globulin. It can be brought about in normal guineapig tissues, since the cells will have fixed guineapig γ-globulin, by exposing them to rabbit anti-guineapig-γ-globulin serum. It can also be brought about by sensitizing the tissues with a heterologous γ-globulin and then exposing them to an antibody to that γ-globulin prepared in a guineapig or other animal. This is reversed passive anaphylaxis and has been used in much of the work relevant to this discussion. It will be noted that whether direct or reversed anaphylaxis is concerned sensitization can be effected only by γ-globulin, whether this is to function as antibody or as antigen.

11.9. Resemblances between transmission and anaphylactic sensitization

Hartley (1948) was the first to suspect a similarity between passive anaphylactic sensitization and transmission of passive immunity and that both these processes depended upon the acceptability of the antibody molecules by the cells. Anaphylactic sensitization of guineapigs *in vivo* and of their tissues *in vitro* is a selective process, since γ-globulin is the only effective agent and the antibodies of some species are more effective than those of others. The γ-globulins of guineapig, rabbit and man, for example, are capable of sensitizing guineapig tissues *in vivo* for reversed passive anaphylaxis, whereas that of horses is not (Humphrey and Mota 1959a). Similarly, small amounts of guineapig or rabbit antibodies, and rather larger amounts of monkey, dog, and human antibodies sensitized guineapigs *in vivo* while rat, goat, horse and fowl antibodies did not sensitize, as determined by general anaphylaxis, the Schultz–Dale reaction, or mast cell degranulation.

Hartley (1951) showed that guineapig diphtheria antitoxin when pepsin-refined lost its capacity to sensitize guineapig tissues either *in vivo* or *in vitro*, although it retained its antibody activity virtually unimpaired. Subsequently it was shown that the Fab-fragments of rabbit γ-globulin were incapable of sensitizing guineapig tissues *in vivo* (Humphrey and Mota 1959a) or of sensitizing guineapig skin for either direct or reversed passive cutaneous anaphylaxis (Ovary and Karush 1961). The Fc-fragment readily sensitized skin in reversed passive cutaneous anaphylaxis, or smooth muscle *in vitro* (Liacopoulos, Halpern, Liacopoulos and Perramant 1963).

Non-immune serum interferes with passive sensitization of guineapig tissues by antibodies (Ovary and Bier 1953). The interference is due to the γ-globulin fraction of the serum, the other serum proteins having no effect (Fisher and Cooke 1957). Interference can be demonstrated *in vivo* in passive general anaphylaxis by both human and rabbit γ-globulins in guineapigs and by human γ-globulin in mice, but not by equine or bovine γ-globulins (Halpern and Frick 1962). Passive cutaneous sensitization of guineapigs with rabbit antibody is interfered with by various γ-globulins in the order: rabbit > guineapig > human and rat > horse, the last named having no significant effect (Biozzi, Halpern and Binaghi 1959). Sensitization of guineapig smooth muscle *in vitro* by rabbit antibody is interfered with by non-immune γ-globulin (Halpern, Liacopoulos, Liacopoulos-Briot, Binaghi and Van Neer 1959) and of guineapig lung by guineapig, rabbit and human sera and human γ-globulin, but not by bovine γ-globulin (Mongar and Schild 1960). The effectiveness of various γ-globulins to interfere with the sensitization of guineapig smooth muscle by rabbit antibody is in the order: rabbit > human > dog > guineapig > rat > horse > bovine > pig > fowl > goat. Interference could be detected even with the last five γ-globulins in this series, though as antibodies they are incapable of themselves sensitizing guineapig tissues (Binaghi, Liacopoulos, Halpern and Liacopoulos-Briot 1962). The Fc-fragment of rabbit γ-globulin is even more effective than the whole γ-globulin in inhibiting the sensitization of guineapig smooth muscle *in vitro* by rabbit antibody, whereas the Fab-fragment is entirely without effect (Liacopoulos, Halpern, Liacopoulos and Perramant 1963). The quantity of γ-globulin firmly bound by chopped guineapig lung is in the order: sheep > pig > bovine > horse > human > rabbit (King and Francis 1967), which is the opposite of that in which these γ-globulins interfere with passive sensitization so that it must be concluded that binding by the tissue of γ-globulin does not necessarily involve sensitization.

Attention was drawn (Brambell 1963) to the resemblances between passive anaphylactic sensitization and passive transmission of immunity and to the way in which further knowledge of these processes had reinforced Hartley's early suggestion (1948) that both processes depended on the acceptability of the molecules of immunoglobulin to the cells. Both processes are selective of γ-globulins and between one γ-globulin and another; one γ-globulin can interfere with sensitization by, or in rats and mice with transmission of, another; the activity of the molecules resides in the Fc, not the Fab parts. Even the sequences of relative effectiveness of the various heterologous γ-globulins are remarkably similar, the probability that these similarities are not fortuitous being high. Immunologists working in both these fields have seen fit on quite independent evidence to adopt hypotheses of receptors for γ-globulins on the cells.

Recently, as the methods of distinguishing varieties of 7S γG-globulins have developed, some very interesting facts have come to light concerning their functions. Nussenzweig, Merryman and Benacerraf (1964) found that the γ_2G-antibodies of mice were complement fixing and able to sensitize guineapigs, but not mice, for passive cutaneous anaphylaxis, whereas the γ_1G-antibodies could not do either, but did sensitize mice for cutaneous anaphylaxis which the γ_2G-antibodies could not. Thus, the capacities for homologous and heterologous sensitization reside in different components. This finding was confirmed by Ovary, Barth and Fahey (1965), who distinguished two varieties of 7S γ_2G-globulins, γ_{2a}G- and γ_{2b}G-globulins. They found that heterologous skin sensitizing activity was confined to the γ_{2a}G-globulin. Carretti and Ovary (1969) showed that both mouse γ_{2a}G- and γ_{2b}G-globulins fix complement and are transmitted from mother to foetus in mice, and Irvin, Eustace and Fahey (1967) found that both enhancing and cytotoxic activity of mouse serum resided in the 7S γ_2G-globulins, not in the 7S γ_1G-globulin. Jones (1969) isolated chromatographically from rats two antigenically distinct fractions of 6.9S immunoglobulins containing antibodies to 2,4-dinitrophenyl, which were identified as γ_2G- and γ_1G-globulins. The γ_2G-globulin sensitized homologous rat skin for passive cutaneous

anaphylaxis. Both lysed sensitized sheep red cells in the presence of complement, the γ_1G-globulin being the more active. They behaved similarly in
passive cutaneous anaphylaxis in mice. It is suggested that they correspond
to the 7S γ_2- and 7S γ_1-globulins of guineapigs and mice, except for their
behaviour in homologous passive cutaneous anaphylaxis and in haemolysis.

It was found with human myeloma proteins (Terry 1965) that γ_1G-, γ_3G-
and γ_4G-globulin were able to sensitize guineapig skin for reverse passive
cutaneous anaphylaxis, but that γ_2G-globulin was not able to do so. The
Fc-fragments of the myeloma proteins, and the proteins of 'heavy chain
disease', which resemble them, sensitized guineapig skin but neither the
Fab- nor the F(ab')$_2$-fragments of myeloma protein could do so. Ishizaka,
Ishizaka, Salmon and Fudenberg (1967) showed that γ_1G-, γ_2G-, γ_3G- and
γM-globulin fixed complement, whereas γ_4G- and γA-globulin did not fix
complement. Augustin (1966) pointed out that the reagins responsible for
homologous anaphylactic sensitization in man are not found in cord blood
and are not γG-globulins, and Patterson, Roberts and Pruzansky (1969)
suggest that the reaginic antibodies of dogs and monkeys, and possibly of
rats, are also in a distinct fraction, analogous to γE-globulin of man.

These considerations suggest that it may be necessary to think of different
receptors for different varieties of 7S γG-globulins and for reagins, a population of various kinds of receptors as was hinted at earlier. These might not
be uniformly distributed amongst the cells, but some kinds of cells might
specialise in one or more kinds of receptors and other kinds of cells in other
kinds of receptors.

11.10. An hypothesis of γ-globulin catabolism based on that of transmission

Other properties of γ-globulins that have certain resemblances to those involved in transmission are concerned with its catabolism. Fahey and Robinson (1963) found that in mice the rate of catabolism of γ-globulin increases
with its concentration. Their strain of BALB/C mice were used at a size of
25 g body weight and an average plasma volume of 1.25 ml. The normal
serum concentration was 5 mg/ml with a normal half-life of $T_{\frac{1}{2}} = 4.1$ days,
but the half-life decreases to a minimum of $T_{\frac{1}{2}} = 1.8$–2.0 at a γ-globulin concentration of 20 mg/ml. The concentration was raised by hyperimmunization,
by transplantation of myelomas or by injection of various γG-globulins.
Increased concentrations of γM-, γA-globulins or albumin had no effect.

The Fc-fragment of γG-globulin was as effective on a molar basis as the whole molecule, whereas the Fab-fragment did not shorten, and even seemed to lengthen slightly, the half-life of γ-globulin. Only γG-globulin was effective, heterologous γG-globulin had a similar effect to homologous, the Fc-fragment was as effective as the whole molecule and no other serum proteins nor the Fab-fragment of γG-globulin had any effect. These resemblances to transmission and the shape of the curve relating half-life to concentration suggested that a similar mechanism might be involved (Brambell, Hemmings and Morris 1964; Brambell 1966). The hypothesis is that the serum proteins were being pinocytosed at a constant rate and that γG-globulin receptors on the walls of the vesicles were being saturated with γG-globulin molecules and subsequently were returning them to the circulation, while all the protein in the vesicles not attached to receptors was being degraded. Thus the proportion of γG-globulin catabolised would rise with the concentration in excess of that required to saturate the receptors, as represented diagrammatically in fig. 11.1. This idea permits of mathematical treatment. The fractional rate of γ-globulin catabolism, F, is the amount catabolised in unit time divided by the total amount in the system. If V is the total γ-globulin space and c is the concentration, then the total amount in the system is Vc. The proportion catabolised will be the proportion pinocytosed less the proportion saved by the receptors. If a is the proportion of the total γ-globulin solution pinocytosed per day and b is the minimum concentration of γ-globulin that will saturate the receptors, then

$$F = \frac{Vac - Vab}{Vc}. \tag{1}$$

Since the half-life, $T_{\frac{1}{2}}$, is related to the fractional rate of catabolism as

$$T_{\frac{1}{2}} = \frac{\ln 2}{F}, \tag{2}$$

then by substitution,

$$T_{\frac{1}{2}} = \frac{c \ln 2}{a(c - b)}. \tag{3}$$

The values for the constants a and b can be estimated graphically from the data on the simplest assumption that the rate of pinocytosis is constant irrespective of concentration, since when $T_{\frac{1}{2}} = \infty$, $c = b$, and when $c = \infty$, $a = \ln 2/T_{\frac{1}{2}}$. Fig 11.4 represents Fahey and Robinson's data of their normal and immunized mice, with the curve derived from eq. (3), using values of $a = 0.34$ and $b = 2.5$. The theoretical minimum half-life is 2.05 days. The resulting curve is a reasonably good fit for their data, allowing for the errors inseparable from determinations of concentration in small samples.

Sell (1964a), using low-pathogen and germ-free mice, confirmed that the half-life of the γ-globulin was shortened when the γ-globulin concentration

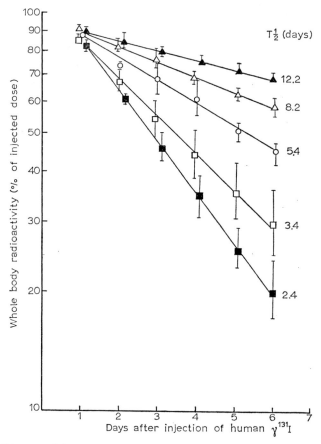

Fig. 11.2. Diagram of the rates of elimination of ^{131}I-labelled human γ-globulin in mice with different serum γ-globulin concentrations due to different antigenic exposures or hyperimmunization. Each symbol represents the mean value of 3 to 5 animals. The symbols represent mice with serum γ-globulin levels of: ▲, 3.4 mg/ml (low pathogen); △, 2.9 mg/ml (germ-free); ○, 7.6 mg/ml (conventional); □, 12.9 mg/ml (hyperimmune); ■, 15.5 mg/ml (high pathogen). (From Sell 1964a.)

was raised and lengthened when it was below normal (fig. 11.2). He showed also that human, rabbit or guineapig γG-globulins were as effective as mouse γG-globulin, but that bovine γG-globulin was less effective and human

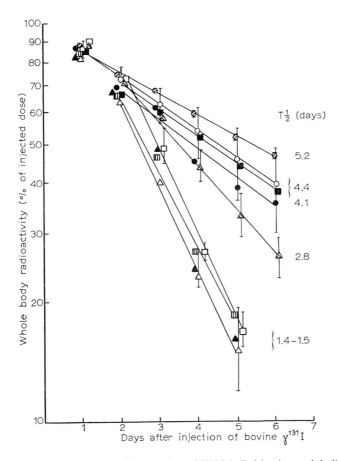

Fig. 11.3. Diagram of the rates of elimination of ^{131}I-labelled bovine γ-globulin in mice receiving exogenous serum proteins. Each symbol represents the mean value of 3 to 4 mice and the brackets, when given, the range within each group. The unlabelled exogenous protein or saline was injected 2 days after the labelled bovine γ-globulin. The symbols represent mice with total serum γ-globulin levels due to injection of the named exogenous protein of: ⊘, 6.6 mg/ml (saline); ○, 7.6 mg/ml (none); ▨, 8.0 mg/ml (bovine serum albumin); ●, 6.1 mg/ml (human serum albumin); ▲, 18.7 mg/ml (bovine γ-globulin); □, 14.0 mg/ml (guineapig γ-globulin); ▥, 13.5 mg/ml (rabbit γ-globulin); △, 12.4 mg/ml (human γ-globulin); ▲, 14.9 mg/ml (mouse γ-globulin). (From Sell 1964a.)

albumin was without effect on the half-life (fig. 11.3). Fahey and Sell (1965) then compared the effects of the different varieties of mouse immunoglobulins. They found that 7S γ_1G-, γ_{2a}G- and γ_{2b}G-globulins had different half-lives in the normal mouse, but the half-lives of all three were lengthened at low serum γ-globulin concentrations and shortened at high concentrations (fig. 11.5). The half-life of each variety of γG-globulin is influenced by the concentrations in the circulation of all three and by human γG-globulin, but not by the concentration of γA-globulin. Both γA-globulin and γM-globulin have much shorter half-lives which are independent of the serum concentration. These authors, commenting on the suggested mechanism, state that 'The present data are in accord with this hypothesis and indicate that the γ_{2a}-, γ_{2b}- and 7S γ_1-globulin molecules may be protected from catabolism in a similar way'. The differences in the half-lives of these three varie-

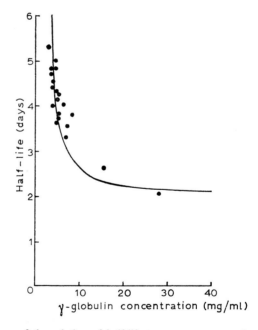

Fig. 11.4. Diagram of the relation of half-life to serum concentration of γ-globulin in mice. The data are of mice that were normal, hyperimmunized or injected with human serum albumin only, extracted from Fahey and Robinson (1963). The curve is derived from the equation $T\frac{1}{2} = (c \ln 2)/a \ (c-b)$, where c is the concentration in mg/ml and the constants $a = 0.34$ and $b = 2.5$. (From Brambell, Hemmings and Morris 1964.)

ties of mouse γG-globulins suggest that the receptors available to each are not identical, yet the concentrations of any one effect the half-lives of all three suggesting common receptors. Largely, but not completely, overlapping populations of receptors available to each and to heterologous γG-globulins might account for this.

It would be of great interest to know if a similar relationship between concentration and half-life of γG-globulins held for other species. Unfortunately there are in the literature very few reliable data covering a sufficient range of concentrations. Sell (1964b) found that the rates of homologous γ-globulin catabolism are the same in germ-free and normal guineapigs despite a difference of ×6 in the serum concentration, suggesting that catabolism may be independent of concentration in this species. It is difficult to understand why germ-free guineapigs should be exceptional; possibly a simple pinocytotic mechanism without receptors, which would account for the results, might be involved. Andersen and Bjørneboe (1964) provide data of the half-lives and concentrations of γ-globulin both before and during

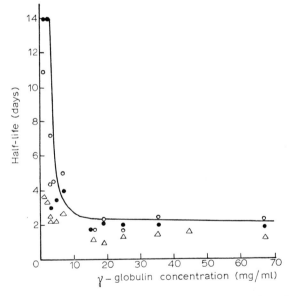

Fig. 11.5. Diagram of the relation of half-life to serum concentration of γ-globulin in mice for each of the three distinguishable 7S γG-globulins. The symbols represent: ●, γ₁G-globulin; ○, γ₂ₐG-globulin; △, γ₂ᵦG-globulin. The curve is the same as that in fig 11.4. The data are from Fahey and Sell (1965). (From Brambell 1966.)

hyperimmunization in seven rabbits. These are shown in fig. 11.6, together with a curve derived from eq. (3) where $a = 0.21$ and $b = 4.74$. Cohen and Mannik (1966) studied the effects on catabolism of severing the disulphide interchain bonds of rabbit γ-globulin, after which the chains remained assembled due to non-covalent forces, and of reassembling molecules *in vitro* from separated chains. They found that these procedures had no effect on the rates of catabolism of the molecules over a range of concentrations. Their data are given in fig. 11.7 together with the curve derived from eq. (3) where $a = 0.2$ and $b = 2.25$. The value of a is very close to that for Andersen and Bjørneboe's data, but the value of b is considerably lower, possibly due to a strain difference.

The evidence in the literature for a relationship between half-life and concentration of γ-globulin in man is conflicting, as might be expected with clinical data. However, Solomon, Waldmann and Fahey (1963) and Wald-

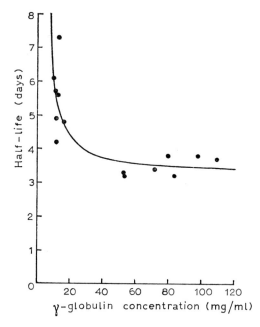

Fig. 11.6. Diagram of the relation of half-life to serum concentration of γ-globulin in rabbits before and after hyperimmunization. The curve is derived from the same equation as that in fig 11.4 using values for the constants of $a = 0.21$, $b = 4.74$. The data are from Andersen and Bjørneboe (1964). (From Brambell, Hemmings and Morris 1964.)

mann and Schwab (1965) appear to have demonstrated a clear relationship. They excluded cases with pathological loss of serum proteins and determined the concentrations of 7S γG-globulins. The half-lives were shorter than normal with high serum concentrations due to myelomas and longer than normal with low serum concentrations due to hypogammaglobulinaemia. This indicates that half-life of 7S γG-globulin in man probably is related to concentration in a similar way to that in the mouse and the rabbit. Wochner, Drews, Strober and Waldmann (1966) found that patients with myotonic dystrophy had γG-globulin concentrations of 7.2 mg/ml, as compared to

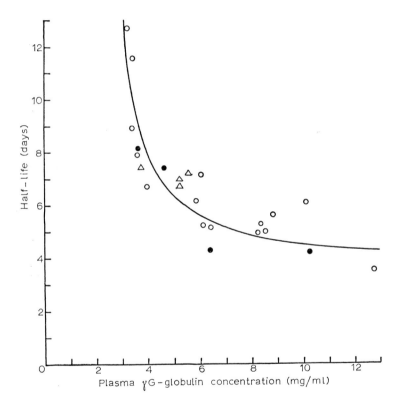

Fig. 11.7. Diagram of the relation of half-life to serum concentration of γ-globulin in rabbits of unaltered, reduced and alkylated γ-globulin molecules and ones reassembled from separated chains. The procedures do not appear to affect the relation. The superimposed cure is calculated from the equation as in fig 11.4 using values for the constants of $a = 0.2$, $b = 2.25$. (Data from Cohen and Mannik 1966.)

12.1 ± 2.6 mg/ml in controls. The γG-globulin half-life in these patients was 11.4 days as compared to 22.9 days in controls. Isolated γG-globulin from the patients had a normal half-life in the controls. The rate of synthesis was normal, as was the γG-globulin synthesized, so the low concentration arose from increased breakdown. The concentrations and half-lives of γM- and γA-globulins were normal. Allansmith, McClellan and Butterworth (1967) showed that the concentrations of γG-, γA- and γM-globulins in healthy individuals are largely independent of each other. Even with diseases causing severe disturbances of the immunoglobulins the levels remained independent of each other. Spiegelberg, Fishkin and Grey (1968) examined the catabolic rates of isotopically labelled γG-myeloma proteins in patients suffering from cancer other than multiple myeloma. On average γ_1G-, γ_2G- and γ_4G-globulins were catabolised at similar rates to normal γG-globulin, whereas γ_3G-globulin was catabolised more rapidly. Significant differences were observed, however, when individual myeloma proteins of a single sub-class were compared. These individual variations in catabolic rates were present within all four sub-classes. The authors suggest that the results could be partially explained on our hypothesis if either (a) a heterogeneity of the site on the γG-molecule attaching to the protective receptor allowing certain molecules to compete better for the receptor and therefore to be catabolised more slowly, or (b) variation in susceptibility to proteolysis of individual proteins resulting in different rates of catabolism. It was pointed out that γ_3G-myeloma protein, with a more rapid average rate of catabolism, is known to be more susceptible to papain digestion than those of the other sub-classes. Wochner, Strober and Waldmann (1967) showed that the kidneys are the main site of breakdown of Bence-Jones proteins and of isolated L-chains, but not of γG-molecules or Fc-fragments and even Fab-fragments were only partially catabolised in the kidneys.

Significant evidence has been forthcoming in another way. Spiegelberg and Weigle (1965, 1966) have studied the half-lives of homologous and of heterologous 7S γG-globulins and of their fragments and isolated chains in several species of normal animals (table 11.1). In each of several species γG-globulins have half-lives characteristic of the species that produced them. In the rabbit, for example, the half-lives decline in the order: rabbit > man > guineapig > horse > bovine > mouse. The rates of transmission from the uterine lumen to the foetal circulation of antitoxins prepared in five of these six species are known (p. 70) and decline in the same order; the probability of the identity of two sequences of five occurring by chance is 0.0083 and the cor-

TABLE 11.1

Half-lives of different gamma globulins and gamma globulin fragments.* (From Spiegelberg and Weigle 1965.)

Animal	Source of gamma globulin	7S gamma globulin average (range)	Gamma globulin fragments		
			Pepsin 5S	Papain 3.5S	
				I (S)	III (F)[†] average (range)
Rabbit	Rabbit	6.0 (4.5–7.5)	<0.5	<0.5	4.7 (4.1–5.6)
Guineapig	Rabbit	4.3 (4.0–4.7)	<0.5	<0.5	4.0 (3.9–4.1)
Mouse	Rabbit	5.7 (5.3–6.4)	<0.5	<0.5	4.4 (3.6–5.9)
Guineapig	Guineapig	4.2 (3.4–5.0)	<0.5	<0.5	2.2 (1.7–2.5)
Rabbit	Guineapig	3.3 (2.9–3.7)	<0.5	<0.5	2.1 (1.6–2.5)
Mouse	Guineapig	4.9 (4.6–5.2)	<0.5	<0.5	2.2 (2.0–2.4)
Mouse	Mouse	4.0 (3.0–5.2)	<0.5	<0.5	1.0 (0.8–1.1)
Rabbit	Mouse	1.5 (1.2–1.7)	<0.5	<0.5	1.4 (1.3–1.5)
Guineapig	Mouse	2.3 (2.2–2.5)	<0.5	<0.5	1.5 (1.4–1.7)
Rabbit	Human	5.0 (3.7–5.8)	<0.5	<0.5	3.8 (2.6–4.9)
Guineapig	Human	3.8 (3.7–3.9)	<0.5	<0.5	3.1 (3.0–3.4)
Mouse	Human	4.5 (4.2–4.9)	<0.5	<0.5	2.9 (2.6–3.6)
Rabbit	Horse	1.7 (1.6–1.8)	<0.5	—	—
Rabbit	Bovine	1.6 (1.4–1.8)	<0.5	—	—

* Half-life given in days.
† Half-life of F papain fragment (III) obtained after 5 min digestion with papain.

respondence is significant. It was shown also that the Fc-fragments and γ-chains of the γG-globulins of all the species tested had much longer half-lives than the Fab or F(ab')$_2$ or L-chains, which are eliminated rapidly (fig. 11.8). The elimination of the Fc-fragment or γ-chain is slow and related to that of the intact γG-globulin. It was concluded that the molecular structure responsible for γG-globulin catabolism is located in the Fc-piece. Spiegelberg and Grey (1968) studied next the catabolism of human myeloma proteins in mice, rabbits, guineapigs, monkeys and man. It was found that γ$_1$G-, γ$_2$G- and γ$_4$G-globulins were catabolised at similar rates to each other in all these animals, whereas γ_3G-globulin was catabolised more rapidly. Individual myeloma proteins of a given subclass differed significantly in their catabolic rates in mice and monkeys but, with the exception of γ_3G-globulin, did not differ in rabbits or guineapigs. It was concluded that in gross aspects of catabolism the homologous and heterologous species handle human γG-immunoglobulins in a similar fashion, but that there are subtle differences between species that allow some, but not others, to recognise structural differences between individual myeloma proteins which have an effect on their catabolism.

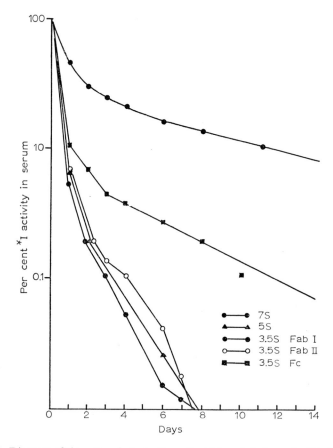

Fig. 11.8. Diagram of the rates of elimination of rabbit γ-globulin and of its fragments produced by papain or pepsin digestion from the circulation of rabbits. (From Spiegelberg and Weigle 1965.)

The transmission of various γ-globulins from mother to foetus in the mouse was determined by Koch, Boesman and Gitlin (1967), as was mentioned previously (p. 95). The rates of transmission declined in the order: guineapig $\geq$ human $>$ rat $>$ bovine $=$ mouse. The half-lives of these γ-globulins in the circulation of the mouse decline in the same order, but whereas there is a difference of *c.* 22.5 times between the extremes of the series in transmission the differences in the half-lives are much less, being only $\times 3$ between the extremes. They conclude that 'a possible similarity in underlying mechanisms of the two processes is not precluded by these data, but it is apparent that there are specific kinetic differences between plasma protein catabolism and maternofoetal transfer'. We have suggested no more than that the underlying mechanisms of the two processes are similar, not that they are identical; they may be mediated by different kinds of cells, with different rates of pinocytosis and different densities of receptors and consequently different proportions of the protein saved and catabolised. Even if the mechanisms were quantitatively identical they would result in similar differences between the rates of transmission and the half-lives only in the special case when the quantities of the absorbed protein that were saved and degraded were equal. This is because transmission depends on the proportion saved and half-life on the proportion degraded. We do not know the proportion of the protein absorbed by the foetus which is transmitted to the circulation in the mouse but, for example, in the rabbit it is *c.* $\frac{1}{5}$ for that γ-globulin which is transmitted most rapidly, leaving $\frac{4}{5}$ degraded (p. 73). The lowest rate of transmission of any γ-globulin in the rabbit was 1% of this or about $\frac{1}{500}$ of the γ-globulin absorbed. The amounts of γ-globulin degraded in these two extreme cases would be $\frac{4}{5}$ and $\frac{499}{500}$. In this example the same mechanism would account for an extreme difference of $\times 100$ in rates of transmission but only of $\times 1.25$ in half-lives. Therefore, on the information available, the observed differences in the range of rates of transmission and of half-lives in the mouse is consistent with hypothesis.

References

ABBAS, T. M. and J. E. TOVEY, 1960, Proteins of the liquor amnii. Br. med. J. *1*, 476–479.

ADAMSON, C. A., S. LÖFGREN and C. MALMNÄS, 1951, Antibodies in mothers and newborn infants. Scand. J. clin. Lab. Invest. *3*, 52–57.

AIKEN, J. M. and I. C. BLORE, 1964, Immunology of newborn pigs: response to lapinized hog cholera virus in colostrum-deprived and suckling pigs. Am. J. vet. Res. *25*, 1134–1140.

AITKEN, I. D., 1964, Development of natural anti-Forssman hemolysin in young rabbits. J. infect. Dis. *114*, 174–178.

ALEXANDER, R. A. and J. H. MASON, 1941, Studies on the neurotropic virus of horsesickness. VII. Transmitted immunity. Onderstepoort J. vet. Sci. Anim. Ind. *16*, 19–32.

ALLANSMITH, M., B. MCCLELLAN and M. BUTTERWORTH, 1967, Evidence for the independence of human immunoglobulin class levels. Immunology *13*, 483–488.

AL-NAJDI, M. R., 1965, The transfer of antibody from mother to foetus in the guinea-pig. Thesis (University of Leeds).

AMOROSO, E. C., 1952, Placentation. *In:* A. S. Parkes (ed.) Marshall's physiology of reproduction. Vol. 2, 3rd. ed. (Longmans, Green & Co., London).

ANDERSEN, S. B. and M. BJØRNEBOE, 1964, Gamma globulin turnover in rabbits before and during hyperimmunization. J. exp. Med. *119*, 537–546.

ANDERSON, J. A. and V. BOLIN, 1949, Congenital antiviral immunity in Swiss mice. Am. J. Hyg. *50*, 200–206.

ANDERSON, J. F., 1906, Simultaneous transmission of resistance to diphtheria toxine and hypersusceptibility to horse serum by the female guinea-pig to her young. J. med. Res. *15*, 259–260.

ANDERSON, J. R., 1956, The experimental production of erythroblastosis foetalis in rabbits. Br. J. Haemat. *2*, 44–60.

ANDERSON, J. W., 1959, The placental barrier to gamma-globulins in the rat. Am. J. Anat. *104*, 403–430.

ANDERSON, J. W., 1964, The use of antiferritin serum in tracing the transport of antibodies. J. Cell Biol. *23*, Abstracts 4A.

ANDERSON, J. W. and J. C. LEISSRING, 1961, The transfer of serum proteins from mother to young in the guinea pig. II. Histochemistry of tissues involved in prenatal transfer. Am. J. Anat. *109*, 157–174.

ANDRESEN, E. and L. N. BAKER, 1963, Hemolytic disease in pigs caused by anti-Ba. J. Anim. Sci. *22*, 720–725.

ASCARI, W. Q., P. LEVINE and W. POLLACK, 1969, Incidence of maternal Rh. immunization by ABO compatible and incompatible pregnancies. Br. med. J. *1*, 399–401.

ASKONAS, B. A., P. N. CAMPBELL, J. H. HUMPHREY and T. S. WORK, 1954, The source of antibody globulin in rabbit milk and goat colostrum. Biochem. J. *56*, 597–601.

ASOFSKY, R., Z. TRNKA and G. J. THORBECKE, 1962, Serum protein synthesis by embryonic and neonatal chicks. Proc. Soc. exp. Biol. Med. *111*, 497–499.

ASPLUND, J. M., R. H. GRUMMER and P. H. PHILLIPS, 1962, Absorption of colostral γ-globulins and insulin by the newborn pig. J. Anim. Sci. *21*, 412–413.

AUGUSTIN, R., 1966, Transmission of maternal immunity. Lancet *ii*, 1312–1313.

AYCOCK, W. L. and S. D. KRAMER, 1930, Immunity to poliomyelitis in mothers and the newborn as shown by neutralisation tests. J. exp. Med. *52*, 457–464.

BALCONI, I. R. and J. G. LECCE, 1966, Intestinal absorption of homologous lactic dehydrogenase isoenzymes by the neonatal pig. J. Nutr. *88*, 233–238.

BALFOUR, W. E. and R. S. COMLINE, 1959, The specificity of the intestinal absorption of large molecules by the newborn calf. J. Physiol., Lond. *148*, 77–78P.

BALFOUR, W. E. and R. S. COMLINE, 1962, Acceleration of the absorption of unchanged globulin in the newborn calf by factors in colostrum. J. Physiol., Lond. *160*, 234–257.

BAMFORD, D. R., 1965, Studies *in vitro* of the passage of serum proteins across the gut walls of young rats. Thesis (University of Wales).

BAMFORD, D. R., 1966, Studies *in vitro* of the passage of serum proteins across the intestinal wall of young rats. Proc. R. Soc., B *166*, 30–45.

BANGHAM, D. R., 1960, The transmission of homologous serum proteins to the foetus and to the amniotic fluid in the rhesus monkey. J. Physiol., Lond. *153*, 265–289.

BANGHAM, D. R., K. R. HOBBS and D. E. H. TEE, 1961, The origin and nature of proteins of the liquor amnii in the rhesus monkey; a new protein with some unusual properties. J. Physiol., Lond. *158*, 207–218.

BANGHAM, D. R., K. R. HOBBS and R. J. TERRY, 1958, Selective placental transfer of serum proteins in the rhesus. Lancet *ii*, 351–354.

BANGHAM, D. R., P. L. INGRAM, J. H. B. ROY, K. W. G. SHILLAM and R. J. TERRY, 1958, The absorption of ^{131}I-labelled serum and colostral proteins from the gut of the young calf. Proc. R. Soc., B *149*, 184–191.

BANGHAM, D. R. and R. J. TERRY, 1957a, The absorption of ^{131}I-labelled homologous and heterologous serum proteins fed orally to young rats. Biochem. J. *66*, 579–583.

BANGHAM, D. R. and R. J. TERRY, 1957b, The survival of globulins absorbed from the gut in suckling rats. Biochem. J. *66*, 584–587.

BARDELLI, P. C., 1930, Sulla trasmissione dell'immunità contro il tetano da madre a figlio nel cavallo. Annali Ig. sper. *40*, 675–680.

BARNES, J. M., 1959, Antitoxin transfer from mother to foetus in the guinea-pig. J. Path. Bact. *77*, 371–380.

BARR, M., A. T. GLENNY, S. HIGNETT, K. J. RANDALL and A. THOMSON, 1952, Antigenic efficiency of fluid and precipitated diphtheria prophylactics in very young babies and lambs. Lancet *ii*, 803–805.

BARR, M., A. T. GLENNY and K. J. RANDALL, 1949, Concentration of diphtheria antitoxin in cord blood, and rate of loss in babies. Lancet *ii*, 324–326.

BARRICK, E. R., G. MATRONE and J. C. OSBORNE, 1954, Effects of administering various blood serum constituents on gamma globulin levels of baby pigs. Proc. Soc. exp. Biol. Med. *87*, 92–94.

BAR-SHANY, S. and V. HERBERT, 1967, Transplacentally acquired antibody to intrinsic factor with vitamin B_{12} deficiency. Blood *30*, 777–784.

BATTY, I., F. W. R. BRAMBELL, W. A. HEMMINGS and C. L. OAKLEY, 1954, Selection of antitoxins by the foetal membranes of rabbits. Proc. R. Soc., B *142*, 452–471.

BATTY, I., A. THOMSON and J. R. HEPPLE, 1954, The active immunization of new born lambs against pulpy kidney disease (*Cl. welchii* type D enterotoxaemia). Vet Rec. *66*, 249–254.

BEALE, D., A. FEINSTEIN and M. J. HOBART, 1968, Gammaglobulins of the cow, sheep, pig and chicken. A.R.C. Institute of Animal Physiology, Babraham, Cambridge, Report for 1966–1967, pp. 92–93.

BEATON, G. H., A. E. SELBY, M. J. VEEN and A. M. WRIGHT, 1961, Starch gel electrophoresis of rat serum proteins. II. Slow α_2-globulin and other serum proteins in pregnant, tumor-bearing and young rats. J. biol. Chem. *236*, 2005–2008.

BECK, F., J. B. LLOYD and A. GRIFFITHS, 1967, A histochemical and biochemical study of some aspects of placental function in the rat using maternal injection of horseradish peroxidase. J. Anat. *101*, 461–478.

BECK, J. S. and N. R. ROWELL, 1963, Transplacental passage of antinuclear antibody. Lancet *i*, 134–135.

BEIER, H. M., 1968, Biochemisch-entwicklungsphysiologische untersuchungen am proteinmilieu für die blastozystenentwicklung des kaninchens (*Oryctolagus cuniculus*). Zool. Jb. (Anat.) *85*, 72–190.

BEIJERS, J. A., J. J. VAN LOGHEM and M. VAN DER HART, 1950, Haemolytische anaemie bij het pasgeboren veulen. Tijdschr. Diergeneesk. *75*, 955–970.

BELLAIRS, R., 1963, Differentiation of the yolk sac of the chick studied by electron microscopy. J. Embryol. exp. Morph. *11*, 201–225.

BELLAIRS, R., 1965, The relationship between oocyte and follicle in the hen's ovary as shown by electron microscopy. J. Embryol. exp. Morph. *13*, 215–233.

BERRY, G. P. and H. B. SLAVIN, 1943, Studies on herpatic infection in mice. I. Passive protection against virus inoculated intranasally. J. exp. Med. *78*, 305–313.

BESSIS, M. and J. CAROLI, 1947, Anticorps anti-mulets incomplets et bloquants chez la jument mère de muleton ictérique. C. r. Séanc. Soc. Biol. *141*, 387.

BESSIS, M. and P. FREIXA, 1947a, Ictère et anémie par ingestion de sérum hémolytique chez le rat nouveau-né. C. r. Séanc. Soc. Biol. *141*, 14–15.

BESSIS, M. and P. FREIXA, 1947b, Études sur l'ictère hémolytique expérimental par injection et ingestion d'antisérum. Revue Hémat. *2*, 114–146.

BESSIS, M. and P. MILLOT, 1949, A propos du rôle du lait et du colostrum dans la physiopathologie de l'ictère grave du muleton nouveau-né. Bull. Acad. vét. Fr. *22*, 291–295.

BILLINGHAM, R. E. and G. H. LAMPKIN, 1957, Further studies on tissue homotransplantation in cattle. J. Embryol. exp. Morph. *5*, 351–367.

BINAGHI, R., P. LIACOPOULOS, B. N. HALPERN and M. LIACOPOULOS-BRIOT, 1962, Interference of non-specific gamma globulins with passive *in vitro* anaphylactic sensitization of isolated guinea-pig intestine. Immunology *5*, 204–210.

BINNS, R. M., 1967, Bone marrow and lymphoid cell injection of the pig foetus resulting in transplantation tolerance or immunity, and immunoglobulin production. Nature, Lond. *214*, 179–181.

BINNS, R. M., 1968, The ontogeny of immune responses in the pig. A.R.C. Institute of Animal Physiology, Babraham, Cambridge, Report for 1966–1967, pp. 89–90.

BIOZZI, G., B. N. HALPERN and R. BINAGHI, 1959, The competitive effect of normal serum proteins from various animal species on antibody fixation in passive cutaneous anaphylaxis in the guinea pig. J. Immun. *82*, 215–218.

BISWAS, E. R. I., 1961, Selective secretion of circulating antibodies in the milk of the rat. Nature, Lond. *192*, 883–884.

BLAKEMORE, F. and R. J. GARNER, 1956, The maternal transfer of antibodies in the bovine. J. comp. Path. Ther. *66*, 287–289.

BLOCK, K. J., Z. OVARY, F. M. KOURILSKY and B. BENACERRAF, 1963, Properties of guinea-pig 7S antibodies. VI. Transmission of antibodies from maternal to fetal circulation. Proc. Soc. exp. Biol. Med. *114*, 79–82.

BOASS, A. and T. H. WILSON, 1963, Development of mechanisms for intestinal absorption of vitamin B_{12} in growing rats. Am. J. Physiol. *204*, 101–104.

BOCKMAN, D. E. and W. B. WINBORN, 1966, Light and electron microscopy of intestinal ferritin absorption. Observations in sensitized and non-sensitized hamsters (*Mesocricetus auratus*). Anat. Rec. *155*, 603–622.

BOFFA, G. A., J. M. FINE, Y. JACQUOT-ARMAND, F. GAUDIN-HARDING and H. SUSBIELLE, 1965, Existence de macroglobulines α_1 et α_2 dans le sérum de rat au cours des périodes foetales et néo-natales. C. r. Séanc. Soc. Biol. *159*, 1342–1347.

BOORMAN, K. E., B. E. DODD and M. GUNTHER, 1958, A consideration of colostrum and milk as sources of antibodies which may be transferred to the newborn baby. Archs Dis Childh. *33*, 24–29.

BOORMAN, K. E., B. E. DODD and P. L. MOLLISON, 1944, The incidence of haemolytic disease of the foetus ('Erythroblastosis foetalis') in different families. The value of serological tests in diagnosis and prognosis. J. Obstet. Gynaec. Br. Commonw. *51*, 1–23.

BOUCEK, C. M., 1928, A study of the placental permeability of the white rat, as determined by its reaction to hemolysins. Am. J. Anat. *41*, 1–24.

BOURNE, G., 1962, The human amnion and chorion. (Lloyd-Luke (Medical Books) Ltd., London).

BOURNE, G. L. and D. LACY, 1960, Ultra-structure of human amnion and its possible relation to the circulation of amniotic fluid. Nature, Lond. *186*, 952–954.

BÖVING, B. G., 1963, Implantation mechanisms. *In:* C. G. Hartman (ed.) Mechanisms Concerned with Conception. (Pergamon Press, New York) pp. 321–396.

BOYD, J. D. and W. J. HAMILTON, 1952, Cleavage, early development and implantation of the egg. *In:* A. S. Parkes (ed.) Marshall's Physiology of Reproduction. Vol 2, 3rd ed. (Longmans, Green and Co, London).

BOYD, J. D., W. J. HAMILTON and C. A. R. BOYD, 1968, The surface of the syncytium of the human chorionic villus. J. Anat. *102*, 553–563.

BRAMBELL, F. W. R., 1925, The oogenesis of the fowl (*Gallus bankiva*). Phil. Trans. R. Soc. Ser. B *214*, 113–151.

BRAMBELL, F. W. R., 1958, The passive immunity of the young mammal. Biol. Rev. *33*, 488–531.

BRAMBELL, F. W. R., 1960, Transmission of immunity from mother to young. The New Scientist, 28th Jan. 1960.

BRAMBELL, F. W. R., 1963, Resemblances between passive anaphylactic sensitization and transmission of passive immunity. Nature, Lond. *199*, 1164–1166.

BRAMBELL, F. W. R., 1966, The transmission of immunity from mother to young and the catabolism of immunoglobulins. Lancet *ii*, 1087–1093.

BRAMBELL, F. W. R., J. BRIERLEY, R. HALLIDAY and W. A. HEMMINGS, 1954, Transference of passive immunity from mother young. Lancet *i*, 964–965.

BRAMBELL, F. W. R. and R. HALLIDAY, 1956, The route by which passive immunity is transmitted from mother to foetus in the rat. Proc. R. Soc., B *145*, 170–178.

BRAMBELL, F. W. R., R. HALLIDAY and W. A. HEMMINGS, 1961, Changes in ^{131}I-labelled immune bovine γ-globulin during transmission to the circulation after oral administration to the young rat. Proc. R. Soc., B *153*, 477–489.

BRAMBELL, F. W. R., R. HALLIDAY and I. G. MORRIS, 1958, Interference by human and bovine serum and serum protein fractions with the absorption of antibodies by suckling rats and mice. Proc. R. Soc., B *149*, 1–11.

BRAMBELL, F. W. R. and W. A. HEMMINGS, 1949, The passage into the embryonic yolk-sac cavity of maternal plasma proteins in rabbits. J. Physiol., Lond. *108*, 177–184.

BRAMBELL, F. W. R., G. P. HEMMINGS, W. A. HEMMINGS, M. HENDERSON and W. T. ROWLANDS, 1951, The route by which antibodies enter the circulation after injection of immune serum into the exocoel of foetal rabbits. Proc. R. Soc., B *138*, 188–195.

BRAMBELL, F. W. R., W. A. HEMMINGS, M. HENDERSON and R. A. KEKWICK, 1953, Electrophoretic studies of serum proteins of foetal rabbits. Proc. R. Soc., B *141*, 300–314.

BRAMBELL, F. W. R., W. A. HEMMINGS, M. HENDERSON and C. L. OAKLEY, 1952, Selective and non-selective admission of various antitoxins into foetal rabbits. Proc. R. Soc. B *139*, 567–575.

BRAMBELL, F. W. R., W. A. HEMMINGS, M. HENDERSON, C. L. OAKLEY and W. T. ROWLANDS, 1951, The accumulation of antibodies in the stomach contents of foetal rabbits. Proc. R. Soc., B *138*, 195–204.

BRAMBELL, F. W. R., W. A. HEMMINGS, M. HENDERSON, H. J. PARRY and W. T. ROWLANDS, 1949, The route of antibodies passing from the maternal to the foetal circulation in rabbits. Proc. R. Soc., B *136*, 131–144.

BRAMBELL, F. W. R., W. A. HEMMINGS, M. HENDERSON and W. T. ROWLANDS, 1950, The selective admission of antibodies to the foetus by the yolk-sac splanchnopleur in rabbits. Proc. R. Soc., B *137*, 239–252.

BRAMBELL, F. W. R., W. A. HEMMINGS and I. G. MORRIS, 1964, A theoretical model of γ-globulin catabolism. Nature, Lond. *203*, 1352–1355.

BRAMBELL, F. W. R., W. A. HEMMINGS and C. L. OAKLEY, 1959, The relative transmission of natural and pepsin-refined homologous antitoxin from the uterine cavity to the foetal circulation in the rabbit. Proc. R. Soc., B *150*, 312–317.

BRAMBELL, F. W. R., W. A. HEMMINGS, C. L. OAKLEY and R. R. PORTER, 1960, The relative transmission of the fractions of papain hydrolyzed homologous γ-globulin from the uterine cavity to the foetal circulation in the rabbit. Proc. R. Soc., B *151*, 478–482.

BRAMBELL, F. W. R., W. A. HEMMINGS and W. T. ROWLANDS, 1948, The passage of antibodies from the maternal circulation into the embryo in rabbits. Proc. R. Soc., B *135*, 390–403.

BRAMBELL, F. W. R. and I. H. MILLS, 1947, Studies on sterility and prenatal mortality in wild rabbits. II. The occurrence of fibrin in the yolk-sac contents of embryos during and immediately after implantation. J. exp. Biol. *23*, 332–345.

BRANDLY, C. A., H. E. MOSES and E. L. JUNGHERR, 1946, Transmission of antiviral activity via the egg and the rôle of congenital passive immunity to Newcastle disease in chickens. Am. J. vet. Res. *7*, 333–342.

BRIDGMAN, J., 1948a, A morphological study of the development of the placenta of the rat. I. An outline of the development of the placenta of the white rat. J. Morph. *83*, 61–80.

BRIDGMAN, J., 1948b, A morphological study of the development of the placenta of the rat. II. An histological and cytological study of the development of the chorioallantoic placenta of the white rat. J. Morph. *83*, 195–215.

BRIERLEY, J. and W. A. HEMMINGS, 1956, The selective transport of antibodies from the yolk sac to the circulation of the chick. J. Embryol. exp. Morph. *4*, 34–41.

BRION, A., 1949, Sur le mécanisme de l'immunisation de la jument mulassière par son produit, et le passage des anticorps antimulet chez son muleton. C. r. hebd. Séanc. Acad. Sci., Paris *228*, 1614–1616.

BRION, A., 1950, Réalisation expérimentale de l'ictère du muleton nouveau-né. C. r. hebd. Séanc. Acad. Sci., Paris *230*, 1547–1548.

BRION, A. and P. GORET, 1949, Les échanges immunitaires entre la mère et le foetus ou le nouveau-né. Conséquences et applications a l'étiologie et à la pathogénie de l'ictère hémolytique du muleton et du poulain. Revue Immunol. Thér. antimicrob. *13*, 325–337.

BRITTON, J. W., 1950, A method of handling hemolytic icterus of newborn foals. J. Am. vet. med. Ass. *116*, 345–347.

BROWN, H., V. C. SPEER, L. Y. QUINN, V. W. HAYS and D. V. CATRON, 1961, Studies on colostrum-acquired immunity and active antibody production in baby pigs. J. Anim. Sci. *20*, 323–328.

BROWN, P., M. W. SMITH and R. WITTY, 1968, Interdependence of albumin and sodium transport in the foetal and new-born pig intestine. J. Physiol., Lond. *198*, 365–381.

BROWN, R. D., 1958a, Rinderpest immunity in calves. I. The acquisition and persistence of maternally derived antibody. J. Hyg., Camb. *56*, 427–434.

BROWN, R. D., 1958b, Rinderpest immunity in calves. II. Active immunization. J. Hyg., Camb. *56*, 435–444.

BRUCE-CHWATT, L. J. and F. D. GIBSON, 1956, Transplacental passage of *Plasmodium berghei* and passive transfer of immunity in rats and mice. Trans. R. Soc. trop. Med. Hyg. *50*, 47–53.

BRUNER, D. W., R. G. BROWN, F. E. HULL and A. S. KINKAID, 1949, Blood factors and baby pig anemia. J. Am. vet. med. Ass. *115*, 94–96.

BRUNER, D. W., E. R. DOLL, F. E. HULL and A. S. KINKAID, 1950, Further studies on haemolytic icterus in foals. Am. J. vet. Res. *11*, 22–25.

BRUNER, D. W., P. R. EDWARDS and E. R. DOLL, 1948, Passive immunity in the newborn foal. Cornell Vet. *38*, 363–366.

BRUNER, D. W., E. F. HULL and E. R. DOLL, 1948, The relation of blood factors to icterus in foals. Am. J. vet. Res. *9*, 237–242.

BRUNER, D. W., F. E. HULL, P. R. EDWARDS and E. R. DOLL, 1948, Icteric foals. J. Am. vet. med. Ass. *112*, 440–441.

BRYCE, L. M. and F. M. BURNET, 1932, Natural immunity to staphylococcal toxin, J. Path. Bact. *35*, 183–191.

BUFFE, D. and P. BURTIN, 1967, Formation des immunoglobulines chez le foetus et le jeune enfant. Annls Inst. Pasteur, Paris *112*, 468–475.

BUXTON, A., 1952, On the transference of bacterial antibodies from the hen to the chick. J. gen. Microbiol. *7*, 268–286.

BUXTON, J. C. and N. H. BROOKSBANK, 1953a, Haemolytic disease of new-born pigs caused by iso-immunization of pregnancy. Nature, Lond. *172*, 355.

BUXTON, J. C. and N. H. BROOKSBANK, 1953b, Haemolytic disease of new-born pigs caused by iso-immunisation of pregnancy. Vet. Rec. *65*, 287–288.

BUXTON, J. C., N. H. BROOKSBANK and R. R. A. COOMBS, 1955, Haemolytic disease of newborn piglets caused by maternal iso-immunisation. Br. vet. J. *111*, 463–473.

CALARCO, P. G. and F. H. MOYER, 1966, Structural changes in the murine yolk sac during gestation; cytochemical and electron microscope observations. J. Morph. *119*, 341–356.

CAMPBELL, C. H., 1960, Transfer of immunity to foot-and-mouth disease virus from maternal mice to offspring. Am. J. vet. Res. *21*, 697–700.

CARMICHAEL, L. E., D. S. ROBSON and F. D. BARNES, 1962, Transfer and decline of maternal infectious canine hepatitis antibody in puppies. Proc. Soc. exp. Biol. Med. *109*, 677–681.

CAROLI, J. and M. BESSIS, 1947a, Sur la cause et le traitement de l'ictère grave des muletons nouveau-nés. C. r. hebd. Séanc. Acad. Sci., Paris *224*, 969–971.

CAROLI, J. and M. BESSIS, 1947b, Immunisation de la mère par le foetus chez la jument mulassière. Son rôle dans l'ictère grave du muleton. C. r. Séanc. Soc. Biol. *141*, 386–387.

CAROLI, J. and M. BESSIS, 1947c, Recherches sur la cause de l'ictère grave familial des muletons. Revue Hémat. *2*, 207–228.

CAROLI, J. and M. BESSIS, 1948, L'ictère grave des muletons. Sem. Hôp. Paris *24*, 535–537.

CARPENTER, S. J. and V. H. FERM, 1966, Electron microscopic observations on the uptake and storage of Thorotrast by rodent yolk sac epithelial cells. Anat. Rec. *154*, 327.

CARRETTI, N. and Z. OVARY, 1969, Transmission of γG-antibodies from maternal to fetal circulation in the mouse. Proc. Soc. exp. Biol. Med. *130*, 509–512.

CASTLE, W. E. and C. E. KEELER, 1933, Blood group inheritance in the rabbit. Proc. natn. Acad. Sci. U.S.A. *19*, 92–98.

CHAMBERLAIN, A. G., G. C. PERRY and R. E. JONES, 1965, Effect of trypsin inhibitor isolated from sow's colostrum on the absorption of γ-globulin by piglets. Nature, Lond. *207*, 429.

CHANG, M. C., 1952, Development of bovine blastocyst with a note on implantation. Anat. Rec. *113*, 143–162.

CHARLWOOD, P. A. and A. THOMSON, 1948, Electrophoretic patterns of lamb serum before and after transfer of colostrum. Nature, Lond. *161*, 59.

CHESNEY, G., 1945, A note on the transmission of diphtheria antitoxin from mother to infant. Mon. Bull. Minist. Hlth *4*, 144–146.

CHIPMAN, W., 1903, Observations on the placenta of the rabbit with special reference to the presence of glycogen, fat, and iron. Rep. Lab. R. Coll. Physns Edinb. *8*, 227–485.

CHODIRKER, W. B. and T. B. TOMASI, 1963, Gamma-globulins: quantitative relationships in human serum and non-vascular fluids. Science, N.Y. *142*, 1080–1081.

CHOWN, B., 1954, Anaemia from bleeding of the foetus into the mother's circulation. Lancet *i*, 1213–1215.

CHOWN, B., 1955, On a search for rhesus antibodies in very young foetuses. Archs Dis. Childh. *30*, 232–233.

CHRISTIAN, R. M., D. M. ERVIN, S. N. SWISHER, W. A. O'BRIEN and L. E. YOUNG, 1949, Hemolytic anemia in newborn dogs due to absorption of isoantibody from breast milk during the first day of life. Science, N.Y. *110*, 443.

CHRISTIAN, R. M., D. M. ERVIN and L. E. YOUNG, 1951, Observations on the in vitro behavior of dog isoantibodies. J. Immun. *66*, 37–50.

CHRISTOFFERSEN, A. K., 1934, La superficie des villosités choriales du placenta à la fin de la grossesse. (Étude d'histologie quantitative.) C. r. Séanc. Soc. Biol. *117*, 641–644.

CLARK, S. L., 1959, The ingestion of proteins and colloidal materials by columnar absorptive cells of the small intestine in suckling rats and mice. J. biophys. biochem. Cytol. *5*, 41–50.

CLARKE, C. A., 1968, Prevention of rhesus iso-immunisation. Lancet *ii*, 1–7.

CLARKE, C. A., R. FINN, D. LEHANE, R. B. MCCONNELL, P. M. SHEPPARD and J. C. WOODROW, 1966, Dose of anti-D gamma-globulin in prevention of Rh-haemolytic disease of the newborn. Br. med. J. *1*, 213–214.

COHEN, G. L. and M. MANNIK, 1966, Catabolism of γG-globulin with reduced interchain disulfide bonds in rabbits. J. Immun. *96*, 683–690.

COHEN, P. and S. J. SCADRON, 1943, The placental transmission of protective antibodies against whooping cough by inoculation of the pregnant mother. J. Am. med. Ass. *121*, 656–662.

COHEN, P., H. SCHNECK and E. DUBOW, 1951, Prenatal multiple immunization. J. Pediat. *38*, 696–704.

COHEN, S. G., 1950, The placental transmission of antibodies and serum γ-globulin. J. infect. Dis. *87*, 291–298.

COLES, B. L., 1957, Serum protein pattern in normal kittens. J. Physiol., Lond. *136*, 37P.

COMLINE, R. S., R. W. POMEROY and D. A. TITCHEN, 1953, Histological changes in the intestine during colostrum absorption. J. Physiol., Lond. *122*, 6P.

COMLINE, R. S., H. E. ROBERTS and D. A. TITCHEN, 1951a, Histological changes in the epithelium of the small intestine during protein absorption in the new-born animal. Nature, Lond. *168*, 84–85.

COMLINE, R. S., H. E. ROBERTS and D. A. TITCHEN, 1951b, Route of absorption of colostrum globulin in the newborn animal. Nature, Lond. *167*, 561–562.

CONNAN, R. M., 1968, An attempt to demonstrate passive resistance in lambs to three species of gastro-intestinal nematodes as a result of sucking the ewe. Res. vet. Sci. *9*, 591–593.

COOMBS, R. R. A., R. C. CROWHURST, F. T. DAY, D. H. HEARD, I. T. HINDE, J. HOOG-STRATEN and H. B. PARRY, 1948, Haemolytic disease of newborn foals due to iso-immunization of pregnancy. J. Hyg., Camb. *46*, 403–418.

COOMBS, R. R. A., J. GORIUS and M. BESSIS, 1950, Diagnostic de l'ictère hémolytique des muletons par le test à l'antiglobuline. C. r. Séanc. Soc. Biol. *144*, 688–691.

COOMBS, R. R. A., A. E. MOURANT and R. R. RACE, 1945, A new test for the detection of weak and 'incomplete' Rh agglutinins. Br. J. exp. Path. *26*, 255–266.

CORNELL, R. and H. A. PADYKULA, 1969, A cytological study of intestinal absorption in the suckling rat. Am. J. Anat., in press.

CRONIN, M. T. I., 1955, Haemolytic disease of newborn foals. Vet. Rec. *67*, 479–494.

CROWTHER, C. and H. RAISTRICK, 1916, A comparative study of the proteins of the colostrum and milk of the cow and their relations to serum proteins. Biochem. J. *10*, 434–452.

CULBERTSON, J. T., 1938, Natural transmission of immunity against *Trypanosoma lewisi* from mother rats to their offspring. J. Parasit. *24*, 65–82.

CULBERTSON, J. T., 1939a, The immunization of rats of different age groups against *Trypanosoma lewisi* by the administration of specific antiserum *per os*. J. Parasit. *25*, 181–182.

CULBERTSON, J. T., 1939b, Transmission of resistance against *Trypanosoma lewisi* from a passively immunised mother rat to young nursing upon her. J. Parasit. *25*, 182–183.

CULBERTSON, J. T., 1940, The natural transmission of immunity against *Trypanosoma duttoni* from mother mice to their young. J. Immun. *38*, 51–66.

CUMMINGS, J. N. and T. P. BELLVILLE, 1963, Studies on fetal physiology in the sheep. Transplacental passage of antibodies and techniques for repeated sampling of the fetal lamb *in situ*. Am. J. Obstet. Gynec. *86*, 504–513.

CURLEY, F. J. and J. E. GORDON, 1948, Immunization of young mice with unmodified MM mouse encephalomyelitis virus under passive protection from immune mothers. Am. J. Hyg. *48*, 81–86.

DAFFNER, H. W. and K. SCHREIER, 1961, Über das verhalten der proteinsyntheserate in verschiedenen organen während der pränatalperiode bei kaninchen. Clinica chim. Acta *6*, 195–204.

DALE, H. H., 1913, The anaphylactic reaction of plain muscle in the guinea-pig. J. Pharmac. exp. Ther. *4*, 167–223.

DANCIS, J., 1960, Transfer of proteins across the human placenta. *In:* C. A. Villee, (ed.) The Placenta and Fetal Membranes. (Williams and Wilkins Co., Baltimore) pp. 185–187.

DANCIS, J., N. BRAVERMAN and J. LIND, 1957, Plasma protein synthesis in the human fetus and placenta. J. clin. Invest. *36*, 398–404.

DANCIS, J., J. LIND, M. ORATZ, J. SMOLENS and P. VARA, 1961, Placental transfer of proteins in human gestation. Am. J. Obstet. Gynec. *82*, 167–171.

DANCIS, J. and M. SHAFRAN, 1958, The origin of plasma proteins in the guinea-pig fetus. J. clin. Invest. *37*, 1093–1099.

DE KROMME, L. and L. A. M. VAN DER SPEK, 1950, On placenta permeability and antibody varieties in rhesus immunization. Maandschr. Kindergeneesk. *18*, 130–145.

DEMPSEY, E. W., 1953, Electron microscopy of the visceral yolk-sac epithelium of the guinea pig. Am. J. Anat. *93*, 331–363.

DEREN, J. J., H. A. PADYKULA and T. H. WILSON, 1966, Development of structure and function in the mammalian yolk sac. II. Vitamin B_{12} uptake by rabbit yolk sacs. Devl Biol. *13*, 349–369.

DEREN, J. J., E. W. STRAUSS and T. H. WILSON, 1965, The development of structure and transport systems of the fetal rabbit intestine. Devl Biol. *12*, 467–486.

DESAI, R. G. and W. P. CREGER, 1963, Maternofetal passage of leukocytes and platelets in man. Blood *21*, 665–673.

DEUTSCH, H. F. and V. R. SMITH, 1957, Intestinal permeability to proteins in the newborn herbivore. Am. J. Physiol. *191*, 271–276.

DICKERSON, J. W. T. and R. A. McCANCE, 1957, The composition and origin of the allantoic fluid in the rabbit. J. Embryol. exp. Morph. *5*, 40–42.

DIXON, F. J., W. KUHNS, W. O. WEIGLE and TAYLOR, P., 1959, The lack of absorption of ingested bovine antibody in humans. J. Immun. *83*, 437–441.

DIXON, F. J., W. O. WEIGLE and J. J. VAZQUEZ, 1961, Metabolism and mammary secretion of serum proteins in the cow. Lab. Invest. *10*, 216–237.

DOLL, E. R. and R. G. BROWN, 1954, Isohemolytic disease of newborn pigs. Cornell Vet *44*, 86–93.

DOLL, E. R. and F. E. HULL, 1951, Observations on hemolytic icterus of newborn foals Cornell Vet. *41*, 14–35.

DOLL, E. R., M. G. RICHARDS, M. E. WALLACE and J. T. BRYANS, 1952, The influence of an equine fetal tissue vaccine upon hemagglutination activity of mare serums: its relation to hemolytic icterus of newborn foals. Cornell Vet. *42*, 495–505.

DU PAN, R. M., J. J. SCHEIDEGGER, P. WENGER, B. KOECHLI and J. ROUX, 1959, Das Verhalten der intramuskulär, intravenös und per os verabreichten gammaglobuline. Blut *5*, 104–114.

DUVAL, M., 1889, Le placenta des rongeurs; le placenta du lapin. J. Anat. Physiol., Paris *25*, 309–342, 573–627.

DUVAL, M., 1890, Le placenta des rongeurs; le placenta du lapin. J. Anat. Physiol., Paris *26*, 1–48, 273–344, 521–592.

DUVAL, M., 1891, Le placenta des rongeurs; le placenta de la souris et du rat. J. Anat. Physiol., Paris *27*, 24–73, 344–395, 515–612.

EARLE, I. P., 1935, Influence of the ingestion of colostrum on the proteins of the blood sera of young foals, kids, lambs and pigs. J. agric. Res. *51*, 479–490.

EDOZIEN, J. C., H. M. GILLES and I. O. K. UDEOZO, 1962, Adult and cord-blood gammaglobulin and immunity to malaria in Nigerians. Lancet *ii*, 951–955.

EDSALL, G., 1956, Active and passive immunity of the infant. Ann. N.Y. Acad. Sci. *66*, 32–43.

EHRLICH, P., 1892, Ueber immunität durch vererbung und säugung. Z. Hyg. Infeckt-Krankh. *12*, 183–203.

EICHHOLZ, A., 1967, Structural and functional organization of the brush border of intestinal epithelial cells III. Enzymic activities and chemical composition of various fractions of trisdisrupted brush borders. Biochim. biophys. Acta *135*, 475–482.

EPP, M., 1962, Penicillin antibody in maternal and cord bloods and its possible relationship to hypersensitivity. J. Immun. *5*, 287–294.

EPSTEIN, W. V., S. W. FONG, and M. TAN, 1966, Naturally-occurring macroglobulin antibody of foetal origin in the normal human newborn. Immunology *10*, 259–270.

EVERETT, J. W., 1935, Morphological and physiological studies of the placenta in the albino rat. J. exp. Zool. *70*, 243–286.

FAHEY, J. L. and J. H. HUMPHREY, 1962, Antibodies with differing molecular sizes in mice. Immunology *5*, 104–109.

FAHEY, J. L. and A. G. ROBINSON, 1963, Factors controlling serum γ-globulin concentration. J. exp. Med. *118*, 845–868.

FAHEY, J. L. and S. SELL, 1965, The immunoglobulins of mice. V The metabolic (catabolic) properties of five immunoglobulin classes. J. exp. Med. *122*, 41–58.

FAMULENER, L. W., 1912, On the transmission of immunity from mother to offspring. A study upon serum hemolysins in goats. J. infect. Dis. *10*, 332–368.

FEINSTEIN, A., 1963, Character and allotypy of an immune globulin in rabbit colostrum. Nature, Lond. *199*, 1197–1199.

FELDMAN, J. D., 1961, Fine structure of the cow's udder during gestation and lactation. Lab. Invest. *10*, 238–255.

FENNER, F., 1948, The epizootic behaviour of mouse-pox (infectious ectromelia). Br. J. exp. Path. *29*, 69–91.

FENNESTAD, K. L. and C. BORG-PETERSEN, 1957, *Leptospira* antibody production by bovine foetuses. Nature, Lond. *180*, 1210–1211.

FENNESTAD, K. L. and C. BORG-PETERSEN, 1958, Fetal leptospirosis and abortion in cattle. J. infect. Dis. *102*, 227–236.

FENNESTAD, K. L. and C. BORG-PETERSEN, 1962, Antibody and plasma cells in bovine fetuses infected with *Leptospira saxkoebing*. J. infect. Dis. *110*, 63–69.

FILKINS, M. E. and D. D. GILLETTE, 1966, Initial dietary influences on antibody absorption in newborn puppies. Proc. Soc. exp. Biol. Med. *122*, 686–688.

FINN, R., C. A. CLARKE, W. T. A. DONOHOE, R. B. McCONNELL and P. M. SHEPPARD, 1961, Transplacental passage of red cells in man. Nature, Lond. *190*, 922–923.

FISCHL, R. and O. VON WUNSCHEIM, 1895, Ueber Schutzkörper im Blute des Neugeborenen; das Verhalten des Blutserums des Neugeborenen gegen Diphtheriebacillen und Diphtheriegift nebst kritischen Bermerkungen zur humoralen Immunitätstheorie. Z. Heilk *16*, 429–482.

FISHER, J. P. and R. A. COOKE, 1957, Passive cutaneous anaphylaxis (PCA) in the guinea pig. An immunologic and pathologic study. J. Allergy *28*, 150–169.

FLORMAN, A. L., B. SCHICK and H. E. SCALETTAR, 1951, Placental transmission of mumps and *streptococcus* MG antibodies. Proc. Soc. exp. Biol. Med. *78*, 126–128.

FOSTER, J. F., R. W. FRIEDELL, D. CATRON and M. R. DIECKMANN, 1951, Electrophoretic studies on swine. III. Composition of baby pig plasma and sow's whey during lactation. Archs Biochem. Biophys. *31*, 104–112.

FRANGIONE, B., C. MILSTEIN and J. R. L. PINK, 1969, Structural studies of immunoglobulin G. Nature, Lond. *221*, 145–148.

FRANKLIN, E. C. and H. G. KUNKEL, 1957, Immunologic differences between the 19S and 7S components of normal human γ-globulin. J. Immun. *78*, 11–18.

FRANKLIN, E. C. and H. G. KUNKEL, 1958, Comparative levels of high molecular weight (19S) gamma globulin in maternal and umbilical cord sera. J. Lab. clin. Med. *52*, 724–727.

FREDA, V. J., 1958, A-B-O(H) blood group substances in the human maternal-fetal barrier and amniotic fluid. Am. J. Obstet. Gynec. *76*, 407–416.

FREDA, V. J., 1962, Placental transfer of antibodies in man. Am. J. Obstet. Gynec. *84*, 1756–1777.

FREDA, V. J. and B. CARTER, 1962, Placental permeability in the human for anti-A and anti-B isoantibodies. Am. J. Obstet. Gynec. *84*, 1351–1367.

FRIEDRICH, F., 1964, Die Entwicklung der sogenannten Dottersackdivertikel in der Placenta der weissen Maus. Z. Anat. EntwGesch *124*, 153–170.

FUDENBERG, H. H. and B. R. FUDENBERG, 1964, Antibody to hereditary human gamma-globulin (Gm) factor resulting from maternal-fetal incompatibility. Science, N.Y. *145*, 170–171.

FULTON ROBERTS, G., 1957, Comparative aspects of haemolytic disease of the newborn. (William Heinemann (Medical Books) Ltd., London).

GALLAGHER, N. D., 1969, Mechanism and site of vitamin B_{12} absorption in suckling rats. Nature, Lond. *222*, 877–878.

GARBY, L., 1957, Studies on transfer of matter across membranes with special reference to the isolated human amniotic membrane and the exchange of amniotic fluid. Acta physiol. scand. *40*, (suppl.) 137, 1–84.

GARNER, R. J. and W. CRAWLEY, 1958, Further observations on the maternal transference of antibodies in the bovine. J. comp. Path. Ther. *68*, 112–114.

GELFAND, H. M., J. P. FOX, D. R. LEBLANC and L. ELVEBACK, 1960, Studies on the development of natural immunity to poliomyelitis in Louisiana. V. Passive transfer of polioantibody from mother to fetus, and natural decline and disappearance of antibody in the infant. J. Immun. *85*, 46–55.

GELFAND, M. M., G. J. STREAN, V. PAVILANIS and J. STERNBERG, 1960, Studies in placental permeability. Transmission of poliomyelitis antibodies, lipoproteins and cholesterol in single and twin newborn infants. Am. J. Obstet. Gynec. *79*, 117–133.

GENCO, R. J. and M. A. TAUBMAN, 1969, Secretory γA antibodies induced by local immunization. Nature, Lond. *221*, 679–681.

GENGOZIAN, N., C. C. LUSHBAUGH, G. L. HUMASON, and R. M. KNISELEY, 1965, 'Erythroblastosis foetalis' in the primate, *Tamarinus nigricollis*. Nature, Lond. *209*, 731–732.

GILLETTE, D. D. and M. FILKINS, 1966, Factors affecting antibody transfer in the newborn puppy. Am. J. Physiol. *210*, 419–422.

GITLIN, D. and M. BOESMAN, 1966, Serum α-fetoprotein, albumin, and γG-globulin in the human conceptus. J. clin. Invest. *45*, 1826–1838.

GITLIN, D. and C. KOCH, 1968, On the mechanisms of maternofetal transfer of human albumin and γG globulin in the mouse. J. clin. Invest. *47*, 1204–1209.

GITLIN, D., J. KUMATE, J. URRUSTI and C. MORALES, 1964a, Selective and directional transfer of 7S γ2-globulin across the human placenta. Nature, Lond. *203*, 86–87.

GITLIN, D., J. KUMATE, J. URRUSTI and C. MORALES, 1964b, The selectivity of the human placenta in the transfer of plasma proteins from mother to fetus. J. clin. Invest. *43*, 1938–1951.

GITLIN, D. and L. G. MORPHIS, 1969, Systems of materno-foetal transport of γG immunoglobulin in the mouse. Nature, Lond. *223*, 195–196.

GOOD, R. A., R. M. CONDIE and R. A. BRIDGES, 1960, Development of the immune response in man and animals. *In:* Mechanisms of Antibody Formation. (Czechoslovak Academy of Sciences, Prague) pp. 118–129.

GOODWIN, R. F. W. and R. R. A. COOMBS, 1956, The blood groups of the pig. IV. The A antigen-antibody system and haemolytic disease in newborn piglets. J. comp. Path. Ther. *66*, 317–331.

GOODWIN, R. F. W., B. H. G. HAYWARD, D. H. HEARD and G. FULTON ROBERTS, 1955, Acquired haemolytic anaemia occurring in newborn piglets. Sang *26*, 24–30.

GOODWIN, R. F. W., D. H. HEARD, B. H. G. HAYWARD and G. FULTON ROBERTS, 1956, Haemolytic disease of the newborn piglet. J. Hyg., Camb. *54*, 153–171.

GOODWIN, R. F. W. and R. SAISON, 1957, The blood groups of the pig. V. Further observations on the epidemiology of haemolytic disease in the new-born. J. comp. Path. Ther. *67*, 126–144.

GOODWIN, R. F. W., R. SAISON and R. R. A. COOMBS, 1955, The blood groups of the pig. II. Red cell iso-antibodies in the sera of pigs injected with crystal violet swine fever vaccine. J. comp. Path. Ther. *65*, 79–92.

GORDON, J. E. and F. J. CURLEY, 1949, Induced latent infection and resultant active immunity to MM mouse encephalomyelitis virus in mice suckled by immune foster mothers. J. infect. Dis. *85*, 259–262.

GORDON, J. E. and J. H. JANNEY, 1941, Antistreptolysin content of the sera of normal infants and children. J. Pediat. *18*, 587–591.

GORINI, I. and G. LANZAVECCHIA, 1955, La livetina dell'uovo di pollo. Rc. Ist. lomb. Sci. Lett, B *88*, 951–959.

GRANEY, D. O., 1968, The uptake of ferritin by ileal absorptive cells in suckling rats. An electron microscope study. Am. J. Anat. *123*, 227–254.

GRASSET, E., H. DE WATTEVILLE and J. WIRTH, 1952, Passage transplacentaire des anticorps grippaux et antirickettsia et titrage comparatif de ces derniers dans la circulation maternelle et foetale. Schweiz. Z. allg. Path. Bakt. *15*, 484–490.

GRAVES, J. H., 1963, Transfer of neutralizing antibody by colostrum to calves born of foot-and-mouth disease vaccinated dams. J. Immun. *91*, 251–256.

GREEN, N. M., 1969, Electron microscopy of the immunoglobulins. Advances in Immunology (Academic Press, New York).

GROSSER, O., 1927, Frühentwicklung, Eihautbildung und Placentation des Menschen und der Sangetiere. (Bergmann, München).

GUGLER, E. and G. VON MURALT, 1959, Über immunoelektrophoretische Untersuchungen au Frauenmilchproteinen. Schweiz. med. Wschr. *89*, 925–929.

GWYNFOR JONES, T., K. L. G. GOLDSMITH and I. M. ANDERSON, 1961, Maternal and neonatal platelet antibodies in a case of congenital thrombocytopenia. Lancet *ii*, 1008–1009.

HAFEZ, E. S. E. and S. SUGAWARA, 1968, Maternal effects on some biochemical characteristics of the blastocyst in the domestic rabbit. J. Morph. *124*, 133–142.

HALASZ, N. A. and M. J. ORLOFF, 1963, Transplacental transmission of homotransplantation antibodies. J. exp. Med. *118*, 353–358.

HALE, J. H. and L. H. LEE, 1954, Transplacental passage of antibody to Japanese B encephalitis virus. J. Path. Bact. *68*, 631–632.

HALLIDAY, R., 1955a, The absorption of antibodies from immune sera by the gut of the young rat. Proc. R. Soc., B *143*, 408–413.

HALLIDAY, R., 1955b, Prenatal and postnatal transmission of passive immunity to young rats. Proc. R. Soc., B *144*, 427–430.

HALLIDAY, R., 1956, The termination of the capacity of young rats to absorb antibody from the milk. Proc. R. Soc., B *145*, 179–185.

HALLIDAY, R., 1957a, The production of antibodies by young rats. Proc. R. Soc., B *147*, 140–144.

HALLIDAY, R., 1957b, The absorption of antibody from immune sera and from mixtures of sera by the gut of the young rat. Proc. R. Soc., B *148*, 92–103.

HALLIDAY, R., 1959, The effect of steroid hormones on the absorption of antibody by the young rat. J. Endocr. *18*, 56–66.

HALLIDAY, R., 1964, The relationship between the occurrence of mortality and the development of active immunity in the young rat. Proc. R. Soc., B *161*, 208–215.

HALLIDAY, R., 1968, Effect of passive immunisation against *Brucella abortus* on active production of *Brucella abortus* agglutinins in young rats. J. Path. Bact. *96*, 137–148.

HALLIDAY, R. and R. A. KEKWICK, 1957, Electrophoretic analysis of the sera of young rats. Proc. R. Soc., B *146*, 431–437.

HALLIDAY, R. and R. A. KEKWICK, 1960, The selection of antibodies by the gut of the young rat. Proc. R. Soc., B *153*, 279–286.

HALPERN, B. H. and O. L. FRICK, 1962, Protection against fatal anaphylactic shock with γ-globulins in guinea pigs and mice. J. Immun. *88*, 683–689.

HALPERN, B. N., P. LIACOPOULOS, M. LIACOPOULOS-BRIOT, R. BINAGHI and F. VAN NEER, 1959, Patterns of *in vitro* sensitization of isolated smooth muscle tissues with precipitating antibody. Immunology *2*, 351–362.

HANSEN, R. G. and P. H. PHILLIPS, 1947, Studies on proteins from bovine colostrum. I. Electrophoretic studies on the blood serum proteins of colostrum-free calves and of calves fed colostrum at various ages. J. biol. Chem. *171*, 223–227.

HANSEN, R. G. and P. H. PHILLIPS, 1949, Studies on proteins from bovine colostrum. III. The homologous and heterologous transfer of ingested protein to the blood stream of the young animal. J. biol. Chem. *179*, 523–527.

HARDING, S. K., D. W. BRUNER and I. W. BRYANT, 1961, The transfer of antibodies from the mother cat to her newborn kittens. Cornell Vet. *51*, 535–538.

HARDY, R. N., 1965, Intestinal absorption of macromolecules in the new-born pig. J. Physiol., Lond. *176*, 19–20P.

HARMON, B. G., E. R. MILLER, D. E. ULLREY, D. A. SCHMIDT, J. A. HOEFER and R. W. LEUCKE, 1959, Antibody production in the baby pig. J. Anim. Sci. *18*, 1559–1560.

HARRIS, J. W. S. and E. M. RAMSEY, 1966, The morphology of human uteroplacental vasculature. Contr. Embryol. *38*, 43–58.

HARTLEY, P., 1948, The behaviour of different types of homologous and heterologous diphtheria antitoxin when administered to pregnant guinea-pigs. Mon. Bull. Minist. Hlth 7, 45–53.

HARTLEY, P., 1951, The effect of peptic digestion on the properties of diphtheria antitoxin. Proc. R. Soc., B *138*, 499–513.

HARTMAN, P. A., V. W. HAYS, R. O. BAKER, L. H. NEAGLE and D. V. CATRON, 1961, Digestive enzyme development in the young pig. J. Anim. Sci. *20*, 114–123.

HAYWARD, A. F., 1967, Changes in fine structure of developing intestinal epithelium associated with pinocytosis. J. Anat. *102*, 57–70.

HEARD, D. H., I. T. HINDE and L. S. MYNORS, 1949, An experimental study of haemolytic disease of the newborn due to isoimmunization of pregnancy. I. An attempt to produce the syndrome in the rabbit. J. Hyg., Camb. *47*, 119–131.

HEIM, W. G., 1961, The serum proteins of the rat during development. J. Embryol. exp. Morph. *9*, 52–59.

HEMMINGS, W. A., 1956, Protein selection in the yolk-sac splanchnopleur of the rabbit: the distribution of isotope following injection of ^{131}I-labelled serum globulin into the uterine cavity. Proc. R. Soc., B *145*, 186–195.

HEMMINGS, W. A., 1957, Protein selection in the yolk-sac splanchnopleur of the rabbit: the total uptake estimated as loss from the uterus. Proc. R. Soc., B *148*, 76–83.

HEMMINGS, W. A., 1961, Protein transfer and selection. *In:* M. Fishhein (ed.) First International Conference on Congenital Malformations, 1960. (J. B. Lippincott Co., Philadelphia and Montreal) pp. 223–229.

HEMMINGS, W. A. and R. E. JONES, 1962, The occurrence of macroglobulin antibodies in maternal and foetal sera of rabbits as determined by gradient centrifugation. Proc. R. Soc., B *157*, 27–32.

HEMMINGS, W. A. and I. G. MORRIS, 1959, An attempt to affect the selective absorption of antibodies from the gut in young mice. Proc. R. Soc., B *150*, 403–409.

HEMMINGS, W. A. and C. L. OAKLEY, 1957, Protein selection in the yolk-sac splanchnopleur of the rabbit: the fate of globulin injected into the foetal circulation. Proc. R. Soc., B *146*, 573–579.

HERTIG, A. T. and J. ROCK, 1945, Two human ova of the pre-villous stage, having a developmental age of about 7 and 9 days respectively. Contr. Embryol. *31*, 65–84.

HERVEY, E. J., 1966, The immunological response to a killed bacterial antigen in foetal and neonatal rats. Immunology *11*, 589–596.

HEUSER, C. H. and G. L. STREETER, 1941, Development of the macaque embryo. Contr. Embryol. *29*, 15–56.

HILL, J. P., 1932, The developmental history of the Primates. Phil. Trans. R. Soc. Ser. B *221*, 45–178.

HILL, K. J., 1956, Gastric development and antibody transference in the lamb, with some observations on the rat and guinea-pig. Q. Jl exp. Physiol. *41*, 421–432.

HILL, K. J. and W. S. HARDY, 1956, Histological and histochemical observations on the intestinal cells of lambs and kids absorbing colostrum. Nature, Lond. *178*, 1353–1354.

HIMENO, K., R. NAGANO, T. MORI, K. MOGI, T. ABE and T. HOSODA, 1968, Studies on haemolytic disease of new-born pigs. V. Changes in agglutination titres of colostrum and serum from sow producing affected litters. Jap. J. zootech. Sci. *39*, 275–280.

HIMENO, K., R. NAGANO, T. MORI, K. MOGI and T. HOSODA, 1967, Studies on the hemolytic disease of newborn pigs. II. Natural occurring isoimmunization of sows and hematological findings of pigs affected with hemolytic disease. Jap. J. zootech. Sci. *38*, 167–175.

HITZIG, W. H., 1959, Über die transplacentare Übertragung von Antikörpern. Schweiz. med. Wschr. *89*, 1249–1253.

HOERLEIN, A. B., 1952, Studies in swine Brucellosis. I. The pathogenesis of artificial *Brucella melitensis* infection. Am. J. vet. Res. *13*, 67–73.

HOERLEIN, A. B., 1957, The influence of colostrum on antibody response in baby pigs. J. Immun. *78*, 112–117.

HOLFORD, F. E., 1930, The placental transmission of foreign proteins in rabbits. J. Immun. *19*, 177–216.

HOWE, P. E., 1921, An effect of the ingestion of colostrum upon the composition of the blood of new-born calves. J. biol. Chem. *49*, 115–118.

HOWE, P. E., 1924, The relation between the ingestion of colostrum or blood serum and the appearance of globulin and albumin in the blood and urine of the new-born calf. J. exp. Med. *39*, 313–320.

HUBER, J. T., N. L. JACOBSON, R. S. ALLEN and P. A. HARTMAN, 1961, Digestive enzyme activities in the young calf. J. Dairy Sci. *44*, 1494–1501.

HUBRECHT, A. A. W., 1889, Studies in mammalian embryology. I. The placentation of *Erinaceus europaeus*, with remarks on the phylogeny of the placenta. Q. Jl microsc. Sci. *30*, 283–404.

HUGGETT, A. StG. and W. F. WIDDAS, 1951, The relationship between mammalian foetal weight and conception age. J. Physiol., Lond. *114*, 306–317.

HUMPHREY, J. H. and I. MOTA, 1959a, The mechanism of anaphylaxis: observations on the failure of antibodies from certain species to sensitize guinea-pigs in direct and reversed passive anaphylaxis. Immunology *2*, 19–30.

HUMPHREY, J. H. and I. MOTA, 1959b, The mechanism of anaphylaxis: specificity of antigen-induced mast cell damage in anaphylaxis in the guinea-pig. Immunology *2*, 31–43.

HURLIMANN, J., M. WALDESBÜHL and C. ZUBER, 1969, Human salivary immunoglobulin A. Some immunological and physicochemical characteristics. Biochim. biophys. Acta *181*, 393–403.

IRVIN, G. L., J. C. EUSTACE and J. L. FAHEY, 1967, Enhancement activity of mouse immunoglobulin classes. J. Immun. *99*, 1085–1091.

ISHIZAKA, T., K. ISHIZAKA, S. SALMON and H. FUDENBERG, 1967, Biologic activities of aggregated γ-globulin. VIII. Aggregated immunoglobulins of different classes. J. Immun. *99*, 82–91.

JAKOBSEN, P. E. and J. MOUSTGAARD, 1950, Investigations of the serum proteins in pigs from birth to maturity. Nord. VetMed. *2*, 812–824.

JAMESON, E., C. ALVAREZ-TOSTADO and H. H. SORTOR, 1942, Electrophoretic studies on new-born calf serum. Proc. Soc. exp. Biol. Med. *51*, 163–165.

JEAL, F., 1965, Functional changes in the intestinal mucosa of the young rat. Thesis (University of Wales).

JENKINSON, J. W., 1902, Observations on the histology and physiology of the placenta of the mouse. Tijdschr. ned. dierk. Vereen. *2*, 124–190.

Jo, K., 1953, On the transmission of antibodies from mothers to their offspring in experimental typhus fever, experiments in albino rats and guinea-pigs. Jap. J. med. Sci. Biol. *6*, 299–310.

Johansson, S. G. O., H. Bennich and L. Wide, 1968, A new class of immunoglobulin in human serum. Immunology *14*, 265–272.

Johnson, E. M. and R. Spinuzzi, 1966, Enzymic differentiation of rat yolk-sac placenta as affected by a teratogenic agent. J. Embryol. exp. Morph. *16*, 271–288.

Johnson, E. M. and R. Spinuzzi, 1968, Differentiation of alkaline phosphatase and glucose-6-phosphate dehydrogenase in rat yolk-sac. J. Embryol. exp. Morph. *19*, 137–143.

Johnson, P. and A. E. Pierce, 1959, Ultracentrifugal and electrophoretic studies on neonatal calf sera and maternal colostrum. J. Hyg., Camb. *57*, 309–320.

Jollie, W. P., 1968, Changes in the fine structure of the parietal yolk sac of the rat placenta with increasing gestational age. Am. J. Anat. *122*, 513–531.

Jonas, W. E., 1969, The distribution and properties of IgM in some body fluids of sheep. Res. vet. Sci. *10*, 83–92.

Jones, R. E., 1966, Studies on the proteolytic enzymes of the foetal yolk sac of the rabbit. Thesis (University of Wales).

Jones, V. E., 1969, Rat 7S immunoglobulins: characterization of γ_2- and γ_1-anti-hapten antibodies. Immunology *16*, 589–599.

Jordan, S. M. and E. H. Morgan, 1967, Albumin, transferrin and gamma-globulin metabolism during lactation in the rat. Q. Jl exp. Physiol. *52*, 422–429.

Jordan, S. M. and E. H. Morgan, 1968, The development of selectivity of protein absorption from the intestine during suckling in the rat. Aust. J. exp. Biol. med. Sci. *46*, 465–472.

Jukes, T. H., D. T. Fraser and M. D. Orr, 1934, The transmission of diphtheria antitoxin from hen to egg. J. Immun. *26*, 353–360.

Jukes, T. H. and H. D. Kay, 1932, The immunological behaviour of the second protein (livetin) of hen's egg yolk. J. exp. Med. *56*, 469–482.

Kaeberle, M. L., 1968, Colostrum and immunologic competence. Vet. Bull. *38*, 695 (abstract).

Kaliss, N., 1968, Transfer from mother to offspring of antifetal antibody induced in the mouse by multiparity. Proc. Soc. exp. Biol. Med. *129*, 83–85.

Kaliss, N. and M. K. Dagg, 1964, Immune response engendered in mice by multiparity. Transplantation *2*, 416–425.

Kaliss, N., M. K. Dagg and J. H. Stimpfling, 1963, Maternal transfer of isoantibody in mice. Transplantation *1*, 535–545.

Kaliss, N. and P. Rubinstein, 1968, Absence of correlation between presence of pregnancy-induced hemagglutinins and stage of pregnancy in mice. Proc. Soc. exp. Biol. Med. *128*, 1214–1217.

Kalmutz, S. E., 1962, Antibody production in the opossum embryo. Nature, Lond. *193*, 851–853.

Kaminski, M. and J. Durieux, 1956, Étude comparative des sérums de poule, de coq, de poussin, d'embryon et de blanc d'oeuf. Expl Cell Res. *10*, 590–618.

Kammeraad, A., 1942, The development of the gastro-intestinal tract of the rat. I. Histogenesis of the epithelium of the stomach, small intestine and pancreas. J. Morph. *70*, 323–351.

KAPLAN, K. C., E. A. CATSOULIS and E. C. FRANKLIN, 1965, Maternal-foetal transfer of human immune globulins and fragments in rabbits. Immunology *8*, 354–359.

KARTHIGASU, K. and C. R. JENKIN, 1963, The functional development of the reticulo-endothelial system of the chick embryo. Immunology *6*, 255–263.

KARTHIGASU, K., C. R. JENKIN and K. J. TURNER, 1964, The nature of the opsonin in adult hen serum and developing chick embryos to certain gram-negative bacteria. Aust. J. exp. Biol. med. Sci. *42*, 499–510.

KEELER, C. E. and W. E. CASTLE, 1933, A further study of blood groups of the rabbit. Proc. natn. Acad. Sci. U.S.A. *19*, 403–411.

KEELER, C. E. and W. E. CASTLE, 1934a, Blood group incompatibility in rabbit embryos and in man. Proc. natn. Acad. Sci. U.S.A. *20*, 273–276.

KEELER, C. E. and W. E. CASTLE, 1934b, The influence of pregnancy upon the titre of immune (blood-group) antibodies in the rabbit. Proc. natn. Acad. Sci. U.S.A. *20*, 465–470.

KEKWICK, R. A., 1959, The serum proteins of the fetus and young of some mammals. Adv. Protein Chem. *14*, 231–254.

KEKWICK, R. A. and M. E. MACKAY, 1954, The separation of protein fractions from human plasma with ether. Medical Research Council Special Report Series No. 286.

KEKWICK, R. A. and P. L. MOLLISON, 1961, Blood group antibodies associated with the 19S and 7S components of human sera. Vox Sang. *6*, 398–408.

KEKWICK, R. A. and B. R. RECORD, 1940, Some physical properties of diphtheria antitoxic horse sera. Br. J. exp. Path. *22*, 29–44.

KELLEHER, P. C., C. D. KENYON and C. A. VILLEE, 1963, Serum protein synthesis by the fetal rat. Science *139*, 839–840.

KELLEHER, P. C. and C. A. VILLEE, 1962, A protein present in fetal but not in maternal rat serum. Science *138*, 510–511.

KELLNER, A. and E. F. HEDAL, 1952, Experimental erythroblastosis fetalis. Am. J. Path. *28*, 539–540.

KELLNER, A. and E. F. HEDAL, 1953a, Experimental erythroblastosis fetalis in rabbits. I. Characterization of a pair of allelic blood group factors and their specific immune isoantibodies. J. exp. Med. *97*, 33–49.

KELLNER, A. and E. F. HEDAL, 1953b, Experimental erythroblastosis fetalis in rabbits. II. The passage of blood group antigens and their specific isoantibodies across the placenta. J. exp. Med. *97*, 51–60.

KELLY, D. F., 1964, Experimental infection of pigs with a porcine enterovirus (F7). J. comp. Path. Ther. *74*, 381–397.

KEMP, T., 1930, Uber den empfindlichkeitsgrad der blutkörperchen gegenüber isohämag-glutininen im fëtalleben und im kindesalter beim menschen. Acta path. microbiol. scand. *7*, 146–156.

KEMPE, C. H. and A. S. BENENSON, 1953, Vaccinia. Passive immunity in newborn infants. I. Placental transmission of antibodies. II. Response to vaccinations. J. Pediat. *42*, 525–531.

KENDRICK, P., M. THOMPSON and G. ELDERING, 1945, Immunity response of mothers and

342   *References*

babies to injections of pertussis vaccine during pregnancy. Am. J. Dis. Child. *70*, 25–28.

KERMAN, R., D. SEGRE and W. L. MYERS, 1967, Altered response to pneumococcal poly-saccharide in offspring of immunologically paralyzed mice. Science *156*, 1514–1516.

KERR, W. R. and M. ROBERTSON, 1946, A study of the passively acquired antibody to *Tr. foetus* in the blood of young calves and its behaviour in agglutination tests and intradermal reactions. J. comp. Path. Ther. *56*, 38–48.

KERR, W. R. and M. ROBERTSON, 1954, Passively and actively acquired antibodies for *Trichomonas foetus* in very young calves. J. Hyg., Camb. *52*, 253–263.

KERSHAW, G. F., 1950, Notes on deaths in young piglets similar to the haemolytic disease in young foals. Vet. Rec. *62*, 383.

KIDDY, C. A., W. H. STONE, W. J. TYLER and L. E. CASIDA, 1958, Immunological studies on fertility and sterility I. An attempt to produce hemolytic disease in cattle by isoim-munization. Acta haemat. *20*, 236–245.

KIM, Y. B., S. G. BRADLEY and D. W. WATSON, 1964, Development of immunoglobulins in germfree and conventional colostrum-deprived piglets. Fedn Proc. Fedn Am. Socs exp. Biol. *23*, 346.

KIM, Y. B., S. G. BRADLEY and D. W. WATSON, 1966, Ontogeny of the immune response. I. Development of immunoglobulins in germfree and conventional colostrum-deprived piglets. J. Immun. *97*, 52–63.

KING, C. A. and G. E. FRANCIS, 1967, Adsorption of heterologous γ-globulins by chopped guinea-pig lung. Immunology *13*, 1–8.

KIRBY, D. R. S., D. M. POTTS and I. B. WILSON, 1967, On the orientation of the implanting blastocyst. J. Embryol. exp. Morph. *17*, 527–532.

KISSLING, R. E., M. E. EIDSON and D. D. STAMM, 1954, Transfer of maternal neutralizing antibodies against eastern equine encephalomyelitis virus in birds. J. infect. Dis *95*, 179–181.

KLAUS, G. G. B., A. BENNETT and E. W. JONES, 1969, A quantitative study of the transfer of colostral immunoglobulins to the newborn calf. Immunology *16*, 293–299.

KLEMPERER, F., 1893, Über natürliche Immunität und ihre Verwerthung für die Im-munisierungstherapie. Arch. exp. Path. Pharmak. *31*, 356–382.

KNIGHT, P. F. and A. M. SCHECHTMAN, 1954, The passage of heterologous serum proteins from the circulation into the ovum of the fowl. J. exp. Zool. *127*, 271–304.

KOCH, C., M. BOESMAN and D. GITLIN, 1967, Maternofoetal transfer of γG immunoglo-bulins. Nature, Lond. *216*, 1116–1117.

KOCHWA, S., R. E. ROSENFIELD, L. TALLAL and L. R. WASSERMAN, 1961, Isoagglutinins associated with ABO erythroblastosis. J. clin. Invest. *40*, 874–883.

KOHLER, P. F. and R. S. FARR, 1966, Elevation of cord over maternal IgG immunoglobulin: Evidence for an active placental IgG transport. Nature, Lond. *210*, 1070–1071.

KOLDOVSKY, O., P. SUNSHINE and N. KRETCHMER, 1966, Cellular migration of intestinal epithelia in suckling and weaned rats. Nature, Lond. *212*, 1389–1390.

KOLODNY, M. H., 1939, The transmission of immunity in experimental trypanosomiasis (*Trypanosoma cruzi*) from mother rats to their offspring. Am. J. Hyg. *30*, 19–39.

KOSUNEN, T. U. and P. HALONEN, 1963, Transmission of maternal tetanus immunity to offspring in mice. Annls Med. exp. Biol. Fenn. *41*, 571–575.

KRAEHENBUHL, J. P., E. GLOOR and B. BLANC, 1966, Morphologie comparée de la muqueuse intestinale de deux espèces animales aux possibilités d'absorption protéique néonatale différentes. Z. Zellforsch. mikrosk. Anat. *70*, 209–219.

KRAEHENBUHL, J. P., E. GLOOR and B. BLANC, 1967, Résorption intestinale de la ferritine chez deux espèces animales aux possibilités d'absorption protéique néonatale différentes Z. Zellforsch. mikrosk. Anat. *76*, 170–186.

KRUSE, V., 1969, Resorption of immunglobulin fra kolostrum hos nyfødte kalve. Afdelingen for Husdyrbrug. Den Kgl. Veterinær- og Landbohøjskole, København.

KULANGARA, A. C., M. K. KRISHNA MENON and M. WILLMOTT, 1965, Passage of bovine serum albumin from the uterine lumen into the human foetus. Nature, Lond. *206*, 1259–1260.

KULANGARA, A. C. and A. M. SCHECHTMAN, 1962, Passage of heterologous serum proteins from mother into fetal compartments in the rabbit. Am. J. Physiol. *203*, 1071–1080.

KULANGARA, A. C. and A. M. SCHECHTMAN, 1963, Do heterologous proteins pass from mother to fetus in cow, cat and guinea pig? Proc. Soc. exp. Biol. Med. *112*, 220–222.

KUTTNER, A. and B. RATNER, 1923, The importance of colostrum to the new-born infant. Am. J. Dis. Child. *25*, 413–434.

KYFFIN, S. E., 1967, Premature termination of the transmission of immunity in the runted mouse. Immunology *13*, 319–322.

LAMBOTTE, R., 1963, Étude immunoélectrophorétique du liquide amniotique de lapin. C. r. Séanc. Soc. Biol. *157*, 1849–1850.

LAMBSON, R. O., 1966, An electron microscopic visualization of transport across rat visceral yolk sac. Am. J. Anat. *118*, 21–52.

LANDSTEINER, K. and A. S. WIENER, 1940, An agglutinable factor in human blood recognised by immune sera for rhesus blood. Proc. Soc. exp. Biol. Med. *43*, 223.

LANMAN, J. T. and L. HEROD, 1965, Homograft immunity in pregnancy. The placental transfer of cytotoxic antibody in rabbits. J. exp. Med. *122*, 579–586.

LARSEN, J. F., 1961, Electron microscopy of the implantation site in the rabbit. Am. J. Anat. *109*, 319–334.

LARSEN, J. F., 1962a, Electron microscopy of the uterine epithelium in the rabbit. J. cell. Biol. *14*, 49–64.

LARSEN, J. F., 1962b, Electron microscopy of the chorioallantoic placenta of the rabbit. 1. The placental labyrinth and the multinucleated giant cells of the intermediate zone. J. Ultrastruct. Res. *7*, 535–549.

LARSEN, J. F., 1963a, Histology and fine structure of the avascular and vascular yolk-sac placentae and the obplacental giant cells in the rabbit. Am. J. Anat. *112*, 269–284.

LARSEN, J. F., 1963b, Electron microscopy of the chorioallantoic placenta of the rabbit. 2. The decidua and the maternal vessels. J. Ultrastruct. Res. *8*, 327–338.

LARSEN, J. F. and J. DAVIES, 1962, The paraplacental chorion and accessory fetal membranes of the rabbit. Histology and electron microscopy. Anat. Rec. *143*, 27–46.

LARSH, J. E., 1942, Transmission from mother to offspring of immunity against the mouse cestode, *Hymenolepis nana* var. *fraterna*. Am. J. Hyg. *36*, 187–194.

LARSON, B. L., 1958, Transfer of specific blood serum proteins to lacteal secretions near parturition. J. Dairy Sci. *41*, 1033–1044.

LARSON, B. L. and K. A. KENDALL, 1957, Changes in specific blood serum protein levels associated with parturition in the bovine. J. Dairy Sci. *40*, 659–666.

LASCELLES, A. K., P. M. OUTTERIDGE and D. D. S. MACKENZIE, 1966, Local production of antibody by the lactating mammary gland following antigenic stimulation. Aust. J. exp. Biol. med. Sci. *44*, 169–180.

LASKOWSKI, M., B. KASSELL and G. HAGERTY, 1957, A crystalline trypsin inhibitor from swine colostrum. Biochim. biophys. Acta *24*, 300–305.

LASKOWSKI, M. and M. LASKOWSKI, 1951, Crystalline trypsin inhibitor from colostrum. J. biol. Chem. *190*, 563–573.

LAURELL, C. B. and E. H. MORGAN, 1965, The relation between the proteins of plasma and milk in the rat. Biochim. biophys. Acta *100*, 128–135.

LECCE, J. G., 1966, *In vitro* absorption of γ-globulin by neonatal intestinal epithelium of the pig. J. Physiol., Lond. *184*, 594–604.

LECCE, J. G. and G. MATRONE, 1960, Porcine neonatal nutrition: the effect of diet on blood serum proteins and performance of the baby pig. J. Nutr. *70*, 13–20.

LECCE, J. G., G. MATRONE and D. O. MORGAN, 1961, Porcine neonatal nutrition: absorption of unaltered nonporcine proteins and polyvinylpyrrolidone from the gut of piglets and the subsequent effect on the maturation of the serum protein profile. J. Nutr. *73*, 158–166.

LECCE, J. G. and D. O. MORGAN, 1962, Effect of dietary regimen on cessation of intestinal absorption of large molecules (closure) in the neonatal pig and lamb. J. Nutr. *78*, 263–268.

LECCE, J. G., D. O. MORGAN and G. MATRONE, 1964, Effect of feeding colostral and milk components on the cessation of intestinal absorption of large molecules (closure) in neonatal pigs. J. Nutr. *84*, 43–48.

LEISSRING, J. C. and J. W. ANDERSON, 1961a, The transfer of serum proteins from mother to young in the guinea pig. I. Prenatal rates and routes. Am. J. Anat. *109*, 149–156.

LEISSRING, J. C. and J. W. ANDERSON, 1961b, The transfer of serum proteins from mother to young in the guinea pig. III. Postnatal studies. Am. J. Anat. *109*, 175–182.

LEISSRING, J. C., J. W. ANDERSON and D. W. SMITH, 1962, Uptake of antibodies by the intestine of the newborn infant. Am. J. Dis. Child. *103*, 160–165.

LEMÉTAYER, E., L. NICOL, L. JACOB, O. GIRARD and R. CORVAZIER, 1946a, Immunité antitoxique diaplacentaire du poulain issu de juments immunisées. C. r. Séanc. Soc. Biol. *140*, 852–854.

LEMÉTAYER, E., L. NICOL, L. JACOB, O. GIRARD and R. CORVAZIER, 1946b, Immunité antitoxique colostrale du poulain issu de juments immunisées. C. r. Séanc. Soc. Biol. *140*, 854–856.

LEVI, M. I., F. E. KRAVTZOV, T. M. LEVOVA and G. A. FOMENKO, 1969, The ability of maternal antibody to increase the immune response in infants. Immunology *16*, 145–148.

LEVINE, P., L. BURNHAM, E. M. KATZIN and P. VOGEL, 1941, The role of iso-immunization in the pathogenesis of erythroblastosis fetalis. Am. J. Obstet. Gynec. *42*, 925–937.

LEVINE, P. and E. M. KATZIN, 1940, Isoimmunization in pregnancy and the varieties of isoagglutinins observed. Proc. Soc. exp. Biol. Med. *45*, 343–346.

LEVINE, P. and R. E. STETSON, 1939, An unusual case of intra-group agglutination. J. Am. med. Ass. *113*, 126–127.

LEWIS, W. H. and C. G. HARTMAN, 1933, Early cleavage stages of the egg of the monkey (*Macacus rhesus*). Contr. Embryol. *24*, 187–201.

LEWIS, W. P. and E. K. MARKELL, 1958, Aquisition of immunity to toxoplasmosis by the newborn rat. Expl Parasit. *7*, 463–467.

LIACOPOULOS, M., B. N. HALPERN, P. LIACOPOULOS and M. F. PERRAMANT, 1963, Comportement des γ-globulines et des fractions I et III de Porter en tant qu'antigènes dans l'anaphylaxie passive in vitro. C. r. Séanc. Soc. Biol. *57*, 76–82.

LICHTY, J. A., C. P. KATSAMPES and W. S. BAUM, 1943, A study of humoral antibodies for staphylococcus aureus in infants and their mothers. J. Pediat. *22*, 549–558.

LIEBLING, J. and H. E. SCHMITZ, 1943, Protection of the infant against diphtheria during the first year of life following the active immunization of the pregnant mother. J. Pediat. *23*, 430–436.

LILLIE, F. R., 1927, The Development of the Chick. (Henry Holt and Co., New York).

LINKLATER, K. A., 1968, Iso-immunisation in the parturient sow by foetal red cells. Vet. Rec. *83*, 203–204.

LIPTON, M. M. and A. J. STEIGMAN, 1957, Neonatal immunity. I. Disparity in maternal-infant poliovirus antibody. Proc. Soc. exp. Biol. Med. *96*, 348–352.

LOCKE, R. F., D. SEGRE and W. L. MYERS, 1964, The immunologic behaviour of baby pigs. IV. Intestinal absorption and persistence of 6.6S and 18S antibodies of ovine origin and their role in the immunologic competence of baby pigs. J. Immun. *93*, 576–583.

LONG, C. H., D. E. ULLREY and E. R. MILLER, 1964a, Alkaline phosphatase studies on sow colostrum and on serum and tissues of the neonatal pig. J. Anim. Sci. *23*, 882 (abstract).

LONG, C. H., D. E. ULLREY and E. R. MILLER, 1964b, Serum protein electrophoresis, immunoelectrophoresis and tagged protein in pigs deprived of colostrum. J. Anim. Sci. *23*, 882 (abstract).

LONGSWORTH, L. G., R. M. CURTIS and R. H. PEMBROKE, 1945, The electrophoretic analysis of maternal and fetal plasmas and sera. J. clin. Invest. *24*, 46–53.

LUNSFORD, L. and H. F. DEUTSCH, 1957, Human milk whey proteins. Proc. Soc. exp. Biol. Med. *96*, 742–744.

LUSE, S. A., 1958, The morphologic manifestations of uptake of materials by the yolk sac of the pregnant rabbit. *In:* C. A. Villee (ed.) Gestation, Transactions of the Fourth Conference, 1957, (Josiah Macy Jr. Foundation, New York) pp. 115–141.

LUTWAK-MANN, C., 1954, Some properties of the rabbit blastocyst. J. Embryol. exp. Morph. *2*, 1–13.

LUTWAK-MANN, C., J. C. BOURSNELL and J. P. BENNETT, 1960, Blastocyst-uterine relationships: uptake of radioactive ions by the early rabbit embryo and its environment. J. Reprod. Fert. *1*, 169–185.

LUTWAK-MANN, C. and H. LASER, 1954, Bicarbonate content of the blastocyst fluid and carbonic anhydrase in the pregnant rabbit uterus. Nature, Lond. *173*, 268.

MCALPINE, J. G. and L. F. RETTGER, 1925, Serological studies on bovine infectious abortion. J. Immun. *10*, 811–828.

McArthur, C. L., 1919, Transmissibility of immunity from mother to offspring in hog cholera. J. infect. Dis. *24*, 45–50.

McCance, R. A. and J. W. T. Dickerson, 1957, The composition and origin of the foetal fluids of the pig. J. Embryol. exp. Morph. *5*, 43–50.

McCance, R. A., A. O. Hutchinson, R. F. A. Dean and P. E. H. Jones, 1949, The cholinesterase activity of the serum of newborn animals and of colostrum. Biochem. J. *45*, 493–496.

McCance, R. A. and E. M. Widdowson, 1959, The effect of colostrum on the composition and volume of the plasma of new-born piglets. J. Physiol., Lond. *145*, 547–550.

McCarthy, E. F. and R. A. Kekwick, 1949, The passage into the embryonic yolk-sac cavity of maternal plasma proteins in rabbits. Addendum. J. Physiol., Lond. *108*, 184–185.

McCarthy, E. F. and E. I. McDougall, 1949, Absorption of immune globulin by the young lamb after ingestion of colostrum. Nature, Lond. *164*, 354.

McCarthy, E. F. and E. I. McDougall, 1953, Absorption of immune globulin by the young lamb after ingestion of colostrum. Biochem. J. *55*, 177–182.

McDiarmid, A., 1946, The transference of agglutinins for *Brucella abortus* from cow to calf and their persistence in the calf's blood. Vet. Rec. *58*, 146–149.

MacDonald, A., 1950, Incidence of toxoplasma infection in north-west England. Transmission of antibody from mother to foetus. Lancet *ii*, 560–562.

MacDougall, D. F. and W. Mulligan, 1969, The distribution and metabolism of fast IgG immunoglobulin in the neonatal calf. J. Physiol., Lond. *201*, 77P.

Mackenzie, I. L., R. M. Donaldson, W. L. Kopp and J. S. Trier, 1968, Antibodies to intestinal microvillous membranes. II. Inhibition of intrinsic factor-mediated attachment of vitamin B_{12} to hamster brush borders. J. exp. Med. *128*, 375–386.

Magara, M., 1936, On natural and immune antitoxin of diphtheria in the newborn and sucklings. Jap. J. exp. Med. *14*, 355–370.

Malkinson, M., 1965, The transmission of passive immunity to *Escherichia coli* from mother to young in the domestic fowl (*Gallus domesticus*). Immunology *9*, 311–317.

Malkinson, M. H., 1967, Transference of maternal passive immunity to vaccinia virus in mice. Nature, Lond. *216*, 1117–1118.

Mancini, R. E., O. Vilar, J. J. Heinrich, O. W. Davidson and B. Alvarez, 1963, Transference of circulating labeled serum proteins to the follicle of the rat ovary. J. Histochem. Cytochem. *11*, 80–88.

Mandy, W. J., M. E. Woolsey and F. B. Lewis, 1968, A new serum factor in normal rabbits. IV. Occurrence in neonatal rabbit sera. J. Immun. *100*, 15–23.

Manville, I. A. and R. W. Lloyd, 1932, The hydrogen ion concentration of the gastric juice of fetal and newborn white rats. Am. J. Physiol. *100*, 394–401.

Manzallo, A. and A. O. L. Martino, 1963, Estudio de transmision transplacentaria de la immunidad antidifterica y ensayos de vacunacion en el cobayo recien nacido. Revta Asoc. méd. argent. *77*, 423–428.

Mårtensson, L., 1962, Anti-Gm molecules with distinctly different physicochemical properties. Acta path. microbiol. scand. *56*, 352.

Mårtensson, L. and H. H. Fudenberg, 1965, Gm genes and γG-globulin synthesis in the human fetus. J. Immun. *94*, 514–520.

MARZA, V. D. and E. V. MARZA, 1935, The formation of the hens egg. Q. Jl microsc. Sci. *78*, 133–249.

MASON, J. H., T. DALLING and W. S. GORDON, 1930, Transmission of maternal immunity. J. Path. Bact. *33*, 783–797.

MATHOT, C. and S. SCHER, 1968, Transmission through milk of antibodies against the Friend virus in mice. Nature, Lond. *219*, 82–83.

MAUNG, R. T., 1963, Immunity in the tortoise, *Testudo ibera*. J. Path. Bact. *85*, 51–66.

MAUSS, E. A., 1940, Transmission of immunity to *Trichinella spiralis* from infected animals to their offspring. Am. J. Hyg. *32*, 75–79.

MAYERSBACH, H., 1958, Zur frage des proteinüberganges von der mutter zum foeten. I. Befunde an ratten am ende der schwangerschaft. Z. Zellforsch. mikrosk. Anat. *48*, 479–504.

MEADER, R. D. and D. F. LANDERS, 1967, Electron and light microscopic observations on relationships between lymphocytes and intestinal epithelium. Am. J. Anat. *121*, 763–774.

MELNICK, J. L., N. A. CLARKE and L. M. KRAFT, 1950, Immunological reactions of the Coxsackie viruses. III. Cross-protection tests in infant mice born of vaccinated mothers. Transfer of immunity through milk. J. exp. Med. *92*, 499–505.

MILLER, E. R., B. G. HARMON, D. E. ULLREY, D. A. SCHMIDT, R. W. LUECKE and J. A. HOEFER, 1962, Antibody absorption, retention and production by the baby pig. J. Anim. Sci. *21*, 309–314.

MILLER, H. M., 1932, Transmission to offspring of immunity against infection with a metazoan (cestode) parasite. Proc. Soc. exp. Biol. Med. *29*, 1124.

MILLER, J. J., H. K. FABER, M. L. RYAN, R. J. SILVERBERG and E. LEW, 1949, Immunization against pertussis during the first four months of life. Pediatrics, Springfield *4*, 468–478.

MILLER, W. T. and J. O. HEISHMAN, 1943, Staphylococcal antitoxin in the blood, milk and colostrum of cows. Am. J. vet. Res. *4*, 265–269.

MILLOT, P. and J. GORIUS, 1950, Considérations sur la physiopathologie de l'ictère hémolytique du muleton. – Rôle de l'allaitement. – Importance du colostrum. Revue Path. comp. Hyg. gén. *50*, 85–107.

MILSTEIN, C. P. and A. FEINSTEIN, 1968a, Structural differences and similarities between two bovine immunoglobulins, IgG1 and IgG2. A.R.C. Institute of Animal Physiology, Babraham, Cambridge, Report for 1966–1967, p. 41.

MILSTEIN, C. P. and A. FEINSTEIN, 1968b, Comparative studies of two types of bovine immunoglobulin G heavy chains. Biochem. J. *107*, 559–564.

MINETT, F. C., 1937, Staphylococcus antitoxin in the blood and milk of cows and other animals. J. comp. Path. Ther. *50*, 173–190.

MINNING, W., 1936, Zur frage der auf dem Wege über die plazenta und durch den saugakt erworbenen immunitätgegen *Trypanosoma lewisi*. Zentbl. Bakt. ParasitKde (Abt I) *135*, 469–472.

MITCHISON, N. A., 1953, The effect on the offspring of maternal immunization in mice. J. Genet. *51*, 406–420.

MOGI, K., T. HOSODA and K. HIMENO, 1966, Studies on the haemolytic disease of newborn pigs. Jap. J. zootech. Sci. *37*, 296–301.

MOLLISON, P. L., 1967, Blood Transfusion in Clinical Medicine. 4th ed. (Blackwell, Oxford).

MONGAR, J. L. and H. O. SCHILD, 1957, Effect of temperature on the anaphylactic reaction. J. Physiol., Lond. *135*, 320–338.

MONGAR, J. L. and H. O. SCHILD, 1960, A study of the mechanism of passive sensitization. J. Physiol., Lond. *150*, 546–564.

MOOG, F., 1951, The functional differentiation of the small intestine. II. The differentiation of alkaline phosphomonoesterase in the duodenum of the mouse. J. exp. Zool. *118*, 187–207.

MOOG, F., 1953, The functional differentiation of the small intestine. III. The influence of the pituitary-adrenal system on the differentiation of phosphatase in the duodenum of the suckling mouse. J. exp. Zool. *124*, 329–346.

MOOG, F., 1961, The functional differentiation of the small intestine. VIII. Regional differences in the alkaline phophatases of the small intestine of the mouse from birth to one year. Devl Biol. *3*, 153–174.

MOOG, F. and E. R. THOMAS, 1955, The influence of various adrenal and gonadal steroids on the accumulation of alkaline phosphatase in the duodenum of the suckling mouse. Endocrinology *56*, 187–196.

MOORE, D. H., R. M. DU PAN and C. L. BUXTON, 1949, An electrophoretic study of maternal, fetal and infant sera. Am. J. Obstet. Gynec. *57*, 312–322.

MORGAN, D. O. and J. G. LECCE, 1964, Electrophoretic and immunoelectrophoretic analysis of the proteins in the sow's mammary secretions throughout lactation. Res. vet. Sci. *5*, 332–339.

MORGAN, E. H., 1964, Passage of transferrin, albumin and gamma globulin from maternal plasma to foetus in the rat and rabbit. J. Physiol., Lond. *171*, 26–41.

MORRIS, B., 1950, The structure of the foetal yolk-sac splanchnopleur of the rabbit. Q. Jl microsc. Sci. *91*, 237–249.

MORRIS, B., 1953, The yolk-sacs of *Erinaceus europea* and *Putorius furo*. J. Embryol. exp. Morph. *1*, 147–160.

MORRIS, B., 1957, Some histochemical observations on the endometrium and the yolk-sac placenta of *Erinaceus europea*. J. Embryol. exp. Morph. *5*, 184–200.

MORRIS, B., 1959, Transmission of passive immunity in an insectivore. Nature, Lond. *184*, 1151.

MORRIS, B., 1960, The transmission of anti-Brucella agglutinins from the mother to the young in *Erinaceus europaea*. Proc. R. Soc., B *152*, 137–141.

MORRIS, B., 1961a, Some observations on the breeding season of the hedgehog and the rearing and handling of the young. Proc. zool. Soc. Lond. *136*, 201–206.

MORRIS, B., 1961b, The transmission of anti-Salmonella agglutinins from the mother to the young in *Erinaceus europaea*, with some observations on the active immunization of suckling hedgehogs. Proc. R. Soc., B *154*, 369–376.

MORRIS, B., 1963, The selection of antibodies by the gut of the young hedgehog. Proc. R. Soc., B *158*, 253–260.

MORRIS, B. and R. W. BALDWIN, 1962, The distribution of antibody activity in hedgehog serum. Proc. R. Soc., B *155*, 551–556.

MORRIS, B. and E. D. STEEL, 1964, The absorption of antibody by young hedgehogs after treatment with cortisone acetate. J. Endocr. *30*, 195–203.

MORRIS, B. and E. D. STEEL, 1967, Gastric and duodenal differentiation in *Erinaceus europaeus* and its relationship to antibody absorption. J. Zool. Lond. *152*, 257–267.

MORRIS, I. G., 1956, Studies on the effects of immunological incompatibility on the young in mice. Thesis (University of Wales).

MORRIS, I. G., 1957, The effects of heterologous sera on the uptake of rabbit antibody from the gut of young mice. Proc. R. Soc., B *148*, 84–91.

MORRIS, I. G., 1958, Experimentally induced haemolytic disease in young mice. J. Path. Bact. *75*, 201–210.

MORRIS, I. G., 1961, The effects of anti-leucocyte-platelet serum on young mice, J. Path. Bact. *81*, 209–224.

MORRIS, I. G., 1963a, Transmission of anti-*Brucella abortus* agglutinins across the gut in young mice. Nature, Lond. *197*, 813–814.

MORRIS, I. G., 1963b, Interference with the uptake of guinea-pig agglutinins in mice due to fractions of papain hydrolyzed rabbit γ-globulin. Proc. R. Soc., B *157*, 160–169.

MORRIS, I. G., 1964, The transmission of antibodies and normal γ-globulins across the young mouse gut. Proc. R. Soc., B *160*, 276–292.

MORRIS, I. G., 1965, The transmission of anti-*Brucella abortus* agglutinins across the gut in young rats. Proc. R. Soc., B *163*, 402–416.

MORRIS, I. G., 1967, The transmission of bovine anti-*Brucella abortus* agglutinins across the gut of suckling rats. Immunology *13*, 49–61.

MORRIS, I. G., 1968, Gamma globulin absorption in the newborn. *In:* C.F. Code (ed.) Handbook of Physiology – Alimentary Canal. Sec. 6, Vol. 3 (Am. Physiol. Soc., Baltimore).

MOSINGER, B., Z. PLACER and O. KOLDOVSKY, 1959, Passage of insulin through the wall of the gastro-intestinal tract of the infant rat. Nature, Lond. *184*, 1245–1246.

MOSSMAN, H. W., 1926, The rabbit placenta and the problem of placental transmission. Am. J. Anat. *37*, 433–497.

MOSSMAN, H. W., 1937, Comparative morphogenesis of the fetal membranes and accessory uterine structures. Contr. Embryol. *479*, 129–246.

MOULINIER, J., 1953, L'allaitement maternel des enfants atteints de maladie hémolytique. Sem. Hôp. Paris (Sem. Méd.) *29*, No. 9, 1–6.

MOURANT, A. E., 1954, The Distribution of the Human Blood Groups. (Blackwells, Oxford).

MOUTON, R. F., L.-L. MARGADANT, R. A. COLLET, P. ROWINSKI and M. BEIN, 1957, Transfert oral de gamma-globulines chez le lapin et le nourisson. Bull. Soc. Chim. biol. *39*, 119–134.

MURPHY, F. A., O. AALUND, J. W. OSEBOLD and E. J. CARROLL, 1964, Gamma-globulins of bovine lacteal secretions. Archs Biochem. Biophys. *108*, 230–239.

MURRAY, J. and R. M. CALMAN, 1953, Immunity of the newborn. A study of the transfer of anti-streptolysin from mother to foetus during pregnancy. Br. med. J. *1*, 13–15.

MURRAY, J., R. M. CALMAN and A. LEPINE, 1950, Transmission of staphylococcal anti-toxin (anti-haemolysin) from mother to child. Lancet *ii*, 14–16.

MYANT, N. B. and C. OSORIO, 1959, Serum proteins, including thyroxine-binding proteins, in maternal and foetal rabbits. J. Physiol., Lond. *146*, 344–357.

MYERS, W. L. and D. SEGRE, 1963, The immunologic behavior of baby pigs. III. Transplacental transfer of antibody globulin in swine. J. Immun. *91*, 697–700.

NACE, G. W., 1953, Serological studies of the blood of the developing chick embryo. J. exp. Zool. *122*, 423–448.

NACHTSHEIM, H. and H. KLEIN, 1948, Hydrops congenitus universalis beim Kaninchen, eine erbliche fetale Erythroblastose. Abh. dt. Akad. Wiss. Berl. *5*, 1–71.

NATTAN-LARRIER, L. and L. RICHARD, 1929, Perméabilité du placenta aux sérums hétérologues. C. r. Séanc. Soc. Biol. *101*, 531–533.

NELSON, J. B., 1932, The maternal transmission of vaccinial immunity in swine. J. exp. Med. *56*, 835–840.

NELSON, J. B., 1934, The maternal transmission of vaccinial immunity in swine. II. The duration of active immunity in the sow and of passive immunity in the young. J. exp. Med. *60*, 287–291.

NETER, E., E. RAJNOVICH and E. A. GORZYNSKI, 1960, Study of staphylococcal antibodies of the Rantz type: placental transfer and titres in sera of children of various ages. Pediatrics, Springfield *25*, 21–26.

NEVANLINNA, H. R., 1953, Factors affecting maternal Rh immunisation. Annls Med. exp. Biol. Fenn. *31*, (Suppl. 2), 1–80.

NEWCOMB, R. W., D. NORMANSELL and D. R. STANWORTH, 1968, A structural study of human exocrine IgA globulin. J. Immun. *101*, 905–914.

NISONOFF, A., F. C. WISSLER, L. N. LIPMAN and D. L. WOERNLEY, 1960, Separation of univalent fragments from the bivalent rabbit antibody molecule by reduction of disulphide bonds. Archs Biochem. Biophys. *89*, 230–244.

NOER, H. R. and H. W. MOSSMAN, 1947, Surgical investigation of the function of the inverted yolk sac placenta in the rat. Anat. Rec. *98*, 31–38.

NORDBRING, F., 1957a, The appearance of antistreptolysin and antistaphylolysin in human colostrum. Acta paediat., Stockh. *46*, 481–496.

NORDBRING, F., 1957b, The failure of newborn premature infants to absorb antibodies from heterologous colostrum. Acta paediat., Stockh. *46*, 569–578.

NORDBRING, F. and B. OLSSON, 1957, Electrophoretic and immunological studies on sera of young pigs. I. Influence of ingestion of colostrum on protein pattern and antibody titre in sera from suckling pigs and the changes throughout lactation. Acta Soc. Med. upsal. *62*, 193–212.

NORDBRING, F. and B. OLSSON, 1958a, Electrophoretic and immunological studies on sera of young pigs. II. The effect of feeding bovine trypsin inhibitor with porcine colostrum on the absorption of antibodies and immune globulins. Acta Soc. Med. upsal. *63*, 25–40.

NORDBRING, F. and B. OLSSON, 1958b, Electrophoretic and immunological studies on sera of young pigs. III. Transfer of protein fractions and antibodies to the newborn pigs by ingestion of porcine serum with a study of the effect of bovine trypsin inhibitor. Acta Soc. Med. upsal. *63*, 41–52.

NORDSTRÖM, C., O. KOLDOVSKÝ and A. DAHLQVIST, 1969, Localization of β-galactosidases and acid phosphatase in the small intestinal wall. Comparison of adult and suckling rat. J. Histochem. Cytochem. *17*, 341–347.

NORTON, P. M., H. W. KUNZ and E. L. PRATT, 1952, Electrophoretic analysis of serum proteins in premature infants. Pediatrics, Springfield *10*, 527–532.

NOSSAL, G. J. V., 1957, The immunological response of foetal mice to influenza virus. Aust. J. exp. Biol. med. Sci. *35*, 549–558.

NUSSENZWEIG, R. S., C. MERRYMAN and B. BENACERRAF, 1964, Electrophoretic separation and properties of mouse antihapten antibodies involved in passive cutaneous anaphylaxis and passive hemolysis. J. exp. Med. *120*, 315–328.

OLSSON, B., 1959a, Studies on the formation and absorption of antibodies and immune globulins in piglets. II. The intestinal absorption of antibodies and immune globulins by new-born piglets after the administration of bovine colostrum. Nord. VetMed. *11*, 375–390.

OLSSON, B., 1959b, Studies on the formation and absorption of antibodies and immune globulins in piglets. III. The intestinal absorption of heterologous antibodies and serum proteins in new-born piglets. Nord. VetMed. *11*, 441–460.

ORCUTT, M. L. and P. E. HOWE, 1922, The relation between the accumulation of globulins and the appearance of agglutinins in the blood of new-born calves. J. exp. Med. *36*, 291–308,

ORLANDINI, O., A. SASS-KORTSAK and J. H. EBBS, 1955, Serum gamma globulin levels in normal infants. Pediatrics, Springfield *16*, 575–583.

ORLANS, E., 1967, Fowl antibody. VIII. A comparison of natural, primary and secondary antibodies to erythrocytes in hen sera; their transmission to yolk and chick. Immunology *12*, 27–37.

OSBORN, J. J., J. DANCIS and J. F. JULIA, 1952a, Studies of the immunology of the newborn infant. I. Age and antibody production. Pediatrics, Springfield *9*, 736–744.

OSBORN, J. J., J. DANCIS and J. F. JULIA, 1952b, Studies on the immunology of the newborn infant. II. Interference with active immunization by passive transplacental circulating antibody. Pediatrics, Springfield *10*, 328–334.

OSBORN, J. J., J. DANCIS and B. V. ROSENBERG, 1952, Studies on the immunology of the newborn infant. III. Permeability of the placenta to maternal antibody during fetal life. Pediatrics, Springfield *10*, 450–456.

OSBURN, B. I. and R. K. HOSKINS, 1969, Antibody responses to *Brucella ovis* in maternal and fetal sheep. J. infect. Dis. *119*, 267–272.

OSORIO, C. and N. B. MYANT, 1958, Thyroxine-binding protein in the serum of rabbit foetuses. Nature, Lond. *182*, 866–867.

OVARY, Z., W. F. BARTH and J. L. FAHEY, 1965, The immunoglobulins of mice. III. Skin sensitizing activity of mouse immunoglobulins. J. Immun. *94*, 410–415.

OVARY, Z. and O. G. BIER, 1953, Action empêchante du sérum normal de lapin sur l'anaphylaxie cutanée passive du cobaye. Annls Inst. Pasteur, Paris *84*, 443–445.

OVARY, Z. and F. KARUSH, 1961, Studies on the immunologic mechanism of anaphylaxis. II. Sensitizing and combining capacity *in vivo* of fractions separated from papain digests of antihapten antibody. J. Immun. *86*, 146–150.

OXER, D. T., 1936, The transmission of antitoxic immunity from the ewe, vaccinated against entero-toxaemia, to the lamb. Aust. vet. J. *12*, 54–58.

PADYKULA, H. A., J. J. DEREN and T. H. WILSON, 1966, Development of structure and function in the mammalian yolk sac. I. Development morphology and vitamin B$_{12}$ uptake of the rat yolk sac. Devl Biol. *13*, 311–348.

PAIĆ, M., 1938, Détermination de la constante de sédimentation de l'hémolysine. C. r. hebd. Séanc. Acad. Sci., Paris *207*, 1074–1076.

PANSE, M. V. and N. K. DUTTA, 1964, Cholera vaccines and placental transmission of antibodies. J. Immun. *93*, 243–245.

PARKER, R. H. and W. H. BEIERWALTES, 1961, Thyroid antibodies during pregnancy and in the newborn. J. clin. Endocr. Metab. *21*, 792–798.

PARRY, H. B., F. T. DAY and R. C. CROWHURST, 1949, Diseases of new-born foals. I. Haemolytic disease due to iso-immunisation of pregnancy. Vet. Rec. *61*, 435–441.

PARRY, H. J., 1950, The vascular structure of the extraplacental uterine mucosa of the rabbit. J. Endocr. *7*, 86–99.

PARRY, L. M., F. BECK and J. B. LLOYD, 1968, *In vitro* measurement of intracellular digestion. J. Anat., Proc. Anat. Soc. *103*, 393.

PATTERSON, R., M. ROBERTS and J. J. PRUZANSKY, 1969, Comparisons of reaginic antibodies from three species. J. Immun. *102*, 466–475.

PATTERSON, R., J. S. YOUNGNER, W. O. WEIGLE and F. J. DIXON, 1962a, The metabolism of serum proteins in the hen and chick and secretion of serum proteins by the ovary of the hen. J. gen. Physiol. *45*, 501–513.

PATTERSON, R., J. S. YOUNGNER, W. O. WEIGLE and F. J. DIXON, 1962b, Antibody production and transfer to egg yolk in chickens. J. Immun. *89*, 272–278.

PAYNE, L. C. and C. L. MARSH, 1962, Gamma globulin absorption in the baby pig: the nonselective absorption of heterologous globulins and factors influencing absorption time. J. Nutr. *76*, 151–158.

PERRY, G. C. and J. H. WATSON, 1967a, Sources of variation in the uptake of a marker antibody by piglets. Anim. Prod. *9*, 377–384.

PERRY, G. C. and J. H. WATSON, 1967b, Variation in the absorption of a colostrally secreted marker antibody in piglets. Anim. Prod. *9*, 385–391.

PERRY, G. C. and J. H. WATSON, 1967c, A note on the selective uptake of serum proteins in piglets following dosage with porcine serum. Anim. Prod. *9*, 557–559.

PICKUP, J., 1968, The production and absorption of porcine gamma-globulin. Thesis (University of Wales).

PIERCE, A. E., 1955a, Electrophoretic and immunological studies on sera from calves from birth to weaning. I. Electrophoretic studies. J. Hyg., Camb. *53*, 247–260.

PIERCE, A. E., 1955b, Electrophoretic and immunological studies on sera from calves from birth to weaning. II. Electrophoretic and serological studies with special reference to the normal and induced agglutinins to *Trichomonas foetus*. J. Hyg., Camb. *53*, 261–275.

PIERCE, A. E., 1959, Studies on the proteinuria of the new-born calf. J. Physiol., Lond. *148*, 469–488.

PIERCE, A. E., 1960, β-lactoglobulins in the urine of the new-born suckled calf. Nature, Lond. *188*, 940–941.

PIERCE, A. E., 1961a, Further studies on proteinuria in the new-born calf. J. Physiol., Lond. *156*, 136–149.

PIERCE, A. E., 1961b, Antigens and antibodies in the newly born. *In:* Proceedings of the

Thirteenth Symposium of the Colston Research Society 1961 (Butterworths, London) pp. 189–212.

PIERCE, A. E., 1961c, Proteinuria in the newly born. Proc. R. Soc. Med. *54*, 996–999.

PIERCE, A. E. and A. FEINSTEIN, 1965, Biophysical and immunological studies on bovine immune globulins with evidence for selective transport within the mammary gland from maternal plasma to colostrum. Immunology *8*, 106–123.

PIERCE, A. E. and P. JOHNSON, 1960, Ultracentrifuge and electrophoretic studies on the proteinuria of the new-born calf. J. Hyg., Camb. *58*, 247–260.

PIERCE, A. E., P. C. RISDALL and B. SHAW, 1964, Absorption of orally administered insulin by the newly born calf. J. Physiol., Lond. *171*, 203–215.

PIERCE, A. E. and M. W. SMITH, 1966, The *in vitro* transfer of bovine immune lactoglobulin across small intestines of new-born pigs. J. Physiol., Lond. *186*, 85–86P.

PIERCE, A. E. and M. W. SMITH, 1967a, The intestinal absorption of pig and bovine immune lactoglobulin and human serum albumin by the new-born pig. J. Physiol., Lond. *190*, 1–18.

PIERCE, A. E. and M. W. SMITH, 1967b, The *in vitro* transfer of bovine immune lactoglobulin across the intestine of new-born pigs. J. Physiol, Lond. *190*, 19–34.

PIGOURY, L. and J. CHARNY, 1951, Reproduction expérimentale de l'ictère hémolytique du muleton. Bull. Acad. vét. Fr. *24*, 399–404.

PLUMMER, H., 1938, Studies in scarlet-fever immunity. J. Immun. *35*, 235–244.

POLANO, O., 1904, Der Antitoxinübergang von der Mutter auf das Kind. Ein Beitrag zur Physiologie der Placenta. Z. Geburtsh. Gynäk. *53*, 456–476.

POLSON, A., 1943, Variation of serum composition with the age of horses as shown by electrophoresis. Nature, Lond. *152*, 413–414.

POLSON, A., 1952, Comparative electrophoretic studies of bovine and human colostrum in relation to neonatal immunity. Onderstepoort J. vet. Res. *25*, 7–12.

PORTER, P., 1969, Transfer of immunoglobulins IgG, IgA and IgM to lacteal secretions in the parturient sow and their absorption by the neonatal piglet. Biochim. biophys. Acta *181*, 381–392.

PORTER, R. R., 1958, Separation and isolation of fractions of rabbit gamma-globulin containing the antibody and antigenic combining sites. Nature, Lond. *182*, 670–671.

PORTER, R. R., 1959, The hydrolysis of rabbit γ-globulin and antibodies with crystalline papain. Biochem. J. *73*, 119–126.

PORTER, R. R., 1967, The structure of antibodies. Scient. Am. *217*, 81–90.

QUINLIVAN, L. G., 1964, Transplacental passage of gamma globulin-I[131] in the rat. Am. J. Physiol. *207*, 782–786.

QUINLIVAN, W. L. G., 1967, Gamma globulin-^{131}I transfer between mother and offspring in the rhesus monkey. Am. J. Physiol. *212*, 324–328.

RACE, R. R., 1944, An 'incomplete' antibody in human serum. Nature, Lond. *153*, 771–772.

RACE, R. R. and R. SANGER, 1968, Blood Groups in Man. 5th ed., (Blackwell, Oxford).

RAMIREZ, C. G., E. R. MILLER, D. E. ULLREY and J. A. HOEFER, 1963, Swine hematology from birth to maturity. III. Blood volume of the nursing pig. J. Anim. Sci. *22*, 1068–1074.

RAMON, G., 1928, Sur le passage de la toxine et de l'antitoxine tétaniques de la poule a l'oeuf et au poussin. C. r. Séanc. Soc. Biol. *99*, 1476–1478.

RAMSEY, E. M. and J. W. S. HARRIS, 1966, Comparison of uteroplacental vasculature and circulation in the rhesus monkey and man. Contr. Embryol. *38*, 59–70.

RANSOM, F., 1900, The conditions which influence the duration of passive immunity. J. Path. Bact. *6*, 180–192.

RATNER, B. and H. L. GRUEHL, 1929, Transmission of respiratory anaphylaxis (asthma) from mother to offspring. J. exp. Med. *49*, 833–845.

RATNER, B., H. C. JACKSON and H. L. GRUEHL, 1927a, Transmission of protein hypersensitiveness from mother to offspring. III. The role of milk. J. Immun. *14*, 275–290.

RATNER, B., H. C. JACKSON and H. L. GRUEHL, 1927b, Transmission of protein hypersensitiveness from mother to offspring. IV. Passive sensitization *in utero*. J. Immun. *14*, 291–302.

REEVES, W. C., J. M. STURGEON, E. M. FRENCH and B. BROOKMAN, 1954, Transovarian transmission of neutralizing substances to western equine and St. Louis encephalitis viruses by avian hosts. J. infect. Dis. *95*, 168–178.

REIF, A. E., H. J. NORRIS, N. MAHONEY, E. KLEIN and L. M. McVETY, 1964, Experimental erythroblastosis foetalis in rabbits due to A incompatibility. Br. J. exp. Path. *45*, 226–234.

REMLINGER, P., 1899, Contribution expérimentale a l'étude de la transmission héréditaire de l'immunité contre le bacille d'Éberth et du pouvoir agglutinant. Annls Inst. Pasteur, Paris *13*, 129–135.

REYMANN, G. C., 1920, On the transfer of the so-called normal antibodies from mother to offspring. I. Agglutinins. J. Immun. *5*, 227–238.

REYNOLDS, S. R. M., 1946, The relation of hydrostatic conditions in the uterus to the size and shape of the conceptus during pregnancy: A concept of uterine accommodation. Anat. Rec. *95*, 283–296.

REYNOLDS, S. R. M., 1947, Uterine accommodation of the products of conception: physiologic considerations. Am. J. Obstet. Gynec. *53*, 901–913.

RICHARDSON, M., C. C. BECK and D. T. CLARK, 1968, Prenatal immunization of the lamb to *Brucella*: Dissociation of immunocompetence and reactivity. J. Immun. *101*, 1363–1366.

RIMINGTON, C. and J. A. BICKFORD, 1947, Pre- and post-natal development of immunity. Lancet *i*, 781–785.

RODOLFO, A., 1934, A study of the permeability of the placenta of the rabbit to antibodies. J. exp. Zool. *68*, 215–235.

ROMANOFF, A. L., 1952, Membrane growth and function. Ann. N.Y. Acad. Sci. *55*, 288–301.

ROMER, P. H., 1901, Untersuchungen über die intrauterine und extrauterine antitoxinübertragung von der mutter auf ihre descendenten. Berl. klin. Wschr. *38*, 1150–1157.

ROOK, J. A. F., J. MOUSTGAARD and P. E. JAKOBSEN, 1951, An electrophoretic study of the changes in the serum proteins of the pig from birth to maturity. Royal Veterinary and Agricultural College, Copenhagen, Denmark, Yearbook 1951.

ROYAL, W. A., R. A. ROBINSON and D. M. DUGANZICH, 1968, Colostral immunity against *Salmonella* infection in calves. N.Z. vet. J. *16*, 141–145.

RUH, H. O. and J. E. McCLELLAND, 1923, Comparison of diphtheria immunity in the mother and in the new-born. Am. J. Dis. Child. *25*, 59–62.

RUOSLAHTI, E., TH. TALLBERG and M. SEPPALA, 1966, Origin of proteins in amniotic fluid. Nature, Lond. *212*, 841.

RUTQVIST, L., 1958, Electrophoretic patterns of blood serum from pig fetuses and young pigs. Am. J. vet. Res. *19*, 25–31.

SAISON, R., R. F. W. GOODWIN and R. R. A. COOMBS, 1955, The blood groups of the pig. I. The interaction of pig red cells of group A and the naturally occurring A iso-antibody in the serum of pigs of blood group O. J. comp. Path. Ther. *65*, 71–78.

SAN CLEMENTE, C. L. and I. F. HUDDLESON, 1943, Electrophoretic studies of the proteins of bovine serums with respect to *Brucella*. Michigan State College, Agricultural Experimental Station, Technical Bulletin *182*, 3–44.

SANDERS, E. and C. T. ASHWORTH, 1961, A study of particulate intestinal absorption and hepatocellular uptake. Use of polystyrene latex particles. Expl Cell Res. *22*, 137–145.

SANSOM, G. S. and J. P. HILL, 1931, Observations on the structure and mode of implantation of the blastocyst of *Cavia*. Trans. zool. Soc. Lond. *21*, 295–354.

SCHECHTMAN, A. M. and K. C. ABRAHAM, 1958, Passage of serum albumins from the mother to the foetus. Nature, Lond. *181*, 120–121.

SCHEINBERG, H., C. D. COOK and J. A. MURPHY, 1954, The concentration of copper and ceruloplasmin in maternal and infant plasma at delivery. J. clin. Invest. *33*, 963.

SCHINCKEL, P. G. and K. A. FERGUSON, 1953, Skin transplantation in the foetal lamb. Aust. J. biol. Sci. *6*, 533–546.

SCHMIDT, W., 1956, Der Feinbau der reifen menschlichen Eihaüte. Z. Anat. EntwGesch. *119*, 203–222.

SCHMITTLE, S. C. and T. W. MILLEN, 1948, Detection of hemagglutination-inhibition antibodies in unincubated eggs. Cornell Vet. *38*, 306–309.

SCHNEIDER, L. and G. PAPP, 1938, Beiträge zur Übertragung der Agglutinine von der Mutter auf das Neugeborene. Arch. Kinderheilk. *114*, 91–98.

SCHNEIDER, L. and J. SZATHMARY, 1939a, Ueber die immunität des neugeborenen lammes. Z. ImmunForsch. exp. Ther. *95*, 169–177.

SCHNEIDER, L. and J. SZATHMARY, 1939b, Ueber die immunität des neugeborenen hundes Z. ImmunForsch. exp. Ther. *95*, 177–188.

SCHNEIDER, L. and J. SZATHMARY, 1940, Ueber die Immunität der neugeborenen meerschweinchen. Z. ImmunForsch. exp. Ther. *98*, 24–30.

SCHOENAERS, F. and A. KAECKENBEECK, 1964, Influence de l'ingestion préalable de proteines ou de glucose sur la résorption des anticorps du colostrum, chez le veau nouveau-né. Annls Méd. vét. *108*, 205–211.

SCHUBERT, J. and A. GRÜNBERG, 1949, Zur frage der Uebertragung von Immun-Antikörpern von der Mutter auf das Kind. Schweiz. med. Wschr. *79*, 1007–1010.

SCHULTZ, W. H., 1910, Physiological studies in anaphylaxis. I. The reaction of smooth muscle of the guinea-pig sensitized with horse serum. J. Pharmac. exp. Ther. *1*, 549–567.

SEGRE, D. and M. L. KAEBERLE, 1962, The immunologic behavior of baby pigs. I. Production of antibodies in three-week-old pigs. J. Immun. *89*, 782–789.

SEKLA, B., 1958, Passive transfer of antitumour factors through milk in rats. Nature, Lond. *181*, 1600–1601.

SELL, S., 1964a, Evidence for species' differences in the effect of serum γ-globulin concentration on γ-globulin catabolism. J. exp. Med. *120*, 967–986.

SELL, S., 1964b, γ-globulin metabolism in germfree guinea pigs. J. Immun. *92*, 559–564.

SETO, F. and W. G. HENDERSON, 1969, Natural and immune hemagglutinin forming capacity of immature chickens. J. exp. Zool. *169*, 501–512.

SHAW DUNN, J., 1967, The fine structure of the absorptive epithelial cells of the developing small intestine of the rat. J. Anat. *101*, 57–68.

SHEPARD, C. C. and G. A. HOTTLE, 1949, Studies of the composition of the livetin fraction of the yolk of hen's eggs with the use of electrophoretic analysis. J. biol. Chem. *179*, 349–357.

SHERMAN, W. B., S. F. HAMPTON and R. A. COOKE, 1940, The placental transmission of antibodies in the skin-sensitive type of human allergy. J. exp. Med. *72*, 611–621.

SHERVEY, P., 1966, Observations on the development and histochemistry of the intestinal inclusion bodies of the suckling rat. Anat. Rec. *154*, 422.

SHIM, B.-S., Y.-S. KANG, W.-J. KIM, S.-H. CHO and D.-B. LEE, 1969, Self-protective activity of colostral IgA against tryptic digestion. Nature *222*, 787–788.

SIBALIN, M. and N. BJÖRKMAN, 1966, On the fine structure and absorptive function of the porcine jejunal villi during the early suckling period. Expl Cell Res. *44*, 165–174.

SILVERSTEIN, A. M., 1962, Congenital syphilis and the timing of immunogenesis in the human foetus. Nature, Lond. *194*, 196–197.

SILVERSTEIN, A. M. and R. J. LUKES, 1962, Fetal response to antigenic stimulus. I. Plasma-cellular and lymphoid reactions in the human fetus to intrauterine infection. Lab. Invest. *11*, 918–932.

SILVERSTEIN, A. M., R. A. PRENDERGAST and K. L. KRANER, 1964, Fetal response to antigenic stimulus. IV. Rejection of skin homografts by the fetal lamb. J. exp. Med. *119*, 955–964.

SILVERSTEIN, A. M., J. W. UHR, K. L. KRANER and R. J. LUKES, 1963, Fetal response to antigenic stimulus. II. Antibody production by the fetal lamb. J. exp. Med. *117*, 799–812.

SKINNER, H. H., W. M. HENDERSON and J. B. BROOKSBY, 1952, Use of unweaned white mice in foot-and-mouth disease research. Nature, Lond. *169*, 794–795.

SMITH, A. E. S. and A. M. SCHECHTMAN, 1962, Significance of the rabbit yolk sac. A study of the passage of heterologous proteins from mother to embryo. Devl Biol. *4*, 339–360.

SMITH, E. L., 1946a, The immune proteins of bovine colostrum and plasma. J. biol. Chem. *164*, 345–358.

SMITH, E. L., 1946b, Isolation and properties of immune lactoglobulins from bovine whey. J. biol. Chem. *165*, 665–676.

SMITH, E. L., 1948, The isolation and properties of the immune proteins of bovine milk and colostrum and their role in immunity: a review. J. Dairy Sci. *31*, 127–138.

SMITH, E. L. and A. HOLM, 1948, The transfer of immunity to the new-born calf from colostrum. J. biol. Chem. *175*, 349–357.

SMITH, M. G., 1943, Placental transmission of immunity to St. Louis encephalitis virus inoculated intraperitoneally in mice. Proc. Soc. exp. Biol. Med. *52*, 83–85.

SMITH, M. G. and B. B. GEREN, 1948, Transfer of immunity to the virus of St. Louis encephalitis to suckling mice through the milk, demonstrated by foster nursing. Am. J. Path. *24*, 713.

SMITH, M. W. and A. E. PIERCE, 1966, Protein absorption across intestine of the new-born pig. A. R. C. Institute of Animal Physiology, Babraham, Cambridge, Report for 1964–1965, p. 52.

SMITH, M. W. and A. E. PIERCE, 1967, Effect of amino-acids on the transport of bovine immune lactoglobulin across new-born pig intestine. Nature, Lond. *213*, 1150–1151.

SMITH, M. W., R. WITTY and P. BROWN, 1968, Effect of poly-L-arginine on rate of bovine IgG transport by newborn pig intestine. Nature, Lond. *220*, 387–388.

SMITH, R. T., 1960a, Discussion. *In:* Mechanisms of Antibody Formation (Czechoslovak Academy of Sciences, Prague) p. 148.

SMITH, R. T., 1960b, Studies on the mechanism of immune tolerance. *In:* Mechanisms of Antibody Formation (Czechoslovak Academy of Sciences, Prague) pp. 313–328.

SMITH, T. and R. B. LITTLE, 1922a, The significance of colostrum to the new-born calf. J. exp. Med. *36*, 181–198.

SMITH, T. and R. B. LITTLE, 1922b, Cow serum as a substitute for colostrum in new-born calves. J. exp. Med. *36*, 453–468.

SMITH, T. and R. B. LITTLE, 1924, Proteinuria in new-born calves following the feeding of colostrum. J. exp. Med. *39*, 303–312.

SMITH, V. R. and E. S. ERWIN, 1959, Absorption of colostrum globulins introduced directly into the duodenum. J. Dairy Sci. *42*, 364–365.

SMITH, V. R., R. E. REED and E. S. ERWIN, 1964, Relation of physiological age to intestinal permeability in the bovine. J. Dairy Sci. *47*, 923–924.

SMYTH, D. S. and S. UTSUMI, 1967, Structure of the hinge region in rabbit immunoglobulin-G. Nature, Lond. *216*, 332–335.

SOBOTTA, J., 1903, Die Entwicklung des Eies der Maus vom Schlusse der Furchungsperiode bis zum Auftreten der Amniosfalten. Arch. mikrosk. Anat. *61*, 274–330.

SOBOTTA, J., 1911, Die Entwicklung des Eies der Maus vom ersten Auftreten des Mesoderms an bis zur Ausbildung der Embryonalanlage und dem Auftreten der Allantois. Arch. mikrosk. Anat. *78*, 271–352.

SOLOMON, A., T. A. WALDMANN and J. L. FAHEY, 1963, Metabolism of normal 6.6S γ-globulin in normal subjects and in patients with macroglobulinemia and multiple myeloma. J. Lab. clin. Med. *62*, 1–17.

SOLOMON, J. B., 1964, The onset of immunological competence in the chicken. Folio biol., Praha *10*, 268–274.

SOLOMON, J. B., 1966a, The appearance and nature of opsonins for goat erythrocytes during the development of the chicken. Immunology *11*, 79–87.

SOLOMON, J. B., 1966b, Induction of antibody formation to goat erythrocytes in the developing chick embryo and effects of maternal antibody. Immunology *11*, 89–96.

SOOTER, C. A., M. SCHAEFFER, R. GORRIE and T. A. COCKBURN, 1954, Transovarian passage of antibodies following naturally acquired encephalitis infection in birds. J. infect. Dis. *95*, 165–167.

SOROKIN, S. P. and H. A. PADYKULA, 1964, Differentiation of the rat's yolk sac in organ culture. Am. J. Anat. *114*, 457–478.

Speer, V. C., H. Brown, L. Quinn and D. V. Catron, 1959, The cessation of antibody absorption in the young pig. J. Immun. *83*, 632–634.

Spiegelberg, H. L., B. G. Fishkin and H. M. Grey, 1968, Catabolism of human γG-immunoglobulins of different heavy chain subclasses. I. Catabolism of γG-myeloma proteins in man. J. clin. Invest. *47*, 2323–2330.

Spiegelberg, H. L. and H. M. Grey, 1968, Catabolism of human γG-immunoglobulins of different heavy chain subclasses. II. Catabolism of γG myeloma proteins in heterologous species. J. Immun. *101*, 711–716.

Spiegelberg, H. L. and W. O. Weigle, 1965, The catabolism of homologous and heterologous 7S gamma globulin fragments. J. exp. Med. *121*, 323–338.

Spiegelberg, H. L. and W. O. Weigle, 1966, Studies on the catabolism of γG subunits and chains. J. Immun. *95*, 1034–1040.

Staley, T. E., E. W. Jones and L. D. Corley, 1969, Fine structure of duodenal absorptive cells in the newborn pig before and after feeding of colostrum. Am. J. vet. Res. *30*, 567–581.

Staley, T. E., E. Wynn Jones and A. E. Marshall, 1968, The jejunal absorptive cell of the newborn pig: an electron microscopic study. Anat. Rec. *161*, 497–516.

Stäubli, C., 1903, Zur frage des ueberganges der typhusagglutinine von der mutter auf den fötus. Zentbl. Bakt. ParasitKde (Originale) *33*, 458–461.

Steigman, A. J. and M. M. Lipton, 1958, Neonatal immunity. II. Poliocidal effects of human amniotic fluids. Proc. Soc. exp. Biol. Med. *99*, 576–579.

Steinberg, A. G. and J. A. Wilson, 1963, Hereditary globulin factors and immune tolerance in man. Science *140*, 303–304.

Steinmuller, D., 1961, Transplantation immunity in the newborn rat. I. The response at birth and maturation of response capacity. J. exp. Biol. *147*, 233–247.

Stelos, P., 1956, Electrophoretic and ultracentrifugal studies of rabbit haemolysins. J. Immun. *77*, 396–404.

Sterzl, J., J. Kostka, L. Mandel, I. Riha and M. Holub, 1960, Development of the formation of γ-globulin and of normal and immune antibodies in piglets reared without colostrum. *In:* Mechanisms of Antibody Formation (Czechoslovak Academy of Sciences, Prague) pp. 130–145.

Steven, D. H., 1968, Placental vessels of the foetal lamb. J. Anat. *103*, 539–552.

Stiehm, E. R., A. J. Ammann and J. D. Cherry, 1966, Elevated cord macroglobulins in the diagnosis of intrauterine infections. New Engl. J. Med. *275*, 971–977.

Stone, H. D. and W. A. Boney, 1968, Vaccination of congenitally-immune chicks against Newcastle disease virus. Proc. Soc. exp. Biol. Med. *128*, 525–530.

Stone, S. S. and M. Gitter, 1969, Sodium sulphite test for detecting immunoglobulins in calf sera. Br. vet. J. *125*, 68–73.

Strauss, F., 1967, Die normale Anatomie der menschlichen Placenta. Handbuch der Speziellen pathologischen Anatomie und Histologie, Bd 7, T. 5, (Springer-Verlag, Berlin) pp. 1–96.

Strauss, L., N. Goldenberg, K. Hirota and Y. Okudaira, 1965, Structure of the human placenta with observations on ultrastructure of the terminal chorionic villus. *In:* D. Bergsma (ed.) Birth defects original article series 1, (New York, The National Foundation – March of Dimes) pp. 13–26.

STÜCK, B., J. NATZSCHKA and H. WIESENER, 1957, Untersuchungen zum antistreptolysin-gehalt im serum von müttern, neugeborenen und sänglingen. Klin. Wschr. *35*, 924–929.

SUGAWARA, S. and E. S. E. HAFEZ, 1967, Electrophoretic patterns of proteins in the blastocoelic fluid of the rabbit following ovariectomy. Anat. Rec. *158*, 115–120.

SUSSMAN, S., 1961, The passive transfer of antibodies to *Escherichia coli* 0111:B4 from mother to offspring. Pediatrics, Springfield *27*, 308–313.

SVEHAG, S.-E. and J. R. GORHAM, 1963, Passive transfer of immunity to blue tongue virus from vaccinated maternal mice to their offspring. Res. vet. Sci. *4*, 109–113.

SWISHER, S. N. and L. E. YOUNG, 1954, Studies of the mechanisms of erythrocyte destruction initiated by antibodies. Trans. Ass. Am. Physns *67*, 124–132.

SZABÓ, S., T. SZENT-IVÁNYI and A. SZEKY, 1956, Hemolytic disease of newborn pigs. Acta vet. hung. *6*, 313–331.

SZENT-IVÁNYI, T. and S. SZABÓ, 1953, Untersuchungen über die ursache der hämolytischen gelbsucht der neugeborenen ferkel. Acta vet. hung. *3*, 75–80.

SZENT-IVÁNYI, T. and S. SZABÓ, 1954, Blood groups in pigs. Acta vet. hung. *4*, 429–446.

TEN BROECK, C. and J. H. BAUER, 1923, The transmission of tetanus antitoxin through the placenta. Proc. Soc. exp. Biol. Med. *20*, 399–400.

TENNANT, B., D. HARROLD, M. REINA-GUERRA and R. C. LABEN, 1969, Neonatal alterations in serum gamma globulin levels of Jersey and Holstein-Friesian calves. Am. J. vet. Res. *30*, 345–354.

TERRY, R. J., 1956, Transmission of antimalarial immunity (*Plasmodium berghei*) from mother rats to their young during lactation. Trans. R. Soc. trop. Med. Hyg. *50*, 41–46.

TERRY, W. D., 1965, Skin-sensitizing activity related to γ-polypeptide chain characteristics of human IgG. J. Immun. *95*, 1041–1047.

THOMPSON, R. and F. P. MEYERS, 1950, Passive transfer of immunity to *Lansing poliomyelitis* virus from actively immunized mothers to young mice. Am. J. Hyg. *52*, 213–221.

THORBECKE, G. J., 1964, Development of immune globulin formation in fetal, newborn, and immature guinea pigs. Fedn Proc. Fedn Am. Socs exp. Biol. *23*, 346.

THORELL, J. I., 1962, The placental transfer of insulin antibodies. Acta path. microbiol. scand. *56*, 239–240.

THORP, F. and R. GRAHAM, 1933, The persistence of *Brucella* agglutinins in calves of reactor cows. J. Am. vet. med. Ass. *82*, 871–874.

TIGHE, J. R., P. R. GARROD and R. C. CURRAN, 1967, The trophoblast of the human chorionic villus. J. Path. Bact. *93*, 559–567.

TIMMERMAN, W. A., 1931, Zur Frage der Uebertragung des Typhus 'H' und 'O'-Agglutinin von Mutter auf Kind. Z. ImmunForsch. exp. Ther. *70*, 388–399.

TOIVANEN, P., R. MÄNTYJÄRVI and T. HIRVONEN, 1968, Maternal antibodies in human foetal sera at different stages of gestation. Immunology *15*, 395–403.

TOMASI, T. B., 1965, Human gamma globulin. Blood *25*, 382–403.

TOMASI, T. B. and S. ZIGELBAUM, 1963, The selective occurrence of γ_{1A} globulins in certain body fluids. J. clin. Invest. *42*, 1552–1560.

TOOMEY, J. A., 1934, Agglutinins in mother's blood, baby's blood, mother's milk and placental blood. Am. J. Dis. Child. *47*, 521–428.

TRÁVNÍČKOVÁ, E. and J. HELLER, 1963, Plasma and blood volume of infant rats during the first postnatal month. Physiologia bohemoslov. *12*, 541–547.

TRENCH, C. A. H., P. S. GARDNER and C. A. GREEN, 1964, Induction of immunological tolerance to human gamma-globulin in rabbits using the maternal route of inoculation. Immunology *7*, 567–569.

TUCKER, E. M., 1961, An attempt to produce haemolytic disease in lambs. Nature, Lond. *189*, 847–848.

TUFFREY, M., N. P. BISHUN and R. D. BARNES, 1969, Porosity of the mouse placenta to maternal cells. Nature, Lond. *221*, 1029–1030.

ULLREY, D. E., C. H. LONG, E. R. MILLER and B. H. VINCENT, 1962, Sheep hematology from birth to maturity. J. Anim. Sci. *21*, 1031 (Abstract).

USATEGUI-GOMEZ, M. and D. F. MORGAN, 1966, Maternal origin of the group specific (Gc) proteins in amniotic fluid. Nature, Lond. *212*, 1600–1601.

USATEGUI-GOMEZ, M., D. F. MORGAN and H. W. TOOLAN, 1966, A comparative study of amniotic fluid, maternal sera and cord sera by disc electrophoresis. Proc. Soc. exp. Biol. Med. *123*, 547–551.

USATEGUI-GOMEZ, M. and S. STEARNS, 1969, Comparative study of the Rh-D antibody titres of amniotic fluids and corresponding maternal sera in Rh-D sensitized pregnancies. Nature, Lond. *221*, 82–83.

VACEK, Z., 1964, Submikroskopická struktura a cytochemie epithelu tenkého střeva u krysích mláďat. Čslká Morf. *12*, 292–301.

VAHLQUIST, B., 1952, Placental transfer of antibodies in human beings, Étud. néo-natal. *1*, 31–46.

VAHLQUIST, B., 1958, The transfer of antibodies from mother to offspring. Adv. Pediat. *10*, 305–338.

VAHLQUIST, B. and C. HÖGSTEDT, 1949, Minute absorption of diphtheric antibodies from the gastrointestinal tract in infants. Pediatrics, Springfield *4*, 401–405.

VAHLQUIST, B., R. LAGERCRANTZ and F. NORDBRING, 1950, Maternal and foetal titers of antistreptolysin and antistaphylolysin at different stages of gestation. Lancet *ii*, 851–853.

VAILLARD, L., 1896, Sur l'hérédité de l'immunité acquise. Annls Inst. Pasteur, Paris *10*, 65–85.

VALENTINE, R. C. and N. M. GREEN, 1967, Electron microscopy of an antibody-hapten complex. J. molec. Biol. *27*, 615–617.

VALETTE, L. R., 1967, Devenir des anticorps absorbés par la voie digestive chez le veau nouveau-né. Bull. Acad. vét. Fr. *40*, 347–349.

VAN ALTEN, J., 1966, Passive transfer of embryonic immunity in the newly hatched chick by cells of the peripheral blood. Anat. Rec. *154*, 435.

VAN ALTEN, P. J. and A. M. SCHECHTMAN, 1963, Immunity in embryos. Anaphylaxis in young chicks suggests a new explanation for some puzzling properties of embryos. J. exp. Zool. *153*, 187–196.

VAN DURME, M., 1914, Nouvelles recherches sur la vitellogenèse des oeufs d'oiseaux aux stades d'accroissement, de maturation, de fécondation et du début de la segmentation. Archs Biol., Paris *29*, 71–200.

VAN FURTH, R., H. R. E. SCHUIT and W. HIJMANS, 1965, The immunological development of the human fetus. J. exp. Med. *122*, 1173–1188.

VIGNES, H., R. RICHOU and P. RAMON, 1948, De la coexistence, dans les sérums humains, des antitoxines diphtérique et staphylococcique naturellement acquises. Leur transmission de la mère au foetus a travers le placenta. Leur élimination par le lait. Revue Immunol. Thér. antimicrob. *12*, 1–7.

VOGT, E., 1954, Selective filtration of syphilitic reagins through the placenta. Acta paediat., Stockh. *43*, 247–251.

VON MAGNUS, H., 1951, Studies on mouse encephalomyelitis virus (TO strain). V. The effect of passively transferred specific immunity on the infection in baby mice. Acta path. microbiol. scand. *29*, 251–257.

WALDMANN, T. A. and P. J. SCHWAB, 1965, IgG (7S gamma globulin) metabolism in hypogammaglobulinemia: studies in patients with defective gamma globulin synthesis, gastrointestinal protein loss, or both. J. clin. Invest. *44*, 1523–1533.

WASZ-HÖCKERT, O., O. WAGER, T. HAUTALA and O. WIDHOLM, 1956, Transmission of antibodies from mother to foetus. A study of the diphtheria level in the newborn with oesophageal atresia. Annls Med. exp. Biol. Fenn. *34*, 444–446.

WEIDE, K. D., V. L. SANGER and A. LÀGACÉ, 1962, Inoculation of baby pigs with lapinized hog cholera vaccine (1ml.). J. Am. vet. med. Ass. *141*, 464–475.

WELLMANN, G. and H. ENGEL, 1963, Immunbiologische untersuchungen au künstlich aufgezogenen Ferkeln. 3. Über die Fähigkeit neugeborenen Ferkel, Antikörper und γ-globulin aus der Kolostralmilch zu resorbieren. Zentbl. Bakt. ParasitKde (Originale) *190*, 408–414.

WELLMANN, G., H. LIEBKE and H. ENGEL, 1962, Antikörpergehalt der Sauenmilch und Antikörperresorption durch die Ferkel zu verschiedenen zeiten nach der Geburt. Zentbl. Bakt. ParasitKde (Originale) *185*, 215–229.

WELLMANN, G., C. H. SCHWIETZER and H. LIEBKE, 1961, Beobachtungen über die unterschiedliche Fähigkeit von Sauen, Antikörper mit der Kolostralmilch zu übertragen. Zentbl. Bakt. ParasitKde (Originale) *183*, 217–224.

WELLS, H. G. and T. B. OSBORNE, 1921, Anaphylaxis reactions with purified proteins from milk. J. infect. Dis. *29*, 200–216.

WHIPPLE, G. H., R. B. HILL, R. TERRY, F. V. LUCAS and C. L. YUILE, 1955, The placenta and protein metabolism. Transfer studies using C^{14}-labelled proteins in dogs. J. exp. Med. *101*, 617–626.

WIDAL, F. and A. SICARD, 1897, Recherches sur l'absorption de la substance agglutinante typhique par le tube digestif et sur sa transmission par l'allaitement. C. r. Séanc. Soc. Biol. *4*, 804–807.

WIENER, A. S., 1944, A new test (blocking test) for Rh sensitization. Proc. Soc. exp. Biol. Med. *56*, 173–176.

WIENER, A. S., 1948, Rh factor in immunological reactions. Ann. Allergy *6*, 293–304.

WIENER, A. S., 1951, The half-life of passively acquired antibody globulin molecules in infants. J. exp. Med. *94*, 213–221.

WIENER, A. S., H. BERGER and S. LENKE, 1951, Serum gamma globulin in infants. Lab. Dig. *14*, 11–12.

WIENER, A. S. and H. R. PETERS, 1940, Hemolytic reactions following transfusions of blood of the homologous group, with three cases in which the same agglutinogen was responsible. Ann. intern. Med. *13*, 2306–2322.

WIENER, A. S. and I. J. SILVERMAN, 1940, Permeability of the human placenta to antibodies, J. exp. Med. *71*, 21–27.

WIENER, A. S. and E. B. SONN, 1946, Permeability of the human placenta to isoantibodies. J. Lab. clin. Med. *31*, 1020–1024.

WIENER, A. S., I. B. WEXLER and J. G. HURST, 1949, The use of exchange transfusion for the treatment of severe erythroblastosis due to A-B sensitization, with observations on the pathogenesis of the disease. Blood *4*, 1014–1032.

WILD, A. E., 1960, Proteins of the liquor amnii. Br. med. J. *1*, 802.

WILD, A. E., 1961, The association between protein and bilirubin in liquor amnii. Clin. Sci. *21*, 221–231.

WILD, A. E., 1965a, Protein composition of the rabbit foetal fluid. Proc. R. Soc., B *163*, 90–115.

WILD, A. E., 1965b, Serum proteins of the grey squirrel (*Sciurus carolinensis*) Immunology *9*, 457–466

WILLIAMS, H. E., 1961, Colostral antibody to rabies in cattle vaccinated with HEP Flury strain of the virus. Am. J. vet. Res. *22*, 902–905.

WILLIAMS, J., 1962, Serum proteins and the livetins of hen's-egg yolk. Biochem. J. *83*, 346–355.

WILLIAMS, R. M. and F. BECK, 1969, Intracellular association of pinocytotic capacity and lysosomal enzyme activity in the mammalian small intestine. J. Anat. *104*, 175.

WILSON, T. H. and G. WISEMAN, 1954, The use of sacs of everted small intestine for the study of the transference of substances from the mucosal to the serosal surface. J. Physiol., Lond. *123*, 116–125.

WINKLER, E. G., J. G. FITZPATRICK and J. J. FINNERTY, 1958, The permeability of the rabbit placenta to homologous albumin. Am. J. Obstet. Gynec. *76*, 1209–1213.

WISLOCKI, G. B., 1955, The comparative anatomy and histology of the placental barrier by E. C. Amoroso, Discussion. *In:* L. B. Flexner (ed.) Transactions of the 1st Conference on Gestation (Corlies, Macy and Co. Inc., New York) pp. 119–224.

WISLOCKI, G. B. and H. S. BENNETT, 1943, The histology and cytology of the human and monkey placenta, with special reference to the trophoblast. Am. J. Anat. *73*, 335–350.

WISLOCKI, G. B., H. W. DEANE and E. W. DEMPSEY, 1946, The histochemistry of the rodent's placenta. Am. J. Anat. *78*, 281–333.

WISLOCKI, G. B. and E. W. DEMPSEY, 1955, Electron microscopy of the placenta of the rat. Anat. Rec. *123*, 33–63.

WISLOCKI, G. B. and H. A. PADYKULA, 1953, Reichert's membrane and the yolk sac of the rat investigated by histochemical means. Am. J. Anat. *92*, 117–152.

WISSIG, S. L. and D. O. GRANEY, 1968, Membrane modifications in the apical endocytic complex of ileal epithelial cells. J. Cell Biol. *39*, 564–579.

WITEBSKY, E., G. W. ANDERSON and A. HEIDE, 1942, Demonstration of Rh antibody in breast milk. Proc. Soc. exp. Biol. Med. *49*, 179–183.

WOCHNER, R. D., G. DREWS, W. STROBER and T. A. WALDMANN, 1966, Accelerated breakdown of immunoglobulin G(IgG) in myotonic dystrophy: A hereditary error of immunoglobulin catabolism. J. clin. Invest. *45*, 321–329.

WOCHNER, R. D., W. STROBER and T. A. WALDMANN, 1967, The role of the kidney in the catabolism of Bence Jones proteins and immunoglobulin fragments. J. exp. Med. *126*, 207–221.

WOODROW, J. C., C. A. CLARKE, W. T. A. DONOHOE, R. FINN, R. B. MCCONNELL, P. M. SHEPPARD, D. LEHANE, S. H. RUSSELL, W. KULKE and C. M. DURKIN, 1965, Prevention of Rh-haemolytic disease: A third report. Br. med. J. *1*, 279–283.

WOODROW, J. C. and R. FINN, 1966, Transplacental haemorrhage. Br. J. Haemat. *12*, 297–309.

WORTH, C. B., 1951, Transient presence of complement-fixing antibodies against murine typhus fever in the sera of offspring of immune rats. Am. J. trop. Med. *31*, 299–300.

YEIVIN, R., M. SALZBERGER and A. L. OLITZKI, 1956, Development of antibodies to enteric pathogens: placental transfer of antibodies and development of immunity in childhood. Pediatrics, Springfield *18*, 19–23.

YOUNG, G. A. and N. R. UNDERDAHL, 1949, Swine influenza as a possible factor in suckling pig mortalities. II. Colostral transfer of hemagglutinin inhibitors for swine influenza virus from dam to offspring. Cornell Vet. *39*, 120–128.

YOUNG, G. A. and N. R. UNDERDAHL, 1950, Neutralization and hemagglutination inhibition of swine influenza virus by serum from suckling swine and by milk from their dams. J. Immun. *65*, 369–373.

YOUNG, L. E., R. M. CHRISTIAN, D. M. ERVIN, R. W. DAVIS, W. A. O'BRIEN, S. N. SWISHER and C. L. YUILE, 1951, Hemolytic disease in newborn dogs. Blood *6*, 291–313.

YOUNG, L. E., D. M. ERVIN, R. M. CHRISTIAN and R. W. DAVIS, 1949, Haemolytic disease in newborn dogs following iso-immunization of the dam by transfusions. Science *109*, 630–631.

YOUNG, L. E., D. M. ERVIN and C. L. YUILE, 1949, Hemolytic reactions produced in dogs by transfusion of incompatible dog blood and plasma. I. Serologic and hematologic aspects. Blood *4*, 1218–1231.

ZEIDBERG, L. D., R. S. GASS and R. H. HUTCHESON, 1957, The placental transmission of histoplasmosis complement-fixing antibodies. Am. Med. Ass. J. Dis. Child. *94*, 179–184.

ZEULZER, W. W. and E. KAPLAN, 1954a, ABO heterospecific pregnancy and hemolytic disease. A study of normal and pathologic variants I. Patterns of maternal A and B isoantibodies in unselected pregnancies. Am. J. Dis. Child. *88*, 158–178.

ZEULZER, W. W. and E. KAPLAN, 1954b, ABO heterospecific pregnancy and hemolytic disease. A study of normal and pathologic variants. II. Patterns of A and B isoantibodies in the cord blood of normal infants. Am. J. Dis. Child. *88*, 179–192.

ZEULZER, W. W. and E. KAPLAN, 1954c, ABO heterospecific pregnancy and hemolytic disease. A study of normal and pathologic variants. IV. Pathologic variants. Am. J. Dis. Child *88*, 319–338.

ZIPURSKY, A., A. HULL, F. D. WHITE and L. G. ISRAELS, 1959, Foetal erythrocytes in the maternal circulation. Lancet *i*, 451–452.

Addendum

(Publications appearing too late for inclusion in the text)

ANDERSON, J. W., 1969, Ultrastructure of the placenta and fetal membranes of the dog. I. The placental labyrinth. Anat. Rec. *165*, 15–36.

BAZIN, H. and F. MALET, 1969, The metabolism of different immunoglobulin classes in irradiated mice. Immunology *17*, 345–365.

BILLINGTON, W. D., D. R. S. KIRBY, J. J. T. OWEN, M. A. RITTER, M. D. BURTONSHAW, E. P. EVANS, C. E. FORD, I. K. GAULD and A. McLAREN, 1969, Placental barrier to maternal cells. Nature, Lond. *224*, 704–706.

CLARKE, R. M. and R. N. HARDY, 1969, The use of [^{125}I] polyvinyl pyrrolidone K. 60 in the quantitative assessment of the uptake of macromolecular substances by the intestine of the young rat. J. Physiol., Lond. *204*, 113–125.

CLARKE, R. M. and R. N. HARDY, 1969, An analysis of the mechanism of cessation of uptake of macromolecular substances by the intestine of the young rat ('closure'). J. Physiol., Lond. *204*, 127–134.

CORNELL, R. and H. A. PADYKULA, 1969, A cytological study of intestinal absorption in the suckling rat. Am. J. Anat. *125*, 291–316.

FEINSTEIN, A. and M. J. HOBART, 1969, Structural relationship and complement fixing activity of sheep and other ruminant immunoglobulin G subclasses. Nature, Lond. *223*, 950–952.

GENCO, R. J., L. YECIES and F. KARUSH, 1969, The immunoglobulins of equine colostrum and parotid fluid. J. Immun. *103*, 437–444.

GITLIN, D. and A. BIASUCCI, 1969, Development of γG, γA, γM, β_{1C}/β_{1A}, C′ 1 esterase inhibitor, ceruloplasmin, transferrin, hemopexin, haptoglobin, fibrinogen, plasminogen, a_1-antitrypsin, orosomucoid, β-lipoprotein, a_2-macroglobulin, and prealbumin in the human conceptus. J. clin. Invest. *48*, 1433–1446.

GRAY, G. D., M. M. MICKELSON and J. A. CRIM, 1969, The demonstration of two γ-globulin subclasses in the goat. Immunochemistry *6*, 641–644.

HARDY, R. N., 1969, The influence of specific chemical factors in the solvent on the absorption of macromolecular substances from the small intestine of the new-born calf. J. Physiol., Lond. *204*, 607–632.

HARDY, R. N., 1969, The absorption of polyvinyl pyrrolidone by the new-born pig intestine. J. Physiol., Lond. *204*, 633–651.

364

Hardy, R. N., 1969, The break-down of [^{131}I] γ-globulin in the digestive tract of the new-born pig. J. Physiol., Lond. *205*, 435–451.

Hardy, R. N., 1969, Proteolytic activity during the absorption of [^{131}I] γ-globulin in the new-born calf. J. Physiol., Lond. *205*, 453–470.

Jacoby, R. O., R. A. Dennis and R. A. Griesemer, 1969, Development of immunity in fetal dogs: humoral responses. Am. J. vet. Res. *30*, 1503–1510.

Klaus, G. G. B., A. Bennett and E. W. Jones, 1969, A quantitative study of the transfer of colostral immunoglobulins to the newborn calf. Immunology *16*, 293–299.

Kraehenbuhl, J. P. and M. A. Campiche, 1969, Early stages of intestinal absorption of specific antibodies in the newborn. An ultrastructural, cytochemical and immunological study in the pig, rat and rabbit. J. Cell Biol. *42*, 345–365.

Mach, J.-P., J.-J. Pahud and H. Isliker, 1969, IgA with 'Secretory Piece' in bovine colostrum and saliva. Nature, Lond. *223*, 952–955.

Nash, D. R., J. P. Vaerman, H. Bazin and J. F. Heremans, 1969, Identification of IgA in rat serum and secretions. J. Immun. *103*, 145–148.

Porter, P., 1969, Porcine colostral IgA and IgM antibodies to *Escherichia coli* and their intestinal absorption by the neonatal piglet. Immunology *17*, 617–626.

Tuffrey, M., N. P. Bishun and R. D. Barnes, 1969, Porosity of the placenta to maternal cells in normally derived mice. Nature, Lond. *224*, 701–704.

Williams, R. M. and F. Beck, 1969, Demonstration of alkaline phosphatase in the lysosomes of neonate rat ileum. Histochem. J. *1*, 531–538.

Williams, R. M. and F. Beck, 1969, A histochemical study of gut maturation. J. Anat. *105*, 487–501.

Winchurch, R. and W. Braun, 1969, Antibody formation: Premature initiation by endotoxin or synthetic polynucleotides in newborn mice. Nature, Lond. *223*, 843–844.

Witty, R., P. Brown and M. W. Smith, 1969, The transport of various immune globulins by the new-born pig intestine. Experientia *25*, 310–312.

Author index

Subject index